Marlowe's Soldiers

Marlowe's Soldiers

Rhetorics of Masculinity in the Age of the Armada

ALAN SHEPARD

Ashgate

Published by

Ashgate Publishing Limited
Gower House, Croft Road
Aldershot, Hants
GU11 3HR
England

Ashgate Publishing Company
131 Main Street
Burlington
Vermont 05401–5600
USA

Ashgate website: http://www.ashgate.com

British Library Cataloguing in Publication Data
Shepard, Alan
    Marlowe's soldiers: rhetorics of masculinity in the age of the Armada
    1. Marlowe, Christopher, 1564–1593–Criticism and interpretation.
    2. Militarism–Great Britain–History–16th century.
    I. Title
    822.3

US Library of Congress Cataloging in Publication Data
Shepard, Alan, 1961–
    Marlowe's soldiers: rhetorics of masculinity in the age of the Armada /
    Alan Shepard. p.cm.
    Includes bibliographical references and index.
    1. Marlowe, Christopher, 1564–1593–Characters–Soldiers. 2. Marlowe,
    Christopher, 1564–1593–Views on war. 3. Masculinity in literature.
    4. Soldiers in literature. 5. Men in literature. 6. War in literature.
    7. Armada, 1588. I. Title.
    PR2677.S7 S54 2001
    822'.3–dc21   2001032806

ISBN 0 7546 0229 X

Printed and bound in Great Britain by MPG Books Ltd, Bodmin, Cornwall

Contents

Acknowledgments

It's a pleasure to be able to thank friends and colleagues who have read drafts of chapters or helped me in other ways with the project: Emily Bartels, Beth Bjorklund, Joe Black, Rick Bozorth, Gordon Braden, Mark Thornton Burnett, Lisa Celovsky, Kevin Gustafson, Julie Hardwick, Linda K. Hughes, Alexander Leggatt, Katharine Eisaman Maus, Stephen Powell, Simon Shepherd, Paul Whitfield White, Steven Wozniak, an anonymous reader for Ashgate, and especially David Bevington, who generously read the entire manuscript at a critical moment. Erika Gaffney at Ashgate has been splendid to work with.

I am fortunate to have had the opportunity to do some of the research and writing for this project as a Senior Fellow at the Centre for Reformation and Renaissance Studies (CRRS) at Victoria University in the University of Toronto. The Centre provided an ideal atmosphere for scholarship. For his generosity in making my stay there a success, I warmly thank Konrad Eisenbichler, then director of the Centre. Joe Black, Lisa Celovsky, and David Galbraith were also generous CRRS hosts. Some of the claims in this book began to take shape several years ago in Richard Waswo's 'Imperial Themes' seminar at The Folger Library, and I am grateful to him for a stimulating experience and to the library's director and staff for a grant that made it possible for me to participate. For research assistance at TCU, I thank Doug Hollinger and Cathy Gabor; for interlibrary loan assistance, Joyce Martindale. I am grateful to my English Department colleagues, especially Fred Erisman, Linda K. Hughes, and Gary Tate.

For her untold support back in Charlottesville, I remain indebted to Anne MacMaster. And I thank my families, the Shepards and the Powells, especially Stephen.

I have read bits of this project at meetings of the MLA, Renaissance Society of America, Group for Early Modern Cultural Studies, and the Sixteenth Century Studies Conference; at Kalamazoo's Medieval Congress; at the Medieval and Renaissance Studies Conference in Tempe; and at two gatherings at Cambridge University of the Marlowe Society of America. Thanks to fellow participants who have helped me to sharpen my arguments.

The editors of *Renaissance Quarterly* have granted permission to reprint parts of my article on *Tamburlaine* (46 [1993]: 734–53), which form the basis of Chapter 1. A version of Chapter 4, on *The Jew of Malta*, appeared in *History and Sexuality: New Critical Essays on Christopher Marlowe*, ed. Paul Whitfield White (New York: AMS, 1998), 109–30, parts of which are reprinted here by permission of AMS Press.

A Note on Texts

Quotations of Marlowe's plays are taken by permission from The Revels Plays: *Dido, Queen of Carthage* and *The Massacre at Paris*, ed. H.J. Oliver (Harvard University Press, 1968); *Doctor Faustus: A- and B-Texts (1604, 1616)*, ed. David Bevington and Eric Rasmussen (1992; rpt Manchester University Press, 1997); *Edward II*, ed. Charles R. Forker (Manchester University Press, 1994); *The Jew of Malta*, ed. David Bevington (Manchester University Press, 1997); and *Tamburlaine*, ed. J.S. Cunningham (1981; rpt Manchester University Press, 1999).

When quoting early modern materials I generally modernize u/v and i/j and sometimes silently expand elisions, but for the most part I leave the early modern spelling as it is.

Introduction

Trumpets and drums, alarum presently,
And soldiers, play the men; the hold is yours!

2 Tamburlaine 3.3.62–3

When wert thou in the field with banner spread?
But once! And then thy soldiers marched like players,
With garish robes, not armour

Edward II 2.2.181–3

filthie stage plaies have bin suffered even in our chiefest city

Oliver Pigg[1]

When the prominent Puritan divine Oliver Pigg denounces 'filthie stage plays' as inimical to London's well-being, his complaint assumes a deep link between the theater and national security in late sixteenth-century England. It was a link some more or less influential Londoners considered extremely hazardous in the 1580s and 1590s, on the grounds that playing 'the men' on the stage or – even worse, playing 'the soldier' there – would compromise England's military readiness in a period of near-constant anxiety about yet another Spanish invasion of England and Ireland. Other wags in the capital, among them Christopher Marlowe, leveraged that imputed link between the theater and national security for delight and profit. This study reads Marlowe's plays as entertainments that engage and exploit the rhetoric of war fever that had been building in England from the mid-1580s and that continued at a fairly high volume until the end of Elizabeth's reign. Despite the government's efforts to pretend that the attack on England's shores by the Spanish Armada in July 1588 was not a crisis, a stance the queen had intermittently insisted on, the Anglo-Spanish War, the Armada itself, and its fallout across the next fifteen years or so elicited from the English a surge of nationalism, Kenneth Andrews says, 'probably more intense and generally felt than ever before.'[2] If the attack sparked new interest in the strength of England's physical security, it also created a demand for a new kind of public discourse about England's enemies, one that spilled beyond the court at Whitehall, church pulpits, and pubs. Although it is reasonable to assume that the people who inhabit any state or nation talk about its security on occasion, especially when threatened, it is not always the case that they make its security a subject of their own amusement, especially in time of war. But that is what happened in England in the

1

1580s and 1590s. Sometimes obliquely, often not, the security of the state and of the monarchy became topics of public discourse in places designed to entertain the populace – especially in the public theaters and bookstalls. George Peele, Thomas Kyd, George Chapman, William Shakespeare, Christopher Marlowe and a host of other playwrights concocted dramas that put English soldiers or even just soldiers in general on the stage to amuse and astonish ordinary people. What is Peele's *The Battle of Alcazar* if not a complex effort to depict the historical English mercenary Tom Stuckley in service to the king of Portugal as a savvy hero, all the while acknowledging him as a Catholic proteus who could just as well have posed more danger to England's state security than to Morocco's? And in bookstalls at St Paul's, amidst the volumes of romances for sale, ordinary citizens were also able to buy what were virtually the first military handbooks ever published in English. They purported to advise readers as well as the queen and her lieutenants on various subjects, mostly strategy, weaponry, protocol, and the rules of engagement. As never before, England's state security had become a topic fit for the intellectual engagement and the bemused wonderment of ordinary people.

In time of war the government's responses to national security emergencies were by turns lackadaisical, earnest, and intermittently harsh, even despotic. For these were dangerous, extreme times. Between July 1588 and Marlowe's murder in May 1593, for instance, the Privy Council several times declared civilians to be subject to martial law for certain petty crimes, including the act of pretending to be a soldier in order to take advantage of the meager relief offered to veterans of various military campaigns. Under the stresses of war, counterfeiting the guise of a soldier in the streets could bring a death sentence, while in the theater it could bring modest celebrity to a player and, in rare circumstances, wealth to shareholders. Or, if the anti-theatricalists were to be believed, counterfeiting a soldier could unravel the nation's military resolve if not the structure of society itself. The anxieties surrounding counterfeiting soldiers on stage and the efforts to whip up war fever in the streets seem to have run highest in the six or so years Marlowe wrote plays in London, where the government periodically invoked the still-hazy concept of martial law and applied it to domestic civilian life, and where influential writers campaigned for the benefits of militarism in pamphlets, poems, and soldiers' handbooks. In some respects the plays ascribed to Marlowe and his collaborator(s) can also be counted as participating in that campaign. My concern here is to understand how and why Marlowe's plays make entertainment of a wealth of historically and geopolitically divergent fantasies about martial law and its discontents.[3]

The mentality that promotes martial law is often ventriloquized by Marlovian soldiers playing the Übermensch, amazing audiences by thirsting for blood and glory. The playwright is infamous for creating poetic but ruthless soldiers for the Elizabethan stage. Tamburlaine is the best known. But other principals play the soldier too: Barabas is a captain of commerce who tropes the ducats he is forced to surrender in the first act of *The Jew of Malta* as so many troops lost from his command. Faustus vainly hopes to become 'great emperor of the world' (A 1.3.106) without doing the work of a Charlemagne or a Charles V. And while in Marlowe's work there is only one direct notice of the Armada itself (*The Massacre at Paris* 21.104–5), in its own way each tragedy is engaged in exploring the rhetoric of war and the mental architecture of warlords.

Christopher Marlowe arrived in London in 1587 or so, and it is no surprise his plays are preoccupied with the dangers of militarism, intramural as well as international. In part, his robust and often comic tragedies capitalize on the theater-going public's new appetite for manly heroes who perform as invincible fighting machines: witness the commercial success of *Tamburlaine the Great* in the 1590s. The theatrics of masculinity are central to his work, from Tamburlaine's cutting his own forearm to prove his steely manhood and stabbing his son Calyphas for refusing to play the man to the chivalric quarrel between Lodowick and Mathias that leaves both young men dead to Faustus's stabbing himself to prove himself a man to Mephistopheles. Paradoxically, what is suggested in part in these visceral epiphanies is that, for soldiers and civilian dissidents alike, masculinity is a fiction, a performance,[4] not an essence that can be counted on to shield a man from incursions into his psyche, nor to steel the nation's borders from enemy fleets or Jesuit priests, or whatnot.

The Marlowe plays engage in deeply ambiguous, sometimes subtle acts of resistance to the explicit endorsements of martial law (and of militarism as the best foundation of civil society) being furnished in other public texts such as homilies and prayers, royal proclamations, poems, and especially in the contemporary military handbooks that were for sale. Evidence of resistance is lodged in heteroglossic moments of dissent – usually given to minor characters to speak – that rupture the epideictic war rhetoric that otherwise prevails. To draw out those moments I will focus on the treatment of disputes between Marlowe's soldiers and the civilians they bludgeon, impale and otherwise silence. Conflict between them is often ignited by disagreements about the validity of claims regarding state security, mirroring those then being advanced in England in other public venues – namely that state security is strongest in times of martial law, and is strengthened by carefully regulated codes of masculinity, misogyny, and disembodied action; by callous violence, an ironic disrespect for diplomatic and even martial rhetoric, and contempt for any form of theatricalized identity. Civilian voices in these tragedies are by turns restrained, fulsome or inconsistent. Nevertheless they call spectators to scrutinize the assumptions enjoined by stage 'soldiers' and the veterans and others in London's streets that human life deserves to be regulated principally in martial terms and that militarism makes the world safer. While that resistance is neither consistent nor totalized, the plays do bedevil the putative links being widely proposed between state security, prescriptive English masculinity, and the act of playing soldier on the stage. Even as the veterans and others hotly argue for the risks of insurgency raised by mimesis, the Marlowe plays suggest it is soldiers, not players, who most threaten the security of the state by daring to prescribe an England where all kinds of difference ought to be quashed by martial law. Through his dissidents' voices Marlowe toys with the late sixteenth-century anxiety that 'playing the soldier' or 'playing the man' on stage, or on the battlefield, can destroy a city or even an entire civilization. In these ways Marlowe's inquiry into martial law becomes effectively an *apologia* of the theater.

Pigg and other anti-theatricalists in the early modern period object to plays and playing in part because they scorn everything that smacks of what we would call performativity, a vice they knew as Machiavellian cunning from translations of the Italian theorist that had circulated in London as early as Henry VIII's reign. It was a vice condemned as undercutting the foundations of representational truth on which society itself is built. Soldiers-turned-writers echo the anti-theatricalists' complaints. As the Anglo-Spanish conflict in the early 1570s begins to resurface later that decade, Thomas Churchyard warns against cunning in 'A generall rehearsall of warres' (1579). He censures persons who in a Machiavellian fashion pretend to own emotions and allegiances to ensure their own advancement at the expense of society's need for truth telling. Lamenting the decline of moral conduct 'in this crooked age,' Churchyard warns that the practice of counterfeiting emotion is everywhere in the land, and a grave danger to the stability of the state. 'For now is he accounpted no bodie, that can not deceive a multitude,' he asserts in the course of prophesying that performing identity puts ordinary people reaching above their station in life at grave risk of being devoured by metaphoric wolves: 'with artificiall courtezie, and double dessembled countenaunce, plaine people are carried from them selves, and made the bonde slaves of . . . wolves.' Churchyard offers his treatise as an intervention in the moral decline symbolized for him by what he asserts are new-fangled assumptions about the legitimacy of intrigue; the treatise is dedicated to Christopher Hatton, a member of the Privy Council. Churchyard intends his ideas to be read at the highest levels.[5] Some anti-theatricalists and veterans who turned to writing conduct-books also specifically object to figural representations of war and its combatants in the theater, arguing that neither the risks of war nor its high purpose can be adequately conveyed by stage reproduction. For all the bombast of late sixteenth-century theater, to put some strutting 'soldier' on the boards in London seems to have been understood by veterans and other commentators as an unpatriotic act of sabotage. Yet as the contemporary records of entrance fees to performances attest, Londoners turned to the theater in droves in the midst of the stresses of war and the cold war that followed – seeking there entertainment, diversion, solace, courage – while Spain launched or prepared to launch a series of military strikes through the end of Elizabeth's reign.[6] That stress peaked in July 1588, when Her Majesty's ships fended off the first Spanish Armada. But as I hope is implied by my subtitle, 'Rhetorics of Masculinity in the Age of the Armada,' those July 1588 battles were not isolated events but prodigious expressions of hostilities between a superpower and an emerging empire, hostilities that would significantly shape a variety of discourses said to touch on England's safety from enemies foreign and domestic well beyond Elizabeth's death and subsequent peace with Spain.

* * *

Evidence of the paradoxical cultural capital of soldiers in the latter sixteenth century can be found in the proclamations forbidding civilians to pretend that they are or have recently been on active service as soldiers or mariners. In the Privy Council during the 1580s and 1590s the act of impersonating a soldier in the streets of London became rhetorically if not always legally defined as a crime punishable by capital punishment under declarations of martial law; civilians were not exempt. In November 1589, for instance, the Privy Council issued the proclamation 'Placing Vagrant Soldiers Under Martial Law,' which prescribed the execution of 'all soldiers, mariners, masterless men, and other vagrant persons' who did not within two days' time secure a passport 'to repair into their country.'[7] The targets of the proclamation were not only demobilized soldiers who were judged to have run amok, but also those who, in spite of having never served in Her Majesty's army, were now impersonating soldiers in order to profit from the meager succor veterans were eligible for upon returning home. As historians have pointed out, this particular proclamation was one of several issued in the reigns of Elizabeth and Mary that in effect applied the rule of martial law to civilian life. According to Lindsay Boynton, 'This was indeed an "astonishing extension" of the provost-marshal's powers to civilians, and the frequency with which the government stressed its extraordinary nature and limited duration betrayed uneasiness at this peacetime resort to martial law.'[8] In November 1591 the Privy Council further clarified the queen's wishes in a proclamation 'Placing Vagrants under Martial Law.' It condemns 'the common wandering abroad of a great multitude of her people, whereof the most part pretend that they have served in the wars of late on the other side of the seas, though in truth it is known that very many of them . . . have not served at all,' and it prescribes the penalty of death to those 'vagrant persons now wandering abroad under pretense of begging as soldiers.'[9]

In retrospect, the crime of pretending to be a veteran can be considered enormously ironic. Not only were demobilized soldiers not accorded a hero's welcome; many were forced to beg for food or money on their return from abroad, as governmental assistance was minimal. What elevated pretending to be a soldier to the status of a capital crime was its apparent assault on the idea of authenticity – pretending was to be understood as a form of fraudulent misrepresentation, or counterfeiting. The Privy Council took a very dim view of such pretending. In June 1591, for example, it was declared illegal for idle persons, 'some coloring their wandering by the name of soldiers returned from the war,' to congregate; that October the Council warned against Jesuits disguised 'in apparel as soldiers, mariners, or merchantes pretending that they have been heretofore taken prisoners and put into galleys'; that November the Council declared 'vagrant persons now wandering abroad under pretense of begging as soldiers' to deserve to be 'executed'; and so forth.[10] As we shall see in my discussion of *Edward II*, it was not only the Privy Council but also the commoners writing military conduct-books in the period who condemned efforts to counterfeit the profession of soldier, including most efforts to present the soldier on stage.[11]

Responding to the reading public's wartime anxieties, London printers brought out a 'deluge' of treatises, pamphlets, and monographs on military strategy and conduct, some written by veterans and others by theorists of war.[12] Veterans of service in the Low Countries, Ireland and elsewhere began to publish, as never before in English, handbooks of military strategy and deportment, intended to instruct both the public and a queen who was commonly thought to be less aggressive toward foreign enemies than was prudent. These pamphlets and books were composed most often by literate commoners, usually men who had served the queen in the Low Countries or France or Ireland. From the frequent allusions to current events in these writings, they are obviously occasional pieces, though they also comprise the embryonic *apologia* of professional armies, made permanent in England during the Civil War in the next century. Among the soldiers whose works I read here are the well-known and well-published Barnabe Rich and George Whetstone, but also Geoffrey Gates, William Blandy, Giles Clayton, and several others. They provide a contemporary context for understanding Marlowe's own dialectical treatments of militarism; and we have long had evidence that the playwright read at least some of these treatises himself, including *The Practise of Fortification* (1589) by his Cambridge classmate Paul Ive.[13]

In function these military treatises and handbooks vary widely, often performing several tasks that seem to address the concerns of different audiences. Some offer blueprints of combat strategies with schematic maps as appendices, showing where to place the harquebus or the foot soldier; others translate classical military texts by, say, Vegetius or Julius Frontius; some prescribe roles for the various ranks, such as the duties of the sergeant major general; some enter the technical debates of the day – for example, whether gunpowder should replace archery; others busily narrate important military expeditions, implying moralizing conclusions along the way, such as Sir William Slyngisbie's *Relation of the Voyage to Cadiz, 1596*,[14] whose fold-out map of Cadiz and Calais offers geographical military intelligence to general readers. The most interesting treatises theorize the nature of war and warriors, the justifications of war, the rules of martial law, and the relationship of civilians to soldiers in any society. Virtually all the handbooks and treatises depart in tone and content from the romantic reversion to medieval chivalry that is the mainstay of English poetry about war in the late sixteenth and seventeenth centuries.[15] Even when this theorizing of war seems not to be operating explicitly as propaganda, it is still easy to find in the handbooks not only the xenophobic treatment of Spain, France, Italy, and the Turks, but also attacks on various versions of 'the Other,' whom the writers occasionally ask us to imagine could be – probably is – lurking within England's borders. In their opinions, soldiers and mariners are the best prescription for warding off the evil of internecine as well as international strife. With varying candor and skill these soldiers-turned-writers respond to the crises induced by Spain's attacks and threats of attack by endorsing militarism as the preemptive blueprint of national life. They see these threats as an opportunity to shore up the status of fighting men who, in an age of ever-growing commerce, have less and less status.[16]

It is also no surprise that the military handbooks implicitly and sometimes explicitly endorse a narrowly prescriptive code of masculinity to guide and regulate soldiers and mariners. That code can be roughly generalized in these terms: that manhood is immutable rather than continuously performed; valor is intestinal rather than contextual; bloodshed is an inevitable product of immutable manhood, for men must fight 'the Other' lest they fight countrymen in civil war; women drain men's physical strength and moral resolve, so homosocial relationships deserve to be promoted, but homosexual ones vilified and destroyed; murder may satisfy a soldier's need for intimacy; peace is pernicious because it escalates the risk of civil war;[17] soldiers father the nation; war is natural, inevitable, and healthy for the state.

We can see some of these tenets in *The Defense of Military Profession* by Geoffrey Gates, who asserts that soldiers are the bedrock of a civilization:

> There must bee therefore an other state and profession of men, whose power and prudence must comprehend the maintenaunce and defence, not only of the Seate of Justice, but also of the Cowe and Plowe, of the Bed and Cradle, yea of the Altar and of the sovereigne state: which resteth in the profession neither of the Priest nor Lawyer, nor in the occupation of the Housbandmen, Artisans nor Merchants: but lieth in the prowesse and value of them that professe Armes.[18]

Although their 'value' is underappreciated, soldiers deserve to reign over all other vocations, as Gates tells his interlocutor. Their martial values ought to prevail because they defend the farmer, lawyer, priest, and merchant from their enemies; they make the conditions of commerce and civic life possible. For Gates, then, war-making is the matrix *sine qua non* for making and sustaining a culture. An apparently illiterate man who dictated his treatise to an amanuensis, as I discuss in Chapter 4, Gates clearly feels compelled to honor soldiers in print, understanding the potential for greater legitimacy that such public notice may bring. In 1579 Thomas Churchyard likewise had observed in his preface 'To the freendly reader' that 'before all other thynges (excepte the honourying of Prince and publike state) a true writer ought of duetie, to have in admiration and reverence, the valliaunt Soldiours, and men of worthy value.'[19]

There is more than a small element of class consciousness and class antagonism in the apparent aims of the handbook writers. One of the earliest, from Niccolo Tartaglia to Henry VIII but translated into English only in 1588, that auspicious year, apologizes for the gap between its high motives and low style: 'I am emboldened although I lacke the pithie eloquence and fine phraze of speech which is meete for you to heare.'[20] Tartaglia's sentiment, an instance of a routine rhetoric for almost any correspondence with a king, is akin to the *apologia* contained within other handbooks published late in the sixteenth century by those of Marlowe's contemporaries who did not have the advantage of a Cambridge education but nevertheless felt that they had something important to say during a national emergency. Among the handbook writers, Barnabe Rich is most eloquent on the point that civilians treat soldiers respectfully only in military crises. In his preface to *A Path-Way to Military Practise*, 'Greetings to the Friendly Reader,' Rich walks a tightrope between peace and war:

> Yet as I am not ignorant, that quiet peace is to be preferred before bloody warre, so in the time of peace, warlike disciplines must not be omitted in a well governed commonwealth, where so many evil neighbors are so ready to encroach, but especially when both prince, country, religion, law, justice, subjects and altogether are under the protection of arms.[21]

Once his piece begins in earnest, Rich intensifies his claim:

> it may be perceived that it is the soldier, that protecteth the prince in his seat, it is the soldier, that defendeth the divine in his pulpit, it is the soldier, that upholdeth the judge in his place of justice, it is the soldier as *Varo* sayeth, that resisteth the outward force of enemies, *that represseth domestic seditions, and defendeth the liberty of subjects*: if his service be then so beneficial to all, O what pity, he is not better considered of by some, that are so bountiful in rewarding pipers, parasites, singers and dancers and other like ministers of their pleasures, and suffer poor soldiers to beg, and will sooner afford him a payer of stocks, then a single penny for his alms.[22]

Bluntly, Rich subsumes civilian to military life, which is for him, 'naturally,' it would seem, the ultimate paradigm. In this calculus, England's soldiers, glorified as the embodiments of chivalric heroism, are presumed to have a duty to confront the Roman Catholic terror at home and abroad, whatever its form. In this vein, Rich further condemns the papal support of Spain's control of the Low Countries by saying, 'God with his own mouth hath cursed such oppressors.' That same year William Bourne had beseeched God to 'confound' all English Catholics, 'wicked impes' whom he feared would assassinate Queen Elizabeth with the pope's blessing. Against such internal threats Geoffrey Gates posited that true soldiers – English soldiers, much maligned by their civilian benefactors except in times of crisis – would always stand up 'against the violence of tirantes and oppressers.'[23]

A number of the handbooks see England's troubles with Spain as God's punishment for the nation's own sins. Not surprisingly, these tracts make national security contingent on strict obedience to Christian precepts. Sometimes they spell out the ways safety and godliness are weakened by the popularity of the drama, as in, for example, Oliver Pigg's *Meditations Concerning praiers to Almightie God, for the saftie of ENGLAND, when the Spaniards were come into the narrow Seas.*

August 1588. Pigg's tract is a public prayer rather than a military treatise, yet its generic slippage signals that he has both kinds of advice to offer readers. Holding that there is 'no doubt God is highly displeased' with England, he asks God to 'trie us yet once more.' For him the language of building a community is figuratively and literally at odds with the threat of war:

> The ministers which shoulde boldly have reproved these corruptions in al sorts & states, have for the most part ben unable to do this, & many of them corrupt in their conversation, they have winked at disorders, daubing with untempered morter, that will not hold, as if nothing had bin amisse, and no danger toward, when as iniquitie mightily prevailed amongst us, and thou in thy high displeasure didst threaten war.

In choosing to read the Armada as a scourge rather than a sign of bald Spanish ambition, he deflects both praise and blame from the crown and the soldiers, who owed their victory as much to favorable winds as to strategy or skill; he reads the victory as an instance of God's will that England should be afforded another chance to get its house in order. The 'untempered morter' image captures his conviction that disordered speech as much as overt treason can compromise the nation's very foundation, and he confesses that the military threat has not shocked England into moral reform. Indeed, its mortar is being weakened in Pigg's judgment not only by the age-old sins and crimes – 'murthers, slaughters, quarels, adulteries, whoredomes, dronkennes, and excessive pride in apparel' – but by an activity that to him goes hand in hand with these crimes: 'filthie stage plaies,' he says disgustedly, 'have bin suffered even in our chiefest city, & uppon the Saboths.'[24]

Some of the handbooks prescribe war rather than penitence as the proper antidote to the nation's sins. Advocating the role of scourge, as Tamburlaine claims for himself, is rhetorically a tricky maneuver, however. It requires peace itself be demonized. Simon Harward in *The Solace for the Souldier and Saylour*, for example, equates 'Military discipline' with 'the holy handy worke of God,' though he admits it is sometimes 'shamefully abused.' In his estimation, England nevertheless needs even more military discipline. 'Peace,' he says, 'hath increased plenty, plenty hath wrought pride, pride hath hatcht disdayne,' and so the nation is consequently awash. While Harward's formulation of the idea is particularly bold, it's clear that the conduct-book writers harbor deep ambivalence toward peace, even at times a pathological fear of it. In 1578 Thomas Procter simply warns that 'longe peace breadeth idlenes, whiche sucketh the valure out of noble myndes,' and in 1587 Barnabe Rich avows that 'Peace hath been the nourisher of many vices.'[25] Peace is said by several writers to breed 'effeminacy.' A codeword for being under the spell of a woman, that charge also conveys the distress felt by many who served in England's armies and militias of being commanded ultimately by an unmarried queen.

Often these wordsmith-scourges who have taken up writing in order to theorize war are anxious that their exchange of the sword for the pen may induce their readers to regard them as less than manly, or to lack credibility as military advisers. These worries show up early in Matthew Sutcliffe's *The Practice, Proceedings, and Lawes of Armes*. 'Some [readers] percase will mislike this treatise, as all other of like argument, for that they suppose, that skill in armes is rather to be learned by practise, then rule; and that all such discourses, are vaine conceites and supposalles, of men more able to speake, then performe.' Blasting Machiavelli for having written *The Art of War* without having ever been in the field, Sutcliffe proposes that the men who 'deserve most credite' 'are both writers, and doers themselves,' including Francis Guicciardini, the Italian historian whose brother's account of the 1527 sack of Rome figures in my discussion of *Doctor Faustus*.[26] From an opposite tack, Margaret Tyler proposes that writing of war may be performed by women precisely because it is not such manly work. Translating Diego Ortunez de Calahorra's *The Mirrour of Princely deedes and Knighthood* from the Spanish, Tyler begs her reader's indulgence while she transgresses the apparent restrictions of her gender to translate a military manual. For Tyler, war is men's business, but writing about war is a job for both sexes: 'I hope thou wilt friendly accept, rather for that it is a womans woork, though in a story prophane, and a matter more manlike then becometh my sexe. But as for the manlinesse of the matter, thou knowest that it is not necessary for every trumpettour or drumstare in the warre to be a good fighter.'[27] Reductively Tyler figures writers as mere cheerleaders, underestimating or deliberately misreading the extent to which military treatises, including the one she is translating, shape rather than describe the world, both on and off the field of battle. This rhetorical maneuver of forestalling the question of one's own agency as a rhetorician by subsuming a speech act within a promise of martial valor is precisely the maneuver that we will see Marlowe's own soldiers making on any number of occasions.

* * *

While the handbook writers typically prescribe martial law only for soldiers and mariners, during a number of crises in the late 1580s and 1590s the government imposed it selectively on civilians as well. An important precedent for doing so had been set in 1556, Lindsay Boynton notes, when Queen Mary ordered the marshal of the Irish army to 'scour the country and chastise suspects, vagabonds, and all idle and masterless folk by "the law martiall."'[28] In June and July 1558, in the last months of her reign, Mary issued one proclamation 'Placing Possessors of Heretical and Seditious Books Under Martial Law' and another 'Ordering [the] Fleet Manned under Martial Law.' The first prescribes death 'without delay' for those civilian rebels caught with banned Protestant writings. The second commands 'under pain of death' that ordinary mariners with a modicum of experience (at sea or on the Thames) be released from any other service and 'reserved and spared to the public service of her highness and the realm' in support of a navy.[29] As is suggested by these proclamations, 'martial law,' however hazy a legal concept it may have been, was nevertheless seen as an extension of royal prerogative that could be invoked imprecisely but at times fiercely against civilians as well as conscripted or commissioned soldiers or mariners.

Not until 1570 would Elizabeth first avail herself of the precedent Mary had established of imposing capital punishment under martial law upon dissident civilians. That year, in a proclamation 'Offering Pardon to Northern Rebels,' Elizabeth acknowledged that 'sundry of the meaner sort' who had participated in the borderlands rebellion against her reign had already, in Durham, 'by the martial law suffered pains of death according to their just deserts and to the terror and example of others.'[30] It was a fate she would impose more often in the latter decades of her reign against unarmed religious dissidents who were apprehended as 'sowers of sedition' and those caught with religious or political contraband.[31] In a moment of crisis in 1580 the queen invoked martial law to forbid 'murmurers' from rumoring of invasion, asserting that the realm is 'still continued in a readiness to withstand all hostile attempts as well by sea as by land.'[32] And from Greenwich on 1 July 1588, days before the Armada struck, the government issued an order to impose 'Martial Law against Possessors of Papal Bulls, Books, [and] Pamphlets.' This particular document is taut in its tone; and its range is universal: 'Every such offender shall with all severity be proceeded against and punished according to the martial law by her majesty's lieutenants,' and such offenders may be searched for 'in all places, as well exempt as not exempt'; and for those discovered to be guilty, swift punishment is to be instantly carried out, 'any law or statute to the contrary in any wise notwithstanding.' In short, all government officers – the 'lieutenants and deputies . . . judges, sheriffs, justices of peace, mayors, bailiffs, and all other her officers' – were empowered to impose martial law upon anyone and everyone.[33] From 1588 until her death, Elizabeth would formally proclaim martial law to be in effect some thirteen more times. As late as February 1601 the queen was threatening 'pain of death by martial law' to those persons without a fixed address in London who remained in the city.[34]

The extent to which such threatening punishments were actually imposed by the Tudors varies widely. No one discounts that under both Mary and Elizabeth, the sanctions against religious dissidents were often fierce whenever turbulence threatened. Yet the degree to which despotic governance in the form of martial law was actually levied upon civilians in times of peace is still debated. It is clear that in the early modern period the term 'martial law' meant something quite different from our modern understanding, which conjures up an image of tanks with machine-gunners peering out from opened hatches, patrolling a city's streets. But exactly how would the term 'martial law' have been understood in the late Elizabethan period? G.R. Elton for one argues against the charge of despotism levied by many historians of the period, favoring a view of Tudor government as on the whole bound by constitutional principles. 'Tudor thinking and practice on the law subordinated everybody, the king included, to the rule of law,' he asserts, concluding that it is therefore reasonable to see sixteenth-century England as neither '"a free society"' nor 'a despotism.' In particular, Elton resists the notion that the published royal proclamations such as were cited above could carry the force of law. Instead, he writes, they functioned as supplements to law. 'There is no prerogative power of making new laws or abrogating old; legislation is the function of king in Parliament . . . Such was the theory, and such (which is more) the practice.'[35] Further, in a scholarly review of the first of three modern volumes of Tudor royal proclamations, volumes that carry several declarations of martial law by both Mary and Elizabeth, Elton insists that these are not what they seem, nor actually say what they say. All such declarations must be understood in their legal context, he reasonably proposes, and that context forbade a monarch from single-handedly asserting a new law in the ways that, say, a Roman emperor could. As Elton puts it, rather more optimistically than some historians might, 'The traditional conclusion must stand: proclamations could not and did not create new offences punishable by loss of life.'[36]

In the early modern period, however, a strict legal definition of 'martial law' or of its actual consequences such as Elton seems to suppose may be moot. The term's meaning would not be settled until after 1689, despite Parliament's efforts in 1628 to limit the king's ability to invoke martial law on English soil.[37] Whether or not the proclamations imposing martial law on civilians in times of emergency effectually suspended the common law during Elizabeth's reign, as is often asserted in the proclamations themselves, the point is that the whole of England and most particularly London would have received and reacted to such declarations of martial law by the Privy Council and to the corollary discourse of apprehension, even fear, perhaps even terror, these pronouncements created. In short, whether or not martial law was legally imposed on the populace in predictable ways, which it surely was not, such declarations were bound to become a source of deep tension and anxiety, perhaps especially to civilians, who were less accustomed to the martial frame of mind than an experienced conscript or veteran would have been. It is a tension – at times a fierce anxiety – that Marlowe leveraged to his advantage.

* * *

On its face, the argument of this study runs against the grain of casual impressions of Marlowe's soldiers' glorious deeds. I do not dismiss the fact that Marlowe exploited popular demand for jingoistic entertainment in the wake of the Armada; I do not pretend that he is a misunderstood pacifist. But only a few critics in this century have admired his Tamburlaine or his Admiral Bosco without qualification. More often, the spectacular stage violence that is a hallmark of the Marlowe plays has been ascribed to one form or another of 'overreaching,' in Harry Levin's now-worn phrase; which is to say that critics have tried to understand the tragedies from theological or psychoanalytic perspectives, critical positions and analyses that are already fully worked out by others. More recently, Emily Bartels and Simon Shepherd have aimed instead to challenge the way spectators and readers understand the relationships of the historical contexts of Marlowe's work to the plays as we have them. In *Spectacles of Strangeness: Imperialism, Alienation, and Marlowe,* for instance, Bartels elegantly historicizes the tragedies, reading them through notions of orientalism and post-colonial studies, showing again that it is possible to study their historical contexts without reifying Tillyard's England. Bartels's book is a model for my own in the sense that both projects aim to contextualize the tragedies by investigating how imperial acts are represented and resisted in Marlowe's art. Simon Shepherd's *Marlowe and the Politics of Elizabethan Theatre* likewise focuses on Marlowe's aesthetic and political efforts to offer some kind of dissent from the burgeoning assumptions of a protonationalism within contemporary London. His work is explicitly Foucauldian, however, which mine is not, and is also rooted in contemporary stage history, whereas mine looks more to the effects of other kinds of historical texts and the public discourse they created. Nick de Somogyi's *Shakespeare's Theatre of War* expresses interests similar to mine, and its analysis has been very useful to me. Curtis Breight's *Surveillance, Militarism and Drama in the*

Elizabethan Era considers Marlowe's plays as pro-Catholic acts of intellectual resistance in the context of a larger argument about the hegemony of the Cecils in the 1590s and their uses of militarism to gain and keep control over the state; Breight amasses a great number of primary sources that substantiate the kinds of claims I am also making for the signal importance of royal proclamations of martial law in the period, and in that sense his study is also in the background here. Two other kinds of historical, cultural scholarship have provided intellectual stimulation for this project. Paul Kocher's essays on Marlowe's debts to contemporary writers, including military theorists, started me on rethinking the playwright's treatment of war, using the various tools and theories available to those of us who have been trained in a post-structuralist era. Kocher joined a host of scholars such as Leicester Bradner and Paul Jorgenson in writing about Elizabethan militarism in the shadow of the Second World War; their work still proves useful, even if our own preoccupations might well seem to them strangely peripheral. The other kind of stimulation for this project came from Klaus Theweleit's study of the journals and notebooks of the Freicorps, the German soldiers who banded together as mercenaries between the First and Second World Wars. Theweleit's fascinating efforts to explore the imaginations of modern fascists has been instrumental to my own study of the similar but not historically identical artistic expressions of autarchic fantasies in the worlds of martial law that Marlowe's soldiers work so hard to make for everyone in their orbit.[38]

The sequence of chapters is not intended to suggest a chronology of the composition of Marlowe's plays. Instead, the chapters are ordered so as to offer the reader a tour of Marlowe's critique of hypermilitarism that moves us across a spectrum from apparent endorsement of it to apparent repudiation of it; the order is designed to draw out the more local connections among the various plays. The argument as a whole is organized in the shape of a parabola. Its highest points are its first and last chapters on *Tamburlaine* and *Doctor Faustus* respectively: in these plays we can see Marlowe's least and most ironic representations of the culture wars between soldiers and civilians. David Bevington and Eric Rasmussen speculate that *Faustus* 'A' may 'perhaps even [operate as] a recantation' of *Tamburlaine*. Indeed it does, and on several levels. It may recant Marlowe's commitment in *Tamburlaine* to the '"harmony between ambition and salvation"'; I will argue that *Faustus* also recants the anti-theatrical axioms in *Tamburlaine* and elsewhere that players have nothing to contribute to state security.[39] En route to my discussion of state security, playing, and magical realism in *Faustus*, the medial chapters are ordered in such a way as to draw out what I see as an intensifying effort to complicate the representation of the theatrical enterprise itself within contemporary London's war fever. So the farther one reads beyond Chapter 1, the weaker the magnetic pull of *Tamburlaine*'s hypermilitarism; the closer to Chapter 6, the stronger the playwright's skepticism. Along the route, Chapter 2 considers *Dido, Queen of Carthage* as a tragedy whose hero Aeneas shares some of the Scythian shepherd's goals, but who flirts with a dangerously domesticated notion of triumph, thus depicting the degree to which masculinity is a rhetorical function of its contexts, even in epic. Chapter 3 extends that inquiry into a domestic English arena that was being much written about in the 1590s, the feudal England of *Edward II*, where a dissident is paradoxically king, charged to uphold the fictions of masculinity by which England is made safe from enemies both inside and outside the realm. Chapter 4, the lowest point on the parabola, explores the devolution of chivalry into commerce in *The Jew of Malta* and the tensions between contemporary English veterans and the rising class of merchants, whose international trading demands detente. Chapter 5 analyzes *The Massacre at Paris*, Marlowe's study of the use of the rhetorics of masculinity as weapons in the French wars of religion in his own time. That nuanced exposé in *The Massacre at Paris* of the gendered rhetoric of religious controversy prepares for Chapter 6, the high point of the parabola, *Faustus*. Unlike Tamburlaine, who is utterly unconflicted about what he wants and how he gets it, Faustus is paralyzed by desire, as Edward Snow has claimed; among those desires, one of the more insistent is becoming 'emperor of the world' (A 1.3.106).[40] *Faustus* ironizes many of the effects of martial law on civilian community that are treated more straightforwardly in *Tamburlaine*.

Indeed the final chapter, on *Faustus*, stands out as a reversal of my argument. For in that tragedy the playwright also reverses the dynamic of other Marlovian scripts. In those plays the sheer pleasure of theatrical playing (and its concomitant commitment to polyphonic discourse on stage, gender fluidity, and what might be called a symphonic vision of life) had disqualified, often fatally, one or more characters from the worlds they inhabit. In *Faustus*, playing is asserted as an activity that celebrates all of those features, yes, but also as a strategy or activity that is available to instantiate state security too. The play 'recuperates' playing by demonstrating its utility as a patriotic contribution no less valuable than the other forms of public scripts then in circulation to buoy English commitment to state defense during the Armada scares in the 1590s. In presenting playing as a legitimate form of epistemic aggression in its own right, *Doctor Faustus* ironically reclaims for the art of playing a measure of respectability and nationalistic utility that opponents of the theater – including the soldiers who wrote military handbooks – considered impossible.

Notes

1. Oliver Pigg, *Meditations Concerning praiers to Almightie God, for the saftie of ENGLAND, when the Spaniards were come into the narrow Seas. August 1588*, London, 1589, STC 19916, 8–9.

2. Kenneth Andrews, *Trade, Plunder, and Settlement: Maritime Enterprise and the Genesis of the British Empire, 1480–1630* (Cambridge: Cambridge University Press, 1984), 34. There is much recent discussion of the development of English nationalism in the early modern period. I have been especially influenced by Richard Helgerson's *Forms of Nationhood: The Elizabethan Writing of England* (Chicago: University of Chicago Press, 1992). Perhaps it is worth issuing a disclaimer here with respect to my use of the terms 'nation,' 'nationhood,' and 'nationalism' throughout this project. I do not mean to imply that the government or the people of England had already come to understand themselves as a single entity in the more articulated ways they would come to do in later centuries.

   Historians have long discussed Elizabeth's legendary reluctance to declare war, or to pay for it. One of the most poignant contemporary documents urging her to take the Armada threat more seriously is a letter written from Charles Lord Howard, Admiral of the Fleet since December 1587, aboard the *Ark*, on 23 June 1588, which includes the memorable exhortation 'For the love of Jesus Christ, Madam, awake thoroughly, and see the villainous treasons round about you, against your Majesty and your realm, and draw your forces round about you' (quoted in *Englishmen at War: A Social History in Letters, 1450–1900*, ed. Ernest Sanger [Dover, NH: Sutton, 1993], 23).

3. It was once customary for new historicists to claim that Elizabeth's government, lacking a police force or a standing army, used persuasion rather than force to effect rule. In the early 1990s, however, scholars renewed our attention to the tools of literal as well as rhetorical force available to the government, especially torture, which requires the services of provosts-marshal but not the existence of a constabulary as such. On the development of the office of provost-marshal, see Lindsay Boynton, 'The Tudor Provost-Marshal,' *English Historical Review* 77 (1962): 437–55 and 'Martial Law and the Petition of Right,' *English Historical Review* 79 (1964): 255–84. On the rhetoric of torture and its philosophical implications, see Katharine Eisaman Maus, *Inwardness and Theater in the English Renaissance* (Chicago: University of Chicago Press, 1995) and Elizabeth L. Hanson, 'Torture and Truth in Renaissance England,' *Representations* 34 (1991): 53–84.

   Historians and literary critics across the twentieth century paid only modest attention to another form of governmental control, martial law. Searching the scholarly literature, it is difficult but not impossible to find accounts of the imposition of martial law on civilians inside England and Ireland, a subject that, judging by the publication dates of the materials one can find, seems to interest scholars only when a modern war is in progress. Otherwise the topic is absent from or understated in a number of the canonical accounts of the period by major historians. For a recent, polemical account of the domestic applications of martial law against civilians, by which Elizabeth's government aimed to sustain its control over the people, or what he calls a 'state of terror' (43), see Curtis C. Breight, *Surveillance, Militarism and Drama in the Elizabethan Era* (New York: St

Martin's, 1996), especially 81–90 and Chapter 5. Breight offers a cogent narrative buttressed with an impressive array of primary texts to substantiate what had previously been for me only a hunch, that the government 'exploited domestic martial law' in ways too little recognized. I share Breight's conviction that militarism and martial law were used far more effectively and widely than has been studied, but not his deliberately 'polemical' (xi) assumptions as to why that is so in modern historical and literary scholarship; Breight overstates his claims that a good deal of modern scholarship colludes either unwittingly or deliberately in the Protestant propaganda machinery of the Cecils (see, for example, the Introduction, 1–42).

4.   Judith Butler's now-orthodox work on the performativity of gender helped shape my early thinking about Marlowe's notions of masculinity. In *Gender Trouble: Feminism and the Subversion of Identity* (New York: Routledge, 1990) she theorizes gender as an 'ongoing discursive practice' rather than a stable element existing in some pristine state prior to culture (33), a claim implicitly argued against by many of Marlowe's soldiers.

5.   Thomas Churchyard, 'A generall rehearsall of warres,' London, 1579, STC 5235, *iiv.

6.   Many historians have worked on the Anglo-Spanish crises in the early modern period. I am especially indebted to Kenneth Andrews, *Trade, Plunder, and Settlement*; John Guy, *Tudor England* (Oxford: Oxford University Press, 1988); Wallace T. MacCaffrey, *Queen Elizabeth and the Making of Policy, 1572–1588* and *Elizabeth I: War and Politics, 1588–1603* (Princeton: Princeton University Press, 1981, 1992); Anne Somerset, *Elizabeth I* (New York: St Martin's, 1991), 389–490; R.B. Wernham, *The Making of Elizabethan Foreign Policy* (Berkeley: University of California Press, 1980) and *After the Armada: Elizabethan England and the Struggle for Western Europe, 1588–1595* (1984; rpt Oxford: Clarendon, 1986); Garrett Mattingly, *The Armada* (Boston: Houghton Mifflin, 1959); Geoffrey Parker, *The Army of Flanders and the Spanish Road, 1567–1659* (1972; rpt Cambridge: Cambridge University Press, 1995) and 'Spain, Her Enemies and the Revolt of the Netherlands, 1559–1648,' *Past & Present* 49 (1970): 72–95; and Frank Tallett, *War and Society in Early Modern Europe, 1495–1715* (New York: Routledge, 1992).

7.   Elizabeth I, 'Placing Vagrant Soldiers Under Martial Law,' *Tudor Royal Proclamations*, ed. Paul L. Hughes and James F. Larkin, 3 vols (New Haven: Yale University Press, 1969), 3: 47.

8.   Lindsay Boynton, 'The Tudor Provost-Marshal,' 445.

9.   Elizabeth I, 'Placing Vagrants under Martial Law,' in *Tudor Royal Proclamations*, ed. Hughes and Larkin, 3: 96–7. Parker notes that in 1606 Parliament would make it a felony to serve in the army of a foreign prince without first taking an oath of allegiance to James I (*The Army of Flanders*, 52).

10. Elizabeth I, 'Prohibiting Unlawful Assembly under Martial Law [draft]'; 'Establishing Commissions against Seminary Priests and Jesuits'; 'Placing Vagrants under Martial Law,' in *Tudor Royal Proclamations*, ed. Hughes and Larkin, 3: 82, 91, 97. In September 1598, 'Placing Vagrants under Martial Law' was reissued as 'Placing London Vagabonds under Martial Law' (3:196–7).

11. For a wide-ranging analysis of the metaphors of war as theater circulating in late sixteenth- and seventeenth-century England, see Nick de Somogyi, *Shakespeare's Theatre of War* (Aldershot, UK: Ashgate, 1998), especially 90–130, to which I am indebted.

12. J.W. Fortescue, *A History of the British Army* (rpt New York: AMS, 1976), 1: 136.

13. See, for example, Paul Kocher, 'Marlowe's Art of War,' *Studies in Philology* 39 (1942): 207–25.

14. Sir William Slyngisbie [or Slingsby], *Relation of the Voyage to Cadiz, 1596,* ed. Julian S. Corbett, in *The Naval Miscellany*, ed. John Knox Laughton (London: Navy Records Society, 1901), 1: 23–92.

15. Michael Murrin speculates that English poets from Drayton to Milton 'substituted for realism a romantic view of medieval warfare' when writing of war at all, and that they 'lacked direct experience of war and also . . . an audience for the literature of war' (*History and Warfare in Renaissance Epic* [Chicago: University of Chicago Press, 1994], 236, 241). As the profusion of handbooks published by ordinary soldiers suggests, there was, however, an audience for more realistic accounts of contemporary warfare by English soldiers and mariners.

16. Nabil Matar surveys changes to the military career in Elizabethan England and the 'marginalization of the military values by which [soldiers] had lived' (45) in *Turks, Moors & Englishmen in the Age of Discovery* (New York: Columbia University Press, 1999), 44–55.

17. Barnabe Rich, *A Roome for a Gentleman*, London, 1609, STC 20985, blames intramural discord on a country that has enjoyed too much peace: then 'neighbour [turns] against the neighbour, the friend against the friend, the brother against the brother, & somtimes the father against the sonne' (B2v).

18. Geoffrey Gates, *The Defence of Militarie Profession*, London, 1579, STC 11683 (New York: Da Capo, 1973), 10.

19. Churchyard, 'A generall rehearsall of warres,' **iiiv.

20. Niccolo Tartaglia, *Three Bookes of Colloquies Concerning the Arte of Shooting*, trans. Cyprian Lucar, London, 1588, STC 23689.

21. Barnabe Rich, *A Path-Way to Military Practise*, London, 1587 (Amsterdam: Da Capo, 1969), B.

22. Ibid., B2v.

23. Ibid., D2v; William Bourne, *The Arte of Shooting in Great Ordnaunce*, London, 1587 (New York: Da Capo, 1969), vii; Gates, *The Defence of Militarie Profession*, 35.

24. Pigg, *Meditations*, A5v, 14, 8–9.

25. Simon Harward, *The Solace for the Souldier and Saylour*, London, 1592, STC 12923, B3v; Thomas Procter, *Of the Knowledge and Conducte of Warres*, London, 1578, STC 20403, v; Rich, *A Path-Way to Military Practise*, D2v.

26. Matthew Sutcliffe, *The Practice, Proceedings, and Lawes of armes*, London, 1593, STC 23469, A3v–A4r, A4v, Bv.

27. Diego Ortunez de Calahorra, *The Mirrour of Princely deedes and Knighthood*, trans. Margaret Tyler, London, 1578, STC 18859, A3r.

28. Boynton, 'The Tudor Provost-Marshal,' 440.

29. Mary I, 'Placing Possessors of Heretical and Seditious Books under Martial Law' and 'Ordering Fleet Manned under Martial Law,' in *Tudor Royal Proclamations*, ed. Hughes and Larkin, 3: 90–91.

30. Elizabeth I, 'Offering Pardon to Northern Rebels,' in *Tudor Royal Proclamations*, ed. Hughes and Larkin, 2: 326.
31. Elizabeth I, 'Ordering Destruction of Seditious Books,' in *Tudor Royal Proclamations*, ed. Hughes and Larkin, 2: 377.
32. Elizabeth I, 'Suppressing Invasion Rumors,' in *Tudor Royal Proclamations*, ed. Hughes and Larkin, 2: 470.
33. Elizabeth I, 'Ordering Martial Law against Possessors of Papal Bulls, Books, Pamphlets,' in *Tudor Royal Proclamations*, ed. Hughes and Larkin, 3: 16–17. William Garrard, *The Arte of Warre*, London, 1591, STC 11625, warns that murmuring within ranks about the conditions and quantities of food while serving a captain will destroy morale: 'murmure not against thy Captaine with thy tongue' (33).
34. Elizabeth I, 'Placing London Vagabonds under Martial Law,' in *Tudor Royal Proclamations*, ed. Hughes and Larkin, 3: 233.
35. G.R. Elton, 'The rule of law in sixteenth-century England,' reprinted in his *Studies in Tudor and Stuart Politics and Government: Papers and Reviews 1946–1972*, 2 vols (Cambridge: Cambridge University Press, 1974), 1: 277, 282, 271. For an argument against Elton, see J.A. Sharpe, *Early Modern England: A Social History 1550–1760*, 2d ed (London: Arnold, 1997), 9.
36. G. R. Elton, 'Government by Edict?' reprinted in his *Studies in Tudor and Stuart Politics*, 1: 307.
37. The Petition of Right, passed in the Commons in 1628 and accepted by Charles, aimed in part to thwart the king's recent order to suspend the common law in favor of martial law for troops serving under his flag on English soil. Charles's ordering that troops be disciplined by martial rather than by common law was taken by the Commons as a sign that the king was preparing to build a standing army that could be deployed internally. The Petition of Right made any declaration of martial law within England 'technically illegal.' 'Troops in England subject not to common law but solely to military law administered by the King's officers was a danger signal, as was the subjection of civilians to martial law' (Correlli Barnett, *Britain and her Army, 1509–1970* [New York: William Morrow, 1970], 124, 72). What the Commons in 1628 saw as a grave danger had of course been standard practice in time of war or preparing for it in Elizabeth's reign.

     As is made clear by a book first published in the midst of the First World War and republished during the Second World War, the meaning of 'martial law' continued to be a matter of debate long after the seventeenth century. See Garrard Glenn, *The Army and the Law*, revised by A. Arthur Schiller (1918; rpt New York: Columbia University Press, 1943), especially 185, n. 2.
38. Klaus Theweleit, *Male Fantasies*, trans. Erica Carter et al., 2 vols (Minneapolis: University of Minnesota Press, 1987, 1989).
39. David Bevington and Eric Rasmussen, eds, *Doctor Faustus A- and B-Texts (1604, 1616)*, 22.
40. Edward A. Snow, 'Marlowe's *Doctor Faustus* and the Ends of Desire,' in *Two Renaissance Mythmakers: Christopher Marlowe and Ben Jonson*, ed. Alvin Kernan. Selected Papers from the English Institute, 1975–76 (Baltimore: Johns Hopkins University Press, 1977), 70–110.

CHAPTER ONE

The Rhetoric of Soldiers' Desire in *Tamburlaine*

Death and life are in the power of the tongue.

Proverbs 18:21

The historical Tamerlane the Great conquered large chunks of Asia and North Africa in the latter fourteenth century.[1] Some two hundred years later, and well beyond Asia, his reputation as a fierce warrior and unforgiving victor was still very much alive. In late sixteenth-century London, in an era eager to anthropomorphize its fears of invasion, the specter of 'Tamerlane' appeared in military conduct manuals and on the stage as a shibboleth more potent than Ivan the Terrible and almost as awesome as Alexander the Great. 'Tamerlane' was in use as a ready prop, an eastern hero borrowed by western writers eager to promote various nationalist causes – defence of the coastline and other borders; nostalgia for the medieval crusades against infidels; offensive warlike maneuvers to strengthen England's opportunistic patrol of sea routes; and the *ad hoc* efforts to expand the nascent empire.

Indeed, in the Elizabethan military conduct-books that form the context of this study of Marlowe's plays, Tamerlane makes surprisingly frequent appearances, not all of them cameos, to support various nationalist gestures that are sometimes at odds with one another. This is an ironic use of 'Tamerlane,' to be sure. For the military ventures pressed by the fourteenth-century terror of Asia and Africa suggest in their scope and operations that the historical personage had little regard for nationalist agendas or boundaries. Yet in late sixteenth-century England, 'Tamerlane' appears in treatises and plays to shore up agendas that, however contradictory, all point toward greater nationalism. A floating signifier, 'Tamerlane' puts a face on a pet project or agenda: In *Certain Discourses Military*, for example, John Smythe invokes Tamerlane's defeat of the Turkish king Bajazeth to defend the longbow, Smythe's preferred weapon, from extinction; by the early years of the seventeenth century it would be supplanted by gunpowder-based weapons. On religious rather than strategic grounds, Geoffrey Gates in *The Defence of Militarie Profession* applauds Tamerlane's scourge of Bajazeth and his infidel Turks. In *The Discovery of a Gaping Gulf*, in contrast, the sometime soldier and royal adviser John Stubbs summons the specter of Tamerlane to warn Elizabeth against marrying any foreign prince, some new Philip of Spain who could be expected not only to wed her, but subdue England, much as Tamerlane, it is said, had conquered Bajazeth. George Whetstone's *The Honorable Reputation of a Souldier* praises Tamerlane's trajectory from humble shepherd to great general, as one able to profit by the otherwise largely illusory opportunities open to common soldiers; William Segar would soon suggest that honorable military service may in some instances raise a common soldier nearly to the rank of gentleman, a virtual gentleman-at-arms. In Whetstone's treatise, however, Tamerlane's reputation is finally as unstable as his social climbing, for unlike Segar, Whetstone disapproves: he is thus presented as being one of those unfortunate modern generals whose viciousness may achieve victory but 'displeaseth God': 'Tamberlaine, and other cruel Tyrants, were neither beloved alive, nor morned after death.' Shortly after Marlowe's own death, Tamerlane is again glorified in 1597 in Jean du Bec-Crispin's hagiography, *The Historie of the Great Emperour Tamerlan*. *The Historie* appeared in print amidst the continuing commercial success of *Tamburlaine the Great*, which periodically held the stage of the Rose Theatre through much of the 1590s. Bec-Crispin's guy is a ferocious but also humane warrior, one whose heart would fill with sorrow at the 'humaine miserie' produced by his sieges, whose temperament 'was very courteous' except in response to Bajazeth's pride.[2] Bec-Crispin envisions Tamerlane as a warrior of noble lineage[3] and great compassion; his singularly focused efforts to cleanse the hero of culpability for the massive bloodshed throws into relief Marlowe's more ambiguous uses of the historical legends.

When such historical personages are used in multiple and mutually contradictory ways in the early modern period, the writers who are conjuring them routinely ignore or even elide these potential contradictions within their own texts. Sometimes these contradictions are inadvertently comic, as when Captain Tom Stuckley, the Irish hero of George Peele's *The Battle of Alcazar* (1589), abandoning a papal mandate to rescue Ireland from England's clutches, abruptly commits himself and his troops to helping King Sebastian of Portugal carry out a foolish and ill-fated strike against a usurping king of Morocco. 'Stuckley' (or Stukley) was commonly held up as an instance of Irish Catholic bravery in contemporary lore. While Peele sometimes plays that game, he also dispels that image of Stuckley as a nationalist by having him disavow any such motivations or loyalties. In a key conversation in Lisbon before sailing for Morocco, Peele's Stuckley speaks from the cynical vantage of the untethered mercenary who is prepared to put himself first, and is utterly un-nostalgic for his country of origin:

Lord governour of Lisborne understand,
As we are Englishmen, so are we men,
And I am Stukley so resolvde in all,
To follow rule, honor and Emperie,
Not to be bent so strictly to the place,
Wherein at first I blew the fire of life,
But that I may at libertie make choise,
Of all the continents that bound the world,
For why? I make it not so great desert
To be begot or borne in anie place,
Sith thats a thing of pleasure and of ease,
That might have bin performd else-where as well.

2.2.409–20[4]

Generally speaking, Marlowe's heroes do not join Stuckley in pursuing careers as mercenaries whose sympathies are so malleable or so easily manipulated. The soldiers to whom Marlowe gives voice are more often caught up in defending turf, even if it be a Mediterranean island and the hero every bit as much of an opportunist as Stuckley. Perhaps *Doctor Faustus* is the preeminent example of Marlowe's acute interest in the nuances of nationalism and the concomitant use of contradictory representations of historical personages by various parties for ideological gain. But Marlowe can also be as apparently inattentive as Peele to the ideological intricacies of displays of nationalism, as in *Tamburlaine*, where the principal hero installs puppet leaders to safeguard the national boundaries of nations his armies have just trounced and now rule under terms of occupation. Much like Peele's Stuckley, Tamburlaine is ultimately less interested in what has been won or could be won than in the immediate circumstances of its winning; in the hands of writers in the late 1580s, neither 'Captain Tom Stuckley' nor 'Tamburlaine the Great' is made to find the abstract pull of the nation-state nearly as compelling as war for its own sake. Both love the heat of combat and the possibility of glory.

Even in the midst of its apparently sincere celebration of war, however, *Tamburlaine the Great* quietly attends to the philosophical horror of war. It treats in complex terms what Bec-Crispin's hagiography and Peele's play about a *coup d'état* in North Africa present almost in monochrome. It's not that Marlowe offers spectators some glib recantation of the carnage he conjures up; his soldiers do not run about the stage saying, in effect, 'war is hell.' Instead it's that Marlowe offers his spectators something much more three-dimensional, more disingenuous in its representation of that sheer delight in combat that Tamburlaine embodies. Of all the several Elizabethans who borrowed or adapted Tamerlane's history, Marlowe's graphic presentation of the trail of blood and brutality is most likely the best known today, and among the more notorious. In ten acts, Tamburlaine's armies roll over several nations and cultures, leaving thousands of civilians enslaved or worse.[5] In the interest of founding his own legend as the hypermasculine 'general of the world' he practices virtual genocide against his enemies, and destroys their cities, religions, and ways of life (1–5.1.452). By no means does he work alone, however. The soldiers who serve in his armies eagerly follow his lead, taking delight in committing mass destruction on levels that approach the practices and scope of ethnic cleansing in the twentieth century. 'From Azamor to Tunis near the sea / Is Barbary unpeopled for thy sake' (2–1.3.133–4), Usumcasane boasts to his supreme commander after yet another victory. His comrade Techelles repeats the formula 15 lines later, altering it only slightly, reiterating the genocidal spirit of Tamburlaine's campaigns.

The sheer amount of blood spilled in the course of the ten acts helps to establish the play's decidedly unusual spirit, but has also troubled several generations of post-war Marlowe critics eager to detect in the aspirations and choices of the hero some solid clues as to the elusive playwright's own sensibility. Few critics have admired the taste for crime or the putative cannibalism exhibited in the play. Indeed, most who have written on *Tamburlaine* have struggled to justify or explain away precisely these elements.[6]

I wish instead to examine its soldiers' desire for violence without end, concentrating on the affective motivations and consequences of the bloodshed. Marlowe's characters – males and females, soldiers and civilians – always experience desire not as a universal, but as a historically and socially constructed force. These terms have been usefully explicated by Jay Clayton, who contrasts universal 'need' to culturally generated 'desire': 'Need is a constant by definition; . . . Desire, on the other hand, is what happens to need when it enters history, language, culture, and society.'[7] This discrimination helps to clarify the disagreements between soldiers and civilians in *Tamburlaine*. Its soldiers insist that desire is physiological – produced by passions, those mysterious forces still considered by many in Marlowe's time to be both ontologically certain as well as trans-historically constant.[8] The general and his men invoke contemporary notions of the passions to justify their aggression against one and all, often insisting that their impulse to raze yet one more kingdom is a physical urge to be ignored at their own peril. That is to say, they rape, pillage, and murder because – they claim – they cannot do otherwise: nations and women exist, and they are soldiers: *ergo*, they must rape and pillage.

Their claim is closely interrogated in the play. In the pauses between battles fought and won, the playwright interjects vignettes of domestic life that compromise our admiration of the soldiers' victories. In these vignettes we hear the discordant voices of minor characters for whom desire is always an emotional rather than a purely physiological experience. Of these renegade figures, it is Agydas and Calyphas who explicitly renounce male hegemony and thus subvert the violent frame of mind enjoined by Tamburlaine and his comrades. Together with the widow Olympia, another dissident, these peripheral figures insist through their actions as well as their speeches that the soldiers' account of the relation between nature and culture does not respect the complexities of the world in which both soldiers and civilians live. Through protests, they attempt to preserve, and in some instances to dilate, the autonomy of thought and movement that the soldiers aim to curb in their enemies and in themselves. For contesting a military regime both brittle and self-serving, they are fatally silenced.

If *Tamburlaine* depicts war as the only avenue of escape from the restraints imposed by culture, it also stresses the futility of the warriors' efforts to escape. For even Marlowe's soldiers depend on the patterns of culture, not only to bestow but also continually to verify their Herculean identities. Like the *Iliad*, *Tamburlaine* captures the human cost of the heroic ethos.

The nature of nature in Tamburlaine's soldiers

Midway through Part One, Tamburlaine articulates the ancient assumption that the human body and the natural universe are congruent.[9] In three lines at the crux of what is probably his most famous speech, the one that glories in the 'sweet fruition of an earthly crown' (1–2.7.12–29), he explains the energies that have driven him to rout Mycetes, king of Persia, and the king's brother Cosroe, Tamburlaine's brief ally: 'Nature, that framed us of four elements / Warring within our breasts for regiment, / Doth teach us all to have aspiring minds' (1–2.7.18–20). Prosaically put, the self-elected scourge of God asserts that the actions of the mind are inescapably grounded in the mechanisms of the body. And that pedagogic 'Nature' – by which Tamburlaine surely means the antithesis of civilization – teaches him to preempt the civil desires of communities, such as the legal acquisition of property. 'Nature' emancipates him from the obligation to express in civilized ways ambition he considers innate. According to his argument, the four elements 'Warring within our breasts for regiment' not only authorize, but demand the sort of aspiration that leaves others defeated, wounded, or dead. As he justifies his sudden double-cross of Cosroe, Tamburlaine further implies that warfare releases pent-up aggression. By directing elements at war within his breast toward the universe at large, he renders self-destructive energies beneficial: they spur him on to his glorious identity as world conqueror. Tamburlaine's speech ventriloquizes a stance toward the naturalness of violence that is readily assumed by many military conduct-book writers of the late sixteenth century. In *The Castle*, for example, William Blandy justifies the inevitability of violence with the same rhetorical maneuver as Tamburlaine's *apologia* of the violent energies scrambling in his chest. Aggression is naturalized and supposedly neutralized in aesthetic terms: 'Dame Nature,' Blandy writes, has framed soldiers in 'the clearnesse and shining glory of vertue and nobility: yet she hath imparted unto them a most sharp wit and ready capacity, great value and singuler providence' (27).[10] It is a bold step requiring a lot of poetic license to claim that soldiers enjoy 'singuler providence,' making them figuratively elect, or perhaps even demigods.

Leonard Barkan offers support for the idea that contemporaries of Marlowe would most likely have taken as orthodoxy Tamburlaine's notion of an innate, chaotic energy that must be harnessed. In his excellent study of the ancient assumption that body and universe are congruent, Barkan writes that 'the poets of the Renaissance are more likely [than not] to see the chemical microcosm in Tamburlaine's terms "of four elements / Warring within our breasts for regiment"' (40). Yet it is also possible to find evidence that the presumed congruence of body and universe was collapsing well before the Civil War. For example, the question of whether 'Nature' sanctions peace or war was hotly debated in the sixteenth century, and along with it, the larger linguistic issues of what is meant by 'Nature.' To cite only some obvious examples from the sixteenth and seventeenth centuries, Erasmus, Montaigne, and Bacon occasionally acknowledge that abstractions such as Truth or Nature derive, as Montaigne says, from 'Custom,' where custom sometimes acts as a benign signifier of a malignant ideology. In the *Adages* Erasmus insists that war is never biologically inevitable, never the result of 'four elements / Warring within our breast for regiment,' as Tamburlaine posits, but a bloody tactic of those who pursue political and economic power. For pious Erasmus, war is the 'universal demoralisation of life' that 'floods like a contagious disease.'[11] And Francis Bacon's very different attack in the *Novum Organum* against the mind's idols – superstitions about its own powers – and against its pretensions to be congruent with the universe of reason are well known.

One of the most apposite passages of early modern literature to refute Tamburlaine's claims about nature comes from the genre of revenge tragedy. In Fulke Greville's *Mustapha*, a Senecan drama about Turkish politics, the Chorus cautions against holding to any notion of a monolithic 'Nature' that supports soldiers:

Forsake not nature, nor misunderstand her,
Her mysteries are read without faith's eye-sight.
She speaketh in our flesh, and from our senses
Delivers down her wisdoms to our reason.
If any man would break her laws to kill,
Nature doth, for defence, allow offences.
She neither taught the father to destroy,
Nor promised any man, by dying, joy.[12]

The Chorus's speech is remarkable for its positivist confidence and its denial of eternal life, two surprises that almost obscure its dispute of the analogy between body and universe traced so fully by Barkan. The Chorus refuses to validate for its audience the idea that men can defend murderous conquest as the inevitable expression of human nature: 'She neither taught the father to destroy, / Nor promised any man, by dying, joy.' And in this heroic couplet that closes the speech, Fulke Greville exposes the pathetic fallacy that sustains Tamburlaine in his quests. However regularly spring shall follow winter, the Chorus implies, we have no certainty that 'joy' shall follow 'death': it is not 'promised.' The Chorus thus cautions us not to read our own fantasies into the 'mysteries' of the natural world.

'To be a soldier! That is at best to be something less than a man': The murder of eros[13]

In *Mustapha* the Chorus teases its audience with insoluble questions of eternal life. In *Tamburlaine* the soldiers constrict their experiences, mostly to murder, so as to evade the anxieties created by such questions. In effect they enter a trance that protects them, as Klaus Theweleit says, from 'the bewildering multiplicity of the living. . . . The more lifeless, regimented, and monumental reality appears to be, the more secure the men feel.'[14] The condition is recognized alike by theorists of culture and by those who have hurled grenades in battle and lived to write about it.[15] A trance curbs the soldiers' compassion for the enemy as well as makes it easier to breach civil customs in favor of the rules of war.

It is through poetry that Tamburlaine conceives his destructive acts, and it is poetry that transports him and his men to a mesmerized state of mind that allows them to deconstruct the universe as it has been, as Elaine Scarry says of torturers' methods, and to build it up again upon principles that favor them and their vision of culture predicated upon martial law.[16] Some critics have argued that in *Tamburlaine* the magnificent poetry itself, especially of martial conquest, contains and subdues the violence, helping playgoers to levitate from the bloody

battlefields into the ethereal regions of the sublime.[17] While it is
impossible to argue that such a reading is categorically wrong, it is not
true to my experience of the poetry, nor to the experiences of all sorts of
characters who are the victims of the armies of Tamburlaine and the
subsidiary monarchs of his territories. To my mind, the imagery of mass
destruction overwhelms the poetry. For every apostrophe to Zenocrate
and every shimmering oration before battle, there is a countering image
of the effects of savage behavior eviscerating the nobility of
Tamburlaine's heroic code.

A catalogue of examples drawn from both parts of the play may
help to recreate the playgoer's or reader's experience of the too-
muchness of the violence: preparing for the Turkish expedition,
Tamburlaine boasts that 'such lavish will I make of Turkish blood' that
the sun shall hide its head, 'for half the world shall perish in this fight'
(2–1.3.165, 171); as the army gets ready to meet the Turk Bajazeth on
the field, 'let him bring millions infinite of men, / Unpeopling Western
Africa and Greece' brags Usumcasane to his general, 'Yet we assure us
of the victory' (1–3.3.33–5). Not to be outdone, Bajazeth imitates
Tamburlaine's methods by ordering 'Let thousands die, their
slaughtered carcasses / Shall serve for walls and bulwarks to the rest'
(1–3.3.138–9); Tamburlaine's sons prove their lineage (which the
general has doubted, seemingly in order to provoke their bravado) by
conjuring a 'sea of blood,' as Celebinus has it (2–1.3.89). His brother
Amyras competes by imagining that, were his father defeated, he
would 'strive to swim through pools of blood / Or make a bridge of
murdered carcasses / Whose arches should be framed with bones of
Turks' (2–1.3.92–4). Tamburlaine out-Babels the people of Babylon by
ordering Techelles to 'drown them all, man, woman, and child; / Leave
not a Babylonian in the town' (2–5.1.169–70). The victims include
'thousands' of burghers who, trussed, are dropped into the city's lake,
much as Protestants are drowned without mercy in the Seine in *The
Massacre at Paris*. In short, piling up images of senseless destruction and
of bloody 'murdered carcasses' makes the deeds virtually overwhelming.
The words themselves do some violence even in expressing the various
modes of death, as Marlowe's soldiers well know, and as we hear by
contrast when Theridamas reports Zenocrate's death. He is as grief-
stricken as his general, but his spare language gives no details of
Zenocrate's final moments: 'If words might serve,' Theridamas laments,
'our voice hath rent the air.' To which Tamburlaine replies: 'For she is
dead! Thy words do pierce my soul. / Ah, sweet Theridamas, say so no
more' (2–2.4.121, 125–6). What is painful to Tamburlaine in this single
instance is on the whole potentially far more devastating to playgoers
as well, who watch as he depopulates half the world, fulfilling his

fantasy of obliterating all evidence that his martial ambition has ever been challenged. As he says of his wife's native Damascus, 'Were in that city all the world contained, / Not one should 'scape, but perish by our swords' (1–4.2.121–2).

Moreover, it is not simply the physical world of cities and nations that is deconstructed, but more radically, the world of human relationships. Aiming to destroy a world in which eros helps to bring about the next generation, the soldiers fuse eros with murder, making murder or the poetic promise of it their principal sources of erotic gratification. As Theweleit observes of the imaginations of fascists, 'Heroic acts of killing take the place of the sexual act' (2:279). The play's insistent return to two recurring images – of hearts extruded and bowels pierced – affirms this link. Here again I think an accumulation of examples helps to recreate the omnipresence of the images voiced on stage. Examples culled from parts One and Two include: 'gastly death / With greedy talons gripe my bleeding heart' (1–2.7.48–9); '(cruel Tamburlaine) I could willingly feed upon thy blood-raw heart' (1–4.4.11–12); 'our murdered hearts have strained forth blood' (2–2.4.123); 'Direct my weapon to his barbarous heart' (1–2.6.38); 'First shalt thou rip my bowels with thy sword / And sacrifice my heart to death and hell / Before I yield to such a slavery' (1–4.2.16–18); 'Leave words and let them feel your lances' points / Which glided through the bowels of the Greeks' (1–3.3.91–2); 'I long to pierce his bowels with my sword / That hath betrayed my gracious sovereign' (2–3.2.152–3); 'Go, villain, cast thee headlong from a rock / Or rip thy bowels and rend out thy heart / T'appease my wrath, or else I'l torture thee, / Searing thy hateful flesh with burning irons' (2–3.5.120–23). This obsession with the penetration of an opponent's bowels in the play seems to extend to Marlovian tragedy Mario DiGangi's observation that in Renaissance comedy the '"ass"' is frequently 'an overdetermined part of the body in which sexual, sadistic, and scatological activities converge.'[18]

Collectively, these tropes convey the distinct impression that soldiers in *Tamburlaine* anatomize the precise sites of their victories and defeats; the last image, indeed, echoes the fate of Edward II, whose violation of the priorities of epic masculinity is punished by captors whose 'burning irons' rip his bowels, a punishment many critics have assumed to be symbolically his just reward for sodomy, and that others have argued is instead proof that Edward's killers were intent on disguising incriminating physical evidence of their treachery; I take up the issue in more detail in Chapter 3. As Richard Rambuss has noted in a related context, however, the politics of 'the scholarship of a previous generation of critics' can be taken to be less significant than the fact that

critics of early modern culture of all persuasions seem to have missed the
tacit assumption that the act of 'Sodomy [is] the natural form of
unnaturalness – for all men.'[19]

As in Edward's murder, in *Tamburlaine* victory is victory over some
specific part of an opponent's body – his heart, his bowels – in ways that
make the human body a metonym of the threats of soldiers to culture,
to peace. Piercing a bowel, mapping a victory onto a foe's body,
Marlowe's soldiers aim to demonstrate the truth of their own monolithic
vision of nature. When they cut open an opponent's chest to clutch his
'blood-raw heart,' they confirm that for them, at least, the body of a
man is merely and conveniently only a physical object located in mere
space and time, not a metaphysical being possessing complex humanist
agency.[20] Through such killing the soldiers make life synonymous with
the corporeal body alone, a point hinted at yet again when Cosroe
comments upon the process of his own death: 'with my blood my life
slides through my wound' (1–2.7.43). Cutting out the heart, soldiers
persuade themselves if no one else that body and soul are reductively a
single thing.[21]

Moreover, to eat the heart of an enemy, as these soldiers promise, is
to make the act of murder literally regenerative. For by consuming
another man's flesh, one may sustain and indeed create one's own body.
In the Tamburlainian universe, soldiers paradoxically do consider
murder more regenerative than (hetero)sexual intercourse. They
regularly turn their male opponents into quasi-sexual partners of unions
that express their own plans for reconstituting the world, as is suggested
by the recurring images of cannibalism and of piercing bowels with
swords. While in *Edward II* the playwright openly imagines the practice
of sodomy, it is even more powerfully present in *Tamburlaine*, as in
Usumcasane's implicitly homophobic expression, 'I long to pierce his
bowels with my sword', which hints at the fusion of sexual longing, anal
sex, and murder.

In thinking about the ambiguous and complex representation of these
male–male quasi-sexual fantasies in *Tamburlaine* and other of
Marlowe's plays, it is worth keeping in mind also Rambuss's recent
caveat that critics who have written about the erotics of a strain of
theological ravishment in early modern culture (which is what we have
here – Tamburlaine and co. espousing a theology of war that centers on
their fantasies of divine intervention and scourging intimacy) have often
switched the gender of one personage in order to evade cultural
proscriptions against sodomitical relations, then and now. The most
famous instance would be the editors of Shakespeare's sonnets who, for
centuries, scrubbed away all hints of sodomitical longings by changing
the addressee's gender in the poems to the erstwhile Young Man. But

what critics have done to 'protect' Shakespeare, or themselves or us, they have not done to Marlowe.

In plays other than *Edward*, characters themselves sometimes engage in gender-switching their enemies, as in *Doctor Faustus*, for example. At the court of Charles V, Faustus transforms the braggart knight of the Holy Roman Empire into a Diana figure; and in contrast to his servant Robin's desire to see 'maidens in our parish dance at my pleasure stark naked' (A 2.2.4), Faustus himself is content to relinquish his early demand for 'a wife' (A 2.1.145) for the surrogate love of Mephistopheles: 'If thou lovest me,' Faustus is told by his tempter, 'think no more of' marriage (A 2.1.155). Working on the war rhetoric of Greek epic, Emily Vermeule notes there a similar though not identical phenomenon of gender-switching or gender-baiting one's opponents, contending of the verbal jousts that precede combat, 'When taunting, the aim is to turn the opposing soldier into a female, or into the weaker animal role.'[22]

Tamburlaine is different in that when the title figure and his men meet their foes, they can openly imagine their lust for war as an erotic same-sex experience. Consider for instance the brief courtship of Theridamas by Tamburlaine when they meet, ostensibly in battle, in Part One. As they come together on stage, each recognizes the other as noble by his speech, standard stuff in Renaissance drama. But typically, we might then expect them to engage in honorable combat as a way to affirm that nobility of spirit. Instead, however, the two principals converse as if they are Edward and Gaveston reunited; their discourse draws heavily from early modern reincarnations of platonic friendship.[23] Tamburlaine is the lover: 'Theridamas my friend, take here my hand, / Which is as much as if I swore by heaven / And called the gods to witness of my vow; / Thus shall my heart be still combined with thine / Until our bodies turn to elements / And both our souls aspire celestial thrones' (1–1.2.231–5). If Tamburlaine's language picks up the tropes we associate with male–male friendship in the early modern period, however, Theridamas speaks not as the beloved is prescribed to do, but as Edward does, emphasizing the very thing platonic friends sought to steer away from – physical pleasure. Even before his new master has offered not only his metaphoric hand but also his heart, gushy Theridamas is declaring himself physically vanquished by same-sex desire. When Usumcasane sums up the game, intoning that 'kings shall crouch unto our conquering swords . . . they shall confess / "These are the men that all the world admires"' (1–1.2.219–22), Theridamas addresses Tamburlaine, responding with words that go beyond what is required by the discourse of surrender: 'What strong enchantments tice my yielding soul?' 'Won with thy words and conquered with thy looks, / I yield myself, my men and horse to thee: / To be partaker of thy good or ill / As long as life maintains Theridamas' (1–1.2.223–5, 227–30). In a battle scene, it's a surprise to recognize that Theridamas and Tamburlaine have just staged a mock exchange of marriage vows. And while the master seems content to think of Theridamas as his friend, invoking the myth of Pylades and Orestes as a warrant for the tender exchange that has just been voiced, Theridamas frames their union in language that hedges the explicit assumption of the platonic friendship tradition that they will not physically consummate their same-sex desire but will understand that desire as philosophically elevating and purifying. But as Theridamas makes plain, he has been viscerally seduced; Techelles had been right to tip off Tamburlaine that Theridamas is a man whose 'deep affections make him passionate' (1–1.2.163). As Theweleit might say of this same-sex mock marriage between battlefield foes, 'The existence of the feminine is hallucinated away in a process whereby one man procreates himself by devouring another.'[24]

But not quite. Women in their reproductive capacities are also able to remake the world, a privilege over which the soldiers in the play want to claim exclusive control. Both on and off the fields of battle, they aim to render women harmless. Even Zenocrate serves only an ancillary role as Tamburlaine's cheerleader. Alive, she privately expresses troublesome reservations about her husband's ambitions,[25] as when she apologizes to the gods Jove and Mohamet for his execution of the virgins of Damascus (1–5.1.363–8). Dead, she serves his cause with silent devotion. Soon after she expires in Jerusalem, he orders that her hearse shall always follow his army, her portrait always hang within his royal tent; her visage inspires him, 'As if Bellona, goddess of the war, / Threw naked swords and sulphur balls of fire / Upon the heads of all our enemies' (2–3.2.40–42).

If the general's peculiar nostalgia elevates Zenocrate from queen to (rotting) goddess, then it also raises the related question of whether she has ever been more than a fantasy to him, a question furthered by his representing Zenocrate as Bellona.[26] In classical mythology Bellona is most often considered the wife of Mars; thus when Tamburlaine chooses Bellona rather than Venus as his figurative mistress, he chooses violence over love. As he explains to the virgins of Damascus, the pleasures of love and gold, intertwined in his imagination as domestic sirens that threaten to disrupt the soldier's ruthless pursuit of conquest, have no hold over him: 'I will not spare these proud Egyptians, / Nor change my martial observations / For all the wealth of Gihon's golden waves. / Or for the love of Venus, would she leave / The angry god of arms and lie with me' (1–5.1.121–5). His armor acting as a Teflon shield against love, Tamburlaine is Aeneas 'perfected.' Unlike the Roman imperialist discussed below in Chapter 2, who must be warned against Dido's Egyptian charms by his lieutenant Achates, who urges him to put his fleet to sea in order to get to Rome, Tamburlaine needs no such coaching from his subordinates. Early in the first play, as Tamburlaine woos Zenocrate, Techelles grows anxious at his general's promise to offer all their 'martial prizes' (Techelles is self-interested), 'then my self to fair Zenocrate' (1–1.2.102, 105). 'What now? in love?' asks Techelles, clearly worried that the army's priorities are being sacrificed to the charms of Venus. Tamburlaine answers his lieutenant with an icy cynicism that undercuts all his later professions of love for Zenocrate: 'Techelles, women must be flatterèd. / But this is she with whom I am in love' (1–1.2.106–108).

If it strikes playgoers as peculiar that, almost in the same breath, Tamburlaine is able to order the virgins of Damascus slaughtered and Zenocrate elevated to the status of a goddess ('Ah fair Zenocrate, divine Zenocrate' [1–5.1.135]), it may seem more peculiar that Zenocrate who inspires him on the battlefield barely exists for him beyond it. In his mind's eye, it is not Bellona who is 'naked,' but the swords she hurls against his enemies.

When Tamburlaine uses his wife's body to inspire him in battle, he not only contaminates his own ideal of marital companionship, but divulges his fetishism of the female corpse. This fetish appears in truncated form in the banquet scene with Bajazeth and Zabina. The episode reminds us not only that soldiers feed off other men, but also that, in general, men feed off women. The tone of the banquet is combative from the first, and grows even more so when Tamburlaine baits his prisoners, who have lost their appetites, by force-feeding them from the end of his sword: 'here, eat sir, take it from my / sword's point, or I'll thrust it to thy heart.' Treading upon the proffered food, Bajazeth further provokes his captor: 'Take it up, villain, and eat it, or I will make / thee slice the brawns of thy arms into carbonadoes, and / eat them.' Usumcasane joins in: 'Nay, 'twere better he killed his wife, and then / she shall be sure not to be starved, and he be provided / for a month's victual beforehand.' 'Here is my dagger,' Tamburlaine replies, 'despatch her while she is fat, / for if she live but a while longer, she will fall into a con- / sumption with fretting, and then she will not be worth / the eating' (1–4.4.40–51). Given Tamburlaine's history, we have no guarantee he is speaking tongue-in-cheek about Zabina's potential to be a tasty meal.

Through this perversion of the activity of eating, 'the starting place of self-artifice,' Marlowe exposes Tamburlaine's tenuous grip on the activity of remaking the world.[27] In a small way, his talk of cannibalism violates a powerful taboo. Jokes about having Zabina for dinner expose the insanity of his very serious urge to carry out genocidal fantasies:

'Then, when the sky shall wax as red as blood, / It shall be said I made it red myself, / To make me think of naught but blood and war' (1–4.2.53–5). This arch-dream illustrates the soldier-male's need to decimate all reality. At once his denial affirms the autarchy of the self, but severely restricts its complexity: as he boasts, he shall 'think of naught but blood and war.'

This fantasy is most notoriously worked out in the episode of the Slaughter of the Virgins, where Marlowe braids together the several elements of the soldier's psyche – his eroticization of murder, his misogyny, his contempt for other people and the laws that bind them together, however imperfectly. In 1–5.1, Damascus is under Tamburlaine's heavy attack. Its governor dispatches four virgins bearing laurel, who hope to dissuade Tamburlaine from further efforts to sack their city. The 'god of war,' as the governor calls the general, already displays over his tents outside Damascus the black flags that signal the expiration of his mercy (1–5.1.1). Not even the virgins' 'unspotted prayers . . . will melt his fury into some remorse' (1–5.1.20, 22). Ensuing speeches from both camps emphasize Tamburlaine's 'custom' (1–5.1.13, 5.1.67) of slaughtering an entire city or garrison once the black flags have been raised on the third day of a siege, black signifying a world of grief and sorrow.[28]

The color triad deployed by Tamburlaine – white on the first day, signifying the promise of mercy to those who surrender; then red, signifying the inevitability of some bloodshed of those who have resisted his attack; then black, signifying the promise of utter destruction of the entire city or garrison – by which he crudely communicates with a city under fire, is significantly denied in Bec-Crispin's revisionist history of Tamerlane's reign discussed earlier. Bec-Crispin considers the legend of the triad of colors to be one of the 'fables' about Tamerlane promulgated by unreliable chroniclers—some unnamed 'foolish' 'Italians.' This denial of the triad is part of Bec-Crispin's efforts to recuperate Tamerlane as a 'very courteous' soldier; unwittingly, the denial may reinforce our perception of the conqueror as formulaically barbaric, inhuman.[29]

Tamburlaine's triad of colors has been analyzed for other circumstances by Victor Turner. He suggests that the color black may signify an individual's 'falling into unconsciousness, the experience of a "black out,"' an observation that illuminates the symbolic import of Tamburlaine's black signal flag.[30] The black flag, of 'last and cruellest hue' (1–5.1.8), portends genocide of a people who shall suffer a loss of communal consciousness. By overrunning Damascus[31] – destroying its indigenous life – the conqueror 'blacks out' its culture, which must submit to his own 'custom' of merciless genocide. Refusing to swerve from his plan, he affirms his vision of biological truth. This truth is importantly not affirmed by Zenocrate, whose dissent is embedded in her recounting the Virgins' deaths in painstaking detail. She sees that, with these executions, the conqueror crosses the imaginary line separating war from sadism:

> Wretched Zenocrate, that livest to see
>
> . . .
>
>   the sun-bright troop
> Of heavenly virgins and unspotted maids,
> Whose looks might make the angry god of arms
> To break his sword and mildly treat of love,
> On horsemen's lances to be hoisted up
> And guiltlessly endure a cruel death.
>
> 1–5.1.320–30

This is a painful moment after which one cannot call Tamburlaine a 'noble savage.'[32] In ordering this atrocity, moreover, the general puts himself well outside the boundaries of what playgoers would have recognized from contemporary treatises as the acceptable treatment of captives, particularly virgins, who are often singled out in such treatises for special mention. Styward, for one, decrees that soldiers – 'of what degree soever' – who rape 'maried wives . . . widdowes, maids or virgins,' 'shall without mercie be punished by death.'[33]

The horror of Tamburlaine's iconoclasm is brought into full relief through the image of virgins penetrated by 'horsemen's lances.' The soldiers desecrate what Damascus takes to be supreme objects of desire – and thus desecrate desire itself. Moreover, they stop life: virgins who have known the fatal iron phallus shall know no other, shall never reproduce. Completing the symbolic equation of woman and land that is invited by the governor's plan to have the women save Damascus, 'We see in the bleeding virgin[s] the savaged body politic.'[34]

The hollow men

Marlowe illuminates the ways in which these most powerful soldiers are paradoxically the play's most vulnerable inhabitants. His studies take place in violent domestic episodes that pit the soldiers against minor characters who struggle to the death against military hegemony. Three such episodes – the murders of Calyphas, Olympia, and Agydas – have received scant critical attention, and what has appeared often privileges the warrior's role. But unlike the Slaughter of the Virgins, say, which occurs as part of the sack of Damascus, military conquest drives none of these three domestic scenes; the exigencies of war offer no defense of the soldiers' brutality. Indeed, what is at stake is more valuable than land to

Tamburlaine and his deputies – their ability to prescribe martial law. The tools of its enforcement have changed a great deal in the four centuries since *Tamburlaine*. But the most effective tool by which civilians may resist martial law has remained constant: the dissenting voice. In an immaterial way, the voice is, as Scarry notes, a crucial 'locus of power'; it constructs and deconstructs whole worlds.[35]

All three characters, whose murders we shall come to shortly, speak out against the soldiers' efforts to impose their deadly, monolithic vision of the world on everybody else. As each dissident recognizes, life under martial law entails not only physical but also mental subjugation. To defy martial law, then, is to refute its version of reality. The threat posed by these dissidents is more grave than simple defiance. At stake in each episode is the soldiers' polestar, their belief that nature precedes culture. Individually and collectively, the soldiers fret about the consequences of its collapse. They worry especially that 'masculinity' may not be a correlative of 'natural' aggression, but a category constructed by language and so subject to its vicissitudes.

This particular anxiety traverses both parts of the play. To ward it off, Tamburlaine and company often speak of war as a game, and of 'the warrior' as a role cast by the commanding general. This very idea was a poetic commonplace in the sixteenth century. It appears, for example, in Sir John Harington's preface to his translation of *Orlando Furioso* published in 1591. In a paragraph arguing for poetic license, Harington quotes in Latin an 'old verse' that he 'will English without rime' because, he says, 'I count it without reason.' Playing that beloved literary game of both endorsing and recanting a position, even a frivolous one, Harington quotes a three-line ditty, the relevant line of which is: 'Militibus, medicis, tortori, occidere ludo est;' which he translates thus: 'Souldiers, Phisicians, and Hangmen make a sport of murther.'[36] In the play, such a trope functions like a vaccine, protecting soldiers from the Protean heresy. Techelles thus urges his troops as they arm for combat against Balsera, 'soldiers play the men' (2–3.3.63). Likewise, his enemy Callapine implores his fellow Turks to 'play the men, / Whet all your swords to mangle Tamburlaine' (2–3.5.14–15). As in these instances, the act of killing is most often metaphorically framed as a theatrical experience just before battle. Preparing to war against the Persians, for instance, Tamburlaine asks his lieutenant Techelles, 'Then shall we fight courageously with them, / Or look you I should play the orator?' (1–1.2.128–9). Techelles responds perfectly to his commander's rhetorical test, affirming the absolute truth of the sword that he believes to prevail over mere words: 'No: cowards and faint-hearted runaways / Look for orations when the foe is near. / Our swords shall play the orators for us' (1–1.2.130–32).

But Marlowe introduces evidence inviting playgoers to speculate that Tamburlaine carries the metaphor too far, drawing playgoers' attention to the excess of his virtù. When he says he shall depose Cosroe to create a 'pretty jest' (1–2.5.90), Theridamas, a figure who in spite of his union with Tamburlaine nevertheless resists his plans at various points in the play, objects: 'A jest to charge on twenty thousand men? / I judge the purchase more important far' (1–2.5.91–2). Rather than defend himself against criticism (thus acknowledging an outside world), however, Tamburlaine responds by pushing his metaphor even harder: 'bid him turn his back to war with us / That only made him King to make us sport' (1–2.5.100–101). The moment is deeply ironic: it is Tamburlaine's command of rhetoric that has moved Theridamas to defect to his camp.

As Stephen Greenblatt suggests, Tamburlaine enjoys '"the magic violence of speech."'[37] That he speaks lines of beautiful poetry, and specifically that he uses language to make his fantasies become real, is one of the play's enduring ironies. In the beginning, for instance, he sheds 'ye weeds that I disdain to wear,' for 'This complete armour and this curtle-axe / Are adjuncts more beseeming Tamburlaine' (1–1.2.41–3). His assumptions are slippery. As usual, he asserts an argument for nature before culture. Armor, a cultural artifact, is 'more beseeming' to his intrinsic self than are shepherd's garments. But to complete the transformation, he feels compelled to pronounce the armor and the ax 'adjuncts.' In itself, the act of donning armor does not make him a soldier. He must articulate why he wears it, and presto, he is a conqueror. It is this attitude toward language as a generative rather than merely descriptive force that girds him to think he keeps company with Jove (1–1.2.198) and Hector (2–3.5.70). As Gordon Braden observes, Tamburlaine literalizes 'the equation of speaking and acting on a scale not quite like anything else in Renaissance theater.'[38]

Off the battlefield, however, Tamburlaine is not always the stalwart general, but is sometimes troubled about the power of speech to shape – or better yet, to warp – his martial persona. We see this most acutely in his panegyric to Zenocrate that follows upon the Slaughter of the Virgins near the end of Part One. His songful praise is far from humble ablution, and seems to hold no hint of self-recrimination, no threat to his masculinity. Yet he stops himself midway through it:

> But how unseemly is it for my sex,
> My discipline of arms and chivalry,
> My nature, and the terror of my name,
> To harbour thoughts effeminate and faint.

1–5.1.174–7

Predictably it is war that cleanses the soldier-male's 'nature' from 'thoughts effeminate,' as if any mental departure from the 'discipline of arms' circulates internally like a poison that must be expelled. Nor can he tolerate it when other men drop the soldier's mask. In Part Two, as his sons grieve the loss of their mother, he cuts them off, offering to teach them the 'rudiments of war.'[39] In both these moments, he displaces grief with thoughts of killing.

This maneuver of becoming emotionally steeled against loss is possible only if one functions like a machine, as Zenocrate enables him to do. To establish her passivity, Marlowe gives her precious few lines to speak in Tamburlaine's presence. Even after she has been transported by the rite of marriage from the position of adoring captive to that of adoring wife, she places few demands upon their relationship; most often, she silently cooperates with his aggression toward her and toward the world. Perhaps the best example of the dynamics of Tamburlaine's manipulation of Zenocrate comes in an exchange in Part Two, where she asks him to give up war for the sake of his family: 'Sweet Tamburlaine, when wilt thou leave these arms / And save thy sacred person free from scathe / And dangerous chances of the wrathful war?' (2–1.3.9–11). His response is entirely revealing. While it begins with his usual grandiose rhetoric ('When heaven shall cease to move on both the poles, and when the ground whereon my soldiers march shall rise aloft and touch the hornèd moon' [2–1.3.12–14]), it quickly dissolves into a not-so-subtle *ad hominem* attack on Zenocrate's character. Eyeing his sons, whose 'looks are amorous, not martial as the sons of Tamburlaine,' the general articulates the anxiety of all men who treat their wives and their wives' wombs as chattel – that his offspring might be 'bastards' (2–1.3.21–2, 32). Even as he plants the idea, however, he retracts it, reassuring Zenocrate, 'but that I know they issued from thy womb, / That never looked on man but Tamburlaine' (2–1.3.33–4). This is a self-serving claim, as Zenocrate was betrothed to Alcidamus of Syria (1–1.2.78) when Tamburlaine had arrested her royal train in Part One. As a whole, the exchange illustrates his strategy of keeping the upper hand in marriage by questioning Zenocrate's fidelity when she edges toward complaining about the dangers of war.

But Marlowe's play itself does not unambiguously endorse the unilateral hegemony of men over women. As Theridamas discovers when he tries to apply his master's methods of courtship to Olympia, not every captive female is as cooperative, nay as collusive, as Zenocrate has been. By contrast, through the development of Olympia Marlowe exposes as grotesque the soldiers' chilling fantasies of owning women. In Part Two, Act 4, Theridamas comes upon Olympia as she finishes cremating the bodies of her late husband who has fallen in battle and her son, who has begged her to take his life in a mercy killing rather than allow him to become a prisoner of Tamburlaine's tyranny. Olympia has not only complied with her son's request, but has burned their bodies, 'lest cruel Scythians should dismember' them (2–3.4.37). Pressed by invading troops, that is, she has incinerated her own world before they can get on to the job. She is attempting to commit suicide as Theridamas and Techelles interrupt her. Seeing the burning bodies, Techelles is full of praise for her efforts – "Twas bravely done, and like a soldier's wife' (2–3.4.38). The compliment measures how far from human feeling is Tamburlaine's army.

If Techelles attempts to reinscribe Olympia's mercy killing as an example of heroic duty consonant with soldiering, his compatriot Theridamas picks up on his praise of Olympia as the perfect soldier's wife. Theridamas begins to reinscribe her affection for her late husband as affection for him. In a galling domestic episode, Theridamas first tries to court, then threatens to rape the unyielding Olympia, whose husband he has just vanquished. As if to heighten the disintegration of Theridamas's martial valor into sheer villainy, their initial exchanges have an air of extraordinary dignity:

OLYMPIA: I buried all affections
                  Save grief and sorrow which torment my heart,
                  Forbids my mind to entertain a thought
                  That tends to love, but meditate on death,
                  A fitter subject for a pensive soul.
THERIDAMAS: Olympia, pity him, in whom thy looks
                  Have greater operation and more force
                  Than Cynthia's in the watery wilderness,
                  For with thy view my joys are at the full,
                  And ebb again as thou departest from me.
                                  2–4.2.23–32

But when his words of love fail to charm, Theridamas vows that,

if nothing will prevail,
I'll use some other means to make you yield.
Such is the sudden fury of my love,
I must and will be pleased, and you shall yield –

                                  2–4.2.50–53

And yield she does, though not in the way he had hoped. She offers to demonstrate the protective magical powers of an ointment she has on hand, surely of interest to a soldier, and tricks him into slashing her throat just where she has applied the compound. He immediately cries out, 'What, have I slain her? Villain, stab thyself! / Cut off this arm that murderèd my love' (2–4.2.82–3), but we know he won't do it. Much like Marlowe's Edward II, who vows to sever his own hand, the one that orders his lover the earl of Gaveston banished from England, Theridamas is also too narcissistic to punish himself. Instead, he eulogizes Olympia as the 'queen of chastity' (2–4.2.96), a self-protecting maneuver made ludicrous by his earlier threats to force her to yield to his 'sudden fury.'

What ought we to make of Olympia's protest of martial (or marital) law as Theridamas understands it? We might first observe that, in spite of his bathetic eulogy, the scene glorifies Olympia's dignity and strength, qualities commensurate with her name. Like Cleopatra evading Caesar, she refuses to service Theridamas as a trophy of his victory over her husband. Moreover, the scene records the conflict between civilians and soldiers as a clash between universal need and socially constructed desire, as we may see in comparing the characters' first, peaceable exchange with their second. In the first, Olympia lucidly volunteers that she is in a state of mourning, hardly a surprise, given that Theridamas's advances follow immediately upon the deaths of her husband and son. Like the soldiers who took away her family, she identifies the 'heart' as the site of pain. But it is now grief and sorrow, not the sword itself, that create the 'torment' she feels. Olympia thus appropriates and reverses their trope of hearts extruded from chests: she signifies her own very different way of thinking.

Theridamas aims to break down the complexities of Olympia's world. He tries, for example, to claim a prominent place in her emotional life by exhorting Olympia to 'pity him,' substituting himself for her late husband and son, the true pronomial subjects of her grief; she keeps her pity for 'My lord and husband's death, with my sweet son's' (2–4.2.22). More directly, Theridamas tries to persuade Olympia that sexual desire – as he understands that force – ought to outweigh her grief. He develops the point in a clever lunar analogy that mimes his master's arguments for nature before culture. Claiming that Olympia's eyes have 'operation' and 'force' over him, he represents his unreciprocated desire for her as a physiological tyranny that, like the high tide, cannot be evaded or stopped. And when coaxing fails, Theridamas's invitations turn to threats. His 'sudden fury' reminds us that, even though he has promised Olympia to 'cast off arms and sit with thee, / Spending my life in sweet discourse of love' (2–4.2.44–5), he and his fellows live far from the complex freedoms of such discourse, as he proves with his words 'must' and 'will'; he has learned well from his master. In the largest sense, Olympia's death confirms that the only escape from soldiers appears to be suicide. Moreover, her death illuminates the brutality of the soldiers' sexuality, which does not 'play itself out between persons [but is only] directed against' them.[40]

The second vignette amplifies this point. In Part One, Act 3, Scene 2

Agydas, Tamburlaine's ensign, engages Zenocrate, then a captive princess, in a rare dialogue that demythologizes war. He depicts soldiers as emotionally sterile and combative partners, explores the source of Zenocrate's affection for the man she marries in Act 5, and speculates on the fortunes of their expected union. In all of this he treats Zenocrate as flesh and blood rather than, like Tamburlaine in his best moments, as 'an abstract Platonic ideal.'[41] He genuinely wants to know why she is 'so wan and pale' (1–3.2.5). Ironically, perhaps, she explains to Agydas that she is not at all troubled by Tamburlaine's arrest of her, but rather by his recent loss of interest in her affections. Indeed, she defends his imprisonment of her, which she beguilingly calls 'entertainment,' 'far from villany or servitude.' As she explains, it 'might in noble minds be counted princely' (1–3.2.37–9). Zenocrate's attitude toward the man who is still her captor makes Agydas's advice appear to be more misguided than it actually is. He advises the 'wan and pale' princess that marriage to a conqueror bodes ill for her future happiness:

> How can you fancy one that looks so fierce,
> Only disposed to martial strategems?
> Who when he shall embrace you in his arms
> Will tell how many thousand men he slew;
> And when you look for amorous discourse
> Will rattle forth his facts of war and blood . . .
>
> 1–3.2.40–45

Although Zenocrate quietly objects to Tamburlaine's compulsive military career in Part Two ('Sweet Tamburlaine, when wilt thou leave these arms / And save thy sacred person free from scathe / And dangerous chances of the wrathful war?' [2–1.3.9–11]), she never ratifies Agydas's acidic assessment of the man she weds in between the two parts of the play.

Agydas foresees trouble in paradise, and at considerable risk to himself, he comments acutely on the problematic nature of the conqueror's affection for his queen. Though Tamburlaine may take her in his arms, Agydas warns, her lover will nevertheless be only and ever intensely absent, singularly focused on his 'facts of war and blood.' Unlike Menaphon, who emblazons Tamburlaine's 'desire, lift upwards and divine' (1–2.1.8), Agydas is unimpressed by the glories of military bearing. In his eyes, Tamburlaine is not more, but less than a man, one who is responsible, for instance, for an 'offensive rape' (1–3.2.6), by which Agydas means the arrest of Zenocrate in Act 1, Scene 2, as she progressed from one court to another. Though editors often hasten to point out that by 'rape' Agydas means seizure rather than forcible sexual intercourse, the malcontent's striking metaphor nonetheless suggests the way soldiers see women as powerless prizes who exist solely for men's pleasure. Moreover, it is not Agydas but Zenocrate herself who introduces the image of rape into the play, when she urges Tamburlaine in their first meeting 'not to enrich thy followers by lawless rapine from a silly maid' (1–1.2.9–10). While Tamburlaine makes clear in this scene that he has higher standards than to misuse a princess, he later awards his common soldiers with women captured in war, whom they may use as their 'queens apiece' (with a pun on quean, or whore). These captives (known as 'comfort women' to modern Japanese armies) are meant to 'equally serve' all the soldiers' 'turns'; Tamburlaine instructs his soldiers to 'brawl not' over them (2–4.3.70, 73, 75); he who 'so offends shall die' (2–4.3.76). Martial discipline cannot be sacrificed to sexual pleasure, but between battles, women may be raped by the armies of a conqueror – who in this instance desires to be seen by his beloved Zenocrate as being morally above such infamy, even when we see he is not so.

The words of other soldiers confirm Agydas's complaint about the misuse of women as war trophies. When Mycetes commissions Theridamas as general, he frames the mission against Tamburlaine by comparing it to the Trojan War: 'Go frowning forth, but come thou smiling home, / As did Sir Paris with the Grecian Dame' (1–1.1.65–6). And in Part Two, Callapine bribes his jailer Almeda by promising, among other gifts, to exchange women for freedom:

> Grecian virgins shall attend on thee,
> Skilful in music and in amorous lays
> As fair as was Pygmalion's ivory girl,
> Or lovely Io metamorphosed.

> 2–1.2.36–9

Callapine's poetic bartering glosses over the transformative force that male hegemony exerts over female identity, as the classical allusions of coerced metamorphosis quietly suggest. The most blunt example of this is Tamburlaine's own order, delivered just after he arrests Zenocrate, that she shall be his queen, like it or not: 'lady, this fair face and heavenly hue / Must grace his bed that conquers Asia' (1–1.2.36–7).

Agydas thus rejects Tamburlaine's world as violently phallocentric, much like the world evoked in the *Iliad*, where 'men abuse women and other men to assure themselves of their own continued capacity to dominate.'[42] The power of such a world Agydas experiences first hand. He commits suicide with a dagger that Tamburlaine supplies moments after interrupting the traitor's tête-à-tête with Zenocrate. Usumcasane, who walks in Tamburlaine's shadow, gives the brief eulogy. Having presided over the discharge of a heretic, he pronounces Agydas's suicide 'manly done' (1–3.2.109), restoring him, albeit posthumously, to the company of soldiers who dictate how others may construct the nature of desire.

Of the three episodes in which dissent is silenced, the most illustrative is also most controversial. In Part Two, Act 4, Scene 1, the general and his men return to camp bearing their most recent prisoners of war, four Turkish kings. His forces have included his offspring Amyras and Celebinus, who responded to the alarm while his third son, Calyphas, continued to sleep, then awoke to play cards and talk of kissing the Turkish concubines he expected to find among his father's prisoners.

The son's lackadaisical interest in war Tamburlaine takes as an egregious affront to the 'argument of arms' (2–4.1.100), and the father's response to a son he thinks of as an 'effeminate brat' (2–4.1.162) forms the core of a vignette depicting grave abuse which compromises Tamburlaine's aim of heroic leadership, as he seems to forget that Calyphas is first his son before he is a wayward soldier.[43] Calyphas's murder violently ends a generational feud that has simmered for three acts, while Calyphas repeatedly rejects his father's model of how males ought to behave and what they ought to desire. What begins as censorious paternal disrespect, in which the son is addressed as an 'Image of sloth and picture of a slave,' ends in a murder of passion (2–4.1.91). Significantly, to stab to death a son he considers 'the scum and tartar of the elements' (2–4.1.124), Tamburlaine must set aside the tense pleas for mercy uttered not by the wayward son, but, surprisingly, by the general's lieutenants and obedient sons, who promise to 'force' Calyphas into the next battle if his life is spared now (2–4.1.102). Their pleas elevate blood kinship over the fellowship of soldiers, suggesting a fault-line in their own obedience to Tamburlainian tenets.

It must be conceded that as a conscientious objector against those tenets, Calyphas is not a particularly high-minded dissident. Fending off his brothers Celebinus, who counts him 'lazy,' and Amyras, who complains of his 'cowardice' (2–4.1.7, 23), Calyphas disputes their premise that he is afraid of battle:

> I know, sir, what it is to kill a man –
> It works remorse of conscience in me.
> I take no pleasure to be murderous,
> Nor care for blood when wine will quench my thirst.
>
> 2–4.1.27–30

Yet even in its simple-minded compromises, this dissent from the son of a ruthless imperialist dangerously challenges two axioms of conquest, namely that murder is the highest pleasure and that 'remorse of conscience' has no place in a soldier's breast; to admit 'remorse' is to acknowledge the intrusion of culture – of a philosophical and moral code. His brother Celebinus registers these threats to the heroic ethos, replying, 'O cowardly boy! Fie, for shame, come forth. / Thou dost dishonor manhood and thy house' (2–4.1.31–2). Calyphas's distemper in this scene has another, related function, too. Through it Marlowe criticizes the solipsism of the 'manhood' whose honor Celebinus feels called to protect. While the obedient sons worship their father's priorities and convictions, emulating those values even less thoughtfully than the conquered kings who self-interestedly become his allies, Calyphas cuts through the hero worship. He understands how Tamburlaine's code of 'manhood' draws its strength from its virtual solipsism:

> Away, ye fools, my father needs not me,
> Nor you, in faith, but that you will be thought
> More childish valorous than manly wise:
> If half our camp should sit and sleep with me,
> My father were enough to scare the foe;
> You do dishonor to his majesty
> To think our helps will do him any good.

                                                    2–4.1.15–21

Calyphas grasps how his father's self-image is predicated. It is not simply that Tamburlaine denies the part played by other men in his victories, but also that his dependencies upon other men are intentionally obscured by marking his competitors inside as well as outside his camp as lesser men than he. This recognition is signified in Calyphas's distinction between being 'manly wise' and 'childish valorous': by the rules of the game, as Calyphas here teaches his brothers, they cannot achieve the equivalent of their father's level of manhood. Perhaps their subordinate status as inferior soldiers is symbolically indicated when Tamburlaine refuses to lance their arms, as he does his own, in order to inhabit his role ('Now look I like a soldier' [2–3.2.117]). It is certainly indicated in the general's denigration of all his sons as 'too dainty for the wars' in his attack on Zenocrate's fidelity discussed above. There he depicts his sons as effeminate vaudevillians who play lutes, 'dance and caper in the air,' and 'hang about a lady's neck,' 'Their hair as white as milk and soft as down – / Which should be like the quills of porcupines, / As black as jet, and hard as iron or steel –' (2–1.3.31, 30, 25–7). These absolutist expectations tell us more about Tamburlaine's psychic interior than about his sons'.

If it seems that Calyphas's explanation to his brothers is infected by his express desire to evade doing battle, there is more proof later in the scene that Marlowe is calling attention to the instrumentality of Tamburlaine's revulsion against any expression of 'difference.' The evidence is embedded in an oration he gives just after fatally stabbing his son and just before he returns to battle (the sequencing is not coincidental). Speaking to the kings of Jerusalem, Trebizond, and Soria, whom he dubs 'ye cankered curs of Asia' (2–4.1.132), he vows that in the battle to come, they 'shall feel the strength of Tamburlaine, / And by the state of his supremacy / Approve the difference 'twixt himself and you' (2–4.1.135–7). As Calyphas suspects, his father's notion of manhood requires an effaceable opponent, whether it be a 'curs of Asia' or an 'effeminate brat.' Paradoxically, in other words, the heroic virtù of the mighty general comes into being only in response to some self-consciously created threat to what is, in effect, a surprisingly brittle code of manhood that feeds off the very difference it aims to obliterate.

Tamburlaine's claims have historically been very seductive in a world that only recently has begun to consider manhood as anything more than a self-evident, natural state to which almost half the species ought to strive, and from which the 'weaker sex' is conveniently barred. Thus while critics have had little sympathy for Calyphas's fate, their analyses have privileged exactly the rules of military hegemony protested through his character's voice. Between the First and Second World Wars, for example, Richard Lindabury observed that 'it is impossible to believe that Marlowe sympathized with such a character as Caliphas in such a play as *Tamburlaine*'; Lindabury's reading took Marlowe's presentation of 'the cause of military exercises' at face value. Most critics have grounded their approval of Tamburlaine's murder of his son in the advice of Elizabethan conduct-books for warriors. Thus Paul Kocher, calling the execution 'misunderstood,' argues that Calyphas deserves to die because he is 'insubordinate, slothful, a gamester, and a lecher' – in short, an exemplar of the wayward soldier's worst vices.[44]

These crimes are sometimes punishable by death, according to the handbooks of such sixteenth-century military strategists as Du Bellay, Digges, Styward, and Sutcliffe. Machiavelli's *Art of War*, the premier manual of its time and available in England in Paul Whitehorne's oft-reprinted 1560 translation, closely follows Roman law in prescribing capital punishment for a host of crimes a soldier might commit against his own nation.[45] Indeed, if we read the English handbooks, it is stunning to see how cavalierly their writers prescribe capital punishment for wayward soldiers.

Yet in some instances, a writer allows for leniency, usually on the premise that the humane treatment of soldiers produces loyalty. In 1581, for instance, even Styward's advice to generals includes his observation, echoing *The Prince*, that 'obedience in soudiours [*sic*] is nourished by feare and love, feare is kept by true justice and equity, & love is gotten by wisdome joyned with liberalitie'; in the *Approved Order of Martiall Discipline* Giles Clayton advocates stern discipline, yet gives commanders leave to show mercy: 'you are to understand that where discipline is bled with lenitie and curtesie, mor prevaileth then furie & rathnes, without discretion or wisedom.' Charles Gibbon urges commanders to adopt 'lenitie, and loving perswasions' over 'rash and rigorous dealing,' which he says 'doth more hurt in the harts of the Souldiers, then in the host of the Enemie.'[46] Styward, Clayton, and Gibbon are arguing for the efficacy of morale over the protection of some absolute standard of conduct commanders must enforce.

It is also true that while sixteenth-century military theorists were quick to prescribe capital punishment for a number of crimes that today would be considered misdemeanors, they discriminated simple violations of martial discipline from those that threatened the viability of the army itself. In the case of dicing and at least fantasizing about whoring, ostensibly the conduct for which Calyphas loses his life, for example, Styward decrees death for those who bet with their horse, armor or weapon, while those who simply cheat at cards or dice may be punished less severely, as the commanding officer sees fit. Sutcliffe notes that 'many offences against God and man doe spring of dicing,' and urges that 'gamesters be admonished'; recidivists should be 'imprisoned.' This was also the opinion of Robert Dudley, earl of Leicester, captain-general of Elizabeth's army in the Low Countries in 1585–86, in rules of war designed to guide the conduct of his troops.[47]

I adduce these examples to counter other critics' defenses of Tamburlaine's murder of his son. Indeed, as I have suggested, in refusing to validate the 'manhood' prescribed by his father, Calyphas functions dramatically as Tamburlaine's foil, whom at one point he provokes into making a statement of paternal expectations that reveals the shape of his militaristic mind. When Calyphas asks to remain with his mother behind the line of battle, his father rages:

> Bastardly boy, sprung from some coward's loins,
> . . .
> [Only] he shall wear the crown of Persia
> Whose head hath deepest scars, whose breast most wounds,
> Which, being wroth, sends lightning from his eyes,
> And in the furrows of his frowning brows
> Harbours revenge, war, death and cruelty;
> For in a field whose superficies
> Is covered with a liquid purple veil
> And sprinkled with the brains of slaughtered men,
> My royal chair of state shall be advanced;
> And he that means to place himself therein
> Must armèd wade up to the chin in blood.
>
> 2–1.3.69–84

This speech is marked by a peculiarity common to all of Tamburlaine's paternal chats with his sons, in which he relates war stories or fantasizes about the future of his kingdoms in ways that exclude their efforts; his stories and prophecies work to shore up his masculinity, not to engage his offspring in fantasies 'through which their own masculinity could be imaginatively secured,' which is how Graham Dawson speculates the genre of war stories typically functions for (England's) sons.[48]

As Tamburlaine's fantasy of his successor demonstrates, he places so great a stress on physical self-sacrifice that his fantasy edges toward masochistic self-mutilation: only he shall rule 'Whose head hath deepest scars, whose breast most wounds.' But the general contradicts himself in a later exchange with Calyphas, boasting that in all his years of mortal combat never has he been wounded. Unlike Coriolanus, say, who bears numerous scars as proof of his valor for Rome, Tamburlaine by his own admission has none:

> Quite void of scars and clear from any wound,
> That by the wars lost not a dram of blood,
> And see him lance his flesh to teach you all.
> [s.d.] He cuts his arm.
> A wound is nothing, be it ne'er so deep,
> Blood is the god of war's rich livery.
> Now look I like a soldier.
>
> 2–3.2.112–17

In a hyperbolic gesture to affirm his status as a warrior, Tamburlaine feverishly mutilates himself, much as Faustus under very different circumstances lances his arm to prove his utter devotion to a mentalité through which he hopes, as Tamburlaine would, 'to make the moon drop from her sphere / Or the ocean to overwhelm the world' (*Doctor Faustus* A 1.3.39–40).

As Karen Cunningham observes of Marlowe's dramatic practice, 'he exaggerates what the ruling figures sought to minimize, the profound ambiguity of artifice.'[49] Thus Tamburlaine slashing his arm, a hyperbolic show of paternal masculinity before his sons, reveals a deep anxiety that he only looks 'like' – but in some ultimate, humanist way is not – a soldier, that he only looks like – but is not – a man. Paying attention to the soldiers' use of artifice in the play, I have argued that *Tamburlaine* condemns its soldiers' strategies for coping with the anxieties of masculinity that are pressurized in the cauldron of military threats to England. It is a critique explored at some geographical and generic distance in *Dido*, to which we are now turning, and discomfitingly revisited in *Edward II*, a tragedy that strikes closer to Marlowe's own time and culture.

Notes

1. For studies of the historical Tamburlaine (Timür the Lame, Tamerlane), see Beatrice Forbes Manz, *The Rise and Rule of Tamerlane* (1989; rpt Cambridge: Cambridge University Press, 1990) and Hilda Hookham, *Tamburlaine, the Conqueror* (London: Hodder and Stoughton, 1962). For a superb new historicist reading, see Richard Wilson, 'Visible Bullets: Tamburlaine the Great and Ivan the Terrible,' *ELH* 62 (1995): 47–68, which aims 'to historicize [Tamburlaine's] *kriegspiel* in relation to the war-game waged by Elizabethan finance' (51).

2. John Smythe, *Certain Discourses Military*, ed. J.R. Hale, Folger Library Series of Documents in Tudor and Stuart Civilization (Ithaca: Cornell University Press, 1964), 105; Geoffrey Gates, *The Defence of Militarie Profession*, London, 1579, STC 11683, 21; George Whetstone, *The Honorable Reputation of a Souldier*, London, 1585, STC 25339, D2v; William Segar, *Honor Military and Civil* (London, 1602), ed. Diane Bornstein (New York: Scholars, 1975), who recommends that 'A Souldier basely borne, having lived in continuall exercise of Armes by the space of ten yeerres, without committing any disobedience, or other reprochfull acte, ought be admitted to fight with any Gentleman borne' (123); John Stubbs, *The Discovery of a Gaping Gulf*, ed. Lloyd Berry (Charlottesville: University Press of Virginia, 1968), 53; Jean du Bec-Crispin, *The Historie of the Great Emperour Tamerlan*, London, 1597, STC 7263, 13, 3.

3. See Bec-Crispin, who argues Tamerlane is not 'the sonne of a shepheard' but instead hails from a line of Tartarian kings (4).

4. George Peele, *The Battle of Alcazar*, ed. John Yoklavich, in *The Dramatic Works of George Peele*, gen. ed. Charles Tyler Prouty, 2 vols (New Haven: Yale University Press, 1961), 2:311. 'Tamburlaine' makes an appearance in Peele's tragedy when the Moore makes the historical figure a conceit for his own arch-enemy Abdelmelech: 'Convey Tamburlaine into our Affrike here, / To chastice and to menace lawfull kings, / Tamberlaine triumph not, for thou must die / As Philip did, Caesar, and Caesars peeres' (1.2.222–5; 2:304).

5. I treat *Tamburlaine* as essentially one play having two parts, but do not mean to align myself with Roy Battenhouse's argument in *Marlowe's Tamburlaine: A Study in Renaissance Moral Philosophy* (Nashville: Vanderbilt University Press, 1941) that the ten acts comprise a homiletic whole.

6. Critics who find orthodoxy ironically affirmed include Douglas Cole, *Suffering and Evil in the Plays of Christopher Marlowe* (1962; rpt New York: Gordian, 1972); Judith Weil, *Christopher Marlowe: Merlin's Prophet* (Cambridge: Cambridge University Press, 1977); and Lawrence Danson, 'Christopher Marlowe: The Questioner,' *ELR* 12 (1982): 3–29.

    Mark Thornton Burnett wavers. Reading through the prism of contemporary conduct-books, he argues Tamburlaine strives to be 'the ideal gentleman,' yet concedes the play may well illustrate the hollowness of 'honour' ('*Tamburlaine* and the Renaissance Concept of Honour,' *Studia Neophilologica* 59 [1987]: 201–6). C.L. Barber calls the play 'a blasphemy' ('The Death of Zenocrate: "Conceiving and Subduing Both" in Marlowe's *Tamburlaine*,' *Literature and Psychology* 16 [1966], 15). A.D. Hope argues for its 'thoroughgoing morality of power, aesthetics of power and logic of

power' ('*Tamburlaine*: The Argument of Arms,' reprinted in *Christopher Marlowe*, ed. Harold Bloom [New York: Chelsea, 1986], 49).
The most persuasive arguments against an ironic reading are based on reception history. See, for example, Richard Levin, 'The Contemporary Perception of Marlowe's Tamburlaine,' in *Medieval and Renaissance Drama in England* 1 (1984): 51–70; and Peter Berek, 'Tamburlaine's *Weak Sons: Imitation as Interpretation Before 1593*,' *Renaissance Drama* 13 (1982): 55–82.

7.   Jay Clayton, 'Narrative and Theories of Desire,' *Critical Inquiry* 16 (1989): 50. See Neal Oxenhandler, 'The Changing Concept of Literary Emotion: A Selective History,' *New Literary History* 20 (1988): 105–21. For detailed accounts of the constructionist argument and competing theories of emotion, see *The Social Construction of Emotions*, ed. Rom Harré (Oxford: Basil Blackwell, 1987).

8.   On early modern theories of the passions, see Lawrence Babb, *The Elizabethan Malady: A Study of Melancholia in English Literature from 1580 to 1642* (East Lansing: Michigan State University Press, 1951).

9.   See Leonard Barkan, *Nature's Work of Art: The Human Body as Image of the World* (1975; rpt New Haven: Yale University Press, 1977).

10.   William Blandy, *The Castle* (New York: Da Capo, 1972), 27.

11.   See Erasmus, 'Dulce Bellum Inexpertis,' in *Erasmus on his times*, ed. Margaret Mann Phillips (Cambridge: Cambridge University Press, 1967), 111.

12.   In the *Selected Writings of Fulke Greville*, ed. Joan Rees (London: Athlone, 1973), 138.

13.   J. Glenn Gray, *The Warriors: Reflections on Men in Battle* (New York: Harcourt, Brace, 1959), 25–6.

14.   Klaus Theweleit, *Male Fantasies*, trans. Erica Carter *et al.*, 2 vols (Minneapolis: University of Minnesota Press, 1987, 1989), 1:218.

15.   Gray writes: 'In mortal danger, numerous soldiers enter into a dazed condition' (102).

16.   I am indebted to Elaine Scarry's *The Body in Pain: The Making and Unmaking of the World* (New York: Oxford University Press, 1985). Janel M. Mueller discusses the validity of applying Scarry's conclusions about torture to early modern literature in 'Pain, persecution, and the construction of selfhood in Foxe's *Acts and Monuments*,' in *Religion and Culture in Renaissance England*, ed. Claire McEachern and Debora Shuger (Cambridge: Cambridge University Press, 1997), 161–2.

17.   From this perspective the audience would be said to participate in what Neil Hertz describes as 'a transfer of power . . . from the threatening forces [i.e., of nature or war] to the poetic activity itself' (cited in Oxenhandler, 'The Changing Concept of Literary Emotion,' 110).

18.   Mario DiGangi, *The Homoerotics of Early Modern Drama* (Cambridge: Cambridge University Press, 1997), 64. His second chapter, 'The homoerotics of mastery in satiric comedy,' substantially discusses the multiple functions of anality in early modern drama.

19.   Richard Rambuss, *Closet Devotions* (Durham: Duke University Press, 1998), 50, 57.

20.   Karen Cunningham, 'Renaissance Execution and Marlovian Elocution: The Drama of Death,' *PMLA* 105 (1990), says Marlowe 'makes Faustus's body the point of articulation for a profound suspicion about the phenomenal world: that world is . . . an untrustworthy landscape inhabited

by chimeras' (219). My point is that soldiers in *Tamburlaine* open their enemies' bodies to reassure themselves that the phenomenal world is trustworthy.

21. Here Tamburlaine's soldiers defy western tradition regarding the value of the human heart. The English heart is the predominant metaphor of England's courage, the locus of its valor, in 'An Exhortacion to all English Subjects, to joine for the defence of Queene Elziabeth [*sic*], and their native country,' London, 1588, STC 7582.

22. Emily Vermeule, *Aspects of Death in Early Greek Art and Poetry* (Berkeley: University of California Press, 1979), 101.

23. One medieval English expression of these ideas is formulated in Aelred of Rievaulx's *De spirituali amicitia* [*Spiritual Friendship*], trans. Mary Eugenia Laker, introd. Douglas Roby (Washington, DC: Cistercian Publications, 1974). The parameters of platonic friendship in the English context have been discussed by many scholars in recent years; among the best are still Alan Bray, *Homosexuality in Renaissance England* (1982), rpt and rev (New York: Columbia University Press, 1995) and Bruce R. Smith, *Homosexual Desire in Shakespeare's England: A Cultural Poetics* (Chicago: University of Chicago, 1991).

24. Theweleit, *Male Fantasies*, 2:279.

25. Roy Battenhouse, 'Protestant Apologetics and the Subplot of 2 *Tamburlaine*,' *English Literary Renaissance* 3 (1973), notes that as her husband's victories pile up, Zenocrate is 'subject to recurrent feelings of wretchedness, curse, anxiety, and depression' (41).

26. Regarding the etymology of Bellona, Erasmus points out, perhaps ironically, that some grammarians trace 'bellum' from '*bellus*', a beast, because it is the action of beasts, not men, to come together to destroy one another' ('Dulce bellum inexpertis,' in *Erasmus on his times*, 111; his emphasis).
    In *A Watch-worde for Warre*, London, 1596, STC 11492, C[harles] Gibbon observes that 'bellum' derives from '*Bellona*, whom the Poets fayned to be the Goddesse of Warre, whose felicity was in the effusion of bloode' (Br).

27. Scarry, *The Body in Pain*, 251.

28. Honoré Bonet calls it '"the lowest and humblest colour"' in his influential heraldic treatise *Arbre des Battailles* (*c.* 1387); in *Le Blason des Couleurs* (*c.* 1416–36) Jean Courtois considers black 'symbolic of sadness . . . and a melancholic temperament' (both quoted in Rodney Dennys, *The Heraldic Imagination* [London: Barrie & Jenkins, 1975], 65, 47).

29. Bec-Crispin, *Historie*, 2–3.

30. Victor Turner, 'Colour Classification in Ndembu Ritual,' in *Anthropological Approaches to the Study of Religion*, ed. Michael Banton (New York: Frederick A. Praeger, 1966), 81. Moreover, he writes, 'the three colours represent products of the human body whose emission, spilling, or production is associated with a heightening of emotion' (80).

31. Jack D'Amico, *The Moor in English Renaissance Drama* (Tampa: University of South Florida Press, 1991), points out how Marlowe takes Damascus as the epicenter of his imaginary African world; by that map, *Tamburlaine* is imaginatively located in a space where 'basic Renaissance values are being redefined' by indigenous African culture (47, 50).

32. Eugene Waith, 'Tamburlaine' in *Marlowe: A Collection of Critical Essays*, ed. Clifford Leech, Twentieth-Century Views Series (Englewood Cliffs, NJ:

Prentice-Hall, 1964), argues Tamburlaine is, '[l]ike his successors, Chapman's Bussy and Dryden's Almanzor . . . an early edition of the "noble savage"' (71). His point is reiterated by James Robinson Howe, *Marlowe, Tamburlaine, and Magic* (Athens: Ohio University Press, 1976), 153. On the ideological practices behind the label of 'noble savage,' see Peter Hulme, *Colonial Encounters: Europe and the native Caribbean, 1492–1797* (London: Methuen, 1986), Chapter 1, 'Columbus and the Cannibals.'

33. Thomas Styward, *The Pathwaie to Martiall Discipline*, London, 1581, STC 23413, 55. The admonition is repeated on p. 140.

34. Thus Simon Shepherd describes 'virgin-martyr' plays on the Jacobean stage in *Amazons and Warrior Women: Varieties of Feminism in Seventeenth-Century Drama* (New York: St Martin's, 1981), 179.

35. Scarry, *The Body in Pain*, 51.

36. Thomas Harington, 'A Preface, or rather a Briefe Apologie of Poetrie,' Preface to *Orlando Furioso*, London, 1591, in *Elizabethan Critical Essays*, ed. G. Gregory Smith, 2 vols (1904; rpt Oxford: Oxford University Press, 1937), 2:201.

37. Stephen Greenblatt, *Renaissance Self Fashioning* (Chicago: University of Chicago Press, 1980), 215.

38. Gordon Braden, *Renaissance Tragedy and the Senecan Tradition* (New Haven: Yale University Press, 1985), 185.

39. Paul Kocher, 'Marlowe's Art of War,' *Studies in Philology* 39 (1942): 207–25. Kocher demonstrates Marlowe's debt to Paul Ive's *Practice of Fortification* (1589) for descriptions of strategy.

40. Theweleit, *Male Fantasies*, 2:61.

41. Constance Kuriyama, *Hammer or Anvil: Psychological Patterns in Christopher Marlowe's Plays* (New Brunswick: Rutgers University Press, 1980), 31. See also Eugene Waith ('Tamburlaine'), who says otherwise: 'Tamburlaine's capacity "to love" Zenocrate is a characteristic Renaissance addition to the classical model of the Herculean hero' (77).

42. W. Thomas MacCary, *Childlike Achilles: Ontogeny and Phylogeny in the Iliad* (New York: Columbia University Press, 1982), 114.

43. By contrast, Braden notes, killing Calyphas ironizes Tamburlaine's claim to Herculean *virtù*: he 'repeats one of the most terrible deeds of the Senecan Hercules. But the parallel also defines Tamburlaine's unprecedented ferocity; Hercules kills his sons while he is mad, whereas Tamburlaine commits his murder in full consciousness of what he is doing, and makes a shining addition to his glory out of an action that desolates the classical hero when he finally understands' (*Renaissance Tragedy*, 186–7).

44 Richard Lindabury, *A Study of Patriotism in the Elizabethan Drama*, Princeton Studies in English 5 (Princeton: Princeton University Press, 1931), 55; Paul Kocher, 'Marlowe's Art of War,' 223.

45. See Niccolò Machiavelli, *The Art of War*, rev. ed., trans. Ellis Farneworth (Indianapolis: Bobbs-Merrill, 1965), 163. In the fourth century BCE, Titus Manlius ordered his son beheaded for refusing to adhere to martial law. Machiavelli argues against Manlius's terror tactics in *Discorsi* 3.22 (*The Discourses*, ed. Bernard Crick [1970; rpt London: Penguin, 1981], 465–71), but Manlius's 'precise' discipline is admired by Barnabe Rich, *A Path-Way to Military Practise*, London, 1587 (rpt New York: Da Capo, 1969), Hr–v.

46. Styward, *The Pathwaie to Martiall Discipline*, 148; Giles Clayton, *Approved Order of Martiall Discipline*, London, 1591, STC 5376, 75; Gibbon, *A Watch-Worde for Warre*, 75.
47. Styward, *The Pathwaie to Martiall Discipline*, 57, 59; Matthew Sutcliffe, *The Practice, Proceedings, and Lawes of Armes*, London, 1593, STC 23468, 305. Leicester, *Lawes and ordinances militarie*, Leyden, 1586, STC 7287.7, decrees, 'no private Souldiour or inferiour Officer shal play at Dice and Cardes, nor any other unlawfull games, upon paine of two dayes imprisonment for the first time'; subsequent violations are to be 'punished by the Judges discretion' (3).
48. Graham Dawson, *Soldier Heroes: British Adventure, Empire and the Imagining of Masculinities* (London: Routledge, 1994), 4.
49. Cunningham, 'Renaissance Execution and Marlovian Elocution', 210.

CHAPTER TWO

Epic Masculinity in Troy, Carthage, and London

Bid Theaters and proude Tragadiens,
Bid Mahomets Poo, and mightie Tamburlaine,
King Charlemaine, Tom Stukeley and the rest
Adiewe: to Armes, to Armes, to glorious Armes.
George Peele, A Farewell[1]

Like many popular writers of his generation, George Peele seems to have wanted it both ways. Responding to the just-concluded imperative to defend England, in his 1589 *Farewell* to admirals John Norris and Francis Drake as they set sail on an ill-fortuned journey of revenge on behalf of Elizabeth, he stands ready on the one hand to repudiate classical tragedies and folk legends that celebrate war in favor of the thing itself, urging his fellow subjects to 'Bid Theaters . . . Tom Stukeley and the rest / Adiewe: to Armes.' On the other hand, Peele the writer is busy calling up these very legends to make sense of England's current plight. As every good soldier and erstwhile rhetorician would know, however, persuading men 'to glorious Armes' may require not only a compelling cause, but also a superstructure of legend or myth to frame that cause in ways that make dying for it explicable to those being asked to make the sacrifice. An inspiring myth may be most necessary when soldiers are being asked to take the offensive; in that circumstance, military leaders cannot count on self-preservation to motivate a soldier to become an aggressor.

Elizabeth's government responded to the Armada in the fifteen years following 1588 with several offensives, most of which failed to achieve their primary objectives but may have helped to contain Spanish threats to England's national security. In those years, not coincidentally, the poets, playwrights and prose writers who took national security as a subject regularly invoked various pieces of the most poignant legend the English writers had available to them – the Trojan War – as vehicles for putting the Armada and Spanish aggression generally into an explicable context, and one that could motivate the nation to take up 'glorious Armes.' In *A Roome for a Gentleman*, for example, Barnabe Rich summons the catastrophe at Troy to warn readers against becoming complacent about England's safety. Flying in the face of the myth popularized by Geoffrey of Monmouth that London had been founded by Brutus, a great-grandson of Aeneas, Rich makes Troy's efforts at self-defense a counter-example to what he believes London should be doing. He singles out Aeneas as an exemplar of how not to fight. For Rich, Aeneas's behavior in Troy had exposed a signal lack of courage and integrity (a medieval tradition thought Aeneas guilty of inviting the Greeks inside Troy's walls), disqualifying him from being a model of manhood; worse, he has falsified his 'faith' to a lady:

> And what shall I say of our great Grandsire *Aeneas*, from whome the Romaines would so faine derive themselves? and from whome (as some of our English writers would perswade) our British nation did discend? . . . but *Aeneas*, after he had betraied his countey [*sic*], he himself with the rest of his treacherous companions, were forced to wander at the sea, robbing and spoyling, attending what Destiny would bestow of him, landed in the end upon the coast of Africa, at new built Carthage, where he likewise falsified his faith, and betrayed *Dido*. . . . I wonder that our English Nation, for the glory of antiquity shoulde bee so fond to recount their Genealogy from such a desteyned progeny.[2]

Rich is quick to judge. With Geoffrey Chaucer, who had also weighed in negatively on Aeneas's courage, Rich shows little sympathy for the Trojan's dilemma of being forced to choose between 'Destiny' and 'faith' – even less sympathy, in fact, than Marlowe allows to seep into the final departure scene of his version of the betrayal at Carthage, where Aeneas apologizes for leaving Dido as he exits the stage. While excommunicating Aeneas from the charmed circle of admirable heroes who can be trusted to inspire the English, Rich subsumes a set of axioms about the nature of epic masculinity into a straightforward assumption that 'Aeneas' and his escapades represent some ill-conceived notions of duty and defense that do not bear emulating in Elizabethan London.

Some of these axioms are lurking in George Peele's pious admiration of Aeneas. Peele gives readers a more admirable reading of the hero and the legend in a boring little poem on the Trojan War that is 'annexed' (his word, twice)[3] to his farewell to Norris and Drake, admirals of Elizabeth's armada of revenge. The poem reiterates the Virgilian rather than the Chaucerian line, taking Dido as a symbolic embodiment of the lustful siren whose ministrations threaten a soldier's dutiful pursuit of honor. Modifying that tradition, Peele crosses it with chivalry: his Dido has 'deceav'd' a 'wandring Knight.' In the poem, the lovers' time together is truncated, as is the narrative space between the hero's arrival in Carthage and his disembarkation in 'Lavine land.' Moreover, Peele inverts the sequencing of these two arrivals, giving pride of place to Aeneas's having been 'so royallie receav'd' by Dido, stressing the trouble in Carthage from which the 'knight' has extricated himself; Peele ignores that knights usually rescue ladies rather than flee them. In the poem's last lines, Dido's wiles are suggestively compounded when Peele wonders aloud if Helen of Troy sincerely loved Paris, 'or no.' 'I cannot tell,' he says slyly, 'but may imagine so.' No woman is trustworthy in love, or so the poet hints (3, 21).

Peele's *Farewell* poem is also suggestive for its ambiguous stance toward the question of whether fictional representations of war can effectively energize militaristic sentiments among an audience of readers or playgoers. On the one hand, his answer would seem to be a simple 'yes': and not only because he tells bits of the Troy story to glorify the mission upon which Drake and Norris are to set sail. As Peele explains in a dedicatory epistle to those two 'knights,' a pair of modern Trojans, his 'olde Poem' is meant as a 'pleasaunt dyscourse, fitly serving to recreate, by the reading the chivalrie of England' (3). Defending his decision to sketch the Trojan War, Peele imagines himself aiding a nostalgic recovery of English heroism that Elizabethan writers were associating, say, with the reign of Edward Longshank.

Yet there is something nevertheless contradictory in Peele's invoking the Trojan War to send off admirals Norris and Drake. For even as he is seeming to fan nationalist and militarist sentiments, he dismisses other mimetic artifacts of military valor that were available for public consumption in contemporary London – plays in particular. In the passage adopted above as my epigraph, for example, he dismisses Tamburlaine's theatricalized stage victories as insubstantial, asking playgoers instead to expect the real thing. Yet even as he seems to endorse some kind of absolute split between theatricalized war and war itself, his poetic bon voyage implicitly admits how making war necessarily requires writers to make fictions about war. This is an important admission, even if unwitting, which it almost certainly is not.

In some other contemporary instances, the metaphor of war as theatrical pageant is more deliberately adopted. Thus is the earl of Essex supposed to have written in a letter published by 'his particular friend' that as he looked about for military expeditions to involve himself in, he had 'determinately purposed to put on this habit of a Souldiour.' In the end Essex chooses to join the retaliatory armada against Portugal rather than see further action in the Low Countries, which are mere 'defensive warres' offering little opportunity to play out the soldier's role.[4] And William Garrard had advised his fellow soldiers not only to feign equanimity, but also to mirror the captain's emotions: 'seeme joyfull whilest thy Captaine is merrie, and sorrowfull when he is grieved.'[5] Together with Rich's acidic revaluation of Aeneas's heroic mantle, Peele's admission, and Essex's metaphor, Garrard's advice prepares us to appreciate Marlowe's scrutiny of the fictions of epic masculinity that are implicitly resident in the Dido–Aeneas myth.

While prose writers were inspired to respond to the Armada with an outpouring of the advice-and conduct-manuals that form the backbone of this study, poets oddly enough were less moved to contribute to the war efforts with verse. Literary historians have puzzled over the fact that poets produced only a handful of poems to celebrate England's victory in 1588. Of that handful, few are English, as Leicester Bradner noted in an essay published in the midst of the Second World War.[6] The best remembered of those poems may be Spenser's dull dedicatory sonnets to Walter Ralegh and Charles Howard, Lord High Admiral of England, that were appended only to the 1590 edition of *The Faerie Queene*. Spenser's sonnets praise Howard for having chased away 'those huge castles of Castilian king,' echoing the commonplace image of the Armada as a floating fortress.[7] A few other celebratory verses were composed by Protestants living on the continent, and a number of ballads in English were composed. But the victory was not glorified much by prominent English poets. Michael Murrin ventures to explain the lack of interest in the Armada as a poetic subject as a consequence of changes in the way war was being conducted in the late sixteenth century. Pointing out that poets had inherited a rich array of literary techniques for representing land battles and even naval battles that included much boarding of enemy vessels, Murrin argues that poetry had not yet caught up with developments in naval warfare, especially the broadside cannon duel. He contrasts poets' responses to the Armada victory with the 1571 sea battle of Lepanto, the greatest showdown in contemporary memory. It had featured a good deal of traditional hand-to-hand fighting that was shortly memorialized in epic verse, unlike the battle against the Armada, an epic event, to be sure, but featuring less familiar kinds of tactical engagement with the enemy (unmanned ships afire, for instance) that would have been of lesser interest to poets steeped in the ways of writing of war that they had inherited from the epic tradition.[8]

An example of a minor poet attempting to frame the Armada within that epic tradition is available in James Aske's 'Elizabetha Triumphans' (1588),[9] where something less interesting than Marlowe's experiment with the Dido–Aeneas legend is created. Prominent in its day, the poem is memorable to us chiefly as an occasional piece of wartime bathos that uses the Trojan War to spice up its otherwise bland narration of the collision course between England and Spain in the 1570s and 1580s. The poem proclaims that the Spanish fleet, its 'bigge-made barkes with huge and mightie mastes' chained to its 'lesser shippes,' 'all in nothing are unlike / Unto the Trojans stately new-built towne, / Which nought did feare the Greeks bewronged by them' (2:575). The double negative 'all in nothing are unlike' temporarily obscures the idea that Aske envisions the Armada as a kind of floating Troy. Its admirals, like Troy's princes, have naively underestimated their opponent's fiery response to the attack. Ironically, at Whitehall in the months just before Spain's attack, it had been precisely the reverse. Then Elizabeth had delayed her nation's preparations for the inevitable war with Spain, seeming not to comprehend the magnitude of materiel and military training that England's troops on land and at sea would need sooner or later. Aske's poem whitewashes Elizabeth's well-known delays in decision making. For elsewhere in the poem, the sign of 'Troy' has been reassigned from the Spanish fleet to London itself. Thus Aske depicts Queen Elizabeth as Troy's best defender; she is praised as an 'Amazonian Queene . . . beating down amaine the bloodie Greekes' (2:570). And some seventy lines later she has become 'most Dido-like' as she boards her 'Royall barge' (2:572) en route to the camp at Tilbury. As these examples illustrate, Aske's representation of Queen Elizabeth fluctuates wildly – sometimes she is a Trojan princess par excellence, sometimes a Carthaginian siren, albeit one who inspires her commanders in the field. That feature of the poem contributes to what I take to be Aske's unwitting parody of heroic ideals as he appropriates the Trojan material.

As these examples from prose, drama and poetry may suggest, the Trojan material, like the legend of Tamburlaine, was understood to be available for a variety of ideological tasks. But whereas Rich continues to think war a good idea even as he defames Aeneas; and whereas Peele takes comfort and joy in men who hunger to 'Hoyse sayles, waie Anckers up, plowe up the Seas / With flying keeles, plowe up the land with swordes, / In Gods name venture on' (6); and Aske seems in favor of duty but is unable to decide what he wants to do with the Trojan War, Marlowe puckishly manipulates the Trojan material, concentrating on the Dido–Aeneas legend, to create an anti-war burlesque. His play invites us literally to see the rhetorical maneuvers of these framing myths of the Trojan War by which English playgoers and readers were being persuaded not simply to defend the nation, but to go on the attack against Spain through action in the Low Countries, English armadas against Portugal, and privateering at sea. Marlowe's play contributes a new branch to the literary tradition that had already been reading the Dido–Aeneas myth and its concomitant values of renunciation and duty as burlesque. The play urges its audience to wonder, as Barnabe Rich puts it, whether 'our English Nation, for the glory of antiquity shoulde bee so fond to recount their Genealogy from such a desteyned progeny.' In doing so, it spoofs the military values of Roman antiquity that other English poets had seemingly sought to recollect and reproduce by championing such a wishful genealogy of Britain's past.

'Had not we fought manfully, I had not told this tale.
Yet manhood would not serve'

The tension between heroic duty and romantic love that is at the heart
of the Dido–Aeneas myth is a major topic in medieval and early modern
English literature, and especially so in the late sixteenth century. Think
of Sidney's *Astrophel and Stella*, its hero eventually choosing arms and
public service; of the burst of plays about Dido and Aeneas from mid-
century; of the Roman plays by Shakespeare, Jonson, and others early
in the next century. Reading the literary trends, it seems that as the reign
of Elizabeth wore on, fewer poets and readers were assuming, as Homer
and Virgil had, that men would inevitably prefer the glory of Mars
before the pleasures of Venus; or that being devoted to a woman was
intrinsically foolish, while being enthralled was certainly tragic but
inevitable. Could it have seemed to late Elizabethan writers, in the wake
of Sidney's death in Zutphen in 1586 and his florid London funeral,
simply too ironic in the 1580s and 1590s to continue calling on the
medium of poetry to celebrate the heroic deeds of men at arms? Had it
become a commonplace that Astrophel, or Sidney himself, had perhaps
made the wrong choice?

   While Sidney's death may have had a chilling effect on a London-wide
confidence in the power of fiction to ward off the risks of military
service, the creeping skepticism toward war and its glorious
representations had begun within the literary tradition well before
Sidney's death or the disastrous French wars of religion, even before
Erasmus and other humanists on the continent began to put some
longstanding classical assumptions about the inherent nobility of war
under new scrutiny. The humanists' rethinking is anticipated most
notably in English in Chaucer's revision of the romance of Dido and
Aeneas that occupies book 4 in the *Aeneid*; it would seem that Chaucer's
versions of the story greatly influenced Marlowe's. In both *Legend of
Good Women* and *The House of Fame*, Chaucer's Aeneas is no Roman
hero, but a cad who runs out on a noble woman who is pregnant with
his child, yet unable to persuade the hero to make a life with her in
Carthage. While it is implausible to read Chaucer's versions as proto-
feminist tales, the question of whether duty ought to preempt love is, in
his hands, undeniably open to rethinking. Chaucer's Dido, brilliantly
sketched, is a sharp departure from the Virgilian tradition. Until
recently, scholars had been agreed that that tradition encouraged
auditors and readers to have little sympathy for the distractions of love.
Recently, however, critics have begun to discover in the *Aeneid* a
dormant authorial sympathy toward Dido's plight.[10] These findings run
counter to the work of Church Fathers and medieval exegetes who

aimed to syncretize Virgil, and who did not find in the poem what modern critics are now seeing, as a quick survey of exegeses by Bernard and Fulgentius, for example, would illustrate. Eager to justify patriarchy as a necessary element of (Christian) empire-building, the Fathers pared the story to an allegory of a struggle between lust and duty.[11]

In the late sixteenth century, in Europe and in England, the romance between the Egyptian queen and the son of Venus was a favorite of playwrights in particular; the myth had enjoyed a kind of renaissance from mid-century.[12] Some of the many scripts in Latin, French, and English adopt or modify the Virgilian line, thus glorifying Aeneas's surrender to duty and honoring his virtù; a few scripts sympathize with the Chaucerian line described above, voicing premonitions about the costs of empire borne by humanity.[13] Marlowe's tragedy is located in the latter tradition, and it extends Chaucer's reversal of the usual conclusion that passion corrodes duty. Whereas Chaucer focuses upon Dido's personal tragedy, Marlowe investigates the ways in which the contemporary rhetoric of masculinity amongst sixteenth-century soldiers and others who look to the Dido–Aeneas legend for guidance or genealogical inspiration not only produces the hero's epic ambition, but also weakens his cause and his effectiveness as a defender, as it were, of the faith.

For dramatic irony, Marlowe best exploits the weakening effects of the axioms of epic masculinity in the scene in which Aeneas narrates the Fall of Troy before an audience at Dido's court. In the *Aeneid*, this moment of narration is a small unit, and even smaller in Chaucer's versions. Here, the eyewitness account, itself a fiction, obviously, is a cornerstone of Marlowe's play. Yet its uneven tone belies its ostensible claims of epic heroism, for it presents an erratic and depleted – and even diminished – hero. Within the narration, while Aeneas is sometimes made to marshal a heroic bravado, more often he exhibits symptoms of what would now be called post-traumatic stress. As he narrates the sack of Troy, he experiences flashbacks to the traumatic scenes, anxious disruptions in his thinking, physical lethargy, and a deep grief that dissuades him from speaking of what he saw and experienced. Collapsing at Dido's feet at an early moment in his story, Aeneas is the very picture of the enervated warrior, resisting the queen's invitation 'to discourse at large, / And truly too, how Troy was overcome' (2.1.106–7).

> AENEAS: A woeful tale bids Dido to unfold,
> Whose memory like pale death's stony mace,
> Beats forth my senses from this troubled soul,
> And makes Aeneas sink at Dido's feet.
>
> 2.1.114–17

Yet his pathetically disobedient pose is extemporaneous; as Dido reminds him, he is giving a command performance of royal Trojan masculinity. Dido insists that Aeneas inhabit a seamless martial persona, for vicariously, through discourse, she is absorbing some of his Trojan valor by succoring the defeated. She is more incredulous than piteous toward the broken hero at her feet:

> DIDO: What, faints Aeneas to remember Troy,
>   In whose defence he fought so valiantly?
>   Look up, and speak.
>
> 2.1.118–20

'Look up, and speak' interrupts his self-pity. It demands a royal performance, serving notice of his being in matriarchal space, his Roman ambition temporarily circumscribed by what Aeneas will later disparage as Dido's 'silver arms' (4.3.51). For now, however, reproach flows the other way. Impatiently, Dido expects Aeneas to resuscitate his martial persona. Instantly he recovers an imperative voice: 'Then speak, Aeneas,' he coaches himself, 'with Achilles' tongue' (2.1.121). In his performance before Dido, as Judith Butler might agree, he exhibits masculinity as an 'ongoing discursive practice.'[14] Yet his performance requires a measure of dissonance rather than abject submission to Dido's will and whim; when he resists, she is given an occasion to exercise her royal power over him, just as he and especially his sailors take Dido's resistance to Trojan fate as occasions to reaffirm their masculinist subject positions. Indeed, choosing to impersonate Achilles is itself an example of staking out his subject position as well as an ironic reminder that Aeneas – and Dido – are fateful victims of the homosocial values of epic masculinity he aims to honor. Attending to such scenes as the one just described, Richard Martin once argued that 'Aeneas assumes a very passive role in the play.'[15] More recently, Emily Bartels has shown that that apparent passivity may be read as a deliberate strategy by which he garners power over Dido and her court. 'It is by scripting himself into a position of dependency,' Bartels writes, 'that Aeneas, paradoxically, can impose his own terms and agendas upon Carthage and erase Dido's.'[16]

Aeneas tells the story of Troy's fall to Dido's court during his first audience with the queen of Carthage, while he is still dazed and defeated. It is a chilling tale of the bloody final hours of a massacre that claimed the lives of innocent civilians as well as seasoned soldiers who knew the risks of war. Unlike *Tamburlaine*, in which the poetry arguably allows playgoers to take pleasure in the hero's victories, in *Dido* Marlowe allows no such complacency: Troy's sack, described by a survivor rather than a victor, is resolutely uncomfortable. Not glory but guts and blood are figuratively at center stage. The graphic language captures the Greeks' savage treatment of Trojan civilians:

> By this, the camp was come unto the walls
> And through the breach did march into the streets,
> Where, meeting with the rest, 'Kill! Kill!' they cried.
> Frighted with this confused noise, I rose,
> And looking from a turret might behold
> Young infants swimming in their parents' blood,
> Headless carcases piled up in heaps,
> Virgins half-dead dragg'd by their golden hair
> And with main force flung on a ring of pikes,
> Old men with swords thrust through their aged sides,
> Kneeling for mercy to a Greekish lad,
> Who with steel pole-axes dash'd out their brains.
>
> 2.1.188–99

From Aeneas's vantage in the turret, the 'headless carcases' piled in the streets testify that victory is always stained with the blood of discrete human beings. Moreover, we are invited to hear what had been silently elided in *Tamburlaine* – the screams from the virgins of Damascus. Like those human sacrifices to Tamburlainian pig-headedness in which an aggressor refused the surrender of the vanquished, again it is reported that a group of virgins has been 'flung on a ring of pikes' (*Dido* 2.1.196; see *1 Tamburlaine* 5.1.319–29). But this time it is not some horror-struck, disenfranchised Zenocrate who is reporting a beastly (symbolic) practice. It is the grief-stricken warrior himself, who disavows the emotional numbness necessary to war that Tamburlaine values so much. Concluding ruefully that during the sack of Troy 'manhood would not serve' (2.1.272), Aeneas more than marks the failure of the Trojan men's efforts. Here at least he seems to disavow the essentiality of the term 'manhood,' for his tale of Troy's collapse undermines the notion that any 'defence' could be marshalled 'valiantly' (2.1.119), considering what is required.

Obviously the process of telling the tale anguishes its teller, who defers to his lieutenant Achates to finish telling it. The recitation also distresses its principal auditor, Dido, who in its midst begs 'O end, Aeneas, I can hear no more!' (2.1.243). Significantly, Dido's request that Aeneas halt his story only encourages him to describe the misfortune of 'the frantic Queen' Hecuba, whom 'at last, the soldiers pull'd . . . by the heels, / And swung her howling in the empty air' (2.1.244, 247–8). The image is of a queen whose focus of attraction is constituted of 'soldiers,' signifying the triumph of martial over monarchic law. This detail and its timing would seem to be less than accidental. It illustrates the ubiquity of the chaos inflicted by the Greek invaders, and perhaps it taunts Dido, as Hecuba has been taunted, for having pressed Aeneas to relive his nightmarish memory of the invasion.

Marlowe has called attention to the performativity of the soldiers' personae even before Aeneas reaches Dido's court. In Act 2, Scene 1, he and Achates, having landed ashore, wander the hills above Carthage in reconnaissance. Aeneas is so distressed he seems to be disoriented or, as he says, 'amaz'd' (2.1.2). As they walk, he leads Achates and Ascanius into a fantasy that the city they see in the valley below is not Carthage, but Troy before its fall. As he does so, he stays conscious of retreating into an imaginary place. Comparing himself to 'Theban Niobe, / Who for her sons' death wept out life and breath,' Aeneas asserts she 'had not such passions in her head as I' (2.1.3–4, 6). At first Achates joins Aeneas in his sentimental journey, commiserating, 'and in this humour is Achates too' (2.1.10). Pretending that Priam is yet alive and Troy is 'not overcome' (2.1.30) brings the men emotional comfort. But as soon as a group of inquisitive Carthaginians approaches the Trojan warriors, Achates interrupts the fantasy. The natives will have more respect for the Trojans if they present themselves as humbled soldiers than if they are seen as, like Niobe, emotionally overwrought. Quickly, Achates stops playing Aeneas's game and insists he too leave off grieving to act like a soldier. No longer does Achates 'see' Priam in the distance, telling his commander instead, 'Thy mind, Aeneas, that would have it so / Deludes thy eyesight: Priamus is dead.' 'Aeneas, see, here come the citizens [of Carthage]; / Leave to lament, lest they laugh at our fears' (2.1.31–2, 37–8). Rather like Charles's knights in *Faustus* B, the Trojan exiles stand on a precipice of shame. Lamentation is not for real men.

When the Trojans are shortly thereafter presented to Dido at court, another lieutenant attempts to protect the hero's public face:

> ILIONEUS: Look where she [Dido] comes; Aeneas view her well.
> AENEAS: Well may I view her, but she sees not me.
> s.d. *Enter* Dido [*with* Anna *and* Iarbus] *and her train.*
> DIDO: What stranger art thou that dost eye me thus?[17]
> AENEAS: Sometime I was a Trojan, mighty Queen;
> But Troy is not, what shall I say I am?
>
> 2.1.72–6[18]

Answering her question with one of his own, Aeneas invites Dido to dictate who he is. Is his question a rhetorical ploy designed to appeal to Dido's maternal and monarchic impulses, or a sincere statement of the bankruptcy of his martial persona? However we may interpret it, Aeneas's men take it to be a sincere admission of his bankrupt identity. Ilioneus moves swiftly to protect his leader's honor by speaking for him:

'Renowmed Dido, 'tis our General: / Warlike Aeneas' (2.1.77–8).
Ilioneus insists upon immutable manhood: Aeneas is always 'warlike,'
never vulnerable.

This is a crucial fiction, not only for Aeneas's men, but as I suggested
earlier, also for Dido, whose respect for the Trojan depends upon the
integrity of his martial persona. When Ilioneus identifies 'warlike
Aeneas,' as if in awe, Dido echoes the adjectival phrase, then orders that
a suitably martial costume be brought him. She does this even while
insisting that 'Aeneas is Aeneas, were he clad / In weeds as bad as ever
Irus ware' (2.1.84–5). The costume change is meant to provide Aeneas
clothing suitable to his station and achievements; but it also visually
reminds playgoers, as when Tamburlaine sheds his shepherd's garb for
battle gear, that epic masculinity is achieved in part by paying attention
to its semiotics.

Whether or not Aeneas's question 'what shall I say I am?' is a ploy, it
puts Dido at ease and in charge. This is an effect aimed at by the Trojans
from their first contact with Carthage. Even Ilioneus professes to
suspend the Trojans' military frame of mind in their first encounter with
the Carthaginians on the beach. Ilioneus promises a wary Iarbus,

We come not, we, to wrong your Libyan Gods,
Or steal your household Lares from their shrines;
Our hands are not prepar'd to lawless spoil,
Nor armed to offend in any kind;
Such force is far from our unweapon'd thoughts.

                                              1.2.10–14

This promise seems straightforward. Only a few lines later, however,
Ilioneus is already complaining of the 'barbarous' natives who 'swarm
unto the shore, / And from the first earth interdict our feet' (1.2.34,
36–7). His complaint belies a presumptive right to unfettered hospitality
that conflicts with the political sovereignty and military security of
Carthage. Ilioneus wills his crew into a different kind of story, with
narrative demands that are opposite those of epic.

Compare Ilioneus's complaints to a similar moment in a very different
kind of story – Beowulf. When Beowulf's fleet arrives at the edge of the
land of the Danes, producing similar anxieties among them that an
attack is imminent, Beowulf and his thanes do not complain about being
treated as potential aggressors until proved otherwise. But in Dido,
Ilioneus feels free to whine immediately, and prompts more effusive
offers of hospitality, not alarm. Only a short time later, Aeneas and
company in effect occupy Carthage and rule over the 'barbarous' souls;
eventually the Trojans' control is so great that Cloanthus proposes
renaming Carthage 'Aenea' (5.1.20). While that shift in power is invited
by Dido and accomplished without bloodshed, it also teaches spectators

that no matter what is said by Aeneas or his men, the Trojans' thoughts
are never 'unweaponed.' Everything is about conquest. It is a maxim by
which Dido also lives. When her sister Anna suggests that some
inhabitants of Carthage may resist her elevation of Aeneas to be their
king, Dido replies in lines worthy of a Tamburlaine facing a recalcitrant
city under siege:

> Those that dislike what Dido gives in charge
> Command my guard to slay for their offence.
> Shall vulgar peasants storm at what I do?
> The ground is mine that gives them sustenance.
>
> 4.4.71–4

This absolutist judgment against dissenters, together with her adoration
of Aeneas and her fantasies of revenge, all point to her express idolatry
of martial law, which is probably as close to absolute violence as she or
any female character in early modern theater usually comes.[19]

Staging a critique of epic masculinity, Marlowe necessarily creates
in Queen Dido a foil for Aeneas who is in strength of will not simply
the playwright's 'nominal subject,' as W. Craig Turner would have it,
but a full participant in the artistic inquiry into the tenets of
masculinity that underlay Greco-Roman history from the Trojan to
the Punic Wars.[20] Bartels has affirmed Dido's centrality to Marlowe's
interrogation of the mental structures of imperialism in the play.
Working from an ethnographical perspective focused upon the West's
representation of the East, Bartels argues that Europe and Africa meet
but do not collide in the play. The continents' 'cross-cultural
encounter' through the characters of Dido and Aeneas is presented
not 'as a monologic domination of colonizer over a silent and
submissive colonized, but as a dialogic competition between two
colonizing authorities.'[21]

Bartels's reading may be extended by considering Dido's
commitment to the fictions of epic masculinity that promote
imperialism in the play. Dido simultaneously colonizes Aeneas and is
colonized by the fictions that also drive her to admire him. The
strongest evidence is given in Act 3. Before Aeneas first appears in
Dido's court, he is little more than a figment of her imperially poetic
imagination. As Anna scours Carthage in search of Aeneas, bearing a
summons, the queen blazons him, with Cupid (disguised as Ascanius)
her sole witness. The blazon anticipates Lady Mary Wroth's 'Pamphilia
to Amphilanthus' (circulating before 1621). Like Pamphilia, Dido
represents aggressive but adoring constancy; like Amphilanthus,
Aeneas is fickle in his devotion. Yet not much is asked of him, for
Dido's adoration requires only that Aeneas submit:

I'll make me bracelets of his golden hair;
His glistering eyes shall be my looking-glass,
His lips an altar, where I'll offer up
As many kisses as the sea hath sands;
Instead of music I will hear him speak;
His looks shall be my only library;
And thou, Aeneas, Dido's treasury,
In whose fair bosom I will lock more wealth
Than twenty thousand Indias can afford.

3.1.84–92

Even as Dido savors her beloved's visage, she imagines performing operations upon it – making bracelets of his locks, kissing him, locking wealth into his bosom. Adoration is laced with a desire to harvest what she so admires; her gaze is possessive. When Aeneas does appear, however, she coyly refuses to admit she has had him summoned, playing a game that soon grows tragic. In Act 4 the imagery of her blazon is uncannily reiterated by Aeneas himself, who, having missed Dido's speech to Cupid, is nonetheless able to echo its language. In front of his men he plays the ventriloquist, offering to explain to them, in Dido's voice, why she has seized the sails and oars given to his fleet by Iarbus:

Yet Dido casts her eyes, like anchors, out,
To stay my fleet from loosing forth the bay.
'Come back, come back!' I hear her cry afar,
'And let me link thy body to my lips,
That, tied together by the striving tongues,
We may as one sail into Italy.'

4.3.25–30

Aeneas fears his lover's gaze and 'striving' tongue, by which he has allowed himself to be detained in Carthage; he fears being further mesmerized – his ambition contaminated, his 'golden fortunes clogg'd with courtly ease' (4.3.8) – by the pleasures of her 'body,' and by the rhetoric of her admiration of the same epic masculinity that drives him toward Rome.

The best evidence of Dido's efforts to colonize Aeneas comes later in Act 3 in his first audience with her. As we have seen in his narrative of Troy's fall, he supplicates well; and Dido responds by enveloping him in her late husband's royal robes. Ghoulishly, the gift gives an 'amaz'd' knight a new identity by making him the literal substitute for the murdered Sichaeus:

Stout love, in mine arms make thy Italy,
Whose crown and kingdom rests at thy command;
Sichaeus, not Aeneas be thou call'd;
The King of Carthage, not Anchises' son.

3.4.56–9

In an instant Aeneas is stripped of his patrimony, no longer, it would seem, his father's son: patriarchal inheritance is suspended. A cognitive caesura between lines 57 and 58 calls attention to the lovers' discursive struggle for control. Dido's strategy is to submit, then to rewrite the terms of her submission, much as Aeneas and his troops humble themselves, then effect a bloodless *coup*.

This metamorphosis of Trojan sailor into Carthaginian king continues in the cave episode outside Carthage. Dido celebrates what she takes to be their eternal union by giving Aeneas 'this wedding-ring, / Wherewith my husband woo'd me yet a maid, / And be thou King of Libya, by my gift [s.d.: *Exeunt to the Cave.*]' (3.4.61–3). Yet Dido's gifts are imperative and coercive; as Marcel Mauss noted in his classic study of gift-giving, 'charity wounds him who receives' it.[22] If Aeneas's dignity is wounded by such presents as the kingdom of Libya and the ring Sichaeus had used to woo Dido, which does make him the one wooed, clearly the more provocative threat is to his martial identity, as we see in Dido's response to his invitation to 'say' who he is. Exercising a benefactor's prerogative, Dido renames Aeneas, anticipating Cloanthus's later recommendation that Carthage be 'conquered' by christening it anew in honor of the Trojan leader, like St Petersburg becoming Leningrad.

For a time, Dido's rearrangement of her lover's identity and destiny seems to hold, for she is 'accounted' (note Aeneas's verb, signifying material property) by him first as 'author' of, then 'patroness of all our lives' (3.1.111, 4.4.55). The material consequence of Dido's patronage is her control of the Trojan fleet restored by gifts from Iarbus designed to usher his rival out of town. Dido confiscates their oars, tackling and sails (4.4.109) after their second attempt to depart; imagery in the episode supports the contention that Dido is an emasculating woman (a term ideologically loaded against women who interrupt a hurtful phallocentric ambition):[23] 'O Dido, blame not him, but break his oars, . . . Now let him hang my favours on his masts, / And see if those will serve instead of sails' (4.4.149, 159–60). The answer, of course, is no. Idle warships signify what is taken to be a dangerous rejection of imperial ambition, a point made by Mortimer in *Edward II*, contrasting the king's lack of interest in making war with Denmark's success: 'The haughty Dane commands the narrow seas,' he tells Edward, 'While in the harbour ride thy ships unrigged' (2.2.167–8).

The Trojans' gratitude toward their hosts turns to contempt in Act 4, once they come to recognize Dido's succor as a self-interested threat to the integrity of their homosocial alliance and its objective of planting a new city in Italy. Agreeing to repair their damaged fleet so they may sail to Italy, Dido has set one condition – that Aeneas remain in Carthage as its king and its queen's lover. Marlowe complicates the dilemma by making Aeneas desire to serve fate and Dido simultaneously. As late as Act 5, Aeneas is resolved to demobilize his men in Carthage, rationalizing that he is as able to reshape the world by making Carthage its fulcrum as by continuing on to Italy:

> Triumph, my mates, our travels are at end;
> Here will Aeneas build a statelier Troy
> Than that which grim Atrides overthrew;
> Carthage shall vaunt her petty walls no more,
> For I will grace them with a fairer frame
> And clad her in a crystal livery
> Wherein the day may evermore delight;
> From golden India Ganges will I fetch
> Whose wealthy streams may wait upon her towers
> And triple-wise entrench her round about;
>
> 5.1.1–10

Boasting that he shall divert the Ganges to Carthage, harnessing the mighty river to serve as a protective moat so that the city might become a center of military power, Aeneas echoes Faustus, Tamburlaine, Edward II, even Barabas, all of whom aim to control geography to signify their power. But Aeneas is playing with a dangerously domesticated definition of 'triumph.' The fleet has arrived in Carthage not in glory but in despair; if they stay, their colors shall be under the thumb of an autocratic queen who seems unlikely to surrender her control of the city to Aeneas, regardless of her promises.

Ironically, until Hermes appears with yet another message of warning from Jove, the sailors are ready to accept their leader's decision to abort their mission to Italy; even Achates enters into the city-planning fantasy by asking, 'What length or breadth shall this brave town contain?' (5.1.16). Writing of Aeneas's fascination with Carthage in Virgil's poem, Mihoko Suzuki points out that before the lovers meet, Aeneas marvels at 'the vital signs' of Carthaginian civilization (*Aen.* 2.421–9), which stand in stark contrast to his own attempts to found 'wrongheaded and pathetic replicas of his once magnificent city, such as Aeneadae (3.18) and Pergamum (3.133).'[24]

The men seem oblivious to the hubris of their plans, as they are utterly invested in predatory power relations. Even if their thoughts were initially 'unweaponed' (1.2.14), then, they have been rearmed by the improvement in their circumstances. They effect a combative rather than collaborative notion of how to improve the city, and seem unwilling to coexist peacefully alongside its inhabitants. Hermes arrives just in time to prevent the execution of the Trojans' plans to remake

Carthage, suggesting that the sailors are metaphorically speaking enslaved to their masculinist/militarist frame of mind. In this light it is worth pointing out that only the male characters cling to a geographically specific site for Aeneas's next city. His mother Venus, for example, cares not whether he 'depart to Italy, / Or else in Carthage make his kingly throne' (2.1.330–31), so long as Dido effects his recovery from shipwreck. But Hermes insists that for Aeneas not to go to Rome is to 'betray thy son's good hap' (5.1.31), a consummate act of betrayal of his male line. Hermes's final message restates Aeneas's dilemma in highly gendered terms: it is not Carthage v. Rome that is at stake, but matrilineal v. patrilineal genealogy. The decision to remain in Carthage has long been recognized by Aeneas's men as an affront to the axioms of epic masculinity. In Act 4, Scene 3, for example, Ilioneus had rebuked Aeneas, 'Why, let us build a city of our own / And not stand lingering here for amorous looks. / Will Dido raise old Priam forth his grave / And build the town again the Greeks did burn?' (4.3.37–40). Implicit in Ilioneus's speech is a palpable hostility toward Dido, whose offers to the Trojans are registered as an affront to the memory of Priam and to patriarchal rule. Ilioneus's conviction that Dido holds no brief for old Priam exposes a psychological connection operative in Marlowe's soldiers' psyches: repressing the feminine becomes an occasion of their own masculinity.

The impetus to return to sea mostly comes from Achates, who most clearly articulates the axioms of epic masculinity in all of *Dido*. Just before Aeneas promises to avenge the loss to the 'hateful Greeks' (4.4.91), Achates shames his general into character, as it were, with a poignant directive that expresses the misogyny of his virtù:

> Banish that ticing dame from forth your mouth,
> And follow your foreseeing stars in all;
> This is no life for men-at-arms to live,
> Where dalliance doth consume a soldier's strength,
> And wanton motions of alluring eyes
> Effeminate our mindes inur'd to war.

4.3.31–6

In this speech Achates extends the Tamburlainian frame of mind, which requires not only submitting to one's destiny ('foreseeing stars'), even if that means dying prematurely in battle, but also immersing oneself in an ascetic community of sorts. Pleasure is said to be detrimental to reserves of strength, women are said to be incompatible with a life 'at arms,' a tenet with which virtually all the Elizabethan military conduct-books would agree. Marlowe stages the misogyny of the tenet elsewhere, as in *Edward II*, where Gaveston's captors joke of the distracting duty to kiss their wives. But the Trojan commanders take seriously the threat women allegedly pose to the homosocial camaraderie of soldiers – or sailors – on a mission.

Achates's anxiety that domestic bliss makes both soldiers and nations 'effeminate' (i.e. too womanish, under a woman's spell) captures the thinking of most sixteenth-century military guides. Reflecting on the dangers of effeminacy, Rich is led to praise war as an act of cleansing the state in *A Roome for a Gentleman*: 'war is the minister of Gods justice . . . it is the surfets of peace, that hatcheth uppe war, and it is the sinnes of the people, that draweth the *Soldiers Sword*, for warres are but as a Corrector to the disorders of peace, it is as fire to the mettell that wants refining, as a phisition to a body overgrowne with grosse and corrupt humors.'[25] Like Rich, who audaciously argues that peace is a 'disorder' in need of medical treatment, Achates has likewise argued to Aeneas that his devotion to Dido is a malady and a calamity. Under this pressure from Achates to conform, Aeneas is shown to be what Rich might say is only so much 'mettell that wants refining.'

Achates's peer pressure works quickly. What Aeneas had once seen as Dido's 'beauty' is reconsidered to be 'female drudgery' that he cannot 'dure' (4.3.46, 55). Instantly, it seems, Aeneas is ready to eschew the temptations and comforts of domestic royal life in favor of one 'at arms.' Thus when Dido fawns again, 'O, how a crown becomes Aeneas' head! / Stay here Aeneas, and command as King' (4.4.38–9), the Trojan leader imitates his lieutenant's scorn for comfort, beauty, and peace:

> How vain am I to wear this diadem
> And bear this golden sceptre in my hand!
> A burgonet of steel and not a crown,
> A sword and not a sceptre fits Aeneas.
>
> 4.4.40–43

In the idea that a sword 'fits' him best, he takes refuge in an essentialist image of manhood, one that simply and safely demands allegiance rather than emotion or even independent thought. But the sword 'fits' best only because Aeneas says so: if a sword is a metonym of epic masculinity, what is in part compressed by that metonymic figure is the soldiers' ruse of using language to insist that words simply describe rather than create reality. Thus it is also with Tamburlaine, whose beautiful poetry belies his scorn for rhetoric as a powerful force in the world. We might recall the lines cited in Chapter 1, as he prepared to attack a Persian army. When he baited Techelles, 'Then shall we fight courageously with them, / Or look you I should play the orator?' Techelles knew the expected answer: 'Our swords shall play the orators for us' (*Tamburlaine* 1–1.2.128–9, 132).

Moreover, the rhetoric of Aeneas's reconversion from lover to soldier draws attention to the impact of rhetoric itself upon the soldier's persona. While some Elizabethan military strategists advocated plainness in speech as an admirable martial attribute, most acknowledged the centrality of persuasive speech to the success of a campaign.[26] Likewise, Marlowe has had Aeneas specifically recognize the power of speech in his earlier account of Troy's fall, but in such a way as to disrupt the fictions of battlefield heroism Achates and others uphold. We must return briefly to the scene in which Aeneas recounts the sack of Troy for Dido's court. He is narrating a pivotal moment of near mutiny in the Greek camp. When the Greek soldiers, 'tir'd with ten years' war, / Began to cry, "Let us unto our ships, / Troy is invincible"' (2.1.126–8), their captains had agreed to retreat, after 'looking on the scars we Trojans gave, / Seeing the number of their men decreas'd, / And the remainder weak and out of heart' (2.1.131–3). The Greeks retreat to Tenedos, where, exhausted and demoralized, they are met by their general, Ulysses. He 'Assay'd with honey words to turn them back'; 'And therewithal he call'd false Sinon forth, / A man compact of craft and perjury, / Whose ticing tongue was made of Hermes' pipe, / To force an hundred watchful eyes to sleep' (2.1.137, 143–6). This vignette allows Marlowe to contest a principal claim of epic masculinity, that valor in battle is a matter of solitary gut fortitude rather than a socially constructed commitment to die. These Greek soldiers do not renew their siege against Troy because of some urge stirring in their breasts to triumph at all cost. They do so because Ulysses manipulates them. It is at his behest that the traitor Sinon 'force[s] an hundred watchful eyes to sleep.' This detail demonstrates that, in the Greek camp at least, fortitude is indistinguishable from catatonia, physical signs of which would include muscular rigidity and mental stupor. Further, the hypnotized Greeks may recall the numb wakefulness, necessary to performing epic acts of murder, observed in Tamburlaine's men.

In the end, Aeneas's preoccupation with rhetoric comes closer to home. He argues with Dido that her words shall be ineffectual against the mandate of the gods that he should found Rome: 'In vain my love thou spend'st thy fainting breath: / If words might move me, I were overcome' (5.1.153–4). But as Dido returns his own resistance, 'It is Aeneas calls Aeneas hence' (5.1.132). Or almost. It is at least the ingrained assumptions about the links among honor, achievement, and masculinity, safeguarded through the play by Achates, that force Aeneas from Carthage. It seems to me that Marlowe refuses to exculpate his Trojan hero, who is in his version guilty if not of 'slaughter of a queen,' as Dido charges, then at least of 'perjury' (5.1.294).

While Dido's idolatry of the warrior does not extend to the once-hopeful Gaetulian king Iarbus whose advances she spurns, she is taught by him how to curse Aeneas. In Act 5 she virtually reproduces Iarbus's fantasies of revenge. Figuratively, she releases a serpent from her breast; recall that Iarbus earlier regretted not having been born a serpent, so he might 'sting' both Aeneas and Dido. Dido diverts the vector of her fury by giving it up to the sea:

> O serpent that came creeping from the shore
> And I for pity harbour'd in my bosom,
> Wilt thou now slay me with thy venomed sting,
> And hiss at Dido for preserving thee?
> Go, go, and spare not, seek out Italy;
> I hope that that which love forbids me do
> The rocks and sea-gulfs will perform at large
> And thou shalt perish in the billows' ways,
> To whom poor Dido doth bequeath revenge.

5.1.165–73

If Dido's point here is that she leaves vengeance to the gods, perhaps Marlowe's is that the code of revenge by which a warrior answers dishonor is not exclusively in the domain of men. In her curse Dido recreates the condition under which Aeneas has entered the play, reinscribing Juno's use of Neptune's waves to pound his fleet against Carthage's rocky shore. If the curse affirms the gendered notion that women may commission but never themselves make war (think of Elizabeth I in armor at Tilbury),[27] in calling on the gods it also affirms violence as part of the 'order' of 'all things' (5.1.303). That assumption is introduced in the play's opening scene by Venus, as she recounts how her son Aeneas had been attacked on the high seas by her enemy Juno. Says Venus, Juno has commanded 'Neptune's waves [to] be envious men of war' (1.1.65): the image implies an innate congruity of soldiers and nature in its rawest energy; hence war is 'natural.' Venus's complaint glosses the violence of shipwreck:

> Then gan the winds break ope their brazen doors,
> And all Aeolia to be up in arms;
> Poor Troy must now be sack'd upon the sea,
> And Neptune's waves be envious men of war;
> . . .
> And Aeolus like Agamemnon sounds
> The surges, his fierce soldiers, to the spoil.

1.1.62–9

Compared to Aeneas's bloody narrative of the sack of Troy, Venus's airy description of Troy 'sack'd upon the sea' – making poetry of 'spoil' – seems grotesquely out of touch with the texture of violence that elsewhere prevails in the play.

Mortal women in early modern theater have a more problematic relationship than either Juno or Venus to their immortal impulses to do violence. Dido's revenge fantasies, prescribed to some extent by the tradition, nevertheless are manipulated by Marlowe into an opportunity to indict the militarist ethos of the Mediterranean itself. That becomes clearer when we hold Dido's deathbed soliloquy up against a similar but not identical speech by Isabella in Kyd's *The Spanish Tragedy*. In a brilliant example of the revenge tragedy genre by Marlowe's close friend at the time of his murder in 1593, the seething Isabella rages against son Horatio's murder at a royal court infected by injustice. Part of her rhetorical strategy for bullying her husband into avenging their familial loss is threatening to do the job herself. In a speech taken from Tamburlaine's book, Isabella literally expresses a scorched-earth response to the court's betrayal of Horatio, vowing to obliterate an arbor on the palace grounds: 'I will not leave a root, a stalk, a tree, / A bough, a branch, a blossom, nor a leaf, / No, not an herb within this garden plot – / Accursèd complot of my misery.' But imagining revenge against a garden, however symbolic that act might be, almost instantly proves to be an unsatisfying and inadequate vehicle for Isabella's rage. So she turns the knife upon herself: 'And as I curse this tree from further fruit, / So shall my womb be cursèd for [Horatio's] sake, / And with this weapon will I wound the breast . . . [s.d. *She stabs herself*]'.[28] Like Isabella, Dido also eventually turns the knife to her own breast. Before doing so, however, Dido has made good her threat to destroy a metonymic token of Aeneas's status, his sword. In burning the sword, Dido complicates the implications of her suicide in ways that Isabella's threat to cut down an arbor never does. In fact, not to make too much of this, psychoanalytically, that is, Dido has a very complex relationship with Aeneas's sword itself. Before her final scene, at the moment in Act 5 where she learns that Aeneas and his men have set sail from Carthage for a third time, she prays to the gods to vanquish the fleet and to eviscerate the lands promised to him:

> And now, ye Gods that guide the starry frame
> And order all things at your high dispose
> Grant, though they traitors land in Italy,
> They may be still tormented with unrest,
> And from mine ashes let a conquerour rise
> That may revenge this treason to a queen
> By ploughing up his countries with the sword!
>
> 5.1.302–308

It would seem momentarily that Dido is advocating what Isabella has advocated in her own act of revenge – scorched earth. But if Isabella and Dido come to the same end – suicide – they bring to that act very different assumptions about the ethos of the dastardly martial world they choose to leave. While Isabella despairs, cursing her womb 'from further fruit,' Dido powerfully envisions from her womb the birth of a conqueror who rises like a phoenix 'from mine ashes' to answer Aeneas's treason 'by ploughing up his countries with the sword.' Her curse anticipates the Punic Wars in which Carthage would later be forced to defend itself again from the imperial ambitions of Aeneas's descendents. In effect, then, Dido never loses faith in epic masculinity, but only in her ability to marshal it in self-interest.

Dido, despite her anguish, then, never stops idolizing warriors and their principles of epic manhood. Yet in the closing moments of the play, by focusing our attention again on Aeneas's sword, Marlowe hints that Dido herself is beginning to exculpate Aeneas. Importantly, she does so by discriminating the role of conqueror as itself a role. Climbing onto the pyre on which she soon immolates herself, Dido eulogizes the furniture of war: 'Here lie the sword that in the darksome cave / He drew, and swore by, to be true to me: / Thou shalt burn first, thy crime is worse than his' (5.1.295–7). Importantly, she blames Aeneas's sword, not him, ascribing to it an anthropomorphic capacity for moral error: 'thy crime is worse than his.' Playgoers have seen Dido make this gesture earlier, too, when Aeneas is prevented from departing Carthage by Dido's having confiscated his sails and so forth. 'O Dido,' she comforts herself then, 'blame not him, but break his oars, / These were the instruments that launch'd him forth' (4.4.149–50). In these two gestures transferring blame from the hero to his equipment and arms, Dido is not simply in denial about the depth of his loyalty and affection. These gestures indict ('crime') a set of assumptions about the primacy of epic duty that has led to her great grief. If his sword is still a metonym of epic masculinity in the final moments of the tragedy, then perhaps her gesture of burning his sword first is not the ultimate emasculating act of a furious woman. Perhaps deflecting her fury onto an instrument of death is, paradoxically, a perverse act of hope. For in spite of her still strong desire for revenge, Dido may well be hoping for a world where an Aeneas finds as much honor in using a scepter as a sword, where domestic bliss and virtù are compatible.

If Dido's rage is being hedged by Marlowe, as I suspect, my explanation would help make sense of an earlier remark tossed off by Dido as, like some tragic Portia, she recollects the parade of undesirable suitors who preceded Aeneas. Pointing to the gallery of ex-suitors' portraits that hang in her court, Dido rehearses the suitors' flaws for the assembled Trojan warriors as a way of declaring her powerful love for Aeneas. One rejected suitor 'was an orator, and thought by words / To compass me'; another a 'Spartan courtier vain and wild'; another a musician; yet another a wealthy king. And coming to the last portrait,

Dido pauses: 'this [is] Meleager's son, a warlike prince, / But weapons gree not with my tender years' (3.1.154–5, 156, 162–3). What qualities do these unrequited lovers have in common? The means to ensnare Dido, to 'compass' her with words or music or gold or a 'warlike' *aura*. Given Dido's tragedy, it is especially ironic that she has rejected both an 'orator' and 'a warlike prince,' as Aeneas, the most dangerous of her lovers, is both. Inexorably, the play closes with the suicides of Dido, her spurned suitor Iarbus, and her sister Anna, who loves Iarbus as much as he has loved Dido.[29] Iarbus dies because he has surrendered his autonomy for a woman's love, as Aeneas never finally does. Iarbus dies almost a caricature of a warrior.

The contrasts between Aeneas and Iarbus help the playwright to reflect what is problematic in soldiers' psyches about honor, duty, and masculinity. Iarbus, in Marlowe's version a figure isolated from an epic community of soldiers, nevertheless owns some of its rhetoric in his bid to be both soldier and lover of Dido. Specifically, he imagines his rivalry with Aeneas as a zero-sum conflict, in which one man must die for the other to live, in spite of evidence that the 'love and duty' (3.3.15) he has shown to Dido is admired by Aeneas, who is refusing to allow himself to be cast as Iarbus's rival. Yet the Gaetulian king seethes with fury to eliminate his competitor: 'Iarbus shall but love. / So doth he now, though not with equal gain; / That resteth in the rival of thy pain, / Who ne'er will cease to soar till he be slain' (3.3.82–5). Expressing himself in the second person, Iarbus is grammatically dissociated from his own feelings, yet even so he is too passionate in his affection toward Dido to be a good soldier. Indeed, like Dido, he plays the Petrarchan lover, suffering Dido's scorn:

> O love, O hate, O cruel women's hearts,
> That imitate the moon in every change
> And, like the planets, ever love to range!
> What shall I do thus wronged with disdain?
>
> 3.3.66–9

But unlike a Petrarchan lover's, his volatile response to 'disdain' twists from the sin of despair to homicidal ideation:

> Nature, why madest me not some poisonous beast,
> That with the sharpness of my edged sting
> I might have stak'd them both unto the earth,
> Whilst they were sporting in this darksome cave?
>
> 4.1.21–4

Iarbus thinks of defiling the lovers to retaliate (*lex talionis*) for the defilement of his roles as lover and rival soldier. Like other of Marlowe's soldiers, he is excited by thinking of penetrating his enemies; he eroticizes murder as a grotesque substitute for intimacy if not intercourse.

Further, Iarbus's perception of being defiled is congruent with, and representative of, Marlowe's criticism throughout the play of the zero-sum nature of epic masculinity. While the most poignant imagery of defilement is articulated in Aeneas's account of Troy's fall, which we surveyed earlier, the play is rife with less-sustained examples of defilement that contribute to the eclipse of martial glory. That eclipse is realistically signalled by the Trojans' experience of hunger, which is repeatedly mentioned. Venus, for example, sends Cupid to kiss up to Dido so as to make sure the queen will 'Victual [Aeneas's] soldiers' as well as 'repair his broken ships' (2.1.329, 328); Venus does so after watching the boy Ascanius complain of being starved ('Father, I faint' [1.1.163]) as the Trojans come ashore; their collective hunger is part of what Achates deems their 'extreme misery' (1.1.157). Two acts later, Achates gets his bearings in a woods by recognizing it as the place where Aeneas 'shot the deer / That sav'd your famish'd soldiers' lives from death' (3.3.51–2). The reality of materiel shortages in Elizabethan military campaigns, including England's retaliatory armada celebrated in my epigraph from Peele, intrudes into the Carthaginian setting through the articulated hunger, which is acknowledged by the plot to be a serious threat to the survival of soldiers whoever they be.

Yet other images of feeding in the play take us beyond the necessity of soldiers' being fed. Again, as in the Bajazeth episode in *Tamburlaine*, symbolic cannibalism expresses the soldiers' desire to dismantle their opponents to remake the world in their own image. To return to the case of Iarbus: through his character Marlowe links the desire for vengeance to a cannibalistic urge to subsume the world by consuming one's rivals. His desire hits its peak as Dido's party sets out for the hunt that ends in the lovers taking shelter in the cave outside Carthage. Dido spurns Iarbus when he refuses to take her hint to get lost. Chivalrously, Iarbus is willing to forgive being mistreated by Dido, but not by Aeneas, he says, proclaiming sententiously that 'Women may wrong by privilege of love; / But should that *man of men* . . . Have taunted me in these opprobrious terms, / I would have either drunk his dying blood / Or else I would have given my life in gage' (3.3.25–9; my emphasis). Iarbus subscribes to what Peggy Sanday calls dialectical cannibalism – he would drink the blood of an enemy, or be drained – through which subjectivity may be generated: 'The flesh or bone marrow is a tangible conduit of social and psychological attributes that constitute the subject.'[30]

This vision of Iarbus drinking Aeneas's blood is located inside the soldiers' discussions of famine amongst them. Moreover, Aeneas responds to Iarbus's threat by projecting his own cannibalistic fantasies of young Ascanius growing up to avenge the sack of Troy, again sidestepping Iarbus's aggressive gesture toward him. Aeneas hopes he may 'live to see [Ascanius] sack rich Thebes, / And load his spear with Grecian princes' heads' (3.3.42–3). Aeneas pictures his son as a bounty-hunter, but Juno has just imagined Ascanius as the bounty. In Act 3, Scene 2 she hovers over the sleeping youth, 'Aeneas' cursed brat' (3.2.1). 'In spite of heaven,' Juno vows, 'I'll murder him, / And feed infection with his let-out life' (3.2.10–11). As in this fantasy, or in its opposite – George Peele's send-off of Norris and Drake in a blaze of Trojan glory – blood is the stuff of lineage and of fame. As *The Tragedy of Dido* suggests, blood is also one form of symbolic capital in the infected game of war. The play makes the hemorrhage of war neither epic nor chivalric, but by turns burlesque and grotesque.

Notes

1. George Peele, *A Farewell Entituled to the famous and fortunate Generalls of our English forces: Sir John Norris & Syr Frauncis Drake Knights*, London, 1589, STC 19537, A3r.
2. Barnabe Rich, *A Roome for a Gentleman*, London, 1609, STC 20985, D3r, D1v.
3. Peele, *A Farewell*, title page and p.3.
4. Robert Deveraux, earl of Essex (attributed to), *A True Coppie of a Discourse written by a Gentleman, employed in the late Voyage of Spaine and Portingale*, London, 1589, STC 6790, 2.
5. William Garrard, *The Arte of Warre*, London, 1591, STC 11625, 33.
6. See Leicester Bradner, 'Poems on the Defeat of the Spanish Armada,' *Journal of English and Germanic Philology* 43 (1944): 447–8.
7. Edmund Spenser, *The Poetical Works of Edmund Spenser*, ed. J.C. Smith and Ernest de Selincourt, 3 vols (1909; rpt Oxford: Oxford University Press, 1961, 1964), 2:495.
8. Michael Murrin, *History and Warfare in Renaissance Epic* (Chicago: University of Chicago Press, 1994), 12, 180–82.
9. James Aske, 'Elizabetha Triumphans,' in *The Progresses and Public Processions of Queen Elizabeth*, ed. John Nichols, 3 vols (rpt New York: Burt Franklin, 1966). Aske's poem is quoted from vol. 2 of this edition.
10. See, for example, Gordon Williams, *Technique and Ideas in the* Aeneid (New Haven: Yale University Press, 1983); R.O.A.M. Lyne, *Further Voices in Vergil's* Aeneid (Oxford: Clarendon, 1987); and Marilynn Desmond, *Reading Dido: Gender, Textuality, and the Medieval* Aeneid (Minneapolis: University of Minnesota Press, 1994). Lyne argues that Virgil's support of Aeneas's *pietas* is less absolute than has been recognized. Lyne notes that Aeneas is emotionally frozen 'at crisis-points' in Creusa's and Dido's lives, yet after their deaths shows great emotion – 'towards Dido he reveals sympathy, love, compassion; towards Creusa a wild, mad love according more with his passionate nature.' This phenomenon of being '*too late*'

(Lyne's emphasis) is a 'device of invention and arrangement by which a further voice discreetly but persistently expresses itself' (177). Lyne's argument is anticipated by Williams (see 43–6 and ch. 8). Desmond focuses upon medieval readings of the *Aeneid* in which she discovers support for a countertradition of feminist and postcolonial positions.

11. Bernard, *Commentary on the First Six Books of Virgil's* Aeneid, trans. Earl G. Schreiber and Thomas E. Maresca (Lincoln: University of Nebraska Press, 1974), makes the literary move traditional to Church Fathers of equating Dido with the slavery of passions: 'Dido, that is, passion rules [Carthage]'; 'in this city [Aeneas] finds a woman ruling and the Carthaginians enslaved, because in this world such is the confusion that desire rules and virtues are oppressed' (13). Fulgentius's 'Translation: The Exposition of the Content of Virgil according to Moral Philosophy,' in *Fulgentius the Mythographer*, trans. Leslie George Whitbread (Columbus: The Ohio State University Press, 1971), takes Dido to be so inconsequential she is never mentioned by name: '[T]he spirit of adolescence, on holiday from paternal control, goes off hunting, is inflamed by passion, and driven on by storm and cloud, that is, by confusion of mind, commits adultery. . . . [I]t is by the urging of the intellect that youth quits the straits of passion. So passion perishes and dies of neglect; burnt to ashes, it disintegrates' (127). As Jerome Singerman notes in *Under Clouds of Poesy: Poetry and Truth in French and English Reworkings of the* Aeneid, *1160–1513* (New York: Garland, 1986), the allegorical tradition represented by Bernard and Fulgentius takes Aeneas's rejection of Dido at the end of book 4 'as the entry into the *virilis etas*' (23).

12. Desmond, *Reading Dido*, counts some 'forty Renaissance dramas about Dido,' 20, 237–8, n.93.

13. See *The House of Fame* (lines 239–432) and *The Legend of Good Women* (lines 924–1367) in *The Riverside Chaucer*, ed. Larry D. Benson et al., 3d ed. (Boston: Houghton Mifflin, 1987); John Lydgate, *Troy Book*, ed. Henry Bergen, EETS, 3 vols (London: Kegan Paul, 1906–35), 2:814. On Chaucer's 'Trojan historiography' see Lee Patterson, *Chaucer and the Subject of History* (Madison: University of Wisconsin Press, 1991), 114ff.

14. Judith Butler, *Gender Trouble: Feminism and the Subversion of Identity* (New York: Routledge, 1990), 33.

15. Richard A. Martin, '*Fate, Seneca, and Marlowe's* Dido, Queen of Carthage,' *Renaissance Drama* 11 (1980): 59.

16. Emily Bartels, *Spectacles of Strangeness: Imperialism, Alienation, and Marlowe* (Philadelphia: University of Pennsylvania Press, 1993), 41.

17. On 'hierarchical observation' see Michel Foucault, *Discipline and Punish: The Birth of the Prison*, trans. Alan Sheridan (New York: Vintage, 1979), 170–71.

18. Compare Virgil's description of Aeneas when the lovers first meet: 'And there Aeneas stood, glittering in that bright light, his face and shoulders like a god's' (*Aeneid*, trans. Allen Mandelbaum [Berkeley: University of California Press, 1971], I.827–9).

19. Katharine in *The Jew of Malta* is another of Marlowe's mothers whose fantasies of avenging her son's murder boomerang toward suicide: 'Lend me that weapon that did kill my son,' she tells Governor Ferneze, 'and it shall murder me' (*The Jew of Malta* 3.2.23–4).

20. W. Craig Turner, 'Love and the Queen of Carthage: A Look at Marlowe's *Dido*,' *Essays in Literature* 11 (1984): 8.

21. Bartels, *Spectacles of Strangeness*, 29–30.
22. Marcel Mauss, *The Gift: Forms and Functions of Exchange in Archaic Societies*, trans. Ian Cunnison, introd. E.E. Evans-Pritchard (Glencoe, IL: Free, 1954), 63.
23. See Constance Kuriyama, *Hammer or Anvil: Psychological Patterns in Christopher Marlowe's Plays* (New Brunswick: Rutgers University Press, 1980), 53–76.
24. Mihoko Suzuki, *Metamorphoses of Helen: Authority, Difference, and the Epic* (Ithaca: Cornell University Press, 1989), 106.
25. Rich, *A Roome for a Gentleman*, B1r.
26. Rich is in the minority in claiming that 'souldiours are but blunte, but sure they love plainnes' in *A Path-Way to Military Practise*, London, 1587, STC 20995 (Amsterdam: Theatrum Orbis Terrarum, 1969), A6, but he is writing more as a poet than soldier. Most soldiers in sixteenth-century dramas of war use rhetoric while scorning it as the refuge of cowards aiming to escape having to go into battle. A more representative position is taken by Leonard Digges in *Stratioticos*, London, 1579 (Amsterdam: Theatrum Orbis Terrarum, 1968): a captain 'should be eloquent, and able compendiously and plainly to utter his minde, and also to perswade and diswade, to recreate and sometimes to provoke and stirre by mennes minds' (93–4).
27. Women did serve in battle, but rarely. In *The Actions of the Low Countries* (Amsterdam: Theatrum Orbis Terrarum, 1968), Sir Roger Williams describes the 1586 battle for Haarlem, noting that 'The women's captain was a most stout dame named Captain Margaret Kenau' (81). See also Barton C. Hacker, 'Women and Military Institutions in Early Modern Europe: A Reconnaissance,' *Signs* 6 (1981): 643–71.
28. Thomas Kyd, *The Spanish Tragedy*, in *Drama of the English Renaissance*, ed. Russell A. Fraser and Norman Rabkin, 2 vols (New York: Macmillan, 1976), 1:199 (4.2.10–13 and 4.2.35–8).
29. Of Virgil's Dido, Lyne, *Further Voices*, notes her suicide method 'involves a suggestion of suttee: the Eastern custom of widows burning themselves to death on the pyres of their husbands, the devoted fanatical death sought, in Greek mythology, by Evadne' (49). Is it a sign of fanatical devotion to militarism or to peace that Marlowe's Dido puts Aeneas's sword on the pyre?
30. Peggy Reeves Sanday, *Divine Hunger: Cannibalism as a cultural system* (Cambridge: Cambridge University Press, 1986), 36.

CHAPTER THREE

Pleasure, Peace, and Performance in Edward's England

The wolf is not so hurtful to the fold,
Frost to the grapes, to ripened fruits the rain,
As pleasure is to princes full of pain.
                    Mary Sidney, *The Tragedy of Antonie*[1]

In the 1590s the story of Edward II, a conniving but vulnerable king, vanquished by foes intent on reclaiming England from an impetuous head of state, would be told by several leading writers; their sudden interest in Edward's fall ought to have given Queen Elizabeth pause – as Mark Thornton Burnett has observed, 'the presence of Elizabeth haunts *Edward II*.'[2] For it was being used to examine the relationship of national security, royal leadership, civil war, and the justifications of war and martial law to protect the commonweal from enemies internal, especially from proud favorites of a besotted monarch. While Marlowe's rendition of the story diverges considerably from other contemporary versions, its focus on the dangers posed by pleasure and effeminacy (being under the spell of a woman, as well as the more modern meaning of the term) to the well-being of the empire mirrors some of these other accounts. Its fantasies of martial law bring spectators somewhat closer to contemporary times and geographically much closer than *Tamburlaine* or *Dido*, whose remote settings make it possible to ignore the disturbing aspects of their portraits of warlords while revelling in their actions. In *Edward II*, of course, the story hits closer to home. While Elizabeth proved to be willfully able to ignore the unflattering imputations of the implicit parallel being drawn by some writers, some years hence King James would not be able to be so above the fray. Angry at Sir Henry Yelverton for comparing his court to Edward's, James is said to have shot back, 'I had rather be no king than such a one as King Edward II.'[3]

Saint Edward

At the end of the fourteenth century Edward II was nominated for sainthood by Richard II, his great grandson.[4] In retrospect, of course, the unsuccessful gesture seems too deliciously ironic, Richard honoring his ancestor for some of the same qualities of character that would allow his own reign to be eclipsed by Henry Bolingbroke. Few of Edward's own contemporaries – or Richard's – or Marlowe's – would have joined Richard in describing the despised son of Edward Longshank as a saint, although Marlowe slyly has his earl of Pembroke call Queen Isabella 'saint' (1.4.190). As the plot goes forward, Marlowe exposes not only the irony of that praise, but also the intense self-interest that motivates the epideictic rhetoric of both praise and blame that suffuses Edward's world.

In the later sixteenth century Edward II was regularly cited by writers as a classic victim of unnatural desire, a diagnosis repeated but not reaffirmed by Marlowe. Raphael Holinshed censures the king for having so fixed 'his hart upon a man of such corrupt humor' as to become an 'addict' to 'filthie and dishonorable exercises.'[5] Holinshed leavens a judgment of immorality by suggesting that Edward, once addicted, could not help himself. Even though Holinshed stops short of rationalizing the king's deposition, declarations of a monarch's mental incompetence open up the possibility, as Marlowe well understands. Early on, he has Mortimer label Edward 'brainsick' in the first staged quarrel between king and peers (1.1.124).[6]

Whereas Holinshed tempers his criticism of Edward by making the problems as much medical as moral, Michael Drayton takes a different tack. In *Peirs Gaveston*, Drayton absolves Edward by demonizing Gaveston – literally – by having him speak from hell.[7] With nothing left to lose, Gaveston, characterized by Drayton as an unrepentant seducer, gleefully turns state's evidence. Driven even in hell by 'Selfe-love, prides thirst, unsatisfied desier,' Gaveston brags about having pursued Edward to steal his crown.[8] His proud confession implicitly rehabilitates the peers' drastic intervention in Edward's government two centuries earlier as an action that saved the state from conflagration. His 'desier' is itself preternaturally demonic – 'A flood that never yet had any boundes, / Times pestilence, thou state-consuming fier.'[9] As the apocalyptic diction may suggest, Gaveston's rhetoric is often righteously biblical. It can also be unexpectedly Petrarchan, as when he depicts his pursuit of the king as sport-fishing for Edward's heart. But even when Drayton seems intent on absolving Edward, the poem reinforces the common vision of the dangers of pleasure and passivity said to infect Edward's reign.

Regardless of each writer's estimation of the reign, the various versions of it circulating in late Elizabethan London helped to air contemporary anxieties about the national security implications of favorites – Essex, let's say – whose charms seduced a monarch into miscalculating the strength of foreign threats or otherwise making poor military choices in governing the nation. Not coincidentally, this is a complaint that Queen Elizabeth faced especially in her relationship with Essex. By 1601, when Elizabeth ordered the Privy Council inquiry into the performance of *Richard II* at the Globe Theater on the eve of Essex's attempt to seize the throne, the queen had become more alert to the national security and personal threats of a play about regicide than when the story of *Edward II* had been proliferating some ten years earlier.

While Essex's failed *coup* cannot be construed as altruistic, some years earlier he had been encouraged to champion martial law to make England more safe from its foreign enemies. In 1593 Matthew Sutcliffe had dedicated *The Practice, Proceedings, and Lawes of Armes* to Essex. Its dedicatory epistle, an effusively epideictic genre in the period, is unusually substantive and bold for that genre. It claims that under Elizabeth's rule, England has lost its distinguished tradition of warfare. This claim subordinates an obvious chunk of contrary evidence – the victory over Spain in 1588 – deeming that 'successe' 'so slender' (C2r). Sutcliffe focuses instead upon the failure of the attack on Portugal led by Essex and Drake in 1589. While acknowledging that public opinion is blaming 'our Generals' for 'breaking that enterprise' (B3v–B4r), he faults the metonym 'England' for sending troops to war inadequately provisioned. It is testimony to Essex's clout in 1593 that Sutcliffe's text was licensed for publication, as it is a thinly disguised indictment of the queen's reluctance to fund soldiers at levels satisfactory to them.

> Through disorder of some, & ignorance in others, to speake nothing of pinching & false reckonings, hitherto her Majestie hath not bene resolved to bring into the field a sufficient armie: and those small forces, if I may so call such smal troupes, that have bene employed in divers services, have wanted much of their necessary provisions.[10]

Sutcliffe is adamant: the problem is not that London cannot afford to equip its troops, for it is as rich and ambitious a city as 'Rome the mistres of the world for warlike discipline' or Sparta or Thebes (B3r). The problem is England's 'want of military knowledge, and not want of meanes' (B3r). To press the point, Elizabeth's leadership is contrasted to 'the good government of *Edward* the first, that so long warred in Scotland, of *Edward* the third, and *Henry* the fift, and eight' (B3r). Notably, Sutcliffe omits both Edward II and Elizabeth from his list of monarchs predisposed to war.

Further, Sutcliffe nominates Essex to be England's savior. The earl is urged to use his 'favour and accesse to her Majestie in whom it lyeth to reforme these abuses' to improve the status of English soldiers, and not to 'cease' until 'the redresse of these disorders' is achieved (B3v). Twice in exhorting Essex to combat 'disorders' Sutcliffe hints that martial law rather than more provisions is the better remedy. What he

finds lacking in Elizabeth's conduct, then, is not exactly the resolve to
pay for provisions, but the resolve to fight as often and as intensely as
the treasury will permit. In his words, 'if wee meane to mainteine our
state, and our reputation; of force we must observe militarie and
martiall orders' (B4v). 'Of all disorders the onely remedie and
medicine is, as I have saide, true discipline of armes' (Cr). How much
Sutcliffe's invitation to Essex encouraged the earl to rebel in 1601 is
impossible to know.

As with Sutcliffe, Elizabethan writers evinced an ambiguous
admiration of their queen's very great skill at keeping England's
enemies at bay with diplomacy rather than by strength of arms. They
paid lip service to the notion that peace is to be preferred before war,
yet promoted the idea that peace weakens the state and the soldiers
who in times of war are called to protect it. In 1590, for example, as
England braced for a second Spanish attack, Sir John Smythe
condemned the unfortunate effects of peace in *Certain Discourses
Militarie*. '[O]ur nation hath very much decayed . . . through long
peace,' he argued; the leisure of peacetime had allowed English men to
give 'themselves to covetousness, effeminacies, and superfluities.'
Moreover, he warned, the decline of the empire of ancient Egypt ought
to be taken as a mirror for magistrates. The Egyptians lost control of
the Mediterranean when, 'enjoying long peace and prosperity,' they did
'give themselves to their delights, covetousness, and effeminacies,
neglecting all orders and exercises military.'[11] Smythe visibly links
pleasure, peace, and national disgrace.

In 1584, more diplomatically, but with equal paranoia, Anthony
Munday had ambiguously praised the queen for heading up a 'heroicall
governement (which no Realme in the world is able to match for
peaceable continuance).' The gist of his treatise *A Watch-woord to
Englande To beware of traytours and tretcherous practises*, however, is
that the state's 'enimies are nowe growne so bolde' that it is in danger of
being overthrown; he urges the adoption of martial law to combat the
threats of internal sedition.[12] In 1592, in *The Solace for the Souldier and
Saylour*, Simon Harward identifies those internal threats. Some are
secret papists, 'English men by name, but Spanyards in heart.'[13] More
alarming is that these villains are indistinguishable from the ordinary
run of 'seditious malcontents' who prefer to 'waste great summes in
ungodlie suites of lawe, then to yeelde one mite towards the
maintenance of the souldier and the publike affaires of the common
wealth' (A3v). From Harward's perspective, these frivolous lawsuits are
the disease of an economic prosperity that has grown self-indulgent and
parasitic. This line of argument is embedded in *Edward II* in the peers'
suspicions that a king who is wallowing in pleasure and spending his

gold cavalierly cannot be trusted to answer the threats to his sovereignty in Ireland or Normandy or along the Scottish border.

Assessing the national risks of self-indulgent prosperity, Harward argues for the slippery slope: 'Peace hath increased plenty, plenty hath wrought pride, pride hath hatcht disdayne, and disdaine hath brought . . . such quarrellings and contentions as never were heard of in any age before us' (B3v). Harward concludes that it is in England's interests to support an army and navy to keep 'the enemie occupied at home' (Ev). Otherwise, Harward believes, England risks being not only attacked by outside enemies, but 'opprest by civill mutinies,' a fate Isabella much laments in *Edward II* (1.2.65). Too much peace, Harward asserts, produces a 'greater danger of stirring up rebellions' amongst the English themselves (Ev); Harward's theory has its corollary in Tamburlaine's argument, discussed in Chapter 1, that soldiers must have a constant supply of enemies, lest they turn their aggressions on one another or worse, on civilians. Barnabe Rich and Sutcliffe agree. In *A Room for a Gentleman* Rich, who signs himself 'Souldier,' warns that when England is too long at peace, it risks war inside Westminster, with 'neighbour against the neighbour, the friend against the friend, the brother against the brother, & somtimes the father against the sonne.' 'These warres are unnaturall wars,' he continues, 'and these wars wil never bee dissolved, but are like to grow every day more violent.'[14] And as Sutcliffe explains to Essex, 'Great countries and states cannot rest. if they have no enemies abroade, yet restles heades seeke worke at home' (A2v).

If Edward's tragedy was commonly used to whip up support for calcifying English masculinity in the shadow of the Armada, it is sometimes appropriated today for virtually diametrical purposes. Modern historians, for example, have used it to illustrate the corrective effects of reading historical data without being prejudiced by homophobia. Charles Nauert and John Boswell, to take two examples, point out that the portrait of national crisis painted by Edward's foes and used to justify his murder is inaccurate. Boswell notes that the king 'inherited [the realm] in debt and turmoil' from his father Edward Longshank, yet kept England at peace some twenty years.[15] But Edward's peers did not want peace – as Marlowe's dramatized retelling of Edward's history insists. In deposing Edward, they aimed to get a monarch who was more malleable to their agenda.

Nauert emphasizes that that agenda privileged war. In 1337, Edward III launched the disastrous Hundred Years War, giving the peers what his father would not. As Nauert writes,

> The greatest force working for the outbreak and prolongation of war was the aristocracy on both sides. The nobles were by profession a military caste. From warfare they sought not only

> personal glory but also some very tangible advantages: ransom of
> captives, booty from invaded territories, military commands[.] . . . In
> an age when general inflation, rising labor costs, and falling farm
> profits made it impossible to live aristocratically from the revenues
> of their landed estates, the nobles could find no other socially
> acceptable occupation than war.[16]

Nauert implies that Edward II's greatest challenge was not from the
Gavestons and other flatterers, but from peers who were anxious to return
the court to the glory days of Edward I, when they had support for
making war upon neighbors and infidels. By contrast, Longshank and
Edward III were so honored by secular writers for making war, and
thereby giving peers of the realm opportunities to achieve honor and
profit. Just as Sutcliffe omits Edward II from the roll of great English
commanders, other commentators likewise ignored him in favor of
Edward I and III, whose reigns were gilded in nostalgia. In *Peirs Gaveston*,
for example, Drayton forces Gaveston to praise Edward Longshank, who
had banished the favorite from his son's company. 'Here sprang the roote
of true gentilitie,' Gaveston is made to crow, a man in whom 'Vertue was
clad in gold and crownd with honor, Honor intitled to Nobilitie.'[17]

In Marlowe's tragedy, this respect for Longshank's memory is slyly
reiterated through Mortimer's voice. As the king is reunited with
Gaveston in Act 1, Mortimer remembers his promise to Longshank
never to allow the favorite to be readmitted to the realm (1.1.82–4).
However, it is Mortimer's compatriots who first make their obedience to
the new king contingent upon being able to keep the oath to Longshank.
On this point Lancaster is vehement. In a heated moment he vows to sell
earldoms to finance a rebellion against Edward II, if Gaveston is
permitted to stay repatriated. 'Either change your mind,' he threatens
Edward, 'Or look to see the throne where you should sit to float in
blood' (1.1.129–31).

Responding to the crisis created by Gaveston's first return to court,
initially Mortimer claims to be poised to 'hang his armour up' ('This
sword of mine . . . shall sleep' [1.1.89, 85–6]); he intends to cancel the
allegiance that would require him to assist Edward II in the face of a
foreign military threat. But egged on by Lancaster's example, Mortimer's
opposition is quickly transformed from passive resistance to promises of
physical violence. 'Come uncle, let us leave the brainsick king,' he urges,
'and henceforth parley with our naked swords' (1.1.124–5). Obviously
Mortimer's verbal threat sexualizes ('naked swords') his resistance to
Edward's reign. Here Mortimer exploits the threat of sodomy to efface
his own agency, as Gregory Bredbeck has argued.[18] A rhetorician of the
first order, Mortimer constantly dissembles, as his uncle well knows:
'But nephew, do not play the sophister' (1.4.255).

Mortimer's threat to 'parley' against the king is an example of the maneuver common to Marlowe's soldiers, in which they speak scornfully of using language as a weapon, all the while using it that way. The illogic of that attitude toward the power of rhetoric is drawn out in an exchange between Warwick and Mortimer in this tense first congress of the peers. When Warwick cautions the hotheaded young earl, 'Bridle thy anger gentle Mortimer,' Mortimer blurts out prophetically that he cannot be contained: 'I cannot nor I will not; I must speak' (1.1.120–21). Four lines later Mortimer is resolved to draw his sword instead.

In making these initial responses to Gaveston so mercurial, Marlowe insinuates how the peers' opposition is being driven by more than the favorite's return, which is only symbolic of their real problem with Edward's reign, that he endorses peace over war as the preeminent episteme of English life. In a soliloquy that is juxtaposed with the peers' first verbal assault upon Edward, Gaveston establishes Edward's appetite for Italian masques and so forth. Rather than the camaraderie of war, the king prefers the gambols of peace. Rather than the company of warlike peers, he likes pages clad as 'sylvan nymphs,' or maybe a 'lovely boy in Dian's shape,' whose 'parts which men delight to see' are only half hidden by the twigs of an olive tree, a traditional symbol of Christian peace (1.1.57, 60, 64). In *Edward II* Marlowe revisits an anxiety at the heart of dramatic tension in *Dido*, namely that effeminacy, theatricality and pleasure can disrupt the pursuit of empire and its entitlements. As Stephen Greenblatt once remarked, Marlowe's Edward II makes a habit of recoiling from the 'sanctified rites and responsibilities of kingship, marriage, and manhood.'[19]

Culture Heroes

By long tradition, the success or failure of a military campaign or even a nation's foreign policy is sometimes pinned on a single figure – some Edward III, Henry V, Lincoln, Churchill. This convention is undoubtedly reductive, but it conveniently concentrates praise or blame. Marlowe's London was no exception. Thus the queen who on the one hand could be excoriated for miserly materiel support of troops could on the other also be credited with having saved England from Spain, virtually single-handedly. Commenting on the 'prognosticated dangers' of 1588, Thomas Tymme praises Elizabeth as a 'Deborah for the Israel of the Lord' for having kept 'manie thousand servants of God' from 'the hands of cruel tormenters.'[20] In 'The fatall yeere of fearefull Eighty Eight,' Maurice Kyffin analogizes England itself as Israel, led out of the pharaoh's clutches into safety by the queen, who is said to be descended from 'a Blessed Branch of Brutus Royall Race.'[21]

Sue Mansfield calls such leaders 'culture heroes' when they anoint themselves the enemies of chaos who must use violence to create peace. Elizabeth might qualify, for cracking down on recusants in the 1590s; Mary I certainly would. Through their efforts, such culture heroes claim, 'the forces of destruction and chaos are themselves destructured.' Mansfield's idea is based on her study of Apache and Papago war myths of the nineteenth-century American southwest, but she suggests that the idea may be universal.[22] Mortimer exhibits the qualities of mind Mansfield describes. Initially he is one voice among many that clamor for Edward to mend his priorities and his judgment. But quickly he emerges as opposition leader, precisely because he is careful to sell his ambition as disinterested concern in the well-being of the commonweal, which to his mind is about to come undone.

As early as Act 1 Marlowe establishes that Mortimer's conduct represents as great a threat of chaos – if not greater – as does Edward's behavior with Gaveston. Recall that in Act 1, Scene 4 Mortimer abruptly reverses his opposition to the favorite's repatriation after conferring on stage with Queen Isabella. Putting their conversation in sight but out of earshot of both the peers of the realm and the spectators, Marlowe brilliantly allows the possibility of a conspiracy against Edward to be hatched without yet confirming it. We are left to imagine the deal Isabella and Mortimer have struck. After their tête-à-tête, though, Mortimer pleads for Gaveston's return: 'not for his sake, but for our avail.' 'Nay, for the realm's behoof and for the king's,' he adds almost as an afterthought (1.4.242–3). In reply, Lancaster protests that Mortimer's reversal makes 'white black and dark night day' (1.4.247). This trope of cosmic disorder, even if an early modern commonplace, is particularly significant here. As Pico writes to his friend Barbaro, 'for what is the office of the rhetor other than to lie, deceive, circumvent, practice sleight-of-hand tricks. It's your business, as you say, to turn black into white and white into black as you will.'[23] The trope does triple duty. It registers the threat Mortimer eventually poses to English society as a usurping demagogue; it anticipates his indictment of the deleterious effects of Edward's repeated promotions of Gaveston to the various titles such as Lord of Man; and it prompts Mortimer himself to reassure Lancaster and the other peers that Gaveston will be readmitted to England only to meet death.

Mortimer's first act of leadership is to propose a blueprint of Gaveston's murder. He envisions a 'base slave' being recruited 'To greet his lordship with a poniard, / And none so much as blame the murderer, / But rather praise him for that brave attempt, / And in the chronicle, enroll his name for / Purging of the realm of such a plague' (1.4.265–70). As the play unfolds, we come to understand this as Mortimer's plan for Edward's, not Gaveston's, death. Even in these early deliberations among the peers, the details of regicide are beginning to run through Mortimer's mind, his violent ambition yet disguised as therapeutic violence that, like the practice of bleeding the patient, will purge England of 'plague.' By Act 5, however, Mortimer's pretense of saving his nation from Edward's despotic caprice has been abandoned. In a speech almost vibrating with Tamburlainian authority (almost, because it is peculiarly qualified by Mortimer's recognition that he is still only the Protector of young Prince Edward and not himself king), Mortimer relishes the naked power of the despot:

> The prince I rule, the queen do I command,
> And with a lowly congè to the ground
> The proudest lords salute me as I pass;
> I seal, I cancel, I do what I will.
>
> 5.4.46–9

The parataxis of the final line here dramatizes a mind that acknowledges little connection between its manic imposition of 'martial law' (5.4.86) and its earlier commitment to 'the realm's behoof' (1.4.243), or what the earl of Warwick once understood to be 'my country's cause' (2.6.10). Thus has Mortimer's therapeutic violence become transformed into sinister autarky. As he puts it, sounding like Edward II at his most capricious, 'Mine enemies will I plague, my friends advance, and what I list command, who dare control?' (5.4.65–6). Over the course of five acts, the crusader against the 'light-brained king' (5.2.2) is exposed by Marlowe as a great deal less than England's savior. In offering this portrait of Mortimer's destruction, omitted from other accounts of Edward's reign by Marlowe's contemporaries, the playwright dramatizes how soldiers may create their enemies, and come to regret it.

Evidence is abundant that Edward's enemies themselves escalate the state crises which Mortimer has set out to quell. They do so by speaking in apocalyptic language that injects more tension into the court, crowding out clear thinking or rational responses to the foreign problems facing the king. Lancaster's speech in Act 2 is the best example. 'Look for rebellion, look to be deposed,' he taunts Edward:

> Thy garrisons are beaten out of France,
> And, lame and poor lie groaning at the gates;
> The wild O'Neil, with swarms of Irish kerns,
> Lives uncontrolled within the English pale;
> Unto the walls of York the Scots made road
> And unresisted drave away rich spoils.
>
> 2.2.160–66

What is most remarkable about Lancaster's anxious report of chaos consuming England's boundaries is its unexpected emphasis upon money. The Scots have carted away 'rich spoils'; worse, English soldiers once garrisoned in France are now 'groaning' at those garrisons' gates, 'lame and poor.' Lancaster's speech undercuts the premise of soldiers in *Edward II* and throughout Marlowe's plays that, as Ferneze says hypocritically in *The Jew of Malta*, 'honor is bought with blood and not with gold' (2.2.56). Richard Lindabury has charted similar bombast across many Elizabethan plays; he calls the sincerity of the idea, even as an ideal, 'highly debatable.'[24]

In *Edward II*, other evidence further compromises the peers' pretense of being more interested in honor than in lucre. In Act 3, Scene 1, for example, Isabella informs Edward that her brother Valois is besieging Normandy 'because your highness hath been slack in homage' (3.1.63). Ironically, Edward is being attacked at home for paying homage to Gaveston, and attacked abroad for not paying off Valois. Evidence elsewhere in Marlowe's canon suggests that tribute was seen as symbolically castrating to the king who pays. In *The Jew of Malta* again, Martin del Bosco, vice admiral to the king of Spain, urges Ferneze to fight the Turk Selim Calymath rather than pay what amounts to protection-money. And in both parts of *Tamburlaine*, tribute is only a lesser form of humiliating defeat.

There is also another sort of homage going unpaid in Act 1 of *Edward II*: the needs of common soldiers are being ignored as usual, except in this case their unmet needs are used to spur the rebellion. Late in Act 1, Scene 4 Edward and the peers have for the time being reached an uneasy concord. In thanksgiving, the king does his usual routine of giving away prize offices and lands. This time he appoints the elder Mortimer general of 'levied troops' who are to be dispatched to beat back the Scots from the north of England (1.4.361); Lancaster has already been named 'High Admiral of our fleet' (1.4.66) and the bishop of Coventry 'Chancellor of the realm' (1.4.65). Yet amidst all these presents, the younger earl grouses to his uncle that Gaveston is still able to 'riot it with the treasure of the realm / While soldiers mutiny for want of pay' (1.4.404–5). Mortimer understands two things: that Gaveston's accumulation of wealth indirectly represents its own military threat to the peers; and that at least some of the unpaid soldiers can be recruited into treason by being bought. 'Know you not Gaveston hath store of gold,' he had asked his uncle earlier in the scene, 'Which may in Ireland purchase him such friends / As he will front the mightiest of us all?' (1.4.258–60). Mortimer's concerns show that martial loyalty, if not honor, is for sale in Marlowe's version of fourteenth-century London.

This is a reality which the peers in *Edward II*, Marlowe's soldiers generally, and Elizabethan poet-soldiers all resist.[25] In 1578, Thomas Procter proclaims that 'Love is the surest armour that a Governour or Captaine can put on, and faithfulnes is not by fee.'[26] But he has explicitly borrowed his opinion from Machiavelli. The Italian's advice, Procter admits, is 'not altogether agreeinge with all mens judgementes,' especially in 'our English warres.' Procter is more sure that 'money is the synewes of warre.'[27] In 1587, Thomas Digges reported that when the earl of Leicester arrived in the Low Countries in 1585 as commander of Elizabeth's army, he found 'great confusion,' the 'soldier in miserie and disorder for want of pay.'[28] In 1595 the anonymous writer of *A Myrrour for English Souldiers* repeatedly mentions the importance of paying mustered men on time: 'The want of money makes Souldiers loose theyr courage.'[29] Along these lines, poet-soldiers also understood that unpaid troops had the weapons to turn upon a former master, as the Spanish troops under the duke of Alva had done in the infamous 1576 sack of Antwerp.

Marlowe acknowledges the demoblized soldier as a potential threat to internal peace as early as Act 1, Scene 1. There Gaveston is approached by three impoverished men asking for preferment at court, the very thing the favorite also seeks. The first knows horse riding; the second has travelled, and Gaveston thinks he might be useful, like More's Hythloday, for telling lies at dinnertime; the third is 'A soldier, that hath served against the Scot.' In an Elizabethan audience this line would have been as likely to invoke the sixteenth-century raids against the Scots by Somerset[30] under Henry VIII and Edward VI as those of the fourteenth century. It is also likely to have triggered the only-recently diminished anxieties associated with defending England against Stuart plots to assassinate Elizabeth and, before 1587, to install Mary Stuart and Roman Catholicism by force. And it may also have aroused images of soldiers demobilized from the Low Countries in the late 1580s who swarmed the English countryside, begging and sometimes robbing in order to survive. Gaveston dismisses the soldier, the Third Poor Man, with a sneer:

GAVESTON: Why, there are hospitals for such as you.
                       I have no war, and therefore, sir, be gone.
THIRD POOR MAN: Farewell, and perish by a soldier's hand,
                       That wouldst reward them with an hospital.
                                                          1.1.34–7

The third man is unmoved by a faint offer of succor that, in effect, warehouses soldiers except in times of war, a frequent complaint of soldiers and their supporters. As Stephen Gosson notes, 'Some there are that make gods of soldiers in open warrs, and trusse them up like dogs in time of peace.'[31] Elizabeth's own solutions to the problem took various forms; perhaps the most ingenious was her claim in November 1589 that the 'vagarant Souldiers' troubling London were often only 'pretending to have served her Highnesse in the warres.'[32] Here, pretending is lying.

Peace, pleasure, performance

Several of the testimonials from Elizabethan poet-soldiers complain that civilian contemporaries were showing an irresponsible lack of gratitude for the military services in which mustered men routinely lost their lives to illness and starvation as well as combat. Their complaint is echoed in the expository material in *Edward II*, where the context (a London theater) draws attention to the question of what exactly the poet-soldiers would want to be represented on stage – their valor? their hunger? the unglorious circumstances of the deaths of men on an early modern battlefield? The veterans-turned-writers clearly struggle with these questions, even if only taking them up in the course of larger narratives aimed at advising the queen or shaping public opinion of their profession. Generally they distinguish between their own uses of theater and other stage metaphors, which they endorse as tropes that help them make sense of their actions abroad, and the representation of those actions on the stage itself, which they largely repudiate. We can see the distinction by comparing two passages published in the mid-1590s. Sutcliffe writes in 1593 that 'souldiers are the principall actors in these tragicall matters,' a sentence demonstrating that for him 'actor' carries a double meaning well before the OED suggests that that would have been the case (C2v). Sutcliffe very deliberately invokes the genre of tragedy and comfortably assigns soldiers to it. In 1596 Charles Gibbon, whose admonitions to captains to temper discipline with lenity I discussed in Chapter 1, addresses the effects of theatricalizing military service. He speculates that many such 'Unskilfull persons' – by which he means civilians – 'rejoyce at war because they know not what it is.' Their cavalier disregard for the welfare of soldiers, he writes, echoing Erasmus's pacifism, follows from their mistaking the performances of battles on the stage for the real thing:

> *Dulce bellum inexpertis*, warre is sweete to such as never taste it, because in ordinary traynings, they use to skirmish for theyr learning: or in theyr May-games for delight; They thinke warre to be a matter of merriment. Alas, it is an easie matter to play *Hercules* in our houses, or *Alexander* uppon the stages: but it is somewhat [*sic*] to follow them in the field, where every bullet doth threaten death.[33]

Gibbon puts forward two interesting points. First, he charges that theaters exacerbate warmongering by making acts of war into entertainment. Second, he claims civilians cannot comprehend the fundamental distinction between a player in the role of Hercules and Hercules himself. One is feigning, the other is not. To be sure, as Gibbon reminds us, stage bullets are, practically speaking, not genuine. Yet he denies the possibility that soldiers in battle are performing a role no less than are players on stage. Importantly, Gibbon is not interested in denying the validity of spectators' analogies between a performance of *Henry V*, let's say, and the battle of Agincourt, in order to glorify war; on the contrary, he believes that a nation at war is being punished by God for its sins. But he is implicitly siding with the claim we first met in the chapter on *Tamburlaine* that martial identity is possessed, not performed.

Edward II is suffused with the assumption that identity is performed. Whereas Gibbon claims that art inadequately imitates life, Marlowe, recreating the tumult of Edward's reign, suggests that life *is* theater. Soldiers invested in essentialist models of identity are, like Gibbon, averse to that idea. Typically, Marlowe's older soldiers are calmer about challenges to essentialism. In *Tamburlaine*, for example, the Scythian's lieutenants, all presumably older than he, are less rabid in pressing forward with the conquest of the world along the narrow lines valued by Tamburlaine. In *Edward II* the age differential is embodied in the relationship between the Mortimers. The elder's calm reply to the new commands he gets from Edward for his 'great achievements in our foreign war' are a case in point. 'In this your grace hath highly honoured me,' he glows, 'for with my nature war doth best agree' (1.4.359, 363–4). While the senior Mortimer is obviously invested in defining his 'nature' as martial, he is less interested than his nephew is in forcing others to concur in his self-assessment or to adopt similar self-definitions. Indeed, I posit that Marlowe creates the contrast between the Mortimers in part to help establish that the question of whether a man's martial nature is possessed or performed is a root conflict of the play.

The lovers mimic the priorities and assumptions that sustain the entitlements of empire in ways that call attention to their extemporaneous artificiality. One small example is Lancaster's enraged report in Act 1, Scene 2 that 'arm in arm, the king and [Gaveston] doth march' (1.2.20). Perhaps unwittingly, Lancaster accuses the lovers of imitating the perambulations of troops. An extended example of a similar complaint appears when Lancaster and Mortimer confront Edward alone outside Tynemouth Castle as Gaveston is returned a second time to England. While Lancaster focuses his criticism upon

concrete examples of crises that have gone unanswered by their lovesick
king, again injecting apocalyptic hysteria into the already-tense
confrontation, Mortimer instead stresses the dangers of fictionality
itself. 'The idle triumphs, masques, lascivious shows' at court have
drained the treasury and 'overstretchèd' the 'murmuring commons'
(2.2.156, 159). His complaint is by now as familiar as Lancaster's.

But this time Mortimer compounds the indictment. Edward is faulted
for having made war itself into a fiction:

> When wert thou in the field with banner spred?
> But once! And then thy soldiers marched like players,
> With garish robes, not armour, and thyself,
> Bedaubed with gold, rode laughing at the rest,
> Nodding and shaking of thy spangled crest,
> Where women's favours hung like labels down.
>
> 2.2.181–6

Mortimer hates Edward for eviscerating the semiotics of battle.
Misogynistically, Edward is dismissed as an effeminate creature content
to wear 'women's favors' in place of the usual signs – a red cross,
perhaps – by which soldiers marked their armor to signify which side
they are on. In preferring distinctive cloth costumes to impenetrable
armor, costumes better suited to a ball than a battle, Edward is seen as
renouncing the Tamburlainian warrior's hardened, numbed, impervious
state of mind. Worse, his choices have set a bad example; he has
corrupted his men: 'thy soldiers marched like players.' In a phrase that
would inevitably have evoked the anti-theatrical controversies swirling
about the London theater scene, Mortimer expresses a soldier's
contempt for the wanton seductions of all fictions, including those in
which a player aims to act as Alexander the Great or Hercules. By a
different route, Thomas Cartelli has reached similar conclusions.
'Mortimer and his confederates are cast as counter-fantasists,' he
observes; they are presented as 'puritanical enemies of pleasure who aim
to suppress violently any deviation from their colorless and self-
interested rule.'[34]

Marlowe has afforded Mortimer an earlier opportunity to complain
of sartorial violations by the king and his minion. In Act 1 the earl had
been quizzed by his uncle, the elder Mortimer, as to the grounds of his
opposition to Gaveston's presence at court. The elder peer suspects it is
their presumed sexual relationship that troubles his nephew, so in a
history lesson he reminds him that even in classical times, from whence
come many of the tenets of masculinity the peers aim to protect and
promote, homoerotic relations between men were compatible with great
martial valor: 'Great Alexander loved Hephestion; / The conquering
Hercules for Hylas wept; / And for Patroclus stern Achillis drooped'

(1.4.391–3).[35] But recently a number of critics have agreed that Mortimer is sincere when he replies, 'Uncle, his wanton humour grieves not me' (1.4.401). As Jonathan Goldberg points out, the Mortimers are pressed into accepting the sexual relationship of king and favorite, for it celebrates the primacy of male entitlement in which the peers are invested.[36] Mortimer explains away his quarrel with Gaveston as centering on the social climbing of 'one so basely born' (1.4.402). In keeping with the animus against theatricality, he specifically objects to Gaveston's clothing, for which he demonstrates an acute memory:

> He wears a lord's revénue on his back,
> And, Midas-like, he jets it in the court
> With base outlandish cullions at his heels,
> Whose proud fantastic liveries make such show
> As if that Proteus, god of shapes, appeared.
> I have not seen a dapper jack so brisk;
> He wears a short Italian hooded cloak
> Larded with pearl, and in his Tuscan cap
> A jewel of more value than the crown.
> Whiles other walk below, the king and he
> From out a window laugh at such as we,
> And flout our train and jest at our attire.
> Uncle, 'tis this that makes me impatient.
>
>   1.4.406–18

Mortimer's long, colorful reply to his uncle tells us more about his own habits of mind than about Gaveston's. It displays an impressive array of prejudices against actors, men-about-town, the nouveaux riches, overly familiar courtiers, and Italians.

As a term of general abuse, 'Italian' was sometimes code for a man whom we would call gay or homosexual, whose 'unnatural' sexual practices were taken as grave threats to the integrity of the state.[37] Mortimer's construction of Gaveston as a courtier who is too much under the sway of Italian fashions, however, emphasizes the danger, not of his sexual practices, but of his political advice to the king. Said by his enemies to be parading about in an 'Italian hooded cloak,' Gaveston is, in Mortimer's eyes, a veritable Machiavelli. Gaveston's condemnation ironically rebounds in Act 5, where Mortimer mouths lines from the seventeenth chapter of *The Prince*, making the point that he and Gaveston have more in common than the good soldier would wish to admit. 'Feared am I more then loved,' he gloats, relishing what he thinks is his supreme victory. '[L]et me be feared' (5.4.50).[38]

For Mortimer, Gaveston's sexual alterity is xenophobically linked as well to his status as a foreigner. Indeed, in early modern England the 'sodomite' was frequently an umbrella term for a host of 'othered' subject positions and practices, including 'bestiality, lesbianism, heterosexual anal intercourse, adultery, minority and alien status, political insurgence, witchcraft and sorcery' and so forth, as Gregory Bredbeck, among others, has demonstrated.[39] It is not surprising, then, that the peers hate Gaveston as much for being French (not Italian) as for being Edward's lover; in this detail Marlowe follows the anonymous writer of *Vita Edwardi Secundi* (1325), who judges the king as being 'incapable of moderate favour' and Gaveston a 'sorcerer.'[40] The writer concludes Gaveston was hated by the peers as much because he 'was an alien of Gascon birth as through envy. For the magnates of the land hated him, because he alone found favour in the king's eyes and lorded it over them like a second king, to whom all were subject and none equal.'[41]

Through Mortimer's antipathy, Marlowe reproduces but qualifies the major criticisms of Edward voiced some two and a half centuries earlier in *Vita Edwardi Secundi*. In Marlowe's portrait of the life, those 'othered' positions listed above represent no greater danger to the state than does the peers' matrix of assumptions about what dangers must be eradicated in order to make England, as it were, safe again. For them, Gaveston embodies the link between pleasure, performance, and impending national disgrace that so agitated Elizabethan soldiers. Among numerous examples from the handbooks, consider again Barnabe Rich in 1587. He had lamented that England's 'continued peace hath bene the nourisher of many vices, we have entertained pride [*sic*] newe fangled fashion, and monstrous attire';[42] his complaint is the poet-soldiers' corollary of the puritans' anti-theatrical prejudice being voiced as Marlowe wrote plays.[43] Stephen Gosson proposes a punishment for social climbers who violate sumptuary laws and so threaten the realm with disease. He believes the theater itself must be 'dismembered' (as Gaveston is) if London is to be saved from the vice of men who imitate their betters:

> [I]n a commonweal, if private men be suffered to forsake their calling because they desire to walk gentleman-like in satin and velvet, with a buckler at their heels, proportion is so broken, unity dissolved, harmony confounded, that the whole body must be dismembered.[44]

For Mortimer, Gaveston's costumes constitute the 'monstrous attire' attacked by Gosson and Rich. His 'short Italian hooded cloak, larded with pearl' and his 'Tuscan cap [with] a jewel of more value than the crown' is, as I suggested earlier, said to bedevil harmony itself by penetrating the court in ways that are scarcely less ruinous than having 'the wild O'Neil, with swarms of Irish kerns,' living uncontrolled inside England.

If Gaveston's presence does not exactly constitute invasion in the physical sense, then his costumes suggest a frame of mind that deeply threatens the mentalité upon which Mortimer's own identity and social privilege – and England's upper class – all rest. Given the stakes, Mortimer's anxiety is, on the one hand, well articulated in the sartorially focused complaint. He resents that the minion and the king of England 'laugh' and 'jest' at the 'attire' of warriors, for this is clearly an affront to their superior tenets and priorities. On the other hand, the anxiety produced by the king's laughter suggests that Mortimer is made to feel helpless in the company of one who behaves more like a 'Proteus' than like a foreign aristocrat or another peer.[45] Mortimer's self-consciousness at the merriment produced by his appearance may remind us of Charles V's knights in *Doctor Faustus* who come unglued by the doctor's irreverent shape-shifting. Like those knights, Gaveston is, in Derek Jarman's words, a character in whom we can see a set of anxieties about 'sexuality and class merged.'[46]

Maddeningly to the peers, Gaveston wins plum titles such as earl of Cornwall by spinning ephemeral fictions for the king's delight that, to the peers anyway, seem to have little to do with the business of running a kingdom. Without having to trouble himself on the field of battle, Gaveston is able to picture himself to be 'as great, as Caesar riding in the Roman street, with captive kings at his triumphant car' (1.1.171–3). Under Gaveston's rules, fictions are as potent an imperial weapon as swords are. He is in the habit of demythologizing not only virtù, but also aristocratic privilege. In doing so, however, he aims not to junk the system, as the Levellers would later aim to do, but to bend the system of aristocratic privilege to his advantage. As a Proteus engineering his own rise at court, he understands social station as being never so fixed as those in power wish to claim. Hence the imagery of his counterattack against peers who accuse him of being a parasite on Edward's commonweal: 'Base leaden earls that glory in your birth, / Go sit at home and eat your tenants' beef' (2.2.74–5). His image of 'leaden' earls reminds Mortimer and his compatriots that, at some point in the past, their families too have mastered the trick of transforming base coins – and lives – from lead into gold. For Gaveston, radically, familial wealth and lineage as well as all sorts of other identities are nothing more than their present performance. That is why Mortimer's charge that Gaveston is like 'Proteus' fits so well. It is also why Gaveston so threatens a man of Mortimer's station and strength, for those qualities depend precisely upon his performing – while pretending not to perform – continuous acts of martial masculinity.

Mortimer's metaphysical anxieties about Gaveston's effects on the kingdom are reinscribed as physical threats that must be answered by

murder or flight or both. This psychological maneuver, which we have previously encountered in the discussions of *Tamburlaine* and *Dido*, helps the Marlovian soldier to pretend that he has no anxieties, or rather, no emotions. The circumstances of both Gaveston's and Edward's murders confirm that, symbolically, their deaths are meant to rid England of pleasure, and in getting rid of pleasure, to restore the Crown's support of the military tenets that sustain empire. Thus in Act 2, Scene 5 Gaveston is arrested by the earl of Warwick's troops. Their pursuit of Edward's minion across open country has for Gaveston a homosocial valence, as his double entendres imply: 'Yet, lusty lords, I have escaped your hands, / Your threats, your 'larums, and your hot pursuits' (2.5.1–2). As soon as these suggestive words are spoken, however, he is captured. His intimation of the soldiers' perhaps unconscious motives are quietly but pointedly substantiated by the playwright through the inclusion of a minor domestic detail from the soldiers' lives that seems distinctly out of place in the episode. It pops up in the conversation that follows Gaveston's capture. None of the earls particularly wants to take charge of him, as he is a political hot potato. Eventually the earl of Pembroke agrees to transport him to a final rendezvous with Edward. Moments after getting under way, however, Pembroke announces that his party will divert its course to his estate, Cobham, to stay the night. Pembroke explains the delay to his prisoner: 'We that have pretty wenches to our wives, / Sir, must not come so near and balk their lips' (2.5.100–101).

The earl's metonymic substitution of the kiss for other conjugal acts strikes a humorous chord in the otherwise tense atmosphere. The joke gives comic expression to a portrait of women as possessive spouses whose sexual demands threaten their soldier-husbands' autonomy, a portrait that is more soberly criticized by Marlowe in Dido's tragic loss of Aeneas's companionship to the demands of empire. The joke also signifies Gaveston's exclusion from the homosocial camaraderie of soldiers whose marriages, even as they prove to be distractions from military obligations, cover up the men's triangulated, mimetic desire[47] for other soldiers.

Pembroke's joke is short-lived. While the earl of Warwick's men presumably frolic with their wives off-stage in pleasure licensed by the state, Gaveston is beheaded. He is, as Gosson might well hope, 'dismembered' for symbolizing the dangers of the sort of illicit self-indulgence that erodes a social order that is both sustained by, and sustains, a stalwart English masculinity. The nature of Gaveston's offense is signified by the material conditions of his imprisonment at Cobham. When Pembroke turns over custody of the miscreant to his stable-boy for the night, he chooses a jailer whose province symbolically matches the prisoner to his crime. The horse, as Edgar Wind reminds us, often shows up as a 'Platonic symbol of sensuous passion or *libido*, or of what Pico called *amore bestiale*.'[48] Lancaster says as much, calling him a 'Monster of men,' a 'Greekish strumpet' (2.5.14, 15).[49] We have seen the rhetoric of unnaturalness before, in *Tamburlaine*, where King Mycetes calls his brother a 'Monster of Nature' for refusing to pay him homage (1–1.1.104). Lancaster regrets that Gaveston's charms, as did Helen's, may cost many 'valiant knights' their lives (2.5.16). Gaveston is so far from being a real man, Mortimer agrees, that the earl has no difficulty in holding back from killing him on the spot. Having an earl deliver the death blow to Gaveston would bring no glory, but 'shame and dishonour to a soldier's name' (2.5.12). Characteristically, Mortimer is busy fashioning his reputation, allowing his actions as a soldier to be dictated by how he imagines other soldiers – his audience – will see him.

By the time Edward's execution is staged, it is even more clear that the barons murder the pair of lovers so as to retake control of the gender fables that authenticate the need for soldiers who protect the nation from its enemies. The scene of the king's death is pitiful. For several days he is held by Mortimer in Killingworth Castle, where he is tortured by being immersed in its sewers, and harangued by drumbeats, and starved. Even Drayton, who is otherwise unsympathetic to Edward, admits the king's enemies acted 'without Humane Pittie.'[50] Eventually, infamously, he is raped with a 'burning yron' poker by Mortimer's confederate, Lightborne.[51] As Harry Levin once observed, Lightborne's spit is 'an unspeakable counterpart for the scourge of the Scythian conqueror.'[52] The manner of Edward's death, in other words, punishes his preferring the literal phallus over its metaphorical extension, the sword.[53]

Yet it is not clear that it is Edward's homosexuality *per se* that is punished by the spit. Had Edward played along with the peers' expectations that he should conform to the public images of a warlike king – had he been the Alexander or the Achilles whom the elder Mortimer wanted him to be – had he been, in other words, a conqueror or a great fighter as well as a homosexual – then the peers could have left him to love 'Hephestion' with impunity, as is the case in John Lyly's *Campaspe* (1584). Lyly's 'Alexander renounces heteroerotic desire altogether,' repudiating what Mario DiGangi says must be read as a 'debilitating love for women [that] clearly interferes with more important masculine pursuits.'[54] So Edward's mistake is not in experiencing homosexual desire but, like Mark Antony, in privileging sexual above martial desire. While all the methods of torture, such as deprivation of food and water, that are used on Edward transform potentially pleasurable sensations into horrors, rape with the hot poker is the consummate punishment of forbidden bodily pleasure. A sensible explanation of the link between soldiers' antipathy for desire and pleasure and their use of anal rape to express their hostility is offered in Klaus Theweleit's study of artifacts from German fascists in the 1920s. (If using Theweleit here is not outrageously anachronistic, it is purposefully essentialist: to a great extent, I would argue, western soldiers often think remarkably alike – that's the point.) Theweleit posits that 'If we accept [Guy] Hocquenghem's account of anal penetration, which he sees as a means of penetrating "forbidden territory" in general – and thus as a step in the direction of the undirected, toward roaming desire – then any violent and persecuting penetration of the same area may be seen as a persecution of desire in general.'[55]

'Bloody Colours'

In obvious, grotesque ways, the circumstances of Edward's execution are designed to raise the playgoer's sympathy for him; the renaissance of Edward's dignity is all the more powerful for its backdrop of Killingworth's sewers. Through that restoration Marlowe helps to give birth to the pattern of reclaiming a once proud, now defeated, military hero, a parabolic trajectory that would become an integral part of the tradition of renaissance tragedy. Significantly, though, this is not Edward's only renaissance. When one takes the world for a stage, as he does, it is possible for a character to have nine lives: identity is being constantly produced.

In this next section, then, I want to consider Edward's construction of himself as a soldier in Acts 2 and 3, where he heroically responds to Gaveston's murder with martial performances that match those of his enemies. Being a commander and a poet are not only *not* incompatible, as Harry Levin had assumed; but indeed being a commander in Marlowe's world requires a poet's control of language and sense of the place of fictions in the construction of imperial power.[56]

Marlowe's soldiers typically have a strong grasp of the utility of oratory, either before battle or after victory, as they consolidate with their tongues the booty they have won with both tongues and swords. The rousing set speech is one of Marlowe's great achievements. Yet its effect upon playgoers is potentially subversive by its very context – being spoken in a theater rather than a theater of war. As the poet-soldier Gibbon had worried, a rousing war speech on stage invites the playgoer to appreciate the power of language as much as, if not more than, the power of arms. Even so, such a speech from the mouth of a stage warrior implicitly acknowledges that, at some level, war *is* theatrical.

This is implied also in many of the Elizabethan handbooks for soldiers, where the point is often made that generals who are also superb orators have the advantage. 'Strive to be eloquent' advises the writer of *A Myrrour for English Souldiers*; Rich urges commanders to prepare men for combat with oratory: 'it taketh away fear, it engendreth obstinacy to fight'; in *Stratioticos* Leonard Digges argues that oratory is integral to military strategy: a captain 'should be eloquent, and able compendiously and plainly to utter his minde, and also to perswade and diswade, to recreate and sometimes to provoke and stirre by mennes minds.'[57]

One of the curiosities of Marlowe's soldiers is that, while they speak eloquently of their plans for victory, as we have discovered in earlier chapters, they often insist that among soldiers, the most manly prefer to fight than to talk of fighting, as if talking somehow threatens their agendas of becoming conquerors. For them, paradoxically, denying the power of the voice becomes an important prelude to battle, a ritual stripping away of the multiplicities that might be articulated by the tongue. Consider one manifestation of this contradiction in Mortimer's attitude toward words. In Act 4, Scene 4 he greets Isabella as she returns from her embassy to her native France, where her brother has refused to send troops or provisions to help her overthrow Edward. Near Harwich, the queen's flotilla is met by Mortimer, and she delivers a regal address to the assembled troops – 'our loving friends and countrymen' (4.4.1) – in which she justifies her decision to rebel against her husband: [It is] 'a heavy case, / When force to force is knit and sword and glaive / In civil broils makes kin and countrymen / Slaughter themselves in others, and their sides / With their own weapons gored. But what's the help?' (4.4.4–8).

Lest Isabella have an opportunity to seem too regal, too much able to command her own troops, however, Mortimer interrupts her in mid-sentence: 'Nay madam, if you be a warrior, / Ye must not grow so passionate in speeches' (4.4.14–15). Silencing her, he proceeds to deliver his own preamble to battle that is just as 'passionate' as the queen's:

> for the open wrongs and injuries
> Edward hath done to us, his queen, and land,
> We come in arms to wreak it with the sword,
> That England's queen in peace may repossess
> Her dignities and honours . . .
>
> 4.4.20–24

Idiotically, Mortimer tells Isabella to shut up so he may get on with the business of restoring her privileges of rank. His reprimand of her passion seems designed to redirect the eyes of the soldiers (and of the playgoers) upon him. It is, in other words, a histrionic gesture denying the efficacy of the drama of self-construction. This strained moment is anticipated in Act 2, Scene 4 as his troops storm Tynemouth Castle. Isabella greets him inside the castle with a short but again passionate speech. She tells him she is exhausted by the Sisyphean task of trying to keep Gaveston and Edward apart, and asks for Mortimer's sympathy. He offers none. 'Cease to lament,' he barks: 'tell us where's the king?' (2.4.30).

Plainly, Isabella is little more than Mortimer's vehicle as he climbs toward the throne; she matters to him even less than Zenocrate does to Tamburlaine. Rebuffed, she nonetheless answers him as she has been taught to answer her husband, with (an unwarranted) faith in the possibilities of intimacy: 'So well hast thou deserved, sweet Mortimer, / As Isabel could live with thee for ever' (2.4.59–60). It is her hunger for what Erasmus calls the 'felowshippe of felicitie'[58] that once led her to accept Edward's renewed vows of marriage ('O how a kiss revives poor Isabel' [1.4.333]), and it is her emotional hunger now that causes her to subsume herself in Mortimer's identity, much as Zenocrate stands in Tamburlaine's shadow. As Isabella puts it, her lover is 'Sweet Mortimer, the life of Isabel' (5.2.15). In spite of being treated callously, Isabella idealizes Mortimer in order to heal the emotional wounds of her marriage. But even in this relationship, perhaps especially here, she is disenfranchised from the very 'dignities and honours' Mortimer claims to be able and ready to restore to her. A 'war bride' of sorts, Isabella, as Mary Beth Rose says of Shakespeare's Cressida, 'is construed, and construes herself, entirely in terms of male desire.'[59] So although Kent reports 'Mortimer / And Isabel do kiss while they conspire' (4.6.12–13), theirs is as bloodless a romance as the royal union had been. In place of intimacy with a woman, Mortimer's desire – the desire of all Marlowe's soldiers – is directed toward conquest:

> Fair Isabel, now have we our desire.
> The proud corrupters of the light-brained king
> Have done their homage to the lofty gallows,
> And he himself lies in captivity.
> Be ruled by me, and we will rule the realm.

                                                        5.2.1–5

Fully autarkic at this point, Mortimer has almost abandoned tropological speech in favor of bald, blunt assertions of his supremacy.

Unlike Tamburlaine, Mortimer seems to take almost no delight in savoring his victory by rendering it into poetry. In fact, as his power grows, his speeches become noticeably less poetic. In Act 2, Scene 2, for instance, he resists Edward's questions about the devices commissioned by the earls to celebrate Gaveston's repatriation. 'You have matters of more weight to think upon,' Mortimer answers Edward: 'the King of France sets foot in Normandy' (2.2.8–9). Dismissing this threat as a 'trifle' (2.2.10), Edward insists on having the earls describe their devices. Mortimer feigns modesty – his is 'a homely one, my lord, not worth the telling' (2.2.13). Mortimer is simply confounding Edward by refusing to cooperate, or else baiting the king; in either case, his response discounts a serious link between royal power and its emblematic fictions.

Pressed again, Mortimer then describes a carefully symbolic device: 'But seeing you are so desirous, thus it is: / A lofty cedar tree fair flourishing, / On whose top branches kingly eagles perch, / And by the bark a canker creeps me up / And gets unto the highest bough of all' (2.2.15–19). Lancaster's device is equally pertinent to the peers' opposition to the 'canker' Gaveston, and more prophetic of the violence to come: 'My lord, mine's more obscure than Mortimer's: / Pliny reports there is a flying fish / Which all the other fishes deadly hate, / And therefore, being pursued, it takes the air; / No sooner is it up, but there's a fowl / That seizeth it' (2.2.22–7). In the next scene, these devices are supplanted by Mortimer's family's colors as he rallies his troops to besiege Tynemouth Castle, in which the king and Gaveston have holed up. The substitution again makes the point that Mortimer's priorities must prevail, or else 'This tattered ensign of my ancestors, / Which swept the desert shore of that dead sea / Whereof we got the name of Mortimer, / Will I advance upon these castle walls; / Drums strike alarum, raise them from their sport, / And ring aloud the knell of Gaveston' (2.3.21–6). Mortimer is using his 'ensign' as Tamburlaine uses his black flag, to signal that his patience with a stonewalling enemy has run out. No longer shall Gaveston have opportunities to leave England safely with his life – his bell is tolling. Yet Mortimer's speech lacks the verve of Edward's own mighty declaration of war.

If Mortimer is a remarkably flat character who, as it were, grows into his flatness, I suggest that that movement is consistent with the portraits of Marlovian soldiers other than Tamburlaine – they are deliberately flat. The effect of flat character here, alongside the dramatic Edward, further raises the playgoers' sympathies toward the king, who manages to be both a commander and a poet. One important distinction between the two characters is that while Mortimer takes a utilitarian approach to the fictions of imperial power (his device of the cedar tree being only a prelude to his assault on Tynemouth), Edward lives almost entirely inside his fictions, and he creates those fictions from the materials of classical literature and history and philosophy. Like Faustus, perhaps, he is dangerously enmeshed in a web of images of how to behave, derived from books, as in, say, Cicero's treatise on friendship between men.

For Edward, fictions constitute reality, a position which alarms the peers perhaps more than it ought. When for instance the king speaks in apocalyptic terms of sacrificing his kingdom for love, promising Gaveston that 'sooner shall the sea o'erwhelm my land / Than bear the ship that shall transport thee hence' (1.1.151–2), or when he tells Mortimer that 'Ere my sweet Gaveston shall part from me, / This isle shall fleet upon the ocean / And wander to the unfrequented Inde' (1.4.48–50), the peers take him at his word. But as in these examples of hyperbole, Edward's threats have few objective correlatives: he is in the habit of issuing threats and promises that seldom come to pass. In Act 1, Scene 4, for example, Edward scapegoats the bishop of Coventry for having granted ecclesiastical approval to the peers' plan to reinstate Longshank's banishment of Gaveston from the kingdom. Edward explodes:

> Why should a king be subject to a priest?
> Proud Rome, that hatchest such imperial grooms,
> For these thy superstitious taper-lights,
> Wherewith thy antichristian churches blaze,
> I'll fire thy crazèd buildings and enforce
> The papal towers to kiss the lowly ground,
> With slaughtered priests make Tiber's channel swell,
> And banks raised higher with their sepulchres.
> As for the peers that back the clergy thus,
> If I be king, not one of them shall live.
>
> 1.4.96–105

This speech is classic Marlowe, echoing *The Jew of Malta* and *Doctor Faustus*, where protagonists also rail against the powers of the Roman Catholic Church by threatening to burn down churches or depose popes.[60] Its first line pays elliptical homage to Henry VIII's split with Rome, and the whole panders to Elizabethan fury at Pius and Sixtus for legitimating and advocating the queen's removal from the throne by murder if necessary.

While the threat is powerfully violent, no fantasy of arson or murder comes to pass. Were Tamburlaine to issue such a threat, Rome ought to worry. Even the slave Ithamore in *The Jew of Malta* comes closer to executing a comparable plan of revenge on Christians when he poisons an entire convent of nuns. In contrast, Edward merely allows Gaveston to rough up Coventry, allowing us to see Gaveston's violent side. And in spite of this venomous threat against the bishop, when it comes down to inflicting revenge against his enemies, Edward is likely to hang fire. In Act 2, Scene 2, for example, after capturing the elder Mortimer, Edward exacts only a ransom, not a pound of flesh, in keeping with the decorum of how to treat medieval and renaissance prisoners of war who are gentlemen or better. When the king does order Lancaster and Warwick executed in Act 3, having given them a fair chance to renew their obedience, Marlowe has those murders take place off stage.

When Edward chooses to play a general, though, he is superb. But he takes the part – as all kings pretend to do – on his own terms. He is not interested in doing so to protect real estate or gold, the principal motivations of the peers who oppose him, but to protect his alternative universe in which men are free to love rather than compelled to slaughter other men in a competition that inevitably and only ends in death.

From an antithetical perspective in which one cannot be too much the soldier, Shakespeare's Coriolanus names the Elysium he seeks as a 'world elsewhere.' Like Coriolanus, Edward cannot help but play the part of Alexander the Great. We see this in Act 2, Scene 2, where he prepares to meet Lancaster and the others in a battle he subsequently wins. Unlike, say, Mortimer, whose assault on Tynemouth was preceded by a half-hearted raising of the colors, Edward engineers a grand entrance into battle:

> How oft have I been baited by these peers
> And dare not be revenged, for their power is great?
> Yet, shall the crowing of these cockerels
> Affright a lion? Edward, unfold thy paws
> And let their lives' blood slake thy fury's hunger.
> If I be cruel and grow tyrannous,
> Now let them thank themselves and rue too late.
>
> 2.2.200–206

Depicting himself as a lion, a traditional emblem of English kings, Edward reveals nevertheless that he understands the lion's part as a role to be inhabited rather than an unassailable humanist identity expressed in metaphor. To 'grow tyrannous' signifies not what he is, but what he is choosing to perform; the distinction is clarified by comparing the use of the lion image in 1 Tamburlaine. As Tamburlaine arrests Zenocrate and her train, his lieutenant Techelles depicts him as one of the 'princely lions when they rouse themselves, / Stretching their paws and threatening herds of beasts, / So in his armour looketh Tamburlaine' (1–1.2.52–4). Such praise prompts Tamburlaine to worry that Scythian soldiers may 'scorn' his own arias as mere 'prattle,' so he resolves to keep these soldiers as 'our forcèd followers / Till with their eyes they view us emperors' (1 Tamburlaine 1.2.61, 62, 66–7). Paradoxically, Tamburlaine is not investing himself in the character of a lion, but is instead demanding that other soldiers perceive him correctly: a single 'view' of his character exists, and his prisoners must bend to it.

Lacking Tamburlaine's iron will, Edward seldom projects such a steely self-image. Even in representing himself as a lion he manages to step into quicksand. In the lines above, he is not merely speaking subjunctively of a course of action we expect to come to pass, but also seeming to contemplate the range of his available responses to tyranny ('If I be cruel'), as when he depicts himself as a 'lamb, encompassèd by wolves' (5.1.41); moreover, the animal imagery belies Edward's obsession with seeing all his relations with other men in metaphorical terms as ways of imaginatively holding at bay the imperative to kill them.

'Lakes of gore'

It is significant but perhaps surprising that Edward becomes his most fierce after his beloved is executed; his response comes in Act 3, Scene 1. Swearing by his 'father's sword' (3.1.130), an ironic gesture considering Longshank's banishment of Gaveston from the court, Edward delivers a magnificently vile oration before riding into combat. The prevailing image is of copious quantities of spilled blood, and the punishment he imagines inflicting on the rebels – decapitation – neatly matches Gaveston's fate; the penalty is as symmetrical with their crime as Edward's own fatal punishment in Act 5 is said to be parallel with his 'crime.' On the eve of battle, the king kneels, and visualizes his victory:

> in lakes of gore
> Your headless trunks, your bodies will I trail,
> That you may drink your fill and quaff in blood,
> And stain my royal standard with the same,
> That so my bloody colours may suggest
> Remembrance of revenge immortally
> On your accursèd traitorous progeny –
> You villains that have slain my Gaveston.
>
> 3.1.135–42

Here Edward *is* Tamburlaine. To a surprising extent, his hyperbolic prophecy becomes reality, as the earls hardly expect. They have underestimated his martial skills and his commitment to carrying through his threats of revenge not only because Edward's preferred mode of action is typically more figurative than physical, but also because they have categorized him as a sodomitical, 'brainsick' and 'light-brained' king who, by definition, cannot be as strong as they in battle. In Act 3, Scene 2 he makes good his earlier threat against Lancaster to 'plane the furrows of thy brows / And hew these knees that now are grown so stiff' (1.1.93–4) when he now has Lancaster and Warwick executed.

In spite of ordering revenge against two of his most vocal opponents, however, Edward does not continue to occupy a martial-law frame of mind – unlike Mortimer, whom he significantly spares, Edward cannot sustain a martial persona. Admittedly, the role of soldier is plainly not his preferred mode of playing – if he must be Hercules, he would rather weep for Hylas than charge an enemy. Defeating the barons proves Edward capable of brave battle; but being able to perform as a soldier and wanting to do so are not the same thing. Early in the play, in fact, Edward stages a mock abdication, through which Marlowe shows us not only that Edward sees his own life as a spectacle to be composed and managed, but also that from within that perspective, the king does not intend to honor the militarist priorities and commitments the peers aim to make him endorse. In Act 1, Scene 4 Edward invites Mortimer to take the throne. 'Sit thou in Edward's throne,' he says prophetically; 'Warwick and Lancaster,' he adds, 'wear you my crown' (1.4.36–7). This rhetorical offer to abdicate is famously redone in Shakespeare's *Richard II*, where the king is in fact a poet and no soldier; in Marlowe's play, however, the rebels do not presently accept what is insincerely offered. After considerably more fist-shaking by both sides, the peers retreat nervously, bombastically, into speeches that celebrate the order of militarist hegemony, which dictates their own obedience. They are peers, after all, because they serve their king; otherwise their conduct would make them no better than marauding villains. In their renewed oaths of allegiance, we may hear both their commitment to the violent enforcement of the tenets of militarism and some ironic intimations of the next crisis: Warwick urges the king to 'slay me, my lord, when I offend your grace' (1.4.348) and Mortimer vows, 'I'll marshal so your enemies / As England shall be quiet and you safe' (1.4.356–7). This scenario is repeated in Act 5 when the earl of Leicester and the bishop of Winchester demand Edward's crown; several times, Edward gives up and takes back his crown, understanding that the king's power depends upon his symbols of office. 'But what are kings,' Edward asks nobody in particular, 'when regiment is gone / But perfect shadows in a sunshine day?' (5.1.26–7).

* * *

Posthumous honor came again to Edward in the late twentieth century when his story was taken up once more by artists and historians. In the 1990s they were searching not for moral tales of national security, but for signs of incipient gay subjectivity.[61] The best-known effort is Derek Jarman's 1991 film, a free adaptation of Marlowe's play. In Jarman's retelling, the alterations of tone and outlook are summed up in changes Jarman makes to the role of the assassin, Lightborne. No longer is he Edward's executioner, a sodomitical sadist, but a sexual partner who, unlike the peers, now refuses to see murder as a substitute for sexual relations. Mortimer and his men, costumed by Jarman to resemble Nazi soldiers, are portrayed as jack-booted thugs who seem bent on eliminating difference itself from the kingdom, literalizing the theme of martial law that runs just below the surface of Marlowe's version of events. Picking up on Marlowe's hunch that soldiers sometimes create their enemies so as to advance their own agenda of militarist necessity, Jarman accentuates the brownshirts' threat to internal order in the film by keeping the mention of foreign threats to the king's sovereignty to a minimum. In Jarman's world, Edward needn't watch Normandy so much as his own back. With its anachronistic appearances by the queer activist group Outrage, the film does what Richard II could not accomplish – canonizes Edward as a (modern) gay saint.[62]

Jarman's film delights in the artifice of gender identity. In a notably misogynistic moment, to take one example of the director's efforts to fracture spectators' commitments to an essentialist model of gender identity, Gaveston pretends to coax a kiss from Isabel. As she begins to respond, he pulls away, laughing cruelly. Unlike Drayton's Gaveston, for whom 'desier' is ideally contained within ideologically acceptable limits, Jarman's character uses sexual orientation playfully as a floating fiction; Gaveston is equally capable of seducing king or queen. Jarman's point about the performativity of masculinity is intensified in the closing frames of the film, which concludes with a tableau of the warrior as drag artist. Adorned in elaborate earrings and brilliant red lipstick, Edward III, an astute child with a penchant for wearing his mother's clothes, squats atop a bamboo cage that imprisons her with Mortimer. (Does Warwick get it wrong in the play by declaring *Gaveston* rather than little Edward to be 'like Phaethon' [1.4.16]?) Jarman's decision to put Edward in drag invites us to imagine a new history of Edward III's reign. In Jarman's version of things, it is not only the king's life that has been spared. Young Edward III in drag opens up the fantasy of an England governed by a monarch who shared his father's appreciation of the fluidity of gender identity, and who, rather than don the brownshirt of his 'protector' Mortimer, has chosen a costume entirely unsuitable for battle: suede pumps are a long way from army boots. As Judith Butler says, 'in imitating gender, drag implicitly reveals the imitative structure of gender itself – as well as its contingency.'[63] Under the rule of a transvestical Edward III, Jarman teases, England might have permitted men to celebrate the theatricality of gender identity without having to pretend, as Mortimer does, that their identities are made of steel. Instead, of course, the historical Edward III was to give the English peers what Charles Nauert says they wanted from his beleaguered father – lots and lots of war.

* * *

Jarman's film will hold up well. It's got just the right mix of art and gay propaganda, and enough emotional distance from its title figure to keep it aesthetically alive beyond its historical moment. At the time of its making in the early 1990s it seemed daring (or foolhardy, to the nervous) to have Jarman doing a film celebrating little Edward's transvestical eroticism and an orgy of naked sailors, when AIDS hysteria, wild-eyed anxieties about the purported pederastic impulses of gay men, and gay-bashing writ large had made it again vital to resurrect Edward II's story. Jarman's film took risks, to be sure. But I imagine Marlowe's play at the time of its first performances took more. Curtis Breight has speculated that Marlowe was murdered on orders of the Privy Council for what could be read as the implicit endorsement of regicide in the play.[64] Without necessarily joining Breight, I would agree that Marlowe resurrected Edward's story for a complicated set of purposes that put him at odds with other writers and at risk of government scrutiny. If he did not aspire to make Edward a saint – and he is not one in the play – he did attempt to recover a story that would push back against the efforts of militarists such as the Cecils and other like-minded peers who hoped to use martial law against civilians to crush dissent in a roiled land. The play shows how that could work, and how even a pansy like Edward can become a lion who dons the role of a brutal despot, and also why spectators ought not to think that that's the safer world to live in, or the better part of valor.

Notes

1. Mary Sidney, *The Tragedy of Antonie*, in *Renaissance Drama by Women: Texts and Documents*, ed. S.P. Cerasano and Marion Wynne-Davies (New York: Routledge, 1996), 33 (Act 3, lines 336–8).
2. Mark Thornton Burnett, '*Edward II* and Elizabethan Politics,' in *Marlowe, History, and Sexuality: New Critical Essays on Christopher Marlowe*, ed. Paul Whitfield White (New York: AMS, 1998), 93. Burnett reads the play in relation to various tracts on the royal succession in the 1580s and 1590s, attending to numerous parallels in the contemporary iconic representation of Elizabeth and Edward.
3. David M. Bergeron, *Royal Family, Royal Lovers: King James of England and Scotland* (Columbia: University of Missouri Press, 1991), 184. I am indebted to Mario DiGangi's chapter 'The homoerotics of favoritism in

tragedy,' in *The Homoerotics of Early Modern Drama* (Cambridge: Cambridge University Press, 1997), 100–133.

4. Anthony Tuck, *Richard II and the English Nobility* (London: Edward Arnold, 1973), argues Richard was keenly conscious of the parallels between his and Edward II's reigns (103).

5. Raphael Holinshed, *Chronicles of England, Scotland, and Ireland*, ed. Vernon F. Snow, 6 vols (New York: AMS, 1976), 2:549, 2:547. For a brief analysis of Holinshed's presentation of Parliament's decision to depose Edward in 1327, see Annabel Patterson, *Reading Holinshed's* Chronicles (Chicago: University of Chicago Press, 1994), 110–11.
    Semantically, the word 'addict' has greatly changed since the sixteenth century; Holinshed applies a Galenic interpretation in medicalizing Edward's desire as diseased passion. Emily Bartels offers a sophisticated reading of links between Marlowe's and Holinshed's versions, focusing on the latter's 'discoveries' of sodomy, in *Spectacles of Strangeness: Imperialism, Alienation, and Marlowe* (Philadelphia: University of Pennsylvania Press, 1993), 143–56.

6. Marlowe has Isabella blaming only 'wicked Gaveston' for most of the play. When she finally censures Edward directly, she charges him with moral 'looseness,' causing England to 'overflow with blood' (4.4.11–12). Like Holinshed's, Isabella's criticism figures Edward's crime as a medico-moral tragedy.

7. *Vita Edwardi Secundi*, trans. and ed. N. Denholm-Young (London: Thomas Nelson, 1957), is an anonymous, influential account of Edward's reign dated 1325. Its writer minimizes Edward's guilt by charging Gaveston with sorcery: 'Indeed I do not remember to have heard that one man so loved another. Jonathan cherished David, Achilles loved Patroclus. But we do not read that they were immoderate. Our king, however, was incapable of moderate favour, and on account of Piers was said to forget himself, and so Piers was accounted a sorcerer' (15).

8. Michael Drayton, *Peirs Gaveston*, in *Works*, ed. J.W. Hebel, K. Tillotson, and B. Newdigate. 5 vols (Oxford: Basil Blackwell, 1961), 1:178, line 715. Here Gaveston imagines himself enthroned as Edward 'yeelds his Scepter.' Note the startling use of the present tense: 'And now the king to rayse me higher yet, / Makes me the Lord-protector of the Land, / And in the Chayre of his estate I sit, / Hee yeelds his Scepter up into mine hand. / Devising still how he to passe might bring, / That if he died, I might succeed as King' (1:180, lines 787–92).

9. Drayton, *Peirs Gaveston*, in *Works*, 1:178, lines 716–17.

10. Matthew Sutcliffe, *The Practice, Proceedings, and Lawes of Armes*, London, 1593, STC 23468, B2v. All subsequent quotations will be cited parenthetically.

11. Sir John Smythe, *Certain Discourses Military*, London, 1590, ed. J.R. Hale, Folger Library Series of Documents in Tudor and Stuart Civilization (Ithaca: Cornell University Press, 1964), 6–8.

12. Anthony Munday, *A Watch-woord to England To beware of traytours and tretcherous practices*, London, 1584, STC 18282a, A2v, A3v.

13. Simon Harward, *The Solace for the Souldier and Saylour*, London, 1592, STC 12923, Bv. Subsequent quotations are cited parenthetically.

14. Barnabe Rich, *A Roome for a Gentleman, or the Second Part of Faultes*, London, 1609, STC 20985, B2v.

15. John Boswell, *Christianity, Social Tolerance, and Homosexuality: Gay People in Western Europe from the Beginning of the Christian Era to the Fourteenth Century* (Chicago: University of Chicago Press, 1980), argues that the 'inordinateness of the favors and promotions [Edward] bestowed upon [Gaveston] has been exaggerated by historians, both then and now, often as a mask for disgust at the nature of the relationship' (298). Boswell emphasizes the timing of Edward's ascension after the twelfth-century renaissance of love, in which homosexual relationships had been legal: 'Between 1250 and 1300, homosexual activity passed from being completely legal in most of Europe to incurring the death penalty in all but a few contemporary legal compilations' (293).

16. Charles G. Nauert, Jr, *The Age of Renaissance and Reformation* (Lanham, MD: University Press of America, 1981), 35.

17. Drayton, *Peirs Gaveston*, in *Works*, 1:160, lines 67–9. Drayton's nostalgia for the reign of Edward I is in harmony with *Vita Edwardi Secundi*. Its writer affirms the justness of Parliament's decision in 1310 to appoint regents to oversee Edward II's decisions, lamenting, 'the state of the king and the kingdom had much deteriorated since the elder king Edward of happy memory had died' (9).

18. Gregory Bredbeck offers a subtle reading of the discrepancies in Mortimer's rhetoric in *Sodomy and Interpretation: Marlowe to Milton* (Ithaca: Cornell University Press, 1991), 62–77. The payoff of Bredbeck's argument is that the character of Mortimer 'demonstrates to us . . . a crucial point of the epistemology of Renaissance sodomy: sodomy does not create disorder; rather, disorder demands sodomy' (77). DiGangi ('The homoerotics of favoritism') makes the shrewd point that 'in contrast to the grotesquely specific architectural and anatomical siting of Edward's torments,' physical intimacy between Gaveston and Edward occurs in the upper bodily regions' (113) as a way for Marlowe to accentuate the physical ambiguities of their friendship.

19. Stephen Greenblatt, *Renaissance Self-Fashioning: From More to Shakespeare* (Chicago: University of Chicago Press, 1980), 203.

20. Thomas Tymme, *A Preparation against the Prognosticated dangers of this yeere, 1588*, London, 1588, STC 24420, A3r.

21. Maurice Kyffin, *The Blessednes of Brytaine, or A Celebration of the Queenes Holyday*, London, 1588, STC 15097, C3v, Bv.

22. Sue Mansfield, *The Gestalts of War: An Inquiry into its Origin and Meaning as a Social Institution* (New York: Dial, 1982), 58. See ch. 4, 'The Destruction of Chaos.'

23. Giovanni Pico della Mirandola, 'Letter to Ermolao Barbaro,' in *Renaissance Debates on Rhetoric*, trans. and ed. Wayne A. Rebhorn (Ithaca: Cornell University Press, 2000), 59.

24. Richard Lindabury, *A Study of Patriotism in the Elizabethan Drama*, Princeton Studies in English No. 5 (Princeton: Princeton University Press, 1931), 47.

25. Soldiers' pay is of notable mention throughout the military conduct-books in the period as well as in *Tamburlaine*, too (see *1 Tamb.* 1.2.85; 1.2.185; 2.2.45; and 3.3.260).

26. Thomas Procter, *Of the Knowledge and Conducte of Warres*, London, 1578, STC 20403, Cap. 7, Fol. 12.

27. Ibid., Preface and Cap. 5.

28. Thomas Digges, *A Briefe Report of the Militarie Services done in the Low Countries, by the Erle of Leicester*, London, 1587, STC 7285, Bv.
29. *A Myrrour for English Souldiers*, London, 1595, STC 10418, Bv.
30. On tensions between soldiers and writers in England's sack of Edinburgh, see Alan Shepard, 'William Patten's *Expedition of Somerset into Scotland* (1547) as English Imperial Discourse,' *Scottish Literary Journal* 22 (1995): 22–34.
31. Stephen Gosson, *The School of Abuse* (London, 1841), 38.
32. Elizabeth I, *Proceedings. A Proclamation against vagarant Souldiers and others*, 13 November 1589, STC 8188.
33. Charles Gibbon, *A Watch-Worde for Warre*, London, 1596, STC 11492, D1v.
34. Thomas Cartelli, *Marlowe, Shakespeare, and the Economy of Theatrical Experience* (Philadelphia: University of Pennsylvania Press, 1991), 129.
35. Boswell, *Christianity*, observes this narrative strategy in late medieval texts of turning to classical myth to defend homosexual relationships. His explanation fits the sixteenth century, too: 'In an age addicted to classical literature, the invocation of Greek mythology to describe homosexual relationships not only tacitly removed the stigma . . . but also evoked connotations of mythological sanctions, cultural superiority, and personal refinement' (253).
36. In *Sodometries: Renaissance Texts, Modern Sexualities* (Stanford: Stanford University Press, 1992), Jonathan Goldberg notes that 'remarkably, what Marlowe allows them to voice is a scandalous acceptance of the friend, the minion, as a sexual partner. They can do this because what they want (to maintain their positions as peers of the realm) cannot be separated from the relationship that Edward and Gaveston have. Thus, the Mortimers give voice to the complicity of friendship and sodomy as sexual acts, and for the sake of maintaining male privilege and privileged male/male relations they mark the possibility of this sexual sphere' (120).
37. Martin Wiggins calls attention to Elizabethan notions of the Italian in *Journeymen in Murder: The Assassin in English Renaissance Drama* (Oxford: Clarendon, 1991), pointing out that Roger Ascham records a well-known Italian saying: '"Engles Italianato, e un diabolo incarnat" – an Englishman Italianate is a devil incarnate' (50).
38. See Niccolò Machiavelli, *The Prince*, trans. Peter Bondanella (New York: Oxford University Press, 1984), 61.
39. Bredbeck, *Sodomy and Interpretation, xi* (Preface).
40. *Vita Edwardi Secundi*, 15.
41. Ibid., 1.
42. Barnabe Rich, *A Path-Way to Military Practise*, London, 1587, STC 20995, D2r. Rich anticipates this argument in *Allarme to England, foreshewing what perilles are procured, where the people live without regarde of Martiall lawe*, London, 1578, STC 20978, where he writes, 'peace is the nourisher of vices, the roote of evils, the proppe of pride, and to be short, it is the mother of al mischiefes' (B4v).
43. See Jonas Barish, *The Anti-Theatrical Prejudice* (Berkeley: University of California Press, 1981).
44. Stephen Gosson, *Plays Confuted in Five Actions*, quoted in Julia Briggs, *This Stage-Play World* (Oxford: Oxford University Press, 1981), 171.
45. Edgar Wind, *Pagan Mysteries in the Renaissance*, rev. ed. (New York:

Norton, 1968), discusses a link between Proteus and androgyny in the Renaissance. He suggests neo-Platonism led many thinkers to agree with Philo and Origen 'that the first and original man was androgynous; that the division into male and female belonged to a later and lower state of creation' (212). On androgyny in classical and sixteenth-century texts, see 191–217.

46. Mike O'Pray, 'Damning Desire,' An Interview with Derek Jarman, *Sight and Sound* 1:6 (Oct. 1991): 9. See also Mark Breitenberg, *Anxious Masculinity in Early Modern England* (Cambridge: Cambridge University Press, 1996), 9.

47. See Rene Girard, 'The Politics of Desire in *Troilus and Cressida*,' in *Shakespeare and the Question of Theory*, ed. Patricia Parker and Geoffrey Hartman (New York: Methuen, 1985), 208.

48. Wind, *Pagan Mysteries*, 145.

49. Edward uses this strategy in Act 5, condemning his captors as 'Inhuman creatures' and 'monsters' (5.1.71, 74).

50. Michael Drayton, *The Barrons Warres* (Canto V, 65), cited in Christopher Marlowe, *Edward the Second*, ed. W. Moelwyn Merchant, New Mermaids Series (London: Black, 1987), *xxi*. Mortimer's intent to torture the king is underscored as he instructs Matrevis and Gurney, 'Let no man comfort him if he chance to weep, / But amplify his grief with bitter words' (5.2.63–4).

51. Michael Drayton, *Mortimeriados*, in *Works*, 1:367, lines 2052–5.

52. Harry Levin, '*Edward II*: State Overturned,' reprinted in *Christopher Marlowe*, ed. Harold Bloom, Modern Critical Views Series (New York: Chelsea, 1986), 28. Merchant's edition rehearses the scholarship in which Lightborn is taken to be Lucifer's surrogate (*xxi*).

53. See Michel Foucault, *Discipline and Punish: The Birth of the Prison*, trans. Alan Sheridan (New York: Vintage, 1979), 45.

54. DiGangi, *The Homoerotics of Early Modern Drama*, 136.

55. Klaus Theweleit, *Male Fantasies*, trans Erica Carter et al., 2 vols (Minneapolis: University of Minnesota Press, 1987, 1989), 2:319.

56. 'Edward is not a soldier or a commander, he is an aesthete and a voluptuary . . . a king with the soul of an actor' (Levin, *Edward II*, 21).

57. *A Myrrour for English Souldiers*, Ev; Barnabe Rich, *A Path-Way to Military Practise*, H2r; Leonard Digges, *Stratioticos*, London, 1579 (Amsterdam: Theatrum Orbis Terrarum, 1968), 93–4.

58. Erasmus, 'An Epistle to a young jentleman,' quoted in Thomas Wilson, *Arte of Rhetorique*, ed. Thomas J. Derrick, Vol. 1, The Renaissance Imagination Series, ed. Stephen Orgel (New York: Garland, 1982), 100.

59. Mary Beth Rose, *The Expense of Spirit: Love and Sexuality in English Renaissance Drama* (Ithaca: Cornell University Press, 1988), 206.

60. See *The Jew of Malta*, 2.3.206 and 5.1.62–8 and *Doctor Faustus*: 'Never to name God or to pray to him, / To burn his Scriptures, slay his ministers, / And make my spirits pull his churches down' (A 2.3.96–8).

61. Among the considerable number of recent efforts to discuss what Bruce Smith calls 'the possibility of a homosexual subjectivity' (223) in the play, see his *Homosexual Desire in Shakespeare's England: A Cultural Poetics* (Chicago: University of Chicago Press, 1991); and Goldberg, *Sodometries*, who cautions that Marlowe is not exactly 'a spokesman for modern gay identity' (124); and Bartels, *Spectacles of Strangeness*, 143–72.

62. Jarman's film has prompted a flurry of film scholarship. See, for example, J. Horger, 'Derek Jarman's Film Adaptation of Marlowe's *Edward II*,' *Shakespeare Bulletin* 11 (1993): 37–40; Colin McCabe, 'A Post-National European Cinema: A Consideration of Derek Jarman's *The Tempest* and *Edward II*,' in *Screening Europe: Image and Identity in Contemporary European Cinema*, ed. Duncan Petrie (London: British Film Institute, 1992), 9–18; O'Pray, 'Damning Desire'; C.P. Seabrook Wilkinson, 'The Transmutation of Rhetoric in *Edward II*,' *Shakespeare Bulletin* 14 (1996): 5–7; and Deborah Willis, 'Marlowe Our Contemporary: *Edward II* on Stage and Screen,' *Criticism* 40 (1998): 599–622.
63. Judith Butler, *Gender Trouble: Feminism and the Subversion of Identity* (New York: Routledge, 1990), 137.
64. Curtis C. Breight, *Surveillance, Militarism and Drama in the Elizabethan Era* (New York: St Martin's, 1996), especially 133–45.

CHAPTER FOUR

Paying Tribute in Occupied Malta: From Chivalry to Commerce

Gold 'is such a weapon of so much might.'[1]

In 1585 an ordinarily dovish Queen Elizabeth dispatched troops commanded by the earl of Leicester to aid fellow Protestants said to be suffering under Spain's rule in the Low Countries. She justified her provocative action by invoking England's 'lawful commerce and entercourse of friendship and marchandise' with them.[2] Although the action was obviously deliberate, and much encouraged by many hands, the royal proclamation points casually to a deep material and psychic link between matters of war and international commerce that the queen and her advisers well understood. As J.R. Hale once observed, in early modern Europe 'war can be seen not only as extending the scope of capitalistic enterprise but of inducing reverberations of its spirit, however faint, in society at large.'[3]

In this chapter I examine some of the ways *The Jew of Malta* parleys these rich links between war and commerce in early modern London into entertainment that swerves back and forth between amusing and disturbing an audience. As a tragicomedy the play, I will argue, presents an oblique pageant of the contemporary rivalry between a cohort of English war hawks and an ever-growing accumulation of merchants, who have gradually become a threat to the chivalric code that still sustained even ordinary veterans, and who come to vie for control of the ethos of London in the wake of the Armada. By 'ethos' I mean the fundamental spirit of the working assumptions to be made about England's national defense, principally by the government but also by the people, particularly in the context of international trade, which requires ecumenical, irenic conditions if merchants and governments are to maximize profits. National defense on the scale thought to be necessary to thwart Spain was proving to be expensive to the Crown, and governmental provisions for defense were substantially affected by England's experience of defeating the Armada. Whereas the queen had reluctantly made ready for war against Spain in the months and years prior to July 1588, in part by sending Leicester to the Low Countries, almost as soon as the threat had passed she began to embrace a strategy that shifted to private merchant adventurers both the responsibility and the rewards for keeping Spain and its allies too weakened to constitute

113

a continuing threat. Those merchant vessels that had been pressed into royal service in 1588, for example, were shortly thereafter returned to their private owners, but with their status as mere merchant ships permanently altered; sometimes their top decks continued to hold the weaponry placed there during war. For after 1588, government policy not only allowed but even encouraged offensive micro-attacks against Spanish ships at sea; theoretically, at least, privateering would make it unnecessary to drain the exchequer again to repel another invasion from Spain.

Within this shifting landscape of mostly *ad hoc* military policy in the 1580s and 1590s, English veterans of military campaigns in France and the Low Countries found themselves engaged in an internecine battle with a relatively new breed of mercenary adventurers, who were as eager to profit from war as any chivalric crusader or pressed Englishman would be; but who saw the chivalric code that had once provided cover to these activities as becoming now an obstacle to the ecumenical ways and means of an increasingly international commercial world. Under the guise of a play about an internecine war between merchants and soldiers for control of another island, *The Jew of Malta* opens up that contemporary conundrum in which hawkish English veterans find it necessary to go on the attack against merchant adventurers so as to preserve their own agency and legitimacy in a world increasingly given to commerce rather than crusades. The play stages for our amusement and consternation the disintegration of a militarist ethos that has long since stopped working effectively as the governing paradigm on the island of Malta, and by extension in England itself.[4] By the 1580s, indeed, the two islands were being commercially linked by regular visits to Malta by English merchant ships.[5]

The military handbooks that form the background for this study of Marlowe's plays have a great many negative things to say about these rising merchants. Not too surprisingly, many of the handbooks also take a dim view of the present state of English manhood – and blame its decline on a combination of the unfortunate lull of peace and the greed of effeminate merchants. An inflammatory pamphlet discounting Spain's public version of the events in 1588, for example, introduces the figure of the merchant to signify what it utterly despises: 'you [Spain] would be so wholy a marchant, that you have plaied bankrout with truth.'[6] The hostility toward the merchant class did not recede when peace came shortly after Elizabeth's death, however, because soldiers-turned-writers continued to identify merchants as a rival group bidding in effect for epistemic control over the nation; soldiers continued to suggest that a nation more interested in its secular materialism than in its defense remained a vulnerable target. As Barnabe Rich remarks some six years into James's reign, in a time of peace with Spain and France, '*Peace* breedes Cowards, it effeminates our mindes, it pampers our wanton wils, and it runs headlong into all sorts of sinne. . . . The Souldiour, who in the time of warre savoreth of sweat, (the true testimony of exercise and labour) in the time of Peace, is all to bee spiced with perfumes (the witnes of effeminate and womanish nicite.)'[7] Perversely, Rich champions the idea that peace is more injurious than war in part because, self-reflexively, a peaceful nation can wound itself.

On the one hand, the veterans' gloom and doom may recapitulate the medieval idea that civilizations inevitably spiral toward decay. On the other hand, it often becomes a catalyst for proposing that martial law could remedy what was commonly seen as England's disintegration, by purging various sources of infection (such as perfumed men, in several examples) from the commonweal. Under martial law, these handbooks hold, a chivalric episteme could be resurrected, and England could be made safe again from enemies both foreign and domestic. Ironically, however, as Maurice Keen reminds us, such prognostications about the decline of chivalry, down to the familiar claims that its adherents are being emasculated by new customs, are 'as old as chivalry itself.' But whereas medieval writers had inveighed against 'black knights'[8] who violated a set of chivalric ideals, sixteenth-century commentators who tried to police the exercise of English manhood were being faced with an unprecedented shift toward the commercial organization of life.[9]

In the contemporary military treatises it is possible to see how the ground is shifting. No longer is the battle understood to be between honorable knights and 'black' miscreant ones, but between common soldiers and merchants, whom the soldiers – taking the high ground – paint as the gravest internal threat to a strong England. Signal examples of soldiers' efforts to revoke the role of merchants as arbiters of the direction in which England was headed include a pair of pamphlets by Geoffrey Gates and William Blandy, authors respectively of *The Defence of Militarie Profession* (1579) and *The Castle of Pollicye* (1581). Using a notary as his amanuensis, Gates presents himself as an 'unlettered man' who defends the integrity of a life at arms by claiming that soldiers pursue a 'profession' as specialized as any career in the law or the Church.[10] Further, in times of military conflict, Gates writes, then England will 'know the value of a soldier, & lick the dust off the feete of her men of prewesse: then would the lawer [sic] and the marcheant humble themselves to the warriers, & be glad to geve honour and salary to the martialist' (18). Gates's special antipathy to merchants becomes even more apparent when his pamphlet is read in tandem with his friend Blandy's *The Castle*. In Blandy's text, Gates appears as a interlocutor, playing the role of an eager but naïve pupil in a socratic dialogue that draws out Blandy's ostensible wisdom about war in contemporary life. If *The Castle*'s structure harks back to medieval monastic dialogues between a master and novice, its *apologia* of common soldiers and invective against merchants are quintessentially modern.

Dedicated to Philip Sidney, whose implied patronage must be supposed to supply a patina of aristocratic privilege and chivalric glory, *The Castle* moves in a few pages from such obligatory topics as the nobility of reason to mundane pronouncements about tactics. But the dialogue really comes alive only when Gates asks Blandy to describe his vision of a 'perfect commonwealth.'[11] Answering what is in effect his own question, Blandy spins out a soldier's fantasy of paradise. Rather than consign the responsibility for making war to mercenaries, as does the archetype of a 'perfect commonwealth' in the sixteenth century – More's *Utopia* – Blandy's own text enthusiastically embraces the profession of arms. In *Utopia* mercenaries are presented as merchants of death, whose ambiguous outsider status as hired killers is tied to their rapacious appetite for lucre, which is said to overwhelm all honor; even Barabas the Jew claims to have worked as a mercenary, as an 'engineer . . . in the wars 'twixt France and Germany, / Under pretence of helping Charles the Fifth' (2.3.189–91): in other words, as a kind of Faustus. Like the magician, Barabas is a go-between, committed to mercenary mischief rather than empire. In *The Castle*, by contrast, soldiers are positioned just below the king. There, by 'skill and vertue in warlike practices,' they help rule the 'multitude' (27, 26). Blandy situates them near the apex of the hierarchy because of their central role in making a nation safe. They deserve such exalted status in his opinion because neither they nor their services are for sale to the highest bidder.

Thus Blandy's handbook substantially elaborates and embellishes the argument made in miniature by his friend Gates. Blandy presents himself as a philosopher: 'Dame nature . . . [has bestowed upon soldiers] the clearnesse and shining glory of vertue and nobility: yet she hath imparted unto them a most sharp wit and ready capacity, greate value and singuler providence' (27). The bloody material consequences of war are erased and the soldiers' aggression naturalized by an appeal to the lexicon of natural philosophy, which presupposes a sublunary interdependence of soldiers and nature that is then belied by the phrase 'singuler providence.'

What little respect Blandy has for merchants in *The Castle* is bestowed upon the international adventurers who take risks with their lives as well as their capital on the seas. These merchants earn his respect in part because their successes bring England glory:

> for the magnificence of theyr prince, weale of theyr countrey, honor
> of theyr City . . . [they] will, by land, be the perill never so great, by

sea, be the daunger never so deepe and difficult, with the hazzard of
unknowen goods & deepe expence of a rich pursse, adventure
straunge and untried vioges. Herehence the famous companies of
adventuring Marchauntes floweth, which are the Princes of all other
which buy and sell wares. (27)

Along similar lines, Sir Walter Ralegh once advised the queen that the
merchant vessels based in Dover, if 'set forth to Scour the Seas of
Pirates,' constituted a 'Navy of Merchants,' whose successes were
helping 'the great Strength and Wealth of the Realm' to 'flourish.'[12]

However, ordinary merchants who do not risk their lives to do
business and whose work cannot be construed as a form of crusading
are treated viciously in Blandy's treatise. When his interlocutor Gates
asks where merchants ought to be placed in the all-important chain of
being, the question opens Blandy's valve. The Castle moves in its last
pages to a withering attack on English merchants. As scapegoats they
are alleged to have engaged in behaviors so heinous that they justify a
permanent return to martial law and the renewal of a chivalric ethos.
Indeed, the charges against them in the pamphlet closely resemble a
formula of charges that James Shapiro has shown was frequently
attributed to Jews in England, and that is thoroughly expressed in The
Jew of Malta.[13] Blandy indicts these merchants for showing a reckless
disregard for England's moral and even physical integrity. Sometimes
they are like vampirish predators, sucking the blood of their
aristocratic betters by selling them their own fantasies, as when Blandy
says a merchant 'harkeneth after the wants, phantasies, spending
humors of gentlemen of his owne countrey. . . [They] geve theyr
Countrye to often most unnaturally a deepe and deadlye wound' (28).
This not-so-subtle appeal to gentlemen's anxieties about the
diminishing of class privilege in an age increasingly commercial is
followed by appeals to religious and gender prejudices. Some
merchants, he intones, are popish, effeminate, or worse. Even speaking
about them may be enough to compromise Blandy's standing among
true men, or so he feigns in an outburst against Gates's demand that the
status of merchants be stated more precisely:

> Will you that I write more then I have spoken? Would you [have] me
> attempt the commendation of theyr state: If so, I shall hardly avoyd
> the suspition of feare, or flattery: acknowledging notwithstanding
> how unable a man I am to yelde to the good and vertuous
> Marchaunt the true guerdon of his due desert. Would you [have] me
> instruct them in theyr kinde of life? Should my pen pinch or improve
> their daynty fare? Should I be so bolde, as to enter into theyr house-
> chappell, and mangle theyr to to much carved Imagery, nipp theyr
> soft & nice nightbeds? (28)

Blandy fears that if he were to give merchants even a modicum of respect, he might be contaminated by their soft habits of mind as well as by the material comforts they hawk as part of their new world order of peace for profit.

And the Middle English noun 'guerdon' reminds playgoers that in the new world of international trade – think of Barabas's trading range, from Malta to 'Florence, Venice, Antwerp, London, Seville, Frankfurt, Lubeck, Moscow, and where not' (4.1.75–6) – soldiers are reduced to vying with merchants for the accolades once almost exclusively available to knights, whose international exchanges had focused on pummeling enemies, as in the Crusades, and on bringing home booty gained by violence.[14] Yet outrageously, Blandy hints that merchants, not soldiers, are the destroyers: 'theyr kinde of life' has its 'to to much carved Imagery' and private chapels. He aims to tar merchants by suggesting they share the supposed desire of English Catholics to sabotage the nation from within.[15] This exchange between Gates and Blandy typifies the notion of many veterans-turned-writers that, to keep England safe from Spain or its lesser enemies its soldiers must beat back the advancing merchants, whom the soldiers perceive as too greedy ever to be trusted to put the nation's defense before their own profit. As we shall see, this charge is caricatured in the early scenes of *The Jew of Malta*, where Barabas's greed is but one reason he dismisses all obligation to defend Malta from the Turks. As he proclaims to his fellow Jews as they prepare to meet Ferneze in Act 1, Scene 1, 'If anything shall there concern our state, / Assure your selves I'll look – [*Aside*] *unto myself*' (1.1.171–2). As the aside helps us see, the confiscation of property without due process inflicts an affective injury to those who measure their worth in such terms, and it unleashes a civic alienation from the state and its objectives that not even martial law can restore as the play ends.

The Jew of Malta thus profits theatrically by staging a collision between ancient and contemporary models of empire, the one depending upon military plunder from, say, the Roman legion or the Hospitallers, the other requiring the suspension of the impulse to conquer in favor of voluntary commercial exchanges and international cooperation. As a sly critique of the reactionary efforts of hawkish veterans and their allies to delay or even reverse such a momentous cultural transition, the play seems implicitly to privilege such commercial exchange as is taking place in its first scenes. Marlowe's favorable treatment of commerce, if not of Barabas as its most successful but 'alien' representative, anticipates the response of Enlightenment philosophers, who theorize the spread of commerce as a civilizing phenomenon.[16] *The Jew of Malta* glances toward a world of great merchants (not epic warlords) who are the engines of peaceful contact among nations. The fact that Barabas imagines himself as a merchant-cum-combatant accentuates his outsider status: he is neither a warlord nor an irenic trader, but consumed by both roles, as his figurative language makes plain at several key moments. For to sustain a successful business venture a merchant must not only be able to set aside prejudice while in pursuit of transnational opportunities, but also genuinely able to reciprocate in business deals with merchants from other nations while keeping his defenses, mental and otherwise, intact. As early modern traders well knew, commercial exchange could easily regress into war.

Marlowe jests that war may even scare away opportunities to profit from the most literal kind of promiscuous commerce – the commercialized pleasure customarily available from a prostitute who is selling experiences more corporeal than chivalric to merchant seamen and other travellers arriving in port with goods to sell. As the courtesan Bellamira complains in Act 3, the Turkish warships anchored off the coast of Malta are keeping away clients, especially merchant sailors from Padua and Venice, who would ordinarily have come into port: 'Since this town was besieged, my gain grows cold' (3.1.1). As Bellamira opens her body to any man who can pay, regardless of his nationality or faith, Barabas likewise initially demonstrates an ecumenical pragmatism in his business affairs that sets aside the nationalist concerns of the state. Ignoring the incompatible mishmash of religious and political philosophies of nations, his argosies are said to call at ports across the globe; he trades promiscuously, even with Persians, the sworn enemies of Malta, thus cultivating an ever-expanding network of relations that supersedes traditional boundaries. As when Barabas names the 'scattered nation' of great Jews, those of Greece, Portugal, Bairseth and the like (1.1.120), it is suggested that wealth creates an identity independent of, sometimes contrary to, the state's interest; while the two are not necessarily incompatible, the prospect of commercially gained wealth and the ancient model of the state as a superstructure for raiding wars are clearly so. Marlowe implies what Enlightenment scholars would later say, that peaceful contact among nations usually diminishes prejudice and violence in the world. Montesquieu's treatment of the idea is representative of the eighteenth-century belief that merchants, taken as a group, are in effect ambassadors among cultures and humanitarians who can promote peace. In *The Spirit of Laws* he writes, 'Commerce is a cure for the most destructive prejudices.'[17]

Christian Knights

Malta is a brilliant choice of setting for Marlowe's concerns. In the sixteenth century it was the second Mediterranean base of the Hospitallers (later, the Knights of Malta), one of three Roman Catholic orders of monk-soldiers who were commissioned by the pope in the twelfth century to crusade against the infidels. Over time their mission was reduced to patrolling the Mediterranean Sea, for which they got control of a number of islands to use as staging areas. They received Malta from Charles V in 1530; survived a long siege of Malta by 200 Turkish warships and 30,000 men in 1565; and surrendered it to none less than Napoleon in 1798.

For more than two centuries the Knights protected Christian merchant ships and pirated Turkish and other Islamic ships in the region. The Knights made Malta 'virtually a school for war.'[18] Lest we imagine, however, that all Christians were united in the idea that crusades against the Turks were inevitable, and violence the only recourse, we may consider what Erasmus has to say about the issue of such crusading in *Enchiridion militis christiani*. There he proposes that infidels are conquered not by the sword, but instead by examples of righteous conduct in the name of Christ. One of Erasmus's strategies for pressing the point is to define anew the relationship between war, faith, and masculinity:

> People generally describe as strong and courageous one who is violent and uncontrolled, who seethes with anger at the slightest injury and returns abuse for abuse, evil deed for evil deed. . . . How much more courageous it is for a lofty and generous mind to be able to ignore all injury and indeed return good for evil! For my part I should not call a person brave because he exhibits daring against the enemy, scales the walls, or exposes himself to all dangers with no regard for his own life, which are things that any gladiator could accomplish.[19]

Although Erasmus rethinks the concept of battlefield bravery, stripping epic manhood of a few of its garlands, he preserves evangelism as an imperative and calls attention to its role in strengthening and preserving national security. Of the threat of the Turks to expand the Ottoman Empire, the Erasmian adage 'Dulce bellum inexpertis' asks readers, 'Are you anxious to win the Turks for Christ? Let us not display our wealth, our armies, our strength. Let them see in us . . . the unmistakable marks of a Christian: . . . the wish to do good even to our enemies, a tolerance which will withstand all injuries, contempt of money.'[20] It must be said that Erasmus revised his thinking about war with the Turk after the Turkish army abandoned its siege of Vienna in October 1529. In an essay 'On the War against the Turks/*De bello turcico*,' he asserts that Christian war need not be merely rhetorical or non-violent:

> Someone will perhaps deduce from all this that I have undertaken the task of arguing *against* a Turkish war. Not at all; on the contrary, my purpose is to ensure that we make war against them successfully and win truly splendid victories for Christ. Merely to clamour for war against the Turks, calling them inhuman monsters, traitors to the Church and a race tainted with all kinds of crime and villainy, is simply to betray the ignorant mob to the enemy.[21]

Erasmus's notion that the Turks may be won over by good deeds, or at least not be alienated by 'ignorant' representations of them, was still in common parlance by the time Marlowe was writing plays.[22] Nabil Matar, for one, has made a compelling argument that several early modern English plays present Muslims sympathetically – especially as the employers of out-of-work English soldiers, so long as the Englishmen agree not to do battle against other Christians.[23]

Consistent with Marlowe's effort to diminish respect for a militarist ethos on the island, his Knights of Malta have shrugged off an ideological commitment to fight Turks and have reduced themselves to an indolent if not cowardly existence. Put alongside other Marlovian soldiers whose self-defined mission includes saving the world from real or even imaginary phantasms – the Tamburlaines, the Achates, the Mortimers – the Knights' virtù is shrunken; martial valor in this play is just so much firewood. Super-sized crusades for the greater glory of God have been replaced by the occasional sea battle, and even those acts of piracy are a fading memory. Deliberately, of course, these Knights embody every English stereotype of the Catholic mercenary; their slanted representation is Marlovian propaganda-making at its best. As Emily Bartels comments,

> [t]he Knights stood as a threat to Elizabethan England because of their militant Catholicism and their control over Mediterranean commerce, and the play encourages its audience's prejudices against them as it erases the one historical event (their success in freeing Europe from the Turks) which secured what was already very limited English support after the Reformation.[24]

Under all the grandstanding about religious and military honor is their appetite for what the Basso names as 'The wind that bloweth all the world besides: / Desire of gold' (3.5.3–4). Ironically, only the Turks consistently acknowledge this truth; everyone else speaks from both sides of their mouths. Yet only Barabas the Jew seems to revel in the opportunities created by the gap between false and authentic speech, in the free play of language that is itself, through his counterfeiting, epistemologically unmoored. As the consummate outsider in Malta, he takes up chameleonic self-fashioning not simply to advance himself, but eventually as a way to collude with the state apparatus while simultaneously undermining it, a goal that is necessarily shared by few of the island's other inhabitants. He prizes opportunities to practice his skill at extemporaneously shaping his identity to the moment: 'We Jews can fawn like spaniels when we please, / And when we grin, we bite' (2.3.20–21). As something of an outsider, an alien, it is in his interest to check the state's power. Yet as its most prominent merchant he also has an interest in keeping the state viable as a commercial marketplace. And so through much of the play he pictures his adversarial relationship with Malta as a game, as an endless loop of what he sees as interdependent transactions.[25] This helps to explain, for example, his otherwise puzzling decision to resign the governorship of Malta in Act 5. Though he has previously expressed a desire to see Ferneze 'whipped to death' (5.1.68), he bargains away his new powers only a few lines into his office. Giving it back, Barabas chats up his enemy, pretending nonchalance while throwing down a merchant's gage, daring the governor to pay him back: 'let me see what money thou canst make' (5.2.94); the challenge imitates Ferneze's own jest in Act 1 as the Jew's estate is seized. The resignation from the office he has just won is consistent with the Jew's idea that the more powerful man is one who makes kings, as he tells us: 'Why, is not this a kingly kind of trade, to purchase towns by treachery and sell 'em by deceit?' (5.5.46–8).

However, as is clear in Act 5, Barabas pushes the game too far, and the denouement traps spectators in a uncomfortable critique of the hypocrisy surrounding all the Knights' presumptive moral authority as monk-soldiers. While we may not feel pity as he boils to death in a trap of his own design, we must ask why Ferneze and his fellow Hospitallers do not rescue him when he pleads for Christian mercy.[26] Sacrificing him, they affirm solidarity with the fraternity of soldiers everywhere, even their arch-enemies the Turks. The merchant is sacrificed in symbolic recompense for the Turkish sailors whom he orders 'massacred' even as they showed faith in the hospitality of a victors' banquet (5.5.106). Moreover, the Knights' refusal to extend succor to the one figure who most passionately subscribes to the commercial paradigm clears the way to remake Malta as a sanctuary for the weakened traditions of chivalry, an island of the old school amidst irremediable social change. No one else there, least of all Barabas's fellow Jews Zaareth and Temainte, will stand in the way of its reincarnation as a port for warships that will displace the commercial seascape conjured up in the exchanges of Barabas and his factors in Act 1, Scene 1, where argosies arrive with silk and spice and diamonds in their holds. The final moments of Act 5 press the idea of a nostalgic return to a golden age of chivalry. Following the accepted treatment of noble prisoners, Ferneze spares Calymath's life but holds him for ransom. Proud of himself, Ferneze contrasts his own generosity to 'a Jew's courtesy' (5.5.107); he is unable to imagine that any merchant who would immolate a squadron of soldiers at a victory banquet is capable of respecting the protocol for the treatment of subdued nobles, even though that is exactly what Barabas has just done in treating the imprisoned Ferneze with charity. Yet there is some earlier evidence that the tradition itself is waning: with no trace of regret, Admiral Martin del Bosco has reported 'slain' the captain of the sailors he sells as slaves in Malta (2.2.17).

Further, the term courtesy itself has been robbed of significant meaning over the course of the play. In Act 1, Scene 2, for instance, Calymath has upbraided the basso who demands in a niggardly way the instant payment of Malta's tribute – 'What, Callapine, a little courtesy' (1.2.23), though Calymath himself has just twice said he 'dare not dally' and 'shall not tarry' waiting for the tribute to be paid (1.2.12, 16). In Act 2, Scene 3 Lodowick, negotiating for Abigail's hand, has said that as a suitor he expects to be put through some ritual test so as to 'deserve it' (2.3.68), yet has spoken crudely of her with rival Don Mathias; Barabas has likewise aided in bankrupting the custom of chivalric courtship by directing Abigail to *'make love'* to Lodowick 'with all the courtesy you can afford, / Provided, that you keep your maidenhead' (2.3.241, 229–30). Within both private and public arenas, from diplomacy to love, courtesy is being detached from any signified meaning; it is indiscriminately available to all, regardless of honor, nationality, religious faith, or economic status.

The disintegration of chivalry and its implied militarist ethos is most on display in the seizure episode in Act 1, Scene 2. The Jews summoned to appear are forced to part with half their wealth on the grounds of 'a common good' and their own 'inherent sin' and 'monstrous sin' of 'covetousness' (1.2.99, 110, 125). But these Jews have long been allowed to do business and amass wealth in Malta, and in any case the Knights show little regard for the 'common good,' far less than is expected of them. More to the point is that the Hospitallers, operating within a medieval economy fed by the spoils of war, have been profligate losers at their own game of piracy.[27] As Ferneze explains it, with the tribute ten years in arrears, the sum cannot now be raised 'By reason of the wars, that robbed our store; / And therefore are we to request your aid' (1.2.48–9). In other words the Knights have failed to collect enough loot from pirated ships, presumably because of their 'tributary league' (2.2.23) with the Turks: they find themselves in a catch-22. Barabas seems deliberately to misinterpret the 'request' as an invitation to become a soldier. 'Alas, my lord, we are no soldiers' (1.2.50), he replies, turning back on them their cherished image of themselves as superior to the civilians they protect. Taking the bait, the First Knight answers with sarcastic envy: 'Tut, Jew, we know thou art no soldier; / Thou art a merchant, and a moneyed man, / And 'tis thy money, Barabas, we seek' (1.2.52–4). Pragmatically, the Second Knight explains it as the cost of doing business in a foreign land: 'Have strangers leave with us to get their wealth? Then let them with us contribute' (1.2.60–61). We must remember, however, that Barabas is not much more of an outsider than the Knights themselves; indeed, they are arguably colonialists in ways he is not, for as he points out elsewhere, merchants are less interested in 'principality' than in profit (1.1.134).

The confiscation might have called to mind similar treatment of 'aliens' in London in the years just before the Armada sailed up the English Channel. In 1586 Elizabeth's government had demanded of the 'merchant strangers' who were working and living in London a sum of almost £5000 to help prepare for war with Spain; the government had also relied upon some forced loans and confiscations in order to repay huge debts from military campaigns against Scotland and France that had been concluded decades earlier but not yet fully paid for.[28] But the government's actual demands and the fictional ones that Marlowe stages are fundamentally unlike in one respect – these imaginary Knights of Malta do not as yet intend to fight.

Into the midst of the public and private crises occasioned by Calymath's return to Malta arrives Admiral Martin del Bosco. Like all great military officers in Marlowe's plays, Bosco is a subtle rhetorician, and in a brief exchange in the Senate House manages to reform the Knights into fire-breathing warriors who are again 'at deadly enmity with Turks' (2.2.33). He comes into port fresh from burning and sinking a Turkish fleet. The battle had been joined after he refused to lower his topsails as a sign of respect. In Marlowe's world, no sailor wants to submit to any other, though soldiers (or sailors) are in solidarity against merchants across national boundaries, as when Calymath and Ferneze become temporary allies in Act 5. Within the context of the soldiers' scorn for merchants that runs through the play, we may likewise think of the reward Tamburlaine promises Theridamas while recruiting him for his drive to be 'the monarch of the East.' Tamburlaine offers the plum of 'Christian merchants,' whose ships 'Plough up huge furrows in the Caspian Sea,' being forced to 'vail to us as lords of all the lake' (1–1.2.184, 193, 194–5).

In Malta, Admiral Bosco is shocked to find fellow Catholics submissively in 'league' with the infidels (2.2.23). In fact, their acquiescence ironizes Calymath's false flattery of them in Act 1, Scene 2 as he withdraws to await their payment with 'Farewell, great governor and brave knights of Malta' (1.2.32). The dialogue sparked by Bosco's arrival abruptly ends the cosy deal that has been struck between the Knights and the Turks. It gives theatergoers a taste of Marlowe's rhetorical signature – the inflammatory set piece of war fever – as the Admiral takes charges of Malta's defense. He scarcely need be invited into this catalyzing role, as he is by the First Knight, who is now inspired to fight, though earlier he had goaded Ferneze to submit to the Turks (1.2.157–9). Sounding remarkably akin to the Younger Mortimer wresting command of a beleaguered England from Isabella, Bosco insists that Malta 'be ruled by me' (2.2.39). His tactics are to raise their hopes of becoming a viable military unit again, then to shame them by telling a story of their Order's defeat in the battle of Rhodes (1513), the Hospitallers' first Mediterranean base, lost after a long Turkish siege. Historically, the Order had eventually surrendered Rhodes and negotiated safe passage for its surviving members. Bosco misrepresents the outcome, claiming they had fought to the death, so that 'not a man survived / To bring the hapless news to Christendom' (2.2.50–51). The defeat had been 'Europe's shame' (2.2.30). Implied in Bosco's narrative is the potential for that shame to be compounded now, as if he were Aeneas retelling the fall of Troy to Dido's court. He appeals not only to the Knights' sense of duty, but to their fear of being emasculated in the eyes of a visibly successful warrior. Under this strain, Ferneze declaims as if he were playing Hercules at the Rose Theater:

> So will we fight it out. Come, let's away.
> Proud-daring Calymath, instead of gold,
> We'll send thee bullets wrapped in smoke and fire.
> Claim tribute where thou wilt, we are resolved.
> Honour is bought with blood, and not with gold.
>
> 2.2.52–6

In spite of Bosco's tutelage, however, the Knights are allowed to be seen as only belligerent, not brave. In Act 3 a defiant Ferneze rallies the troops by encouraging them to 'profitably take up arms' (3.5.32), a little joke on what motivates them, and then they virtually disappear until Act 5. In other words, no opportunity to recuperate their honor comes their way, as Marlowe shifts our attention to domestic matters, tracing militarism's impact upon the affective life of Malta's other inhabitants.

* * *

Marlowe is careful to suggest that the language of war has penetrated all of Maltese culture, as civilians construct images of themselves by imitating the Knights of Malta at their peak; they do so, sometimes unwittingly, as a way of joining the dominant group, in this case, soldiers. As even Ferneze grasps, transmitting war fever to the demoralized or the young depends upon simple acts of imitating those who worship arms, as the governor advises the rejuvenated 'warlike' Bosco (2.2.45). Barabas, for example, despite his occupation as a merchant adventurer, persists in representing himself as a soldier instead. After his goods are seized he borrows the vocabulary of war, specifically the vocabulary of the vanquished, to characterize his emotional state, asking his compatriot Jews for the 'liberty at least to mourn / That in a field amidst his enemies / Doth see his soldiers slain, himself disarmed, / And knows no means of his recovery' (1.2.203–6), and later speaking of his 'former richs' as being 'like a soldier's scar, / That has no further comfort for his maim' (2.1.9–11). While some of this talk may simply be a Machiavellian attempt to position himself inside the charmed circle of warriors, from whence revenge would be more accessible, there is too much material in the play suggesting that Barabas takes the confiscation as he does because – like Bosco – he is still invested in a zero-sum vision of the world, in which a man can only win or lose. As Stephen Greenblatt once observed, 'Barabas is brought into being by the Christian society.'[29]

Other than Barabas, martial law's deleterious effects are principally suffered upon Abigail and, to a lesser extent, Bellamira. The female bodies function as focal points in the struggle between chivalry and protocapitalism. Upon these bodies, the civilian men in Malta strive to replicate at least figuratively the absolutism that equates masculine strength with the lack of all human compassion, what Barabas says is the Knights' ability to have their 'unrelenting flinty hearts / Suppress all pity in [their] stony breasts' (1.2.142–3), an image repeated in his advice to Ithamore about how to succeed in Malta (2.3.171–2).

Throughout the play, Abigail and particularly the representation of her body are treated with grave disrespect. In a series of what might easily be considered figurative sexual assaults, her priest confessor; her suitors, including her 'love,' Don Mathias (2.3.240); and her father fantasize about the pleasures of disfiguring, penetrating, and defiling her body. While their fantasies are regularly couched in the language of commerce – getting, selling, profiting, and so forth – I would argue that the transgressive treatment of her body critiques and usually condemns the men's martial fantasies of dominion; and that these fantasies have less to do with commercial than chivalric ideas about gender, though at first study the language might seem to confirm the early modern complaint that the triumph of a commercial mode over more ancient ways of organizing social life threatens to cheapen all human relationships.

To take the series of fantasies in ascending order of complexity, we may begin with the moment of Abigail's death. Like Edward II, she has taken sanctuary in a monastic house to escape a life saturated with violent, ambitious men who, as Michael Drayton says of Edward's foes, have acted 'without Humane Pittie.'[30] Admittedly Abigail's death is not nearly the spectacle Edward's is, and playgoers have less sympathy invested in her character. After all, she had joked ironically with her abbess of expecting to 'profit' when she was first admitted to the convent (1.2.334). Yet it is appalling when her confessor Father Bernardine answers her very last words, 'And witness that I die a Christian,' with a callow reply: 'Ay, and a virgin, too; that grieves me most' (3.6.40–41).[31] Elizabethan jokes about corrupt Roman Catholic priests notwithstanding, this moment records in a perversely serious way the contrast between Abigail's sincere spirituality and Bernardine's false ministry. In one line he manages not only to offend the doctrine of conventual abstinence by presenting her virginity as an occasion of grief, but more importantly, I think – because Marlowe shows more respect for, say, a Piconean rendition of human dignity than for any canonical expression of that idea – Bernardine visually penetrates Abigail in an act of symbolic necrophilia.

Like the good father, Abigail's suitors Don Mathias and Lodowick also take pleasure in imagining sexual intercourse with her, in which the prize of her virginity is again an integral part of their initial fantasies. Their interest in her body has two distinct movements in the play. In Act 1 they are aligned as homosocial pals who from a distance glibly imagine the pleasure of sexual intercourse with Abigail; and in Acts 2 and 3, they become jealous rivals in an unwinnable, fatal competition orchestrated by Barabas. As the play proceeds, then, these gallants are transformed from cads into gentlemen-at-arms, which as Barabas draws out, makes them rather more than less vulnerable because their fantasies about chivalric honor overwhelm good sense. In Act 1, united in their schoolboy banter, they seem invincible. They are economically advantaged and socially privileged, and Mathias in particular shows little compassion for Barabas and Abigail's new circumstances. It seems he might be speaking of himself as he tells Lodowick that Abigail is so 'matchless beautiful; / As had you seen her, 'twould have moved your heart / Though countermured with walls of brass – to love, / Or at the least to pity' (1.2.382–5). Later in Act 2, Lodowick will seem impervious to Barabas's effort to ensnare him with images of Abigail's 'diamond,' while Mathias lacks all discretion. He instantly deduces how Barabas's 'sudden fall' has 'humbled' Abigail into holy orders (1.2.365, 366). Word is out, and it is perceived to shame them both. Lodowick is surprised. She is, he protests to Mathias,

> A fair young maid scarce fourteen years of age,
> The sweetest flower in Cytherea's field,
> Cropped from the pleasures of the fruitful earth
> And strangely metamorphosed to a nun.
>
> 1.2.376–9

Mathias, who is Abigail's '*love*' (2.3.237), is chagrined by the prospect of eternal chastity. Extending the seizure of Barabas's property to include his daughter, Mathias takes charge of Abigail's virtual body, rejecting the idea of the convent as a form of life unnatural to her:

> Become a nun? Her father's sudden fall
> Has humbled her and brought her down to this.
> Tut, she were fitter for a tale of love
> Then to be tirèd out with orizons;
> And better would she far become a bed,
> Embracèd in a friendly lover's arms,
> Than rise at midnight to a solemn mass.
>
> 1.2.365–71

His ribald puns tease out the physical pleasures of sexual intercourse, juxtaposed with the meager spiritual rewards of faith. In his eyes Abigail is thus only a fantastical body, a vessel more fit for the phallus than for prayer, which he stands ready to penetrate with his 'tale of love.' Given this kind of talk it is somewhat difficult to comprehend that in Act 3 the suitors kill one another in a duel they think designed to preserve honor – their own and Abigail's – for as they become gentlemen-at-arms she necessarily becomes their chivalric inspiration. Sons of the aristocracy prove mindlessly vulnerable to the machinations of a merchant who resurrects an aristocratic rite as a weapon in his class war, while the status of Abigail's virtual body is again staged as a function of the fictions surrounding an ancient model of plunder.

The father-daughter relationship is affectively the most complex in the play. She is devoted to him, at least in part by his design – in Hebrew, the name 'Abigail' means 'my father's joy.' He, however, is devoted to victory at all costs. A harbinger that Barabas customarily thinks of even his domestic life in the vocabulary of the militarism that dominates Malta arrives in his oath, said without perceptible irony, that he holds Abigail 'as dear as Agamemnon did his Iphigen' (1.1.136–7). As an expression of paternal love this offers cold comfort. It does, however, reveal a fascinating piece of his fantasy life in which he casts himself as a great Greek general.[32] As Patricia Joplin says about the sacrifice of Iphigenia in Euripides, however, the 'unmaking of Homeric heroes is also the unmasking of the cultural fictions that veil the sacrificial violence at the basis of political domination.'[33] We may see this unmasking in Barabas's epithets for his daughter at various stages of cooperation with his schemes. When compliant, she is judged an erstwhile 'loadstar' (2.1.42); in rebellion she is 'Catzo diavola' (4.1.21), her decision to return to the convent 'Spurca' (3.4.6).[34] The curses – glossed as 'penis, she-devil,' and 'filthy' – capture a synaptic link between sexuality, women, and filth that is fundamental to Barabas's frame of mind.

Initially it is Abigail not her father who proposes a response to the seizure of their estate that dares to contest the veiled fictions of martial law. As a first response she advocates mutilating herself in a public forum, 'not for myself, but agèd Barabas.' She shall 'with fierce exclaims run to the senate-house, / And in the senate reprehend them all / And rend their hearts with tearing of my hair / Till they reduce the wrongs done to my father' (1.2.230, 234–7). But as Barabas knows, Malta has become a place where persuasive speech counts for little, even in the Senate; he teaches Abigail that 'things past recovery are hardly cured with exclamations' (1.2.238–9). From this point father and daughter are never again so united as dissidents. For while she may be ready to injure herself in her father's cause, as a woman in a highly patriarchal world she is unable to injure anyone else, even when she discovers that her father has plotted against her suitors' lives. That, she says, has had the hyperbolic effect of 'murdering me' (3.3.52), '*yet never shall these lips bewray thy life*' (3.3.81).

While Abigail's injury remains effectively unarticulated, Barabas' rage against his forced submission to the Knights' absolute authority is eventually inscribed onto Abigail's body. For men in the play, submitting is always shameful, as we are reminded by the force of Bosco's allusion to the battle of Rhodes and Barabas's disgust with his fellow Jews (and himself) who 'basely thus submit yourselves' to Malta's soldiers (1.2.80). By abusing Abigail, Barabas seeks to erase his shame by projecting it onto her; and this process takes place entirely inside the convent that had served as their home before it was confiscated too. In a state run by a monastic order, the nunnery is inevitably part of the state apparatus, here a place where religious and military disciplines meet, a site in which the power of the capricious state is naturalized as religious piety.[35] In the first attack on the convent Abigail is a reluctant but cooperative accomplice. While Barabas feigns condemning her supposed entry into the novitiate by calling her 'thy father's shame' (1.2.342), she colludes not only with his plan, but unwittingly with his effort to transfer his shame to her through incestuous expressions of a desire for gold. Late at night, awaiting his return to the window where she will hand down the booty, she prays, 'gentle sleep, where'er his body rests, / Give charge to Morpheus that he may dream / A golden dream, and of the sudden walk, / Come, and receive the treasure I have found'

(2.1.35–8). She prays that he may experience a nocturnal wet dream so powerful it would awaken him into a state of acquisitive satisfaction. As if in answer, at midnight he returns to the window to hail her success with sexually charged praise:

> Welcome the first beginner of my bliss!
> O Abigail, Abigail, that I had thee here too,
> Then my desires were fully satisfied,
> But I will practise thy enlargement thence.
> O girl, O gold, O beauty, O my bliss!
> [s.d.] *Hugs his bags.*

2.1.50–54

The paratactic ecstasy of the final line makes fatherhood, sex, pleasure, and wealth grammatically contiguous, emotionally fused. While his promise of Abigail's forthcoming 'enlargement' has a straightforward denotative meaning, in its context it also opens up more than one bawdy connotation for a virginal nun – would it be vaginal dilation? pregnancy? emancipation from the cloister? We are teased by Marlovian ambiguity again as Abigail responds to his speech, sending him away so as 'to shun suspicion' (2.1.57). In a study of incest in early modern drama, Richard McCabe reminds us that the topic 'served as a powerful focus for scrutinising all forms of allegedly "natural" authority.'[36] In the midnight exchange of gold and parental affection through the windows of the convent, indeed, the tableau of a lovers' rendezvous invites playgoers to contemplate not only the potential dangers of absolute paternal authority (where is Abigail's mother, anyway?),[37] but also the righteousness of Christian dogma that naturalizes violent conquests, as in the capture of this real estate that has been gladly converted into church property, as the inevitable and laudable victory of Christ's soldiers. In Barabas's final engagement with Abigail he protests the entitlement expressed in the Church's use of his house. Scheming to injure his daughter and her sisters, he sends alms in the form of poisoned porridge, mocking the nuns who have displaced him as being privileged and unwary consumers of charity, and in effect taking back his house by making it over once more into an erotic zone, but now also a site of mass murder.

Mary Douglas observes that 'food is not likely to be polluting at all unless the external boundaries of the social system are under pressure. . . . [Then] [w]e should expect the orifices of the body to symbolise its specially vulnerable points' in the symbolic economy of that society.[38] To express such pressure on stage, Marlowe frequently relies upon the motif of contaminated food. Usually it signifies that tyrants achieve new heights of control over a community by making the act of eating a shameful expression of submission instead of a regenerative act of self-mastery. Thus Tamburlaine tries to humiliate Bajazeth by forcing him to eat from the tip of a sword; Dr Faustus mocks the Vatican by throwing around its wine; Gurney reports having been almost overcome by the stench of the sewer as he threw meat to Edward II; and Barabas impregnates a pot of porridge with the 'blood of Hydra, Lerna's bane; / The juice of hebon, and Cocytus' breath, / And all the poisons of the Stygian pool'; then speaking, it seems, of himself, he says, 'and in this / Vomit your venom, and invenom her / That like a fiend hath left her father thus!' (3.4.102–7). Metonymically Barabas replaces his daughter's mouth for her vagina.[39] Particularly powerful is his trope of evacuating his 'venom' by vomiting it into the porridge and indirectly into his daughter's mouth: again he is transferring the rage bred in him by having been forced to yield not only his estate, but his dignity too. As late as Act 5 he is continuing to decry the loss of his goods and land and vowing to help Calymath 'slay' women and children and 'fire the churches [and] pull their houses down,' acts that signify a Tamburlainesque rage directed against the community that has betrayed him, but provoked solely by its soldiers' own aggression (5.1.64–5). Calymath well understands this. When he meets Barabas outside the city's walls in Act 5, he asks a rhetorical question: 'Art thou that Jew whose goods we heard were sold for tribute-money?' (5.1.73–4).

The play's second-best merchant thrives amidst Barabas's distress because she collaborates with the state. Bellamira the courtesan regulates access to a female body to turn a profit, pursuing the capitalist game at its most physical. Neither enslaved to her procurer Pilia-borza nor exploited by Ithamore, Bellamira might appear to be in charge of her destiny. Yet she is nonetheless answerable to the Knights of Malta, in part by reifying their Manichean vision of women, who may be only as pure as Abigail or as public as she. In this way as Augustine observed prostitutes are localized sites of disorder, mistresses of order: 'Remove prostitutes from human affairs, and you will destroy everything with lust.'[40] We see Bellamira's collusion with authority in Act 5. Once she learns that Ithamore and Barabas are responsible for setting up Lodowick and Mathias and strangling the friars, she hastens to report their deeds to Ferneze, even though doing so shall stop the flow of ducats to her purse: she acts not in her own, but in the state's best interest. Her interview with Ferneze captures Bellamira's ambiguous status in Malta and explains in part why she makes an effort to associate herself with what Ferneze duplicitously refers to as having the 'law'; even before she is able to speak he tries to dismiss her, so she is forced to assert herself: 'Whate'er I am, yet, governor hear me speak' (5.1.40, 9).

If Bellamira is in abstract ways exploited by the systematic

oppression of women in Malta, in a concrete way she also profits from it by manipulating Ithamore. Unlike her Venetian and Paduan clients who are free traders, Ithamore is still a prisoner of war, a galley slave who seeks to find in intimacy with Bellamira more than sexual gratification. So we might see their 'relationship' as a metaphor for the mutual dependence of merchants and soldiers. The parody of Ithamore's petrarchan pursuit of the courtesan magnifies the deleterious effects of commerce and war both. Under the spell of a quean, Ithamore looks to a strong woman to have his war-torn identity repaired and restored, much as Aeneas does in *Dido, Queen of Carthage*. Ithamore seems to believe that physical intimacy offers an escape from a violent world in which he takes himself to be 'not worthy to look upon her' (4.2.40). This is in fact his first response to Bellamira's letter, delivered by courier, stating her 'interest' in him. Perhaps 'she sees more in me than I can find in myself,' he marvels, 'for she writes further that she loves me ever since she saw me, and who would not requite such love?' (4.2.36–8). As Jacques Rossiaud explains of late medieval Dijonnais who used prostitutes, 'there were images of a golden age suspended at the deepest level of consciousness among the poor; there was a desire to return to the primitive community.'[41]

In *The Jew*, likewise, money becomes the vehicle of a primitive golden age fantasy: Ithamore is metamorphosed from slave to gentleman, from soldier to Petrarchan poet. When the lovers meet, Ithamore finds that he also loves her at first sight, as the tradition dictates, proclaiming hers 'the sweetest face that ever I beheld!' (3.1.27), and he revels in his lady's exalted gaze – her eye 'twinkles like a star' (4.2.138). 'Come, gentle Ithamore, lie in my lap' (4.4.28) she coos, not for the first time, facetiously bestowing upon him the rank of gentleman. As with Ben Jonson's Dol-Common, the clever con in *The Alchemist*, Bellamira feeds herself by feeding a gull's fantasy of vaulting material and sexual limits.[42] But as is made clear by Ithamore's cavalier use of his master's ducats, he values 'love' above gold. When she demands payment for her affections, Ithamore is quick to respond (in an aside): 'I'll go steal some money from my master to make me handsome' (4.2.56–7). We might conclude that underneath the comedy, Ithamore's entanglement with Bellamira exposes the insidious mental violence done by capitalism upon those who worship at its altar as a matter of survival: the disenfranchised poor, for example, like Ithamore, who discover in affluent Malta that poverty is degrading. Ithamore signals as much when he reflects upon how Pilia-borza appeared to him at the (unjust) public execution of friar Jacomo: Pilia-borza 'gave me a letter from one Madam Bellamira, saluting me in such sort as if he had meant to make clean my boots with his lips' (4.2.32–4). Self-reflexively, Ithamore indulges in a comic but coyly sadomasochistic fantasy of being served by another slave.

In responding to Bellamira, Ithamore hopes to create himself as someone other than a soldier or slave. Repeatedly his aim is spoofed. He is so lost in 'imaginative aggrandizement' that he mistakes her name as 'sweet Allamira' (4.2.53), accessible to all.[43] Pilia-Borza jokes that the slave would 'make a rich poet' (4.2.132). Indeed, Ithamore has just finished an aria to his beloved that is the quintessence of all that a prisoner-of-war-become-slave might hope to escape into: 'we will leave this paltry land / And sail from hence to Greece, to lovely Greece' (4.2.96–7). It seems that he is making a promise to himself as much as to Bellamira, somewhat like Faustus in summoning Helen of Troy. Casting himself as a pastoral Adonis who shall live in perpetual ecstasy in a classical paradise, Ithamore transports himself far from the bloody world of infanticide and sadistic torture that his master claims to solicit from him. He spins a fantasy of new life with Bellamira:

> I'll be thy Jason, thou my golden fleece.
> Where painted carpets o'er the meads are hurled
> And Bacchus' vineyards overspread the world,
> Where woods and forests go in goodly green,
> I'll be Adonis, thou shalt be Love's Queen.
> . . .
> Thou in those groves, by Dis above,
> Shalt live with me and be my love.
>
> 4.2.98–106

Suddenly Ithamore's violent impulses have been redeemed by the prospect of escape into a life of peace and pleasure. Yet even in this fantasy, Bacchus is a conqueror. We cannot but keep in mind that the diminishing of Ithamore's violent streak is induced by a mercantile relationship with a quean, and that his abandoning the ways of war is a mirage, albeit a pleasingly comedic one.

While Ferneze and Bellamira carve the world into those who sell and those who fight, the play resists that dichotomy by showing how a mercantilist epistemology is indebted to the mental structures of warmaking, by showing how deeply the ideals of war lurk in the interstices of civilian life. In a city in which human beings are sold at market, their prices marked on their bodies, it makes sense that Ithamore would praise his master for engineering a revenge tragedy against Lodowick and Mathias this way: 'Faith, master, I think by this you purchase both / their lives' (2.3.368–9).[44]

And how differently this internecine struggle between merchants and warriors is treated on the English stage only a few years later by Ben Jonson and Francis Beaumont once the war with Spain is resolved. For this next generation of playwrights, a decline of chivalric manhood and an apparent triumph of crass commercialism become sources of deep if sometimes rueful comedy during what Philip J. Finkelpearl, writing on Beaumont and Fletcher, has called a 'postheroic age.'[45] Sir Epicure Mammon, the effete gull at the center of *The Alchemist*, whose legacy in Jonson's comedy is gutted by a trio of petty thieves, cannot defend himself against these illicit merchants of fantasy in the newly commercial world: it would seem to be just as William Blandy had feared. And the veterans' anxieties that merchants would rise above them, and the merchants' efforts to better themselves, produce much of the comic energy in Beaumont and Fletcher's *The Knight of the Burning Pestle*, where the apprentice 'knight' Rafe laments that '[t]here are no such courteous and fair well-spoken knights in / this age.' Through a cornucopia of misadventures with princesses and giants he grandly and ironically aims to fill that lacuna, to recast English manhood to make it again 'as true as steel.'[46] As Rafe can only ape the chivalric code, however, not actually live it, Beaumont hints that by 1607, the ancient idea of chivalric manhood exists as no more than a pale fiction, beyond the ken of all but the commercially minded playwright. And no playwright in the period understood that better than the prolific Philip Massinger, whose 1624 tragicomedy *The Renegado* resurrects and restores the Knights of Malta to a position of glory on the English stage. The renegade Grimaldi, a sometime mercenary, makes an appeal to the Knights' legendary heroism in battle against the Turks in a heated exchange with Asambeg, the Turkish viceroy of Tunis:

> These knights of Malta, but a handful to
> Your armies that drink rivers up, have stood
> Your fury at the height, and with their crosses
> Struck pale your horned moons. These men of Malta,
> Since I took pay from you, I have met and fought with,
> Upon advantage, too; yet to speak truth,
> By the soul of honor I have ever found them
> As provident to direct and bold to do
> As any trained up in your discipline,
> Ravished from other nations.[47]

The juxtapositions in Grimaldi's speech recall the principal axes of the contests in *The Jew of Malta* – between mercenaries interested primarily in 'pay' and tribute versus knights who claim to be bound by 'the soul of honor'; between 'armies that drink rivers up,' as if in memory of Tamburlaine, and those who at least say they will meet such 'fury at the height' but do not; between aliens who have turned Turk, as it were, and Christians who fear that they too will be 'ravished from other nations' by infidels. Massinger's tale exploits all of the myths about aliens, soldiers, and merchants that Marlowe had worked with more than three decades earlier. But whereas Marlowe had invited spectators to take sides in the struggle between hawks and merchants for control of London's civic identity and its defense, Massinger offers a very different kind of pageant. His tragicomedy of conversion can return the Knights of Malta to center stage because by 1624 the merchant adventurers have effectively defeated the war hawks to become the engines of international commerce, leaving it to playwrights such as Massinger to appeal to a hoary nostalgia that can celebrate rather than denigrate a Roman Catholic order of monk-soldiers on a London stage, and turn a profit doing so.

Notes

1. Thomas Styward, *The Pathwaie to Martiall Discipline*, London, 1581, STC 23413, 3.
2. Elizabeth I, *Proclamations. A Declaration of the Causes Mooving the Queene of England to give aide to the Defence of the People afflicted and oppressed in the lowe Countries*, London, 1585, STC 9189, 19. N.I. Matar, 'English Renaissance Soldiers in the Armies of Islam,' *Explorations in Renaissance Culture* 21 (1995), cites a Bill passed in Parliament in November, 1575, forbidding Elizabeth's '"subjects from engaging in the service in the Low Countries, or of any other foreign prince or state, as mariners or soldiers"' (81 [*Calendar of State Papers, Domestic* 1:506], a proclamation repeated under James I).
    For an exhaustive study of merchants' status and expanding roles in sixteenth- and seventeenth-century England, see Robert Brenner, *Merchants and Revolution: Commercial Change, Political Conflict, and London's Overseas Traders, 1550–1653* (Princeton: Princeton University Press, 1993).
3. J.R. Hale, *War and Society in Renaissance Europe, 1450–1620* (New York: St Martin's, 1985), 230.
4. Richard Helgerson observes that 'the theater was deeply involved in the process' of adjudicating class status in the early modern period, and by what Peter Burke has dubbed the '"withdrawal of the upper classes"' from public life, once their role as military leaders had declined, by participating, for example, in the creation of high and low entertainment. See Richard Helgerson, *Forms of Nationhood: The Elizabethan Writing of England* (Chicago: University of Chicago Press, 1992), 241–2.
5. Godfrey Wettinger, *The Jews of Malta in the Late Middle Ages* (Malta: Midsea, 1985), 147, writing briefly about Marlowe's play.
6. D.F.R. de M., 'An Answer to the Untruths, Published and Printed in Spaine,' trans. I.L., London, 1589, STC 17132, 11.
7. Barnabe Rich, *A Roome for a Gentleman*, London, 1609, STC 20985, B1r–v.
8. Maurice Keen, *Chivalry* (New Haven: Yale University Press, 1984), 233, 234.

9. While there are problems with calling what goes on in Malta 'capitalism,' alternate terms – mercantilism, for example – are not necessarily more accurate. Moreover, in *Worlds Apart: The Market and the Theater in Anglo-American Thought, 1550–1750* (Cambridge: Cambridge University Press, 1986), Jean-Christophe Agnew notes that some historians argue for 'the presence of a protocapitalist market in England almost from the moment of the Conquest' (44). He offers a short bibliography on the question (260, n. 90).

10. Geoffrey Gates, *The Defence of Militarie Profession*, London, 1579, STC 11683, 6. Subsequent quotations are cited parenthetically.
    In *Lords of all the World: Ideologies of Empire in Spain, Britain and France, c. 1500–1800* (New Haven: Yale University Press, 1995), Anthony Pagden observes that early modern nobles complained that merchants 'lacked "a noble idea of their profession,"' and therefore did not possess the moral foundation to lead (183).

11. William Blandy, *The Castle, or picture of pollicy shewing forth . . . the duety, quality, profession of a perfect and absolute souldiar, the martiall feates, encounters, and skirmishes lately done by our English nation*, London, 1581 (New York: Da Capo, 1972), 26. All subsequent quotations are cited parenthetically.

12. Sir Walter Ralegh, *A Discourse of Sea-Ports; Principally of the Port and Haven of Dover*, London, 1700, Wing D1458, 6–7. Modern historians are split on the assessment of the financial impact of English privateering. In *Merchants and Revolution* Brenner, for instance, argues that in the 1580s and 1590s England's war against Spain 'proved to be a blessing' for those merchant-traders whose vessels were pressed into privateering (19), while Robert Wernham calls this practice a 'commerce-destroying war' in *The Making of Elizabethan Foreign Policy, 1558–1603* (Berkeley: University of California Press, 1980), 61.

13. James S. Shapiro, *Shakespeare and the Jews* (New York: Columbia University Press, 1996). See his third chapter, 'The Jewish Crime,' which locates *The Jew of Malta* in the context of scary Christian myths about contemporary Jews, who were alleged to do all of the monstrous actions Barabas proudly claims as his own in his 'I walk abroad o'nights' speech (2.3.177–204).

14. The contiguity of 'Antwerp, London' in Barabas's list of trading cities may be more than happenstance. In 1576 Antwerp was sacked by Spanish troops. In London, to which the news of the assault quickly spread, pamphleteers seized on the event as proof not only of Spain's infamy, but of the dangers of allowing a city to become the province of merchants at soldiers' expense. Nick de Somogyi is one of few critics to take seriously the fascinating play made about the episode and performed by Shakespeare's company, *A Larum for London; or, the siege of Antwerpe*, discussed in *Shakespeare's Theatre of War* (Aldershot, UK: Ashgate, 1998), 31–9.

15. Blandy was removed from a fellowship at New College, Oxford, shortly after becoming B.A. in July 1566, for popery (*DNB*).

16. Shapiro, *Shakespeare and the Jews*, 184: 'Marlowe had anticipated Shakespeare in identifying Jews as aliens, and Elizabethan theatergoers in 1593 would surely have been alert to how closely Barabas' activities in *The Jew of Malta* resembled those attributed to the dangerous aliens in their midst.'

17. Montesquieu, *The Spirit of Laws*, trans. Thomas Nugent (New York, 1900), 1:XX.i.316. For discussion of the issue, see Pagden, *Lords of all the World*, especially chs 6 and 7.

18. Alison Hoppen, *The Fortification of Malta by the Order of St. John, 1530–1798* (Edinburgh: Scottish Academic Press, 1979), 69. A general history of the Hospitallers is in Desmond Seward, *The Monks of War: The Military Religious Orders*, rev. ed. (Harmondsworth: Penguin, 1995).

19. Desiderus Erasmus, *Enchiridion militis christiani* [*The Handbook of the Christian Soldier*], trans. Charles Fantazzi and ed. John W. O'Malley, in *The Collected Works of Erasmus* (Toronto: University of Toronto Press, 1988), 66:91.

20. Erasmus, *Erasmus on his Times: A Shortened Version of* The Adages, ed. Margaret Mann Phillips (Cambridge: Cambridge University Press, 1967), 133. Erasmus had even less sympathy for merchants than soldiers, however: 'The merchant class hold nothing sacred except financial profit, to which they devote themselves entirely, as if to God. By this alone they assess godliness, friendship, honour, reputation, everything either in heaven or earth. The rest is nonsense' (34).

21. Erasmus, *The Erasmus Reader*, ed. Erika Rummel (Toronto: University of Toronto Press, 1990), 325.

22. Precisely these lines of thinking are observed by Stephen Marx in Shakespeare's battle plays. See his 'Shakespeare's Pacifism,' *Renaissance Quarterly* 45 (1992): 49–95. For an older but thorough account of the literary aspects of humanist pacifism, see Robert P. Adams, *The Better Part of Valor: More, Erasmus, Colet, and Vives, on Humanism, War, and Peace, 1496–1535* (Seattle: University of Washington Press, 1962).

23. Matar, 'English Renaissance Soldiers,' 81–94.

24. Emily C. Bartels, 'Malta, the Jew, and the Fictions of Difference: Colonialist Discourse in Marlowe's *The Jew of Malta*,' *English Literary Renaissance* 20 (1990): 9.

25. Stephen Greenblatt, *Renaissance Self Fashioning* (Chicago: University of Chicago Press, 1980), points out that Marlowe's heroes frequently engage in repetitive acts that signify their efforts constantly to reproduce themselves in a universe where theatricalized identity is as much identity as one ever possesses (206).

26. Lloyd Edward Kermode reminds us not to allow 'our modern sensitivities [to] mislead us on the question of whether we expect [the other characters in the play] to object to the ferocity of Barabas' punishment' during the confiscation or, presumably, in the final scene ('"Marlowe's Second City": The Jew as Critic at the Rose in 1592,' *SEL* 35 [1995], 219). While it is valuable to remember that Marlowe's culture was indeed steeped in anti-Semitism, nevertheless it seems to me that the play offers spectators an opportunity (at least) to reframe that prejudice in the denouement, especially if we are able to hear Barabas's screams, much as we might hear the screams from other disenfranchised characters across all of Marlowe's plays.

27. On the medieval view that honor in battle and the plunder of profit are reconcilable, see John Barnie, *War in Medieval Society: Social Values and the Hundred Years War, 1337–99* (London: Weidenfeld & Nicolson, 1974), especially 67–70.

28. Raymond de Roover, *Business, Banking, and Economic Thought in Late*

Medieval and Early Modern Europe, ed. Julius Kirshner (Chicago: University of Chicago Press, 1974), 347; Geoffrey Parker, *The Military Revolution: Military Innovation and the Rise of the West, 1500–1800* (Cambridge: Cambridge University Press, 1988), 62.

29. Greenblatt, *Renaissance Self Fashioning*, 206.

30. Michael Drayton, *The Barrons Warres*, cited in *Edward the Second*, ed. W. Moelwyn Merchant, New Mermaids Series (London: Black, 1987), xxi.

31. Erasmus complains of real-life priests such as are caricatured in Jacomo and Bernardine: 'The Romanists of today have become market-stall holders. What is it they sell? It is male and female pudenda, goods most worthy of these merchants whose avarice and irreligion are worse than the most sordid obscenity imaginable' (Phillips, *Erasmus on his times*, 74).

32. Simon Shepherd, *Marlowe and the Politics of Elizabethan Theatre* (Brighton: Harvester, 1986), 172, sees it as evidence of Marlowe's critique of Barabas's imperial notion of paternity. I prefer his reading to that of Alan Friedman, 'The Shackling of Accidents in Marlowe's *Jew of Malta*,' *Texas Studies in Language and Literature* 8 (1966): 155–67, who argues that in conjuring Agamemnon's sacrifice of Iphigenia, Barabas reveals a naïve grasp of the impact of sacrificing Abigail (159).

33. Patricia Klindienst Joplin, 'The Voice of the Shuttle is Ours,' in *Rape and Representation*, ed. Lynn A. Higgins and Brenda R. Silver (New York: Columbia University Press, 1991), 44.

34. Bowers's edition of the play silently emends '*Catho diobola*' to '*Cazzo diabole*.'

35. In recent years, the intersection of state power and anti-Semitism has received much attention from scholars. In the post-Second World War period, G.K. Hunter was among the first critics to meet such questions head on; his scholarship on these questions has been reprinted in *Dramatic Identities and Cultural Tradition* (Liverpool: Liverpool University Press, 1978). Shapiro, *Shakespeare and the Jews*, offers a convincing critique of Hunter's scholarship, 83–5. Regarding Marlowe's depiction of anti-Semitism, see also Bartels, 'Malta, The Jew'; Stephen Greenblatt, 'Marlowe, Marx, and Anti-Semitism,' *Critical Inquiry* 5 (1978): 291–307; and Thomas Cartelli, 'Shakespeare's *Merchant*, Marlowe's *Jew*: The Problem of Cultural Difference,' *Shakespeare Studies* 20 (1987): 255–60.

36. Richard A. McCabe, *Incest, Drama and Nature's Law, 1550–1700* (Cambridge: Cambridge University Press, 1993), 292.

37. Jean-Louis Flandrin, *Families in Former Times: Kinship, Household, and Sexuality*, trans. Richard Southern (Cambridge: Cambridge University Press, 1979): 'It seems that the authority of parents and their powers of coercion of their children increased from the sixteenth century onwards' as a result of renewed faith in absolute monarchy, Roman law, and the ideas of antiquity (130).

38. Mary Douglas, *Purity and Danger: An Analysis of Concepts of Pollution and Taboo* (1966; rpt New York: Routledge & Kegan Paul, 1970), 126–7, 121.

39. For analysis of cultural assumptions about bodily fluids and functions in early modern England, see Gail Kern Paster, *The Body Embarrassed: Drama and the Disciplines of Shame in Early Modern England* (Ithaca: Cornell University Press, 1993), to which my reading of the poisoning episode is indebted.

40. Augustine, *De Ordine* 2.4, in *Patrologiae Cursus Completus Series Latina*, ed. J.P. Migne (Paris, 1845), 32:1000. Quoted by Aquinas in *Summa Theologica*, 2.2.10.11, in *Opera Omnia* (Rome, 1895), 8:93.

41. Jacques Rossiaud, *Medieval Prostitution*, trans. Lydia G. Cochrane (London: Blackwell, 1988), 42.

42. Rossiaud, ibid., speculates that a courtesan was 'held to be infinitely more dangerous than other women of easy virtue . . . because she demanded ever more money and fine clothing' (132).

43. William Kerrigan and Gordon Braden, describing the Petrarchan lover in *The Idea of the Renaissance* (Baltimore: Johns Hopkins University Press, 1989), 160. T.W. Craik's edition of *The Jew of Malta*, New Mermaids Series (1966, rpt New York: Norton, 1983), prints 'Allamira' for Bellamira at 4.2.53.

44. For an elegant argument about the ways *The Jew of Malta* employs the 'literary genre of the revenge play' to explore 'the popular conception of the Jew' and usury in the early modern period, see David H. Thurn, 'Economic and Ideological Exchange in Marlowe's *The Jew of Malta*,' *Theatre Journal* 46 (1994), especially 161–5.

45. Philip J. Finkelpearl, *Court and Country Politics in the Plays of Beaumont and Fletcher* (Princeton: Princeton University Press, 1990), 92–3.

46. Francis Beaumont, *The Knight of the Burning Pestle*, ed. John Doebler, Regents Drama Series (Lincoln: University of Nebraska Press, 1967), 1:242–3, 4:70.

47. Philip Massinger, *The Renegado*, ed. Daniel J. Vitkus (New York: Columbia University Press, 2000), 2.5.64–73.

CHAPTER FIVE

The Death of Ramus and Rhetoric in *The Massacre at Paris*

> Let us confess the truth: if anyone should sift out of the army . . .
> those who march in it from the pure zeal of affection for religion . . .
> he could not make up one complete company of men-at-arms out of
> them.
>
> Montaigne, *Apology for Raymond Sebond*[1]

The tattered manuscript of *The Massacre at Paris* survives in what J.B. Steane has rightly called a 'much maimed and abbreviated form.'[2] My reading of what we do have suggests the play to be a less vile and more subtle response to the 1572 slaughter of Protestants in Paris than critics have allowed, especially when *The Massacre* is located amidst other English responses to that horror. For the most part, contemporaries who told the story of the day that shocked and galvanized all of Protestant Christendom did so in the context of delivering to partisan English readers bellicose, propagandistic narratives of the wars of religion that had plagued France since the 1560s. Rather than follow the saber-rattling narrative strategies and ideological partisanship of contemporaries such as Anne Dowriche, George Whetstone, François Hotman, and John Stubbs, Marlowe treats the episode less passionately, which is a surprise. It's true that he supplies the requisite stock of Catholic villains (Catherine de Medici and the duke of Guise, for starters) for whom many in his audiences would have had a proven appetite. Yet the play is strangely far from the Marlowe we are familiar with. The brutality here is seldom encapsulated in glorious poetry, and the men of war are not only taciturn, but unambiguously vile. Some wags might say that that is always true of Marlowe's soldiers, but his soldiers are generally treated more ambiguously in his other plays, where they may be pumped up with bloodlust, but can articulate its value with golden tongues.

Marlowe's greatest departure from English accounts of the massacre is his assumption that the events were not fundamentally motivated by genuine disagreements about religion. His play dissolves that pretense. It does this in part by staging vignettes featuring high-profile historical personages (of both religious persuasions) whom we get to see actively resisting being bullied by military fanatics, and who get murdered for the rhetorical and physical resistance they have mounted. Among them are the logician and regius professor of rhetoric Peter Ramus, France's lord admiral Jasper Coligny, Charles IX, and Henry III. Even the duchess of Guise is subject to the terror inflicted upon France by her fanatical husband and his family, the Medici. The particulars of their murders, the threatened uxoricide of the duchess, and the evocation of the slaughter of thousands of nameless Protestants all take us down the path of the play's contempt for religious practice as little more than a façade for worldly ambition and its related temporal desires. If that were the sum of the playwright's vision of the troubles in France, however, then *The Massacre at Paris* would stand out among English discourses on the topic for its thick cynicism toward religion as a whole, but its largely orthodox anti-Catholic sentiments would otherwise mark it as so much Protestant propaganda that pervades the period. I would contend on several scores that *The Massacre* is not at all propaganda. In part it invites us to consider what is explored in more artful ways in *Doctor Faustus*, namely the impact of the European wars of religion on contemporary attitudes toward individual, intellectual, and state security, especially as it relates to the status and the future prospects of the ordinary soldiers impressed to carry out those internal and international wars.

In a way these wars revived old opportunities for holy crusades against an infidel that medieval Christians had had available as a way of warding off internecine strife and solidifying their state or other governmental structure, whatever that was. But now things are different: the opportunities for jihad against Protestants or Catholics are often available on home turf rather than far away in the Middle East or elsewhere, and can be construed as 'opportunities' only in some limited and ambivalent senses of that word. As we will see again in the analysis of *Faustus* in Chapter 6, a play in which Marlowe attends to similar concerns, the opportunities for Christian holy war against other Christians in the sixteenth century narrowed the gap between the two groups of men who had carried out the earlier medieval crusades: priests and soldiers. Both *The Massacre* and *Doctor Faustus* develop the common ground between the two retinues. One occupation was (is) a highly organized profession endowed with the power to administer the sacraments and for the most part enjoying the status that goes hand in hand with moral rectitude, or its appearance, at least in Catholic nations; the other occupation in Marlowe's time was not yet a profession, as any number of Elizabethan handbook writers complain, but instead a motley collection of fickle bands of opportunists and, in England, more often, the conscripted poor and the down-and-out. In a casual bid on behalf of soldiers for increased social respectability, in fact, Barnabe Rich asserts that priests and soldiers deserve to be recognized as fellow warriors. It occurs to him that they are made from the same mold, and he invokes the language of Platonism to press his point: 'But what profession is free from counterfeites,' he asks,

> when Divinity it selfe is sometimes made but a cloke for hipocrites: And here if I might but crave a litle licence, I might speake of a kinde and manner of affinity, that is between the Devine and the Souldier, sympathizing and concurring so nearly together, that both their vertues and their vices might bee saide to bee a kinne, and to have proceeding from one originall: they are both warriors, the one with the word, the other with the sword.[3]

Rich is working against the grain, cheerfully hoping that the Platonic association he is asserting will help steer public opinion. For in spite of the flourishing of orders of monk-soldiers earlier in the sixteenth century, for the most part at the end of the century and in the first half of the next, the gap between English divines and English soldiers was as wide as that between the Roman Catholic priests and Catholic soldiers. It was in effect a lacuna that allowed the Roman Catholic Church in particular to have its way, by force if necessary, in secular affairs, with which bishops and priests were often deeply entangled, while still preserving its claims of transcendental authority and of *pax christi*. As we have seen in *The Jew of Malta* and to a lesser extent in *Edward II*, the incongruity of the priests' commitments can be exploited by Marlowe for its endless entertainment value with English audiences, usually by igniting its comic potential energy. In a performance of *The Massacre*, of course, there would be precious little laughter or the social leveling it sometimes provides. But a subtle form of leveling would still be in play on the stage as Catholics and Protestants went about murdering and mayhem. Paradoxically, what is targeted for leveling is the mental architecture of militarism shared by prelates and soldiers in the play who are tools of the state and, even more so, the mentalité of kings and dukes who use soldiers to support the Church in a façade for worldly ends. Seeing a performance of *The Massacre* might persuade us that the play works by negation, pitting its soldiers, priests, prelates, and kings against the few poor souls who try to escape their mindless wrath, and suggesting to us, as Rich proposes but in a way he most likely never intends, that perhaps priests and soldiers are cut from the same mold after all.

Historical contexts

In 1572 Catherine de Medici, dowager queen of France, arranged for her Roman Catholic daughter Margaret of Valois to marry the Protestant king Henry of Navarre. On 18 August on the steps of Notre

Dame in Paris the couple exchanged vows, hoping by their union to create détente in the religious wars that had wracked France for two decades. The fragile peace collapsed four days later. On the morning of 22 August, a sniper wounded France's most beloved Protestant, a military officer of the highest rank, Jasper Coligny Shatillion. As Lord Admiral of France,[4] Coligny had come to Paris with a group of veteran soldiers to see Henry and Margaret wed. On the 24th, St Bartholomew's Day, assassins struck Coligny again, fatally this time, in his residence. His corpse was thrown from a window into the street, his head cut off and genitals mutilated. The corpse was paraded through the city.

The admiral's murder was only the first of several thousand to be committed in the week following, known collectively as the St Bartholomew's Day Massacre. At the time, chroniclers had difficulty separating facts from rumors, and anxieties of conspiracy abounded; centuries later, the massacre continues to pique modern historians.[5] Contemporary Protestant pamphleteers put the number of deaths in the tens and sometimes hundreds of thousands,[6] but historians have now reduced those estimates. Regardless, everyone agrees that a frightening number of civilians were murdered in Paris and around France during several days of bloodletting. Children were sacrificed alongside Protestant adults who believed that religious dissent had protection under the law. Several leading public figures were among the casualties. One was Peter Ramus, some of whose work on logic and rhetoric had argued along Calvinist lines for radical religious freedom.[7] Later in this chapter I will argue that the dramatized murder of Ramus, while brief, is nevertheless a crux of the play.

When news of the event reached the Vatican, Giorgio Vasari was commissioned to make frescoes glorifying the Catholic victory over heretics; Gregory XIII celebrated a *Te Deum*.[8] In England, of course, the massacre was greeted with anything but prayers of thanksgiving. That October, the Church of England published a prayer alluding to the débâcle. Composed by royal command, the prayer petitions God to spare England from an external enemy, whose identity is artfully metaphorical: 'O Lorde, the counsayle of the wicked conspireth agaynst us: and our enemies are daylye in hande to swalowe us up . . . Save us from the Lions mouthes, and from the hornes of the Unicornes: leste they devour us and teare us in peeces.'[9] This image of unicorns is tricky. By literary convention they may symbolize purity; and they are capable of being tamed when folded into the arms of a virgin (such as Queen Elizabeth, perhaps?).[10] The lion imagery is more obvious. Like the Christians thrown to the lions in ancient Rome, the prayer suggests that England ought to see itself as being pitted against a corrupt Roman empire. Moreover, the prayer is accompanied by the royal command that until further notice, Englishmen and women must all gather for worship not only on Sundays and holidays, but also Wednesdays and Fridays.[11] Presumably this new obligation is imposed to promote national unity by inhibiting religious dissent of the sort that is then tearing France apart.

As the creation of a special prayer suggests, the official government response to the massacre was more sorrowful (and perhaps fearful) than condemnatory. Unlike what might be the case in modern diplomacy, the abuse of human rights in France did not prompt England to decide to intervene in its neighbor's internal affairs.[12] Yet England was watchful. One way to measure its interest is to count books published in London having to do with matters French. Excepting a handful of books on the Turks or about voyages to Brazil or Florida, virtually all English books on foreign affairs published in the latter half of the sixteenth century[13] focus on France, Spain, or the Spanish Netherlands. For the decade 1571–80, A.G. Dickens counts 38 books on France. And for the years 1589–90 alone, 117 such titles. Yet as Dickens notes, more than 85 percent of those 117 titles were translations of French texts.[14] That percentage points to a climate of intellectual curiosity in the turmoil surrounding the succession of Henry IV upon the murder of Henry III. It may also imply little tolerance for books about the troubles by English authors, lest they interfere with the queen's enigmatic diplomacy that often turned upon the tantalizing possibility of a dynastic marriage uniting the thrones of England and France. Dickens reminds us that Elizabeth aimed for neutrality toward France's disposition of its internal strife. She did so in part because she needed France as an ally to keep Spain, a more aggressive Catholic adversary, in check.[15] To this end she had as suitors, after failing to come to terms with Philip, not only Henry III of France but also Catherine de Medici's younger son, the Protestant François, duke of Alençon. In making a play about the French royal family, then, Marlowe took a risk by writing about historical personages who had had such close dealings with Elizabeth's government.

In contrast to Marlowe's diplomatic rendering of the Medicis a decade later, John Stubbs had published a vitriolic attack on the French royal family in 1579, the year Elizabeth was engaged to marry Alençon. In *The Discovery of a Gaping Gulf*, Stubbs dissuades the queen from that alliance by interpreting the massacre as a divine signal warning against trusting the French in any way:

> A king falsified his sworn word; the marriage of a king's sister imbrued with blood; a king murdered his subjects; many noble and honorable gentlemen shamefully used; valiant men surprised by cowards in their beds; innocents put to death; women and children without pity tossed upon halberds and thrown down windows and into rivers; learned men killed by barbarous soldiers. (26)

Stubbs's language recollects Virgil's descriptions of Troy in defeat, anticipating the tale of bloody chaos that Marlowe's Aeneas will narrate in *Dido*. The lesson of Troy is embedded in Stubbs's imagination, for he quotes a salient bit of wisdom from the *Aeneid*: '*Timeo Danaos vel dona ferentes* (I fear the Greeks, even when they offer gifts)' (40, citing *Aeneid* 2:49). In Stubbs's text, the maxim becomes even more haunting when we remember how the English traced their ancestry to Aeneas.[16] Building on fantasies of horror in his treatise, Stubbs concludes that the union of Queen Elizabeth and a French prince – even a Protestant one bearing dynastic gifts – would lead to disaster for England:

> And if intermarriages amongst themselves in their own family cannot stay this fury of theirs, but that for religion only and none other quarrel their very pity is cruelty even upon their own bowels, murdering and massacring one another by thousands and ten thousands, how shall any marriage make them friends to us. (26, 40)

It is well known that the Privy Council punished Stubbs for his unauthorized advice by amputating his right hand and confiscating the copies of his book that could be located. His punishment is a reminder of Elizabeth's capacity for invoking martial law, as when in 1588, for example, she proclaimed 'death by Marshall Lawe' to those English soldiers who refused to serve in the Low Countries after accepting money for being conscripted.[17] In efforts to abort the engagement of Elizabeth and Alençon, then, Stubbs and others inflamed nationalism by claiming that under Alençon's projected command as king of England, English soldiers might become as 'barbarous' as the French troops who had carried out the massacre. Worse, English soldiers might be sacrificed in foreign campaigns led by inept or malignant commanders. Again, John Stubbs: if the marriage comes to pass, 'our soldiers of necessity must be sent out under some Joab for some more desperate service than Saint-Quentin, one way or other to be dispatched and cut in pieces' (90). As it is, he says, those French soldiers who effected the bloodletting in 1572 had won only a 'barbarous, *unmanlike*, and treasonous' victory (81; my emphasis).

In 1576 George Gascoigne had issued a parallel warning of threats to martial English manhood in his eyewitness account of the sack of Antwerp by troops commanded by the duke of Alva, a Spaniard. The 1576 sack was widely viewed by Protestants as companion proof of Catholic infamy. Moreover, political tensions surrounding the question of who would hold military command in the Low Countries may also have figured in the attack on Admiral Coligny.[18] In his report, Gascoigne implored the English to 'learn to detest the horrible cruelties of the Spaniards in all executions of warlike strategems, lest the dishonour of such beastly deeds might bedim the honour wherewith English soldiers have always been endowed in their victories.'[19] In these terms Gascoigne and Stubbs project a distinctive, nationalist innocence upon English militarism and English manhood. Some ten years later, Barnabe Rich again attempts to indemnify English soldiers in print. In *A Path-way to Military Practise* (1587) he argues that soldiers also protect society from civil war. 'It is the soldier as *Varo* sayeth, that resisteth the outward force of enemies, that represseth domestic seditions, and defendeth the liberty of subjects.'[20] *The Massacre at Paris* dramatizes Marlowe's skepticism toward that claim.

In the wake of the attacks on Protestants in both Antwerp and Paris, those English commentators who were not directly affiliated with court seem to have been more or less of one mind that royal union with either Spain or France would vitiate national security. Adopting a medical paradigm, Stubbs diagnoses France as having a 'contagion,' a 'sickness of mind' that threatens to 'infect our minds' (3). This image of infection is used by other writers to reinforce an English nationalist dogma of purity; in Marlowe's play, as I discuss in the next section, it is used by both sides to justify ethnic cleansing. What shall save England from going the way of France, George Whetstone says, continuing Stubbs's medical trope in 1586, is none other than Queen Elizabeth herself: 'Her mercy is the Phisition of forraine afflictions.'[21] This trope of France as a diseased body – its soldiers figuratively emasculated (rendered 'unmanlike') in effect by their own form of cruelty – reiterates an ancient Anglo-Gallic hostility.[22] Surveying the troubles in France, Whetstone arrives at ultimate conclusions: 'For where was there a more savage crueltie ever committed, then the massacre of *Paris*.'[23] While George Whetstone couches his judgment in the pretense of a rhetorical question, the poet Anne Dowriche, his contemporary, speaks more directly: 'ages new and olde have never seene the like in Christendome.'[24]

Most critics of *The Massacre at Paris* have assumed it replicates Protestant propaganda. Among its detractors, David Bevington remains the most eloquent: '*The Massacre at Paris* is an appallingly savage catalogue of atrocities, committed by the Catholic Guises against the Huguenots, with no attempt to explore historical complexities or to soften the rabid prejudices of the pamphlets on which the play is based.'[25] More than a decade ago, however, Julia Briggs made it difficult to read *The Massacre at Paris* quite as Bevington and others have done. Attending to its structure as well as its presentation of historical material, Briggs argues convincingly that the play is not '"obviously" a piece of crude Protestant propaganda.'[26] Focusing on the ways Marlowe handles his historical material, Briggs presses the script for its ironic moments. 'What makes the policy of religious intolerance advocated in the play's final scenes look suspiciously ironic,' she writes, turning to John Stubbs,

> is that the effects of such policies had themselves already been vividly dramatized in the earlier scenes showing the massacre. Marlowe, faced with the apparently endless cycle of retaliation that characterized the French civil wars, like many of his contemporaries, must have come to doubt whether 'one more act of violence could cure a world whose malady was aimless violence.'[27]

Following Briggs, in this chapter I take it as axiomatic that the play, even in its 'maimed' form, is more subtle in its allegiances and more sophisticated in its critique of violence than literary critics have understood. Bloody? Yes. Exultant? No. I suggest that what has seemed to critics to be Marlowe's 'failure' in this script may have been on his part a deliberate strategy of refusing to sentimentalize civil war, much as Wilfred Owen, say, had refused the invitation to write the kind of nationalist poetry that could have been used as an aesthetic unguent for the wounds of world war in the twentieth century.[28]

The interrogation of violence in *The Massacre* proceeds as much by spectacle as by dialogue or soliloquy. In fact the play contains surprisingly little of the grandstanding we expect to hear in the voices of Marlovian soldiers; when they do deliver justifications of their actions, their voices are at low decibels. Dissidents' voices are likewise the most feeble of any in Marlowe, an irony considering that Peter Ramus, famous as an intellectual debater and trouble-maker, should be one of the many victims in 'Paris.' On stage, Catholic and Protestant factions alike quietly cut down their enemies in cold blood, without expressing much remorse or joy. The world is thus remade by their violence without the benefit of that violence first being sanitized through poetry. That absence alone may help explain part of the play's negative critical reception, compared, say, to *Tamburlaine*, which is just as bloody but, in its rich language, has also been more beautiful to literary critics. The absence of ennobling speeches by soldiers does allow playgoers to hear well the voices of characters who protest a militarist mentalité. Yet those characters' resistance to 'Caesar,' as Guise styles himself, is no less perfunctory than the soldiers' justifications of their murders. Guise fancies himself a modern Tamburlaine. Although he sometimes shares the Scythian's habits of mind discussed in Chapter 1, more often he reminds us of Mortimer Junior – that is, a lesser Tamburlaine. One of the duke's liabilities is his bad habit of mocking his principles. In soliloquy, Guise admits his plot to slaughter the Protestants is not impelled by any sort of theological dispute. To say it is, is a joke:

Religion: *O Diabole!*
Fie, I am asham'd, however that I seem,
To think a word of such a simple sound,
Of so great matter should be made the ground.

2.63–6

Speaking with Mortimer's arrogant pragmatism, Guise divulges a
related but more powerful motive for deconstructing the present world
as Charles IX has composed it. Using his tongue not his sword, Guise
expects to rescue France from the leadership of a king who is not
sufficiently invested in the mental habits of martial law, and who is,
instead, like Edward II, invested in a dangerous ideal of gentle pleasure:

The gentle King, whose pleasure uncontroll'd
Weak'neth his body and will waste his realm,
If I repair not what he ruinates:
Him, as a child, I daily win with words,
So that for proof he barely bears the name.

2.67–71

Like Mortimer, Guise convicts Charles of ruining France, and elects
himself its culture hero. He justifies the chaos of the massacre as an
antidote to the turmoil extant in the kingdom.

Genocide?

s.d.: *with their swords drawn, chasing the* Protestants

GUISE: *Tue, tue, tue!*
           Let none escape, murder the Huguenots!
ANJOY: Kill them, kill them!   *Exeunt.*   6. s.d., 1–3

Historians disagree as to whether the massacre constituted an episode
of 'genocide' proper. Janine Estebe, calling it 'un crime rituel . . . un
holocauste,' argues that it was indeed genocide because of the tactics
used: 'Les femmes enceintes constituent véritablement des victimes de
choix; on leur ouvre le ventre et on tue l'enfant à naître. . . . Il s'agit
donc d'éteindre une race étrangère, une race haïe et maudite.' Estebe's
conclusions have been faulted by Natalie Zemon Davis in a well-known
essay on ritual violence in sixteenth-century France. There is 'little
evidence,' she counters, 'that the Catholic killers wished to exterminate
a "foreign race."'[29] While Estebe may go too far in likening the
massacre to the Holocaust, perhaps Davis does not go far enough.
Historical evidence absorbed by Marlowe's play suggests that Catholics
and Protestants were understood to belong not only to different sects
but, in effect, to different races. Roman Catholics especially saw

Protestant reformers as infected by foreign ideas – and so sometimes *as* putative foreigners.[30]

Hotman and Dowriche illustrate how sixteenth-century writers certainly considered the massacre an instance of ethnic cleansing, if that euphemism is not too mild an expression. We may hear that conclusion in the speech Hotman puts in the mouth of Guise as his soldiers assemble to receive their orders for the attack: 'He sayd that the kings meaning was to destroye all the Rebels which had in these late yeares borne armes against his majestie, and *to roote out the race* of those wicked men.'[31] In her poem *The French Historie* Dowriche invents a meeting of the French Privy Council at which Catherine de Medici and Charles IX are addressed by Satan. Fancifully expanding Hotman's version of events, Dowriche has Satan propose that Protestants be 'rooted out.' In her poem, Charles is later condemned by a Protestant martyr for possessing a 'base polluted minde'; Roman Catholics are reviled for being a 'false dissembling race!'[32]

The murder of Admiral Coligny

Keeping in mind Briggs's argument that Marlowe variously presents the massacre from both Catholic and Protestant perspectives, we now turn directly to Marlowe's text, and first to the distinctly Protestant episode of Admiral Coligny's murder. While the pamphlet sources only mention the event in passing, Marlowe seizes upon it as a quintessential illustration of what may happen to soldiers who refuse to collaborate further with warmongers, and who suffer expulsion for their dissent.[33] Guise and other enemies of the admiral come to understand his Protestant faith metonymically as a protest of their totalitarian state control over belief itself. Marlowe gives virtually no exposition of Coligny's life up to the assassination, presumably because his biography was so well known in sixteenth-century London; indeed, as late as 1650 Randle Cotgrave, compiling an English–French dictionary, counted on the martyr Coligny's being a household name in England.[34] It had become one much earlier in France. Jean de Serres reports that in a 1543 battle against the Dauphin, Coligny had so successfully imposed a code of 'warlyke disciplyne' on his men that it had been incorporated into royal statute; he had gone on to other significant military and diplomatic victories.

Understood in the context of Coligny's distinguished military career, a thick irony coats the thin justifications of the admiral's murder in Marlowe's play. He is killed, essentially, for being an obstacle to martial law under Catherine and Guise. Indeed, irony is a pervasive feature of

Marlowe's exposition of events leading up to the assassination, as it seems to have been in the historical Coligny's life. Having once been a prisoner of war in Antwerp under a Protestant army, for example, the historical Coligny remained, and in Marlowe's play is still, a soldier committed to the efficacy of war as the principal means of constructing a community. Having converted from Roman Catholicism during that internment, he remains loyal to a Catholic king and country. And in spite of being a seasoned soldier who knows of Guise's plot to 'murder all the Protestants' (1.30), he is ambushed without much of a fight. In Marlowe's hands, he comes off as politically naïve, even reckless toward his personal safety. Consider his conduct in Scene 1 as an example. He marvels that Guise 'Dares once adventure without the King's consent / To meddle or attempt such dangerous things' as the plot to exterminate Protestants (1.36–7). As is the case with many soldiers, his judgment is better on the high seas or the battlefield than in society. He is no match for Machiavellian forces at court.

Marlowe presses this point in Scene 4, where Charles visits Coligny as he recuperates from the first assassination wound. The scene opens with Catherine figuratively fixing her sights on her prey: 'Now have we got the fatal, straggling deer, / Within the compass of a deadly toil' (4.2–3). Although Charles weakly protests his mother's plan to finish off Coligny in a second attack, he quickly caves in – 'What you determine, I will ratify' (4.25). Remembering his mother's command to 'make a show as if all were well' (4.47), in the rest of the scene Charles falsely chats up Coligny in his bedchamber, promising 'as I am King of France' (4.52) to protect him without fail and to take revenge upon the sniper. In lines bloated with irony that even the soon-to-be-assassinated Charles cannot see, he professes insincerely, 'I am not more secure myself / Than I am careful you should be preserved' (4.61–2). These words acknowledge the role of this – or any – Lord Admiral in the maintenance of state order and in the consequent sanctity of kingship.

Less than 30 lines into the next scene, the admiral is dead by the hand of a minor character, Gonzago. Gonzago might be read, as Lightborne is in *Edward II*, as a harbinger of the rising power of military hard-liners. While the murder of an admiral is not quite the same thing as regicide, both figures are sacrificed in *coups d'état* led by men who intend to eradicate the Other. Whether that Other be a homosexual husband or a Lutheran in the service of Roman Catholics, the aim is roughly the same – to purge from the community a man whose dissent from an arbitrary but definitive set of orthodox fictions has become uncontainable. An independent, dissident voice is intolerable to one such as Guise, who is compelled by his political goals and psychic makeup to see the world in autarkic terms. There is ample evidence of

Guise's ambition to eliminate dissidents in the admiral's murder scene. It begins with solemn oaths from Dumaine, Retes, and Gonzago to do as their leader commands, 'to kill all that you suspect of heresy' (5.3). The duke of Anjoy goes even further. He brags that, being in disguise so 'none knows who I am,' he shall 'therefore mean to murder all I meet' (5.5–6). The admiral is selected for the first strike because, as Guise twice notes, he is 'Chief standard-bearer to the Lutherans' (5.11, 39). The repetition of the line may highlight the faultiness of the text; the image itself is perhaps intended to tarnish the admiral's military reputation by suggesting that he is a traitor not only to Roman Catholicism, but also to martial valor, in caring more about his religion than his life at arms. From that point of view, it is significant that Guise specifically orders Coligny 'murdered in his bed' (5.13). In this way he is disgraced, denied the honor even of a proper fight. Indeed the entire episode lacks the grandeur of an epic death. Coligny is allowed only a hasty single line of prayer as he dies, and plans are immediately laid for having his head and hands sent as a gift to the pope. On stage he is spuriously eulogized by Guise, who 'stamps' the corpse (5.41). In hyperbole reminiscent of Tamburlaine's plans to win Asia Minor, the sight of the admiral's corpse further inspires Guise to declare that if his own troops 'Will be as resolute as I,' 'There shall not a Huguenot breathe in France' (5.49–50).

As if to draw attention to the scale of human destruction that is imagined by Guise in his promise, Marlowe invents two provocative moments in which 100 helpless Huguenots are set up for slaughter. In an age before technology would permit instantaneous wholesale slaughter in war, as it does today, the quick dispatch of 100 persons would likely have seemed mind-boggling to an Elizabethan audience more accustomed to prolonged combat with inefficient methods of inflicting death. Some of Marlowe's critics have seized upon the magnitude of death in the play to condemn what they take to be, in Roy Eriksen's words, his 'crank delight in brutality.'[35] But they ignore that most of the deaths take place off stage in the usual way; and many more are simply fantasized by the Roman Catholic aggressors.

It is arguably those fantasies – not bloody action – that animate the version of events Marlowe presents on stage. In Scene 9, for instance, the conspirator Dumaine remembers his oath from Scene 5 'to kill all that you suspect of heresy.' Guise announces that 100 Protestants have been driven into the river Seine, where they 'swim about and so preserve their lives: / How may we do? I fear me they will live' (9.58–9). Dumaine proposes sharpshooters armed with 'bows and darts' be stationed on the bridge to 'sink them in the river as they swim' (9.61, 62). Scene 11 features a second instance of planning to slaughter defenseless civilians.

Guise has had intelligence reports that 'a hundred Huguenots and more' (11.20) congress daily in the woods outside Paris. There, he informs Catherine, they 'do hold their synogogue' (11.21). As H.J. Oliver notes, 'synogogue' was sometimes applied derisively toward Puritans as well as Jews in the early modern period.[36] As I demonstrate below, however, it is not religious prejudice that motivates Guise to inform Catherine that 'thither will I to put them to the sword' (11.23). Nor is *she* genuinely motivated by religious prejudice:

> Do so, sweet Guise, let us delay no time,
> For if these stragglers gather head again
> And disperse themselves throughout the realm of France,
> It will be hard for us to work their deaths.
>
>   11.24–7

Ericksen has argued that Catherine is little more than a 'mouth-piece' for Guise, but in fact just the opposite seems true.[37] Most of the times when the duke describes the actions of the state as expressing their united will, Marlowe undercuts that chauvinistic assumption by portraying Catherine as keen to contain all who resist her absolute dominion. She is never in doubt about the scope of her power. As she makes plans to have the soft-hearted Charles dispatched, she reminds the cardinal of Lorraine, 'Catherine must have her will in France' (11.38). As the queen is obviously so adept at martial rhetoric, her character also helps to 'prove' the constructedness of martial masculinity for playgoers.

The executions of a hundred Huguenots at a clip may gladden the tyrants. Nevertheless they understand that dissenting speech is best silenced, as it were, by cutting it off at the neck, by decapitating the leadership of the so-called rabble. Thus the admiral's corpse has had symbolic meaning for the tyrants even before his murder. Earlier in Scene 5 the duke of Anjoy had invoked the analogies of the head as governor of the body, and of the body as a correspondent of the body politic, saying that once the admiral is dead, 'the head being off, the members cannot stand' (5.22). This image is a further sign, if any is needed, that Catholics in the play think of French Lutherans as constituting a separate body politic. Like a dragon, the Lutheran must be slain: only thus 'shall Catholics flourish once again' (5.21). We are back to the zero-sum vision of the world.

Scene 5 is not the last we see of the Admiral's body. In Scene 11 it returns to signify the supposed threat of a French Protestant infection, from which the duke of Guise and Catherine de Medici claim to be saving France in ordering the massacre. Two players assigned the task of getting rid of the corpse bring it on stage. The second suggests burning it, the fate of heretics. 'O no,' replies the first, 'his body will infect the fire, and the fire the air, and / so we shall be poisoned with him.' Better that he should be thrown into the river Seine, says the first. 'O,' answers the second, ''twill corrupt the water, and the water the fish, and / by the fish ourselves when we eat them' (11.3–4,7–8). This exchange might easily be played as comedy, but it delivers a serious point. Both players, anxious that the body politic not be infected, believe that a single dissident – a dead one at that – has the power to destroy the state. Even dead, Coligny still possesses for them a totemic influence. We might see their anxieties as the rotten fruit of a virulent nationalism that uses tropes of infection and pollution to motivate soldiers to kill people.

Images of pollution and purification permeate not only Marlowe's script but many of the historical documents collateral to it. These images remind us of the ubiquitous xenophobia that undermined the capacity of early modern states to engage one another peaceably; in the aftermath of the massacre the English people were asked to pray to be spared 'the dreadfull plagues, and afflictions of nations round about us.'[38] In 1579 Stubbs had reiterated a common analogy between sexual disease and disorder in the body politic: 'This sickness of mind have the French drawn from those eastern parts of the world, as they did that other horrible disease of the body, and, having already too far westward communicated the one contagion, do now seek notably to infect our minds with the other' (3). In a mode of paranoia, Stubbs envisions an oriental ('Eastern,' not Asian) plague sweeping toward England. His tactic of scapegoating another country is familiar. Hotman, who in Stubbs's mind is already infected with eastern ideas, has his own candidate for what has caused the present chaos in France's body politic: Italy. Under Catherine de Medici's influence, complains Hotman, so many Italians are being admitted to France that some of the French have begun to call their country 'Fraunce-Italian, and some terme it a Colonie, and some a common sinke of Italie' (XXXIX). Hotman reads immigration as invasion, invasion as defilement. The most immediate English experience of the threat of invasion during Marlowe's stint in London came, of course, from the Armada. Its specter shows up in Scene 21 of *The Massacre at Paris*, which depicts Guise's assassination. His death rids France of a fanatic who, in the words of Henry III, had once caused 'the King of Spain's huge fleet / To threaten England' (21.104–5).[39] Barbara Diefendorf argues that such images of infection and pollution became common in sixteenth-century French religious polemic because they justify genocide. The metaphor of the infected state was 'particularly insidious,' she writes, because it 'could be extended to justify annihilation of the Huguenots in the name of the common good.'[40] In short, the fear of infection, played upon by the right demagogue, enables xenophobia, what Klaus Theweleit calls a 'fear of threatening confrontation with the interior,'[41] a defense against the disintegration of ego boundaries. Marlowe's fanatics, as I have argued in previous chapters, adopt a Tamburlainesque xenophobia in a futile effort to keep their own autarkic psychic interiors pristine. They shun contact with people willing to contend with, rather than fight or flee, the vicissitudes of communal life.

In Marlowe's version of the death of Coligny, the admiral is martyred by soldiers whose violence seems motivated by a fear of life's complexities. Eventually they hang Coligny's body from a tree. If their gesture gives a traitor his due, it also parodies the crucifixion, setting up the Valois as blasphemers. This is confirmed as Guise and Catherine, viewing the corpse on the tree, joke about 'our lusty Admiral' (11.13). Catherine complains of the stench, and Guise orders the body thrown in a ditch. All this stage business about the disposition of a corpse is unusual even in revenge tragedies; it harks back to the play's first murder, of the queen mother of Navarre in Scene 3. There the admiral is seen arranging for her remains to be 'honoured with just solemnity' precisely as he is shot by the sniper (3.30). In an early sign of new queen Margaret's sincerity, she is as disturbed as her husband Henry is by the murder of her mother-in-law. She vows her own 'soul is massacred' by the attack, and begs him not to let it 'Infect thy gracious breast' (3.26–7). Thinking back to the destructive energies surfeiting in Tamburlaine's breast, as discussed in Chapter 1, we may see both of Margaret's images as (perhaps too) heavily ironic.

The queen mother has been poisoned by a gift of gloves sent by Guise through an apothecary, who guaranteed them to 'breed a pang of death' (2.14), in Guise's words. It's worth noting that in *The Honourable Reputation of a Soldier* George Whetstone considers poisoning, among 'damnable pollicies,' no way to win a war.[42] The gift is indeed the first volley in Guise's war, not only upon the house of Navarre but upon peace itself. While waiting for the apothecary to arrive on stage, he waxes poetical in one of the play's rare rhetorical celebrations of violence:

> If ever sun stain'd heaven with bloody clouds
> And made it look with terror on the world;
> . . .
> This day, this hour, this fatal night,
> Shall fully show the fury of them all.
>
> 2.3-4, 7–8

When the apothecary enters, however, Guise's hyperbolic conviction dissolves into bathos. He justifies the queen mother's murder by making her a scapegoat, a tactic that becomes even more ridiculous when we remember that the historical queen mother had died some months before the wedding occurred:

> Go, then, present [these gloves] to the Queen Navarre:
> For she is that huge blemish in our eye
> That makes these upstart heresies in France.
>
>   2.20–22

For this claim there is no evidence. Indeed, as the play unfolds it is possible to read Guise's trumped-up complaint against the queen mother of Navarre metaphorically, as an early expression of an autarkic perspective on the world. Yet Guise is no Tamburlaine, for he lacks absolute will. Instead, his is woven with Catherine de Medici's. Parasitically, he feeds off her power as queen mother of the Valois to nourish his own growth toward despotic rule in ways that recall Mortimer Junior's use of Isabella's status in *Edward II*. Mortimer had convinced Queen Isabella to 'be ruled by me, and we will rule the realm' (5.2.5). That conquest had allowed him to declaim, 'The proudest lords salute me as I pass; / I seal, I cancel, I do what I will' (*Edward II* 5.4.48–9).

Things are different in Paris. Guise sounds more like Gaveston lording it over his fellow nobles in Act 1 of *Edward II* than Mortimer sealing and cancelling in Act 5. Guise boasts of Henry III's troops, 'And all his minions stoop when I command. / Why, this 'tis to have an army in the field' (21.49–50). But it is significant that he himself remains Catherine's minion: he is little more than a military servant who executes her ambitions, and sometimes those are disguised as his own. We have had early notice that Marlowe's Catherine is fully capable of sophisticated dissembling that disguises her tyrannical ambition. This is evidenced in Scene 1, in which she is formally invited into the Cathedral by Charles to witness her daughter's wedding. In reply to his invitation to 'honour' the couple, she hisses an aside: their marriage 'I'll dissolve with blood and cruelty' (1.24, 25). Like Marlowe's Edward II, Catherine conceives of dynastic marriage in the most expedient terms. Moreover, given that a new community is said to be formed in the union of marriage, Catherine's remark may be read as further evidence of her intention to 'dissolve' not simply the religious peace that is promised to France through the marriage, but even the efforts to create the new community she has engineered. There is no rational explanation of Catherine's desire to sabotage her daughter's marriage, nor indeed of her willingness elsewhere in the play to sacrifice her sons to sustain her power. In Scene 14, for example, Henry III has been objecting to the army that Guise has independently mustered. Guise sees Henry's complaint as a worrisome sign that he may not be as pliant a monarch as his mother Catherine expected. To mollify Guise, Catherine promises to persuade the new king to rescind his opposition to the duke's private army, or else: 'And if he do deny what I do say, / I'll despatch him with his brother presently, / Tush, all shall die unless I have my will' (14.62–3, 65). Spectators would recognize this as more than an idle threat, since Charles has just been fatally poisoned in Scene 13.

Strong circumstantial evidence of Catherine's responsibility for Charles's murder emerges in Scene 11, where she mimics Tamburlaine's either/or plans for his sons' own wills. Catherine is an astute observer of faces, asking the cardinal of Lorraine, 'have you mark'd of late, / How Charles our son begins for to lament / For the late night's work' of the massacre (11.30–32)? 'Lament' is no noble quality to someone of Catherine's disposition; a sign of remorse, it threatens to weaken the sovereignty of her ambition. And with the cardinal as her witness, she vows to silence Charles for good:

> Catherine must have her will in France:
> As I do live, so surely shall he die,
> And Henry then shall wear the diadem;
> And if he grudge or crosse his mother's will,
> I'll disinherit him and all the rest:
>
> 11.38–42

Sandwiched between these chilling words and the fulfillment of Catherine's promise is the epigrammatic Scene 12. This scene is a signature tableau of Marlovian despotism in that its violence is thinly disguised as religious zeal. In it Guise kills 'five or six Protestants with books' as they kneel in fear (12 s.d.). As he does so, one pleads, 'O Monsieur de Guise, hear me but speak!' (12.2). The retort from the duke of Guise uses images of the human body to emphasize that despots may visualize dissenting speech as a threat of being penetrated by the dissenter's greatest weapon:

> No, villain, that tongue of thine
> That hath blasphem'd the holy Church of Rome
> Shall drive no plaints into the Guise's ears
> To make the justice of my heart relent.
> Tue, tue, tue! Let none escape.
>
> [s.d.] Kill them.
> 12.3–7

To Guise, a dissident's tongue possesses latent power, and must be diminished, for, unsheathed, it might 'drive' into him like a sword. Faced with the threat of such penetration into his ears – gateways of his mind if not his heart – Guise reacts in a Tamburlainesque fashion. Rather than tolerate the intrusion of dissent, he orders 'Let none escape.'

In Scene 12 Guise has moved to protect his 'heart' from being forced to 'relent'; then in Scene 13 Catherine likewise pretends to fear for her own heart. When the poisoned Charles reports that 'a griping pain hath seiz'd upon my heart; / A sudden pang, the messenger of death,' the queen mother answers, 'O say not so; thou kill'st thy mother's heart' (13. 2–4). At once Catherine articulates shock that her son is ill, yet asks him not to speak – 'O say not so.' That Catherine's affection is ambiguous needs no further proof by this point in the play, yet it is supplied in her frigid lines spoken over Charles's corpse. She is without grief, plotting instead to bring Henry back from Poland to take the throne as quickly as is feasible.

We have examined the image of the heart in earlier chapters. In *Tamburlaine*, for instance, soldiers also insist that it is invested only with physical life, and possesses no symbolic meaning. For them, an extruded heart simply confirms that life is in fact more a physiological event than a complex bond of spiritual and physical forces. Yet even as Tamburlaine's men may unwittingly acknowledge, Elizabethan soldiers who invoke images of the heart, as they incessantly do, are taking it as the locus of their struggle to cover emotion with steely thoughts. Among early modern plays, one of the better-known apostrophes to the heart must be Henry V's during the long night before the battle of Agincourt. Henry prays, but not for his men's souls: 'O God of battles, steel my soldiers' hearts, / Possess them not with fear!' (4.1.289–90). Henry asks for his men to go into battle numbed against the complexity of life, as Tamburlaine's men do. Significantly, in *Tamburlaine* the only character to adopt the heart as a locus of complex, death-defying properties is the widow Olympia, whose attention to her own heart is part of her efforts to resist being raped by Theridamas. Unlike her, Catherine de Medici breaks the stereotype of women as vessels of purity, even as she deceives her son Charles with talk of having her heart broken by his death. Again in *The Massacre at Paris* the heart functions symbolically in conflicts between despots and dissidents. Sometimes it captures sincere physical pain; more often it signifies insincere anguish.

Caesar

Now come thou forth and play thy tragic part.

In several of Marlowe's tragedies, despotism is justified by soldiers as the working out of some biological necessity masked as manifest destiny or heroic duty. In *The Massacre* these claims are voiced by Guise. Far more than a bona fide Roman hero such as Aeneas in *Dido*, Guise desires to live and die a Roman hero. In his own modest estimation he is a

'Caesar,' destined to rule 'all the world' (2.95, 56).[43] 'For this,' he observes, 'hath heaven engender'd me of earth' (2.53). It is clear that he is imagining himself as a global emperor incarnated by the heavens, a fantasy we meet again in *Faustus*, which gives it a more explicitly diabolical twist, suggesting that claims of divine election are instances of self-election. This possibility is insisted upon early and often in *The Massacre at Paris*, too. Although Catherine indulges in speaking in similarly propagandistic tones of her absolute dominion, in the context of sixteenth-century government she has more claim to do so. Guise does not. And through the development of the duke's character, Marlowe illustrates the process of a despot rhetorically constructing himself. The duke's progress toward power punctures the illusion that martial masculinity is merely the mechanical unfolding of fate. More baldly than in any Marlowe play, masculinity and nationalism are said here to be reciprocally instrumental human codes and not divine truths.

Unlike most of Marlowe's conquerors, who surreptitiously fashion their own martial identities through the very poetry they profess to disdain, and who impose complementary identities upon their men, Guise is remarkably translucent about the process. In Scene 2 'Caesar' comes to life on stage in all his autocratic glory. He modifies a commonplace Renaissance trope to assert that it is not chance or fate that he should be king of France. Having catalogued potential allies in Paris – friars, for example, who might be pressed into military service in a *coup d'état* – he concludes, 'Guise, since thou hast all the cards within thy hands / To shuffle or cut, take this as surest thing: / That right or wrong, thou deal thyself a king' (2.85–8). Ordinarily, allusions to card games in drama of the period signify resignation to chance. Here, however, even commonplaces are subject to being commandeered. Guise wills himself to overpower chance, engineer victory. In doing so, he offers a metaphor for the human construction of fate. To his opponent, his rise to glory looks fated; but he is stacking the deck.

For more than half the play, he wins every hand. Yet even as the duke's successes mount, Marlowe is careful to suggest that his protagonist's persona of absolute will is no more than that—a construction. Consider the charged if nevertheless commonplace language in which he commissions the first assassin of Admiral Coligny:

(s.d.: Enter a Soldier.)

SOLDIER: My Lord?
GUISE: Now come thou forth and play thy tragic part:
               Stand in some window opening near the street
               And when thou see'st the Admiral ride by
               Discharge thy musket and perform his death.

2.24–8

The instruction to 'perform his death' takes us beyond the first-order irony of one Elizabethan player saying to another, 'play thy tragic part.' That is merely self-reflexive. But to command the soldier to 'perform' the admiral's murder is to invite spectators to imagine that soldiership itself is fundamentally theatrical, not only literally so, as in this exchange between players, but ontologically so as well.[44] It is also possible to hear the playwright punning on the English meaning of Guise, as in *disguise*.

In keeping with the idea that gendered violence is gender performed, the exchange cited above suggests that warlike valor is virtually an extemporaneous achievement. The duke makes this assumption explicit later in the same scene, as he manufactures his own martial self. In soliloquy he again speaks almost as Tamburlaine might:

> As Caesar to his soldiers, so say I:
> Those that hate me will I learn to loathe.
> Give me a look that, when I bend the brows,
> Pale death may walk in furrows of my face;
> A hand that with a grasp may gripe the world;
> An ear to hear what my detractors say;
> A royal seat, a sceptre, and a crown;
> That those which do behold, they may become
> As men that stand and gaze against the sun.
> The plot is laid, and things shall come to pass
> Where resolution strives for victory.
>
> 2.95–105

Ordinarily I would not want to insist upon the double meaning of 'the plot is laid.' But in this context, given the highly self-reflexive theatrical discourse elsewhere in Scene 2, the phrase calls attention to the idea that victory is scripted. Scripted not only in the narrow sense – laying a plot – but also in the sense that the 'resolution' of one who is marked by epic masculinity is also scripted by the fictions of epic masculinity itself. In that sense Guise is indeed Caesar.

In Scene 21 it is Caesar's turn to play the 'tragic part.' When he meets his own assassin we see that in his imagination, his identity is more than merely metaphorically congruent with Caesar's. The third murderer, deciding to renege on the conspiracy to murder, bursts onto stage to warn Guise about Henry's men who are lurking in an adjacent room. Guise answers imperiously:

> Yet Caesar shall go forth.
> Let mean conceits, and baser men fear death:
> Tut, they are peasants; I am Duke of Guise;
> And princes with their looks engender fear.
>
> 21.67–70

By the ironic logic of revenge plays – *The Massacre at Paris* is consummately of that genre – Guise is instantly set upon and fatally stabbed. As if he is lost in the wrong genre, Caesar the victor has become Caesar the victim. Unlike epics, revenge tragedies punish those who make ruthless grabs for power.

Reading the duke's death speech, Julia Briggs follows Paul Kocher in proposing that Marlowe honors Guise by giving him 'personal courage' in the face of death; Kocher had pointed out earlier that Catholic League pamphlets emphasized the historical duke's bravery at the end.[45] From another angle, however, the duke's speech demonstrates the fatal vulnerability of one so invested in playing 'Caesar' that he cannot appreciate the risk posed by peasants. Though his pride may be Tamburlainesque, in other words, his timing and his judgment are not. As the lieutenant Techelles notes in *Tamburlaine*, 'faint-hearted runaways / Look for orations when the foe is neer. / Our swords shall play the orators for us' (1–1.2.130–32). Guise, rather than fight, only talks of fighting – a sign of cowardice perhaps always under martial law, and a frequent complaint against Queen Elizabeth by her advisers, who asked that she take the Spanish threat more seriously by committing more troops and gold, not more talk, to her defense.

As he lies bleeding, Guise eulogizes himself by spewing forth a last stream of hateful words. Through that performance, Marlowe reminds spectators gathered at the theatre that massacres begin inside the diseased minds of zealots who have no respect for human life:

> To die by peasants, what a grief is this!
> Ah, Sixtus, be reveng'd upon the King;
> Philip and Parma, I am slain for you!
> Pope, excommunicate, Philip, depose
> The wicked branch of curs'd Valois his line!
> *Vive la messe*! Perish Huguenots!
> Thus Caesar did go forth, and thus he died.
>
> [s.d.] *He dies*. 21.81–7

Marlowe gives us the Julianic martyr as a legend in his own mind.

Henry III on the domestic battlefield

> Guise: I daily win with words

We are ready to turn now to episodes in which words explicitly serve as the material capital of the reign of terror. They are its currency; their possession shows who is on top. So dissident speech threatens not only the stability of the state, but also Guise's more personal project of violence. The first example features Henry III ridiculing Guise for his wife's alleged infidelities. It is ironic Henry should do so. Neither of Catherine's sons is especially invested in being in good standing with the code of epic masculinity; neither of them wants to be identified as a Roman conqueror. We may recall that Charles had invited his mother's contempt by lamenting his role in the massacre, and supposedly he even put the entire realm at risk by his pursuits of what Guise condemns as 'pleasure uncontroll'd' (2.67). Yet it is not Charles, but Henry who flagrantly violates the compulsory heterosexuality clause of the code of epic masculinity, a clause implied in the duke's charge of uncontrolled pleasure-seeking.

Historically there was a good deal of contemporary notice of Henry's 'homosexuality.'[46] In the play, its possibility is raised only discreetly. We see it suggested, for example, in Scene 14, where Catherine greets Henry as he returns from Poland to claim the French throne. 'Welcome to France, thy father's royal seat! / Here hast thou a country void of fears, / A warlike people to maintain thy right' (14.3–5). In spite of these public rituals of welcome, however, Catherine soon confides in the cardinal of Lorraine that she expects Henry, as king, to ignore his duties in favor of male playmates: 'His mind, you see, runs on his minions, / And all his heaven is to delight himself; / Thy brother Guise and we may now provide / To plant ourselves with such authority / As not a man may live without our leaves' (14.45–6, 48–50). Later we come to understand how deeply both she and especially Guise underestimate Henry's own powerful will and gift for dissembling. Henry likewise pictures himself as an actor able, like Guise, to construct his face. As Henry observes in Scene 19 quarreling with Guise, 'Epernoun, though I seem mild and calm, / Think not but I am tragical within' (19.88–9).

At the moment of Henry's return to France, however, it would seem that Catherine's judgment may be accurate. Making Edward II's mistake, Henry gives *carte blanche* to 'minions' (14.16) – a nasty word in early modern England – even as he is installed as king:

> No person, place, or time, or circumstance
> Shall slack my love's affection from his bent;
> As now you are, so shall you still persist,
> Removeless from the favours of your king.
>
> 14.19–22

Unlike Charles or Guise, however, Henry is a man of his word. His promise remains intact even after he invokes personal rule in Scene 17 to cope with Guise's mustering of troops. Even then he echoes Edward II, vowing, 'Epernoun, I will be rul'd by thee' (19.81). And there are other signs of Henry's gentle rule. Around the coronation is understandably a period of holiday only briefly sketched in the play. Henry invites well-wishers 'to feast, / And spend some days in barriers, tourney, tilt, / And like disports' (14.39–41). The signal here is that military exercises are the business of show and sport, ceremonial events rather than imperial ventures. They are, in other words, merely theatrical enactments of the physical contests that 'really' matter.

At the coronation festivities, a cutpurse is apprehended for having palmed gold buttons from a cloak. On the certainty of his punishment Guise and Mugeroun are agreed. Mugeroun lops off his ear while asking Henry, *pro forma*, 'to give me leave / To punish those that do profane this holy feast' (14.29–30); meanwhile Guise beckons an attendant to detain the thief. As the arrest is about to be made, Henry intervenes: 'Hands off good fellow; I will be his bail / For this offence' (14.35–6), offering the king's pardon. Speaking directly to the grifter, Henry displays an incisive and compassionate grasp of the exigencies of lower-class existence: 'Go, sirrah, work no more / Till this our coronation-day be past' (14.36–7).

It may be true, as I have argued, that Henry III is, like his brother Charles, only ambiguously invested in the Tamburlainian code that drives Guise toward his goal of the Julianic conquest of France. Yet in Scene 21 Henry is resurrected as a decisive monarch when he orders Guise assassinated. Soon learning that Guise is dead, Henry sighs in relief, 'I ne'er was King of France until this hour' (21.98). Henry has played fast and loose with the demands of martial manhood and still kept his throne; perhaps in Guise's ultimately unsuccessful challenge to the homosexual King Henry, Marlowe is revisiting and recanting Mortimer's defeat of Edward II.

More evidence that *The Massacre at Paris* subverts the code of epic masculinity comes, paradoxically, through Henry's self-defensive response to Guise's mustering of troops. However much Henry prefers to frolic at court than to marshal forces on a battlefield, he understands well how to deploy the fictions of a martial *mentalité* to retain control of his throne. We may see this in his use of the gossip that the duchess of Guise wishes to make her husband a cuckold. Consider the men's confrontation in Scene 17. The scene has begun with Henry solemnly making another peer, the duke of Joyeux – 'sweet Joyeux' (17.1), in Henry's loving words – the commanding general of an army that is about to embark on a campaign against the king of Navarre. (Joyeux is slain in battle between Scenes 17 and 18, reminding spectators of the vicissitudes of combat even for generals.)

Against Joyeux's honor Henry proceeds to juxtapose Guise's domestic dishonor. He needles his adversary with the shame of having lost control of his wife. The stage directions call for the actor playing Henry to make horns at the duke:

> HENRY: So kindly, cousin of Guise, you and your wife
> Do both salute our lovely minions.
> Remember you the letter, gentle sir,
> Which your wife writ to my dear minion,
> And her chosen friend?
> GUISE: How now, my Lord? Faith, this is more than need.
> Am I thus to be jested at and scorn'd?
> 'Tis more than kingly or imperious.
> . . .
> I love your minions? Dote on them yourself!
> I know none else but holds them in disgrace.
> 17.10–17, 21–2

With perturbing bluntness, Henry mocks his rival. More subtly, though, he also mocks the code of epic masculinity. The duke is ridiculed not simply because his wife has written to another man of her affections, but also because that 'other man' is one of the 'lovely minions' saluted by their presumably homosexual monarch. Thus is the duke doubly shamed in being cast off for one of the king's men. Deeply wounded by the king's derision, Guise responds as every man must if he lives by the sword: he vows to kill Mugeroun, though everyone knows him to be innocent, though the desire for cuckoldry exists only in the duchess's heart:

> And here by all the saints in heaven, I swear
> That villain for whom I bear this deep disgrace,
> Even for your words that have incens'd me so,
> Shall buy that strumpet's favour with his blood,
> Whether he have dishonoured me or no!
> *Par la mort dieu, il mourra!*
> 17.23–8

The duke's admission that his king's 'words' have so 'incens'd' him reminds us of the improvisational construction of both the duke's anger and the honor it is designed to defend.

A second instance of Henry's recourse to the fictions of epic masculinity is his plan to have Guise killed; and a third is his own deathbed speech. True to the generic pattern of revenge tragedy, even Henry's murderous plot boomerangs. In Scene 24 he is stabbed by a Jacobin friar – it would seem that Marlowe reserves a special place in hell for friars. As Henry bleeds, his fantasies of revenge also flow very much along the lines uttered by Faustus against Pope Adrian:

> These bloody hands shall tear his triple crown
> And fire accursed Rome about his ears.

I'll fire his crazed buildings, and incense
The papal towers to kiss the holy earth.

24.60–63

An incendiary oath against Rome, this might go over as well in an Elizabethan playhouse as at Henry's now-Protestant, now-Catholic court. We might easily think of echoes elsewhere in Marlowe. In *The Jew of Malta*, for instance, where the slave Ithamore reports that he has been engaged in practicing his skills of 'setting Christian villages on fire, / Chaining of eunuchs, binding galley-slaves' (2.3.206–7). Both characters claim to relish the idea of razing Catholic communities; their claims are outrageous, even surreal. Articulating these claims reaffirms the speakers' allegiances to an agonistic ethos among men. Yet in both cases, that allegiance is conveyed in an oath recognizable as a fiction.

We have seen that while Marlowe's heroes often mean nothing of what is said in such bombastic rantings as those above, they are usually deadly serious in the few domestic sketches included in his plays. Under the terms of martial law, private life is also a battlefield. In vignettes of private life the playwright most effectively challenges the tenets of epic masculinity. Two examples here. First is a soldier's soliloquy as he lies in wait for Mugeroun, the supposed lover of the duchess of Guise; second is Guise's verbal abuse of the duchess in her boudoir. Although the marital confrontation occurs before Mugeroun is killed, the examples are discussed in reverse order because the unnamed soldier articulates a set of assumptions about women and marriage that implicitly animate the duke's attack on his wife.

Bearing a musket, the soldier expounds his vision of gender relations while waiting in a closet for his quarry Mugeroun to show up. His vision is extensively economic:

> Sir, to you, sir, that dares make the Duke a cuckold, and
> use a counterfeit key to his privy-chamber door; and al-
> though you take out nothing but your own, yet you put in
> that which displeaseth him, and so forestall his market,
> and set up your standing where you should not; and
> whereas he is your landlord, you will take upon you to be
> his, and till the ground that he himself should occupy,
> which is his own free land – if it be not too free; there's
> the question. And though I come not to take possession
> (as I would I might), yet I mean to keep you out – which
> I will, if this gear hold. What, are ye come so soon? (19.1–11)

The economic metaphors used here to describe the duke's claim should come as no surprise. They echo claims from Mathias, Lodowick, and Barabas in *The Jew of Malta*; and they echo countless medieval and early modern texts. What is perhaps surprising is the link drawn between a commercial mode of signifying marital relations and martial law. The 'landlord' does not simply have a right to 'occupy' his wife sexually ('till') and affectively; he subsumes her. While this merging may be in harmony with Catholic doctrine, in Marlowe's play it carries sinister connotations, as the whole episode in the boudoir insists.

The soldier's sly allusion to his own sexual desire for the duchess helps to eroticize his murder of Mugeroun. The soldier, constricted in his closet, awaits a tryst with death. As Nancy Huston has observed of modern armies, 'male sexuality in the Army is rigorously controlled, not to say eliminated, with the evident intention of increasing the soldiers' capacity for murder.'[47] While *Othello* is the most powerful example I can think of from the early modern period in which an experienced soldier eroticizes murder (visualize Othello hovering over Desdemona on the bed), Guise experiences some similar mental gyrations in his wife's boudoir in Scene 15. He enters as she is writing sweet nothings to Mugeroun. Immediately Guise suspects her. He asks for – then demands – her letter. Snarling 'I must see' it (15.20), he snatches it away. Even this small detail reminds us of the disrespect for women's privacy and property that is a hallmark of martial law. An abusive husband, he is determined to control her every move, including all communications to the outside world. She cannot hold any thought, any desire, to herself. The psychology of the duke's response may be plausibly read as part of Marlowe's critique of militarism. When the duke's worst fear is confirmed, he at first derides himself, asking the gods if his sexual performance or age have left the duchess unsatisfied: 'Am I grown old, or is thy lust grown young, / Or hath my love been so obscur'd in thee / That others needs to comment on my text?' (13.24–6). Further, this scene draws attention to the humanist project of attempting to control women's literacy in the period as a means of preserving the hierarchical authority of men. As Eve Rachele Sanders has demonstrated, the theater played an enormous if ambivalent role, both transmitting those hierarchies as enshrined in contemporary 'educational treatises and conduct manuals,' but also offering the theatergoing-public plenty of opportunities to see the humanists' ideas about women's education and literacy being contested by way of tense spectacles such as this moment when Guise barges into his wife's boudoir to discover her penning a note to a lover. Writing the scene this way, Marlowe is participating in a new phenomenon in English drama, that of having a woman writing on stage, and is enacting one of the common fears of women's literacy as the humanists expressed it – fear of cuckoldry. 'According to *The Education of a Young Gentlewoman* (1598), women who know how to write are likely to engage in illicit affairs: "there is no lesse danger than they will sooner learne to be subtil & impudent lovers, than learnedly to write verses, poetrie, ballads and songs."'[48]

Faced with a recalcitrant and literate wife, the Guise quickly dismisses his anxieties about his own performance. Even the language in which they have been raised shows him taking refuge in the discursive regulatory practices of gender fictions that protect him from blaming his own behavior for what is happening. In snatching away his wife's letter, he imagines himself thus to be aborting her efforts to script her own sexual desire. Posing the rhetorical question of whether he has invited other men 'to comment on my text' by showing the duchess nothing more than an 'obscur'd' love, Guise activates a long western tradition in which men are authors while women are texts to be inscribed, blank spaces to be marked with tropes that assure the continued survival of a gendered hierarchy of power. Analyzing one formulation of that language in a Richard Lovelace poem, where the speaker imagines Ben Jonson responding in fright to the spectacle of a wife with pen in hand, Sanders concludes that 'underlying the poet's invective is terror at the prospect of ceding to women this instrument with all its correlative powers, its potential for violence, deception and secrecy, its reach into the inner recesses of heart and mind.'[49]

In activating that tradition, Guise quickly dashes all doubt of his own sexual or affective inadequacies. All anxieties are displaced by misogynistic rantings about the 'wicked sex' (15.36), another trope in that long western tradition. It is the tradition itself that authorizes him to threaten her:

> Mort dieu, were't not the fruit within thy womb,
> Of whose increase I set some longing hope,
> This wrathful hand should strike thee to the heart!
> Hence, strumpet, hide thy head for shame
> And fly my presence if thou look to live!
>
> 15.31–5

In the face of such terror, the duchess is silent. How to read that silence? Ordinary fear leading to submission, or more? Fear must be part of the answer. But we might also see this episode as a metaphorical statement about the power and danger of speech to soldiers who would attempt to impose a militarist code upon civilians. We have a woman attempting to script a life for herself outside the autocratic existence imposed by her husband. She is cut off from engaging in an ancient form of dissent – infidelity. As Natalie Zemon Davis has observed of women in sixteenth-century France, 'a strategy for at least a thread of female autonomy may have been built precisely around this sense of being given away, that women sometimes turned the cultural formation around, and gave themselves away.'[50]

Here an idea from Monique Wittig, as theorized by Judith Butler, helps to emphasize what is at stake in the boudoir scene. 'In its ideal sense, speaking is,' says Butler, 'a potent act, an assertion of sovereignty that simultaneously implies a relationship of equality with other speaking subjects.'[51] In the boudoir scene the duchess does claim such equality, only to relent. She exhibits a divided mind. To understand that phenomenon here, we might also think of Patricia Parker's work in *Literary Fat Ladies* on early modern prohibitions against women learning to write or speak for themselves. Parker finds these prohibitions in medieval and early modern handbooks of rhetoric, in which women's access to rhetoric is explicitly proscribed. Such positions were justified by tracing to Aristotle the idea that women 'were to be not only silent but identified with the property of the home and with the private sphere.'[52] And as Mugeroun's assassin asserted, the duchess is her husband's 'privy-chamber,' his 'market,' his 'ground,' his 'own free land.' This episode – in effect an instance of domestic abuse – may well suggest to spectators that the soldier who exercises martial law on the job also brings it home.

The murder of Peter Ramus

I want to suggest, finally, that the silencing of the duchess of Guise and the murder of Peter Ramus are not unrelated acts of violence, but instead of a piece. However much domestic abuse may differ practically from the murder of a public figure, the two are related in Marlowe's play by the solipsism of soldiers who do not recognize the human rights of other persons, or even their rights to exist separately. In two scenes – 7 and 9 – the playwright stages the murders of characters who earn livelihoods by speaking. These scenes reiterate values we usually associate with rhetoric – debate, democracy (in some eras, anyway), admitting the contingency of truth, honoring the reasoned consideration of multiple perspectives, respecting the voice itself as a locus of truth, and so forth. The murder of the Protestant divine at the end of Scene 7 is brief even in comparison with other murders in the play. Within a few lines Guise is able to stab a Protestant[53] who identifies himself as 'a preacher of the word of God' (7.3) and to refuse Anjoy's request to be allowed to recite a psalm. If Anjoy is already softening, his commander lacks guilt as well as heart. Scene 9 presents a modestly longer treatment of soldiers' silencing those who speak for a living. In it the playwright imagines the August 26th confrontation between Peter Ramus and his murderers in his rooms at the Collège de Presles, later to become the Collège de France. Historically, Ramus's murder was apparently carried out against Guise's explicit exemption of the professor of eloquence and

philosophy.[54] For far more than simply shock effect, Marlowe places 'Caesar' at the murder site. Other more certain historical changes introduced into the episode imply that Marlowe is deliberately setting up an anachronistic collision between those who would construct the world in civil terms with the tongue, and those who would do so in martial terms with the sword.

Recalling *Doctor Faustus*, Scene 9 opens upon the scholar in his study, 'sitting at his book' (9.2). Enter Taleus, 'Ramus' bedfellow' (9.12), who urges his longtime friend and collaborator to flee the duke's men. Marlowe would have known, however, of Taleus's death in 1562.[55] His presence in the scene might signify the constitution of a homosocial community beyond the boundaries of the army, as with Edward II and Gaveston, but that is only if we take 'bedfellow' to be suggestive. (Although the historical Ramus and Taleus were lifelong bachelors, my hunch is we should not.) More plausible here is that the appositive 'bedfellow' signifies intellectual compatriots, a community of scholars. Upon being seized, Ramus is immediately separated from Taleus, who is freed by the soldier Retes: 'O let him go, he is a Catholic' (9.15). Never mind that the historical Ramus had also remained a professed Roman Catholic until 1570, some nine years after Taleus had died.[56] By calling attention to the fact that (the historically posthumous) Taleus and Ramus are on opposite sides of the religious fence, Retes unwittingly acknowledges a friendship that transcends religious ideology. As we have seen through this chapter, though, the soldiers' declared motives have been remarkably protean. As soon as Guise has had Ramus identified as 'the King's professor of Logic,' he snaps, 'Stab him' (9.21–2). To the end, Ramus foolishly believes in the persuasive effects of speech. Nervously he delays the inevitable, asking Guise to explain how he has been 'so offensious' (9.23). As a man of words, he clings to the civil ideal that capital punishment is imposed for capital crimes. As if to mock that naïveté, Guise invents a charge of having had incorrect thoughts about that sacred cow Aristotle:

> Marry, sir, in having a smack in all
> And yet didst never sound anything to the depth.
> Was it not thou that scoff'dst the *Organon*
> And said it was a heap of vanities?

> 　　　　　　　　　　　　　　　　　　　9.24–7

Thinking ahead to Doctor Faustus's apparent attacks on Aristotle, we may speculate that here, Guise is defending the Peripatetic's *oeuvre* on the grounds of authority and tradition more than on substance. And by implication, Guise is defending Roman Catholic theology, which through Aquinas has important roots in Aristotelian metaphysics.

Ramus pleads guilty to having read the *Organon* with less than utter reverence. He admits, 'I knew the *Organon* to be confus'd / And I reduc'd it into better form' (9.45–6). But Guise's indictment of the professor for disrespecting the ancient master is a red herring. Not the least proof that it is so comes from Guise's spurious imitation of syllogistic thinking that is Ramus's death warrant. Mocking the condemned man by citing a 'quidditie' (or quibble), Guise momentarily plays the scholastic orator, even inquisitor: 'To contradict which, I say: Ramus shall die. / How answer you that? Your *nego argumentum* / Cannot serve, sirrah. – Kill him' (9.35–7). Guise's own disrespect for Aristotle here reminds us that philosophical and religious contention in the play is little more than a façade for the despot.

Yet Ramus protests further, appealing to Anjoy, 'O good my Lord, let me but speak a word!' (9.38). Others in the play have also been cut down precisely at that moment of begging to speak; two scholars who are killed later in Scene 9 do not even get so much as an opportunity to protest. Guise simply says to them, 'I'll whip you to death with my poniard's point' (9.79), and swiftly does so. By contrast, Marlowe allows Ramus to deliver a relatively lengthy twelve-line *apologia*. In it Marlowe shows us an intellectual softening his ideas to save his life. If he has 'reduc'd' Aristotle's *Organon*, he did so to improve rather than scuttle it, as he explains gingerly: 'And this for Aristotle will I say, / That he that despiseth him can ne'er / Be good in logic or philosophy: / And that's because the blockish Sorbonnists / Attribute as much unto their works / As to the service of the eternal God' (9.47–52). These words of compromise are spoken by a notorious controversialist who is ready to sell his opponents at the Sorbonne down the river in order to diminish his own influential critique of the *Organon*. He is ready to sacrifice his work for his life. Even more telling is that Ramus opens his *apologia* by claiming that he has no interest in saving his own life, only in setting out his position in a quarrel with 'one Scheckius' (9.43). 'Not for my life do I desire this pause,' he proclaims, 'but in my latter hour to purge myself' (9.40–41). Ramus knows that his skill as a rhetorician is needed if he is to save himself; by the logic of epic masculinity, any admission of weakness would simply guarantee Guise's wrath. Yet even his circuitous attempt to cooperate (if not collaborate) with the screwy logic of Guise's code fails to preserve his life. When the *apologia* is ended Guise demands of Anjoy, 'Why suffer you that peasant to declaim? / Stab him, I say, and send him to his friends in hell' (9.53–4). And Anjoy remembers his oath from Scene 5 (5.51–2), and Ramus is dead, and symbolically, in the play, in Paris, rhetoric is dead. As Katharine Maus has put it, Guise's 'dagger provides a "refutation" which is at once a black parody of logical disputation and its most effective implementation. By slaying his opponent, he makes his argument literally unanswerable.'[57]

Obviously Ramus's murder is not some one-liner jab at intellectuals such as we get in a few other places in Marlowe, but an effort to convey symbolically what is at risk when martial law is in force. It's not that Ramus's brief appearance is designed to elicit our sympathy for the historical figure or the stage character, but that Ramus represented in sixteenth-century Paris the voice of the one speaking up against the orthodoxies of the many, to his peril. When the state imposes martial law to regulate such voices, there is no security for the reasoning individual or for the state itself.

Notes

1. Michel de Montaigne, 'Apology for Raymond Sebond,' in *The Complete Essays of Montaigne*, trans. Donald M. Frame (1958; rpt Stanford: Stanford University Press, 1985), 323. Montaigne claimed that 'Navarre, if he did not fear to be deserted by his followers, would be ready to return of his own accord to the religion of his forefathers; and Guise, if there were no danger, would not be averse to the Augsburg Confession' (cited in Peter Burke, *Montaigne* [New York: Hill & Wang, 1982], 30).

2. *Christopher Marlowe, The Complete Plays*, ed. J.B. Steane (1969; rpt Harmondsworth: Penguin, 1986), 600.

3. Barnabe Rich, *A Roome for a Gentleman*, London, 1609, STC 20985, I4v–K1r; see also K1v.

4. Jean de Serres, *The Lyfe of the most godly . . . Capteine . . . Jasper Colignie Shatilion*, trans. Arthur Golding, London, 1576, STC 22248. Serres explains that Coligny, having warred against Henry VIII, was made Lord Admiral of France. That office 'is counted the cheefest dignitie within the Realme, bycause he hathe the cheef rule of the Sea that beateth uppon *Fraunce*, and the charge of the Kings Navie and of all his seamen and seamatters' (A5v).

5. Of the vast literature, see J.H.M. Salmon, *The French Religious Wars in English Political Thought* (Oxford: Clarendon, 1959); *The Massacre of St. Bartholomew: Reappraisals and Documents*, ed. Alfred Soman (The Hague: Martinus Nijhoff, 1974); Natalie Zemon Davis, *Society and Culture in Early Modern France: Eight Essays* (Stanford: Stanford University Press, 1975); Robert M. Kingdon, *Myths about the St. Bartholomew's Day Massacres, 1572–1576* (Cambridge, MA: Harvard University Press, 1988); and Barbara Diefendorf, *Beneath the Cross: Catholics and Huguenots in Sixteenth-Century Paris* (New York: Oxford University Press, 1991).

6. François Hotman, *A True and Plaine Report of the Furious Outrages of Fraunce, & the horrible and shameful slaughter of Chastillion the Admirall*, trans. Ernest Varamund, Striveling, Scotland, 1573, STC 13847, estimates the massacre left 100,000 children and women to beg (86); Serres claims it caused 'almost ten thowsand' Protestants to flee to England,

Ireland, and Germany (H3r); John Stubbs, *The Discoverie of a Gaping Gulf*, ed. Lloyd Berry (Charlottesville: University Press of Virginia, 1968), estimates that 'thousands and ten thousands' of Protestants were killed (40). Hereafter, passages quoted from Stubbs are cited parenthetically.

7. Kingdon, *Myths*, 37.

8. Ibid., 46, 42.

9. 'A Fourme of Common Prayer to be used, by Aucthoritie of The Queenes Majestie, and Necessarie for the Present Tyme and State,' *Church of England Liturgies. Special Forms of Prayer on Various Occasions*, London, 1572, STC 16511, 27 October 1572, B1v. Hereafter cited as '27 October 1572 Liturgy.'

10. Thanks to Kevin Gustafson for this point.

11. '27 October 1572 Liturgy,' A1r.

12. A.G. Dickens, 'The Elizabethans and St. Bartholomew,' notes that Francis Walsingham and Philip Sidney, both in Paris during the massacre, took refuge – Sidney in the English embassy (in *Massacre*, ed. Soman, 52).

13. This may be proved by consulting a chronological STC catalogue such as is available at the Centre for Reformation and Renaissance Studies at Victoria College, University of Toronto.

14. Dickens, in *Massacre*, ed. Soman, 54.

15. Queen Elizabeth may also have been ambivalent toward the plight of French Protestants because of their claim of the right to rebel against Charles IX. See Julia Briggs, 'Marlowe's *Massacre at Paris: A Reconsideration*,' *Review of English Studies* n.s. 34 (1983): 260.

16. In *A Roome for a Gentleman*, Barnabe Rich acknowledges that '(as some of our English writers would perswade) our British nation did discend' from Aeneas (D3r). Rich takes the position that Aeneas – a traitor – admitted enemy Greeks into Troy. This claim is discussed further in Chapter 2 above.

17. Elizabeth I, *Proceedings concerning soldiers pressed for the low countries. 4 October 1588*, London, 1588, STC 8175.

18. The most popular account of the massacre was Hotman's. As he explains, in an effort to make peace between the duke of Guise and Coligny, Charles IX had 'pronounced the Admiral not guiltie of the death of the [elder] Duke of Guise, wherwith he was charged by the yong Duke of Guise' (xxvi); Charles also sent them together to the Low Countries to fight the duke of Alva, hoping to unite them through the pressure of a military campaign. Charles's plan backfired, however, and Guise took Coligny's failures against Alva as further proof of his malignity. Also see Hotman's *De Furoribus* xiiii [*sic*] in Serres's *The Lyfe of the most godly . . . Jasper Colignie Shatilion*, A5v.
    Modern historians agree it is unlikely that Catherine de Medici ordered Coligny's assassination. See Diefendorf, *Beneath the Cross*, 93; and H.G. Koenigsberger, 'Introduction,' in *Massacre*, ed. Soman, 7.

19. George Gascoigne, 'The Spoyle of Antwerpe,' reprinted in *A Larum for London; or The Siege of Antwerpe* (London: Longmans, Green, 1872), 32.

20. Barnabe Rich, *A Path-Way to Military Practise*, London, 1587 (Amsterdam: Da Capo, 1969), B2v.

21. George Whetstone, *The English Myrror*, London, 1586 (New York: Da Capo, 1973), 98. Whetstone is writing specifically about the Paris massacre.

22. In a disarming way, Stubbs argues that the English hatred for the French is in the blood: '[the English] have it sunk so deep and deeply laid up in their heart as the savor wherewith their young shells were seasoned to the sun from grandfather to father, who in teaching them to shoot would have them imagine a Frenchman for their butt, that so in shooting they might learn to hate kindly, and in hating learn to shoot nearly' (*Gaping Gulf*, 37).

23. Whetstone, *English Myrror*, 96. Frank Ardolino, '"In Paris? Mass, and Well Remembered!": Kyd's *The Spanish Tragedy* and the English Reaction to the St. Bartholomew's Day Massacre,' *The Sixteenth Century Journal* 21 (1990): 403, notes that Whetstone exemplifies English Protestant outrage.

24. Anne Dowriche, 'The French Historie,' London, 1589, STC 7159, 18r. A similar claim is used by the bishop of Carlisle to condemn Bolingbroke's seizure of the throne in *Richard II*; its failure has Shakespeare reminding us of the feebleness of the rhetorical capital of ultimate moral claims in the face of martial power.

25. David Bevington, *Tudor Drama and Politics* (Cambridge, MA: Harvard University Press, 1968), 204. I am indebted to his chapter on 'War Fever' (187–211). On the alleged propaganda value of Marlowe's tragedy, see Roy T. Eriksen, 'Construction in Marlowe's *The Massacre at Paris*,' in *Papers from the First Nordic Conference for English Studies*, ed. Stig Johansson and Bjørn Tysdahl, Institute for English Studies (Oslo: Oslo University Press, 1981), 41.

26. Briggs, 'Marlowe's *Massacre*,' 257–78.

27. Ibid., 260, quoting from Stubbs, *The Discovery of a Gaping Gulf*, 25.

28. See Jahan Ramazani, *The Poetry of Mourning* (Chicago: University of Chicago Press, 1994), 69–86.

29. Janine Estebe, *Tocsin pour un Massacre: la saison des Saint-Barthélemy* (Paris: Le Centurion, 1968), 197; Davis, *Society and Culture*, 160. Diefendorf (*Beneath the Cross*) points out that Guise had opened his Paris home to some fleeing Huguenots, showing that the massacre was never intended to be so widespread. She writes, it had been 'aimed at a selective few – the military leadership – and then got out of hand' (105). Contemporary English commentators seem not to have known of Guise's action.

30. In an essay on *The Fair Maid of the West*, Jean Howard has shown how Thomas Heywood uses race as a category to separate Christians from Muslims, but ultimately not Protestants from Catholics. While *The Fair Maid* pits 'merciful' English Protestants against 'rapacious' Spanish Catholics in ways that suggest 'a subterranean fraternal bond between the two nations, a bond defined precisely by rivalrous antipathy,' it marks the Moors who attempt to do business with the English as racially other, and so 'renders them safely inferior to their European visitors' ('An English Lass Amid the Moors: Gender, Race, Sexuality, and National Identity in Heywood's *The Fair Maid of the West*,' in *Women, 'Race,' and Writing in the Early Modern Period*, ed. Margo Hendricks and Patricia Parker [London: Routledge, 1994], 111, 113). In contrast to the strategies of Heywood's exemplary play, I am arguing, *The Massacre at Paris* depicts violence between French Protestants and French Catholics ironically; where spectators might have expected to see a pro-Protestant version of the internecine civil war, the play shows each side abjecting its rival, figuring it as an Other, in maneuvers that spectators would

have been more likely to expect of racially inflected stage presentations of Muslims than of Roman Catholics.

31. Hotman, *A True and Plaine Report*, G2r (my emphasis).

32. Dowriche, 'The French Historie', 19r, 31r.

33. See Paul Kocher, 'Contemporary Pamphlet Backgrounds for Marlowe's *The Massacre at Paris*,' *Modern Language Quarterly* 8 (1947): 151–73 and 309–18, and 'François Hotman and Marlowe's *The Massacre at Paris*,' *PMLA* 56 (1941): 349–68.

34. Randle Cotgrave defines the feminine noun 'Admirale' as an 'Admirallesse (*the late Admirall Chastillons wife is called so in a History of some account among the French*)' in his *French–English dictionary*, London, 1650, Wing C6377B.

35. Eriksen, 'Construction,' 41.

36. Oliver's edition of the play, p.123, n. 21.

37. Ericksen, 'Construction,' 43.

38. '27 October 1572 Liturgy,' B4r.

39. John Michael Archer argues that the play stresses a 'connection between the Guise and Spain' as a way of revisiting earlier misperceptions of the period in Elizabeth's reign 'before the mid-1580's,' when it was commonly assumed by Walsingham and others that France posed a singular threat to England's security; linking the Guise and Spain revises the story of intelligence assessment within spy circles, an arena that Archer suggests is operative in all of Marlowe's plays (*Sovereignty and Intelligence: Spying and Court Culture in the English Renaissance* [Stanford: Stanford University Press, 1993], 91).

40. Diefendorf, *Beneath the Cross*, 150.

41. Klaus Theweleit, *Male Fantasies*, trans. Erica Carter et al., 2 vols (Minneapolis: University of Minnesota Press, 1987, 1989), 2:266.

42. George Whetstone, *The Honorable Reputation of a Souldier*, London, 1585, STC 25339, Diiii.

43. Ironically, Serres tries to fix Coligny as Caesar. Of Coligny's family's property in Burgundy, Serres writes, 'It is an old opinion among the inhabiters there, and it disagreeth not with *Caesars* writings, that it is the same place wherein *Caesar* at his arrivall with his armie in *Fraunce*, heard the *Ambassadors* of the *Burgonions & Nivernoys* complaining of the *Switzers* for comming into *Fraunce* with an armie, and for wastinge their countrey' (*Lyfe*, A2r).

44. My reading of the significance of 'perform' anticipates its first use in a theatrical sense that is recorded in the *OED* (which cites Shakespeare, *The Tempest*). Contemporary evidence from within the competing genre of military conduct-books shows that 'play' was being used by the late sixteenth century in the double sense of performing an action and performing a theatrical part. One bit of evidence is in William Blandy's *The Castle*, London, 1581, STC 3128. Blandy's dialogue between himself and Geoffrey Gates has Gates using the verb 'play' in both senses: 'I perceave by your assertion, that every man in this lyfe (as on a Theatre or Stage) playes one parte or other, which meriteth shame and obloquie, or deserveth (as his owne right) due commendation' (2).

45. Briggs, 'Marlowe's *Massacre*,' 266; Kocher, 'Contemporary Pamphlet Backgrounds,' 152.

46. Briggs, 'Marlowe's *Massacre*,' 264. I am using 'homosexuality' here as a convenient shorthand.

47. Nancy Huston, 'The Matrix of War: Mothers and Heroes,' in *The Female Body in Western Culture*, ed. Susan Rubin Suleiman (Cambridge, MA: Harvard University Press, 1986), 120.

48. Eve Rachele Sanders, *Gender and Literacy on Stage in Early Modern England* (Cambridge: Cambridge University Press, 1998), 171, quoting Giovanni Bruto, *The Necessary, Fit and Convenient Education of a Young Gentlewoman* (London), trans. W.P., F8v–G2r. On Sanders's analysis of the complex presentation of women's stage-literacy, see especially pages 171–80, where she considers Thomas Dekker's *The Whore of Babylon*, among other plays.

49. Sanders, *Gender and Literacy*, 169.

50. Davis, *Society and Culture*, 61.

51. Judith Butler, *Gender Trouble: Feminism and the Subversion of Identity* (New York: Routledge, 1990), 120.

52. Patricia Parker, *Literary Fat Ladies: Rhetoric, Gender, Property* (New York: Methuen, 1987), 104, gives the examples of Fenner's *The Artes of Logike and Rethorike*, Puttenham's *Arte of English Poesie*, and Wilson's *The Rule of Reason*.

53. This is Loreine, not to be confused with the cardinal of Lorraine, brother to Guise.

54. See Walter J. Ong, *Ramus: Method, and the Decay of Dialogue* (Cambridge, MA: Harvard University Press, 1958), 29. Kingdon (*Myths*) repeats the contemporary rumors, dismissed by Ong, that Ramus was murdered at the request of an academic rival (37).

55. Ong, *Ramus*, 27.

56. Ibid., 28.

57. Katharine Eisaman Maus, *Inwardness and Theater in the English Renaissance* (Chicago: University of Chicago Press, 1995), 72.

CHAPTER SIX

Magical Realism and Predatory Playing in *Doctor Faustus*

The fantastic permits us to cross certain frontiers that are inaccessible so long as we have no recourse to it.

Tzvetan Todorov[1]

In this final chapter I propose that the two versions of *Faustus* published in 1604 and 1616 (by custom 'A' and 'B' hereafter) reverse the set of claims I have been developing up to this point, namely that Marlowe's plays generally work on one important level as figurative antidotes to the martial atmosphere that permeated London in the six years or so he was active as a playwright. In his other scripts the theater itself, a polyphonic space intrinsically hospitable to the airing of multiple points of view, is subtly exploited as a counter-military venue. There, I have been suggesting, dissident civilian characters sometimes speak lines and perform other actions that demonstrate resistance to the contemporary worship of the ideals of war and the imposition of those ideals on civilian life via martial law.

The dramatist's concern with the effects of absolutist thinking is central to *Faustus*, but treated very differently. Without perceptible irony, 'A' and 'B' revel in war fever. They depict theatrical playing itself as an aggressive act that has something to contribute to the exigencies of national security in late sixteenth-century England.[2] Thus *Faustus* does not offer spectators a refuge from the frights of war racking contemporary France or England's own shores, but rather instantiates the axioms of martial law proposed by those eager to preserve national security at any price. Theatrical impersonation now becomes an explicitly predatory act by way of what I will call the *magical realism* of various plot devices and the moments they make possible, such as solar chariot rides, apparitions of succubi from Hades, spontaneous tattoos ('*homo fuge*' [A 2.1.81]). How to understand the phenomena of a reattached leg in *Faustus* 'A', a false head in 'B'? Or dragons, a magic girdle, a luminous mirage of a *femme fatale* from the imaginary landscape of epic warfare? These magically real phenomena interrupt the Lutheran–Calvinist plot of the tragedy. Instantaneously these phenomena transport us back and forth across 'certain frontiers' that are variously geographical, visceral, cosmological, ontological. The two *Faustus* plays ask spectators to imagine a series of border-crossings that have the potential to reshape not the geography of Europe or its religious landscape, but more fundamentally the relationship of the fabulous to ordinary civic life, and so the roles of art in defining and securing a state.

While I have argued that other plays such as *Tamburlaine* cast an ambiguous, sometimes negative light on war and warmongering, evidence of that is also necessarily ambiguous: some Marlovian characters in other plays express admiration for the principal's martial deeds within those worlds. In *Faustus* all is different. It is true that the doctor's mind runs quickly and surprisingly often to fantasies of martial glory, and also true that those fantasies resemble no other Marlovian hero's fantasies so much as Tamburlaine's. As Faustus puts it, he too would like to wield an imperial power to reshape the world – perhaps in the manner of Roman and Persian emperors. In fact, saber-rattling rhetoric is integral to his dissent from the orthodoxies of theology right from the start, and it escalates across Act 1. Initially he speculates that with the help of familiars, for example, he will choose to trump the Anglo-Dutch war effort to expel Spanish soldiers, along with Philip's governor general, from the Low Countries: 'I'll levy soldiers with the coin they bring, / And chase the Prince of Parma from our land, / And reign sole king of all our provinces' (A 1.1.94–6). These familiars will be engineers who can 'invent' 'stranger engines for the brunt of war / Than was the fiery keel at Antwerp's bridge' (alluding to a 'fireship used by the Netherlands' forces on 4 April 1585 to destroy a bridge built by Parma' during his blockade of Antwerp [A 1.1.99, 97–8, 98n]). Faustus also keeps company with lesser men who likewise take pleasure in boasting of actions against Spain they might want to perform – 'perform' in the sense that they speak and otherwise enact the 'specific theatrical expressiveness of a multidimensional rhetoric.'[3] Valdes, for example, who envies the ways 'Indian Moors obey their Spanish lords,' plans to conjure elements that can function as privateers to intercept 'from America the golden fleece / That yearly stuffs old Philip's treasury' (A 1.1.123, 133–4). But while Faustus shares Valdes's contemptuous fascination with the Spanish, his dreams run toward the autarkic. So his demonic familiars won't simply intercept argosies of gold – they will 'ransack the ocean for orient pearl' (A 1.1.85). Even 'emperors and kings / Are but obeyed in their several provinces,' he muses in the very first scene, concluding soon that 'By [Mephistopheles], I'll be great emperor of the world,' and 'I'll join the hills that bind the Afric shore / And make that land continent to Spain, / And both contributory to my crown' (A 1.1.59–60; 1.3.106, 109–11). Here the Übermensch idly visualizes having the power to move earth if not heaven, to make northern Africa and the Iberian peninsula, the Muslim shore and

Catholic Spain – touch. Like Barabas, who hopes to make Turks and Catholics bump up against one another on the island of Malta, Faustus anticipates a violent response to the collapse of these physical spaces and geopolitical separations. But for him the fantasy goes farther still. With Baconian vision it looks forward to the modern theory of plate tectonics, but with an early modern demonic twist. Utterly against the axioms that Tamburlaine preaches, the doctor is imagining in effect the (sometimes Satanic) plasticity of matter, space, time, and human identity. Assumptions about the plasticity of those elements are central to the play's claims about theater's utility in a late-sixteenth-century England and Europe that was often at war. In such a world, so his fantasy goes, the black arts can become a vehicle for keeping the doctor's homeland, Germany, safe: 'I'll have [my spirits] wall all Germany with brass / And make swift Rhine circle fair Wittenberg' (A 1.1.90–91).

The subplots concerning militaristic rhetoric and temporal combat among mortals in the tragedy have attracted less attention from critics, especially compared to the ink spilt in discussing the tragedy's infamous theological cruxes. *Flourish*: is the doctor damned already when the plot begins? For decades, that question and variations on it have been parsed by those eager to find definitive evidence for one dogma or another in a play that seems constructed to frustrate airtight explanations of anything.[4] It must be admitted that the warmongering agendas of particular generals, kings, and nations are usually subordinated to its galvanic philosophical and religious themes. Those enigmas have been so worked over, however, that *Faustus* criticism is sometimes declared '"exhausted."'[5] Meanwhile, the Vatican and imperial court episodes in Acts 3 and 4 have been regularly dismissed as slapstick that mars the tragedy. Periodically subjected to intense scrutiny by textual scholars across the twentieth century, these medial episodes, to some ways of thinking, have been rendered even more marginal in the wake of recent general agreement that substantial portions of 'B' do not represent Marlowe's own work, but are instead revisions and elaborations by other hands after his death. Even so, I suggest, these medial episodes merit our continued attention. Not only is it the case that the 'B' version of Acts 3 and 4 expands on actions and themes that are already plotted in 'A', which Marlowe wrote or at least collaborated in writing: so 'B''s extravaganza at the emperor's court and the physical highjinks in the pope's privy chamber are indeed in 'A' in embryonic form, and integral to that version. But also, in expanding on themes and actions present in 'A', 'B' offers us great evidence as to what theatergoers at the turn of the century wanted to see even more of in their entertainment at the close of Elizabeth's reign, before England and Spain made peace. What they wanted was more jingoistic playing.

If the circumnavigation of these medial episodes by critics is partly in response to textual ambiguities enveloping the scripts we call *Doctor Faustus*,[6] it is also explained by expectations established in the Prologue. There we are told that *Faustus* will depart from Marlowe's previous subjects, especially war. 'Not marching now in fields of Trasimene,' the Chorus says, 'where Mars did mate the Carthaginians, / Nor sporting in the dalliance of love / In courts of kings where state is overturned, / Nor in the pomp of proud audacious deeds, / Intends our muse to daunt his heavenly verse' (Prologue A 1–6). Taken at face value, the Chorus readies spectators to watch something completely different. But in what ways different? The rubric of combat is integral to *Faustus's* plot. Beyond the spiritual psychomachia expressed as dialogic combat between the Good Angel and the Evil (or 'Bad' in 'B') Angel, the plot swerves toward physical combat on a number of occasions, and depicts the act of war-making as an act of meaning-making, at least in terms of the frontiers it takes us across. As Elaine Scarry might say, the act of making war in the play constructs new ontological boundaries even as it deconstructs the known world. One elemental difference in *Faustus*, then, is the unparalleled freedom granted the human imagination, which allows Faustus not merely to contend with the play's soldiers and prelates, but to triumph over them in ways that no other Marlovian dissident is able to do.

To read the medial episodes of the two *Faustus* texts as early modern examples of *magical realism*, it may be wise to begin with a cogent definition of that slippery term. One is offered by Lois Zamora and Wendy Faris in a collection of essays on the genre most often associated with it – Latin American fiction:

> magical realism is a mode suited to exploring – and transgressing – boundaries, whether the boundaries are ontological, political, geographical, or generic. Magical realism often facilitates the fusion, or coexistence, of possible worlds, spaces, systems that would be irreconcilable in other modes of fiction. The propensity of magical realist texts to admit a plurality of worlds means that they often situate themselves on liminal territory between or among those worlds – in phenomenal and spiritual regions where transformation, metamorphosis, dissolution are common, where magic is a branch of naturalism, or pragmatism.[7]

As strange as it may sound to borrow what is decidedly a twentieth-century term to read an early modern tragedy with medieval roots, the literary phenomenon we know as magical realism is in fact arguably transhistorical and also an 'international commodity,' as Zamora and Faris note.[8] It offers a vocabulary for talking about early modern texts that fuse fantasy, 'historical allegory,' philosophical self-consciousness, and political criticism. The critic Rawdon Wilson, for example, has used the concept of magical realism and theories related to it to construct persuasive readings of *The Faerie Queene* and *Don Quixote*, particularly of the ways Spenser and Cervantes imagined physical space and bodies as being amorphous in their texts.[9] A magically real moment in a text is a 'transcendental parrot,' as Zamora and Faris coin it, an otherworldly event or device. It interrupts the 'banal reality' that is a text's default setting; yet having interrupted, the parrot is nonetheless inexplicably organic to that default reality, which is not permanently disfigured or fractured by the interpellation of the parrot.[10] In this way, it has been observed, magical realism is available to writers as a subliminal strategy for challenging the *status quo* without seeming to do so, a useful technique in early modern England to be sure.

The magically real in *Faustus* emerges in instances that demonstrate (and make claims for) the plasticity of space, time, and human identity. These fantasies carry dreams of relief from religious and political hostilities, which not only marred late sixteenth-century Europe generally, but preoccupied London in the years Marlowe worked in its playhouses. In 'A' Marlowe draws on magical realism, on the one hand, to mesmerize, thwart, and discredit characters who stand in for the real-life engineers of the acute hostilities in early modern Europe and the anxieties about attack, royal assassination, and enemy infiltration then running through London. On the other hand, the magically real elements transport us beyond representational time and space. The warp allows us to dash in and out of a fantastic world, where the imagination prevails over the laws of ordinary reality. Sometimes the crossing action features ancillary characters such as Wagner the clown. More often, principal figures themselves threaten, inflict, or dodge physical attacks in the playing space, which is repeatedly shot through with sharp noises and the smoke from fireworks: so much so that in 'B' the middle acts almost vibrate from the mimetic religious and political hostilities depicted between, say, Italians and Spaniards, Italians and Germans.

As further preliminary evidence of the applicability of magical realism to *Faustus* I would invoke the historical personage Faust himself, a shadowy figure who has been recalled by writers in the twentieth century as an instance of the early modern magically real. Fifty years ago, in a pioneering essay on the aesthetics of magical realism, Alejo Carpentier named Faust an enigmatic example of what he was calling the *marvelous real* in the modern Americas, in the course of describing Prague as a fantastic cityscape:

> Though the Reformation and Counter Reformation are present in the stones of Prague, its buildings and spaces also speak to us of a past forever suspended between the extreme poles of real and unreal,

fantastical and verifiable, contemplation and action. We know that
Faust, the alchemist, makes his first (imaginary?) appearance in
Prague, where future generations would handle Tycho Brache's [sic]
astronomical instruments, which were exact or nearly so, before
visiting the house of that stargazer named Johannes Kepler, not to
mention those who searched for the philosopher's stone, those who
prepared hermetic mercury – their street is still preserved, complete
with retorts and kilns, in the city of Charles the Great.[11]

Carpentier is pointing to Faust's role as an intermediary between banal
ordinariness and the fantastic. For the historical Faust, so far as we
understand, the journeys back and forth across the border between
ordinary reality and the fantastical were imaginary rather than
genuinely alchemical, and yet no less suggestive or resonant for the
imaginariness of it all. Likewise with Marlowe's protagonist, who is, if
anything, even more marvelous than either the historical legend
celebrated by Carpentier or his prosaic literary cousin known to the
playwright through the English Faust Book. It is one thing for characters
to delude themselves while spectators look on knowingly; it is another
when spectators, to enter fully into the fictional worlds of the play, are
asked to accept as axiomatic the idea that the devil may be summoned,
or that angels may speak to wayward divines, or that the hero may fly
to Rome on a dragon. At any of these moments on stage, something
unusual is being made. These magical moments are not, for instance, the
simple cousins of the puppet show in *Bartholomew Fair*. Whereas
Jonson will call attention to the process of mimesis in ways that take us
'behind the curtain,' in *Faustus* Marlowe gives us magically real space
flight on the backs of dragons that invites us to take mimesis at face
value. 'A dragon in fostes' is among the stage properties recorded in
Henslowe's *Diary*,[12] for example, so we may assume that playgoers were
encouraged to integrate visually and aurally the marvelously real mode
of transport and the 'fact' of space travel with Mephistopheles's and
Faustus's descriptions of the cities underneath their dragons. For what
the players play is simultaneously an illusion of reality beyond the walls
of the theater and yet also magically, fantastically real within the
confines of that theater.[13]

Not coincidentally, I suggest, the magically real moments in *Faustus*
occur when the hero is stressed by being immersed in communities of
men – of priests, then Holy Roman knights. These groups were charged
with defending Roman Catholic orthodoxy in sixteenth-century Europe.
Moving back and forth between what is often simultaneously a
provisional, improvisational membership in these communities and a
liminal status as an outsider, the doctor joyously proclaims the pleasures
of elastic heterodoxy. He works for, and craves, conflict. And when it
leads to hand-to-hand combat in these medial episodes, he relishes it

from a distance, wearing a magic girdle while having others do his dirty work. Yet when the laws of ordinary reality hold sway, Faustus cannot triumph over knights and priests. For he lacks their epistemic privileges and material resources and their expertise in defending these privileges and resources with culturally sanctioned violence. As a way of dramatizing the strength and also the vulnerability of their privileges, the script thus introduces magically real moments that temporarily suspend those privileges and advantages. It does so by transporting both them and us into an invisible subspace where dragons fly through the air. As Faustus goes hand to hand against knights and priests, then, the play offers transcendental parrots that allow him to win. This literary strategy invites us to take seriously the idea that players who impersonate predators on stage become actual predators themselves, able to serve the *ad hoc* English project of defaming Catholicism and in their own way to contribute to the national defense.

My discussion of magical realism in *Faustus* is in three parts. Each considers an episode of realized or imagined impersonation (or identity theft) through which Faustus warps across a border to vie for a temporary transcendental advantage over rivals. The first part studies his brief scheme to play Paris to Helen of Troy in Act 5.[14] The second examines his escapades at Charles V's court, and the third his assault on the pope's privy chamber in Rome.

A putative Homeric hero

Had we been at the Rose Theatre early in 1592 to hear Edward Alleyn of the Admiral's Men as Faustus, the experience might have triggered a memory of the massive armada launched against London, the New Troy, four years earlier. At the time commentators were fond of borrowing images of the Trojan War to give weight to England's troubles with Spain. But as with James Aske's Armada poem 'Elizabetha Triumphans,' discussed in my earlier chapter on *Dido*, the particular literary shorthand of adapting the Trojan War to contemporary purposes was notoriously unstable in accounts of Anglo-Spanish hostilities. However keen Londoners may have been to trace their line through Brutus back to Troy, they were becoming more ambivalent about the intrinsic merits of military glory and less enamored of the Trojan War and the legendary conduct of warriors on both sides as a model for their own conduct, a shift in literary value that Shakespeare's cynical retelling of it in *Troilus and Cressida* would chart a few years after *Faustus* was first staged.

In *Faustus*, Marlowe magnifies that nascent ambivalence through the apostrophe to Helen and the Trojan War that pops up late in Act 5 while a succubus representing 'Helen of Troy' crosses the stage. The apostrophe is an inspired bit of erotic love poetry, much admired by any number of spectators and critics, including me. Yet as a turn in the plot, as a piece of literary shorthand, it paradoxically diminishes Faustus's aspiration to counterfeit a warrior's heroic identity. As he races inexorably toward an end prescribed by earlier versions of his tale, he rashly attempts to bolt from the trajectory of tragedy, to inhabit a genre more favorable to soldiers, but not lovers: epic. We have seen the use of classical encomium as an escape maneuver before. In *Edward II*, for instance, the king retreats into the myth of Hercules and Hylas; in *The Jew of Malta*, Ithamore issues himself a Faustian invitation to become Bellamira's Jason. In each case there is a strong wish on the fantasist's part to leap from an anguished existence into a more hospitable world. Whereas in these other plays the characters travel from one plane of reality to another only in their imaginations, in *Faustus* we are asked to pretend that the doctor has actually experienced 'boundary-skipping between worlds' while flying about the universe, seeing Olympus and the globe with Mephistopheles.[15]

Before going further with an analysis of the apostrophe in Act 5, it will be helpful to set Faustus's impulse to look to heroic poetry as a script for his own fortitude within the late Elizabethan debate about the efficacy of Greek and Latin poetry as didactic material for soldiers. We have some proof in *Faustus* and even better evidence in *Tamburlaine* that Marlowe was at least somewhat engaged by that debate. In both plays, Marlowe invests in it through the ways in which protagonists treat the figure of Helen of Troy and the poetic tradition that gives her life.

To begin with a representative from the most skeptical pole of the debate, we may look once more at Barnabe Rich, who more or less dismisses poetry as inspirational literature before battle or as a weapon in itself. His is a remarkable position in part because Rich excelled at fiction writing, which we might have imagined would incline him toward rather than against the idea that fictions may encourage heroic action. *A Roome for a Gentleman* offers a dialogue between soldiers on the subject of their profession that boils down to this epigrammatic moment: one asks the other 'whether hee had rather to be *Achilles or Homer?*' The question is obviously rhetorical, but unexpectedly provocative, too. It opens up an opportunity for the self-fashioning of ambitious young men, or at least for a reprise of the commonplace dichotomy of martial deeds versus mere words that shows up in so many dramas and prose treatises in the period. But instead, as if to signal the absurdity of the question, the second soldier asks the first 'whether he had rather to be a Captaine or a Trumpeter.'[16] In this pejorative view, the epic poet – a mere horn blower, garnishing with praise the brave deeds of other men – pales in the accumulation of honor alongside the glory earned by the spear thrower, the sergeant of the great works, or the captain of the regiment.

In the debate about the utility of heroic poetry in encouraging valor, at the other end of the spectrum from Rich, I would place as examples two men, both more successful up-and-comers, and both in the Crown's service in the 1580s: Spenser and George Whetstone. Spenser served in Ireland with a number of men who held military positions there, including Rich and Walter Ralegh. The invocation in book one of *The Faerie Queene* begins with Spenser taking up the 'trumpets sterne' to sing of the 'fierce warres and faithfull loues' of the Red Crosse Knight. Its prefatory epistle to Ralegh in the 1590 edition explicitly puts Spenser in the intellectual company of Homer and Virgil.[17] Also adopting Homer's poetry as an inspiration is Whetstone's *The Honorable Reputation of a Soldier*. This volume contains a parable, starring Alexander the Great, that highlights the signal role played by classical texts in producing courage on the battlefield. It depicts Alexander in the midst of hand-to-hand combat. 'Addicted to Homers Iliades . . . being one day in a mortall danger, [Alexander] leaped into the water, and having a Booke in his hande, he had such care thereof as he held that hand upon his head, and wrought for his life with the other.'[18] As Whetstone's image suggests, it was commonplace for Elizabethan writers to envision great generals carrying classical texts into battle. In *The Defence of Poesy*, for example, Sidney posits that the historian would have us remember that Aragon's Alphonso V (1416–58) carried Livy and other poets into battle.[19]

But Whetstone presses the commonplace by describing Alexander as 'addicted.' Modern connotations aside, 'addicted to Homers Iliades' was no compliment; we may remember that Marlowe's contemporaries sometimes described Edward II's love of Gaveston in such terms.[20] Yet clearly Alexander is inspired by Homer, and is not incapacitated or otherwise 'ravished' (A 1.1.6, 1.1.112), as Marlowe says of Faustus, by what he is reading as he fights for his honor and his life. Given the generic context of Whetstone's parable, a military conduct-book, presumably it is implying that Alexander's courage is open for mirroring by Whetstone's readers if they adore Homer – and the values of the *Iliad* – above their own lives. Moreover, implicit in Whetstone's tableau of Alexander with Homer and sword is the idea that soldiering, no less than any other estate, is a part to be played, learned from books. Like another role that one might choose, it is implied, the role of the valorous warrior could be adopted by mimicking epic poetry; this is a strategy that fails in Act 5 when Faustus thinks of playing Paris. Further, in linking virtù to literacy and social class, the parable insinuates that performing as a noble warrior requires not only martial skill and emotional equanimity during battle, but also knowledge of a classical language. We may recall the attention to social degree and learning in the inaugural Chorus of *Faustus*, where it is announced that the doctor, although born of 'parents base of stock,' has become 'glutted more with learning's golden gifts' (Prologue A, 11, 24). The choice of 'glutted' conveys an image of an education marked by an ignoble, ravenous desire said to be typical of members of the lower class, not at all the sort of thing Spenser and Whetstone presumably have in mind.

Somewhere in the middle of this debate about the value of poetry for war is a compromise position articulated by the anonymously authored *A Myrrour for English Souldiers*, published in 1595. On the one hand, this pamphlet looks to the most famous classical poets as guides, praising 'Homer *in his* Achilles, Virgil *in his* Æneas' for their efforts 'to pourtrayt a perfite souldier.' On the other hand, it expresses more skepticism than Spenser's epistle or Whetstone's pamphlet as to whether heroic poetry helps men in 'true attaining of souldierlike immortal vertu.' And it is more alert than Rich's text to the potential danger of being mesmerized by hearing of the heroic deeds that have been sung by Homer and others. For the writer of the *Myrrour*, we may infer, a mimetic reading of the *Iliad*, say, may be lethal. He worries that men who 'over-passe' these '(wel-meaning) Orators, wil the rather be enflamed to marry with Honours maidenhead.'[21] The language of his concern patently sexualizes both the act of war and the act of hearing an epic poem recited. Heroic poetry, it is thus suggested, may well ignite a soldier's passion for victory in ways that put both the ideal of honor and the soldier himself at risk of being defiled; for the imagined union is marred by what may become his compulsive desire to break honor's metaphorical hymen. So as the *Myrrour* presents the debate, poetry may in fact injure rather than protect the soldier or the body politic from harm.

And finally, these epic heroes of classical culture are introduced into evidence in one text as proof that whether or not they once might have inspired martial valor in an Englishman, they no longer can in any case. The seascape of martial valor has been forever altered by the conduct of Charles Lord Howard and Francis Drake in action against the Armada. 'It is good that thou know,' writes D.F.R. de M.,

> that now Julius Caesar liveth not, Pompeie is dead, Scipio forgotten, Alexander banished . . . Hector is slaine, Achilles is no more. Nor none of those whose theaters fame so adorned, live now in remembrance of this present age: and the reason is; for as the stars shine not by reason of the force of the sunne; so all those aforenamed, in respect of the valor of the Lord high Admirall, and Sir Francis Drake, are of no account.[22]

The debate just described is reflected by Marlowe in the ways his titular heroes engage with the icon of Helen of Troy. Marlowe, rather than take a position pro or con in that debate, instead dramatizes a few of the instrumental uses to which the literary tradition of Helen and the Trojan War may be put in the service of tragedy. First let's examine evidence of that use in *Tamburlaine* Part Two. Consider the moment in which the hero delivers an elegy over the body of his wife Zenocrate, who is dying outside their tent on the battlefield. To praise the woman whom he says has inspired his life's work as a warrior, Tamburlaine (and thus Marlowe) puts pressure on the genre of heroic poetry itself by displacing Homer's paean to Helen of Troy with the figure of her superlative rival, Zenocrate:

> And had she lived before the siege of Troy,
> Helen, whose beauty summoned Greece to arms
> And drew a thousand ships to Tenedos,
> Had not been named in Homer's Iliads—
> *Her* name had beene in every line he wrote;
> . . .
> Zenocrate had been the argument
> Of every epigram or elegy.
>
> 　　　　　　　　　*2 Tamburlaine* 2.4.86–90, 94–5

At precisely this moment, melodramatically, '*The music sounds, and she dies*' (*2 Tamb.* 2.4.95 s.d.). With Zenocrate imagined as Homer's muse, his *casus belli*,[23] we might be tempted to extrapolate that Tamburlaine thus comes close to casting himself as Paris, Helen's abductor in the *Iliad*. For much as the Trojan prince has 'raped' Helen, as Marlowe and his fellow poets said,[24] so has the terror of Asia also 'raped' Zenocrate in Part One of the play as she progressed with her 'Soldiers *loaden with treasure*' from Medea to Memphis (*1 Tamb.* 1.2.0 s.d.). Yet even in the throes of grief Tamburlaine stops short of borrowing from the Homeric tradition to give his pain verbal shape. Inspired though he is by the *Iliad*, he in effect revises the poem by projecting onto it a new fictional past, with Zenocrate its star. His treatment of Helen as a displaceable sign of fabulous beauty demonstrates not only autonomy from the canon of classical poetry, but a fascinating kind of solipsism. From his point of view, the literary canon is, if anything, simply one more test of his will to control the world. Tamburlaine bows to no one – no king, genre, or poetic forebear, not even Homer. He suffers no anxiety of influence.

By contrast, in the largest sense, anxiety of influence is perhaps the defining feature of Faustus's psychomachia. From the very first scene, where Faustus throws out the *Analytics* and the *Code of Justinian*, until the last, where he cries out 'come not, Lucifer! / I'll burn my books. Ah, Mephistopheles!' (A 5.2.122–3), a man of action is being strangled by a performative notion of identity, the scripts for which he finds in books. When, for example, he praises Lucifer, he might as well be reading from *Malleus Maleficarum*, so orthodox is his language of rebellion. 'To [*Beelzebub*] I'll build an altar and a church, / And offer lukewarm blood, of new-born babes' (A 2.1.13–14), he says without relish. But as it turns out, Faustus's sacrifice is reflexive. As he confides to his students late in the game, 'O, would I had never seen Wittenberg, never read / book!' (A 5.2.20–21).[25]

Faustus's infatuation with texts as scripts for his own action reaches an apotheosis late in Act 5 when he twice summons Helen of Troy to the stage. In her stead, of course, a dazzling succubus appears in the doctor's room at Wittenberg. The event takes us hopscotching across boundaries metaphysical, ontological, theological, and generic. Her appearance is precipitated by a mundane request from Faustus's pupils that helps to demonstrate how fully they have embraced his fantastically plastic values, which clearly permit shades to be summoned from beyond the River Styx without the students suffering anxiety of Christian damnation. Having talked of 'fair ladies – which was the beautifull'st in all the / world,' they ask their teacher to produce 'Helen of Greece' for their specular satisfaction (A 5.1.10–11, 11–12). He complies, but cautions, 'Be silent then, for danger is in words' (A 5.1.25), an admonition that might serve as an ironic motto of the play, even of the Marlowe canon. On a first pass across the stage Helen evaporates without incident, and the students exit, sated. As they go, the second scholar admits to an anxiety of influence that flatters the Homeric tradition and its presumed ubiquitous dissemination: 'Too simple is my wit to tell her praise, / Whom all the world admires for majesty' (A 5.1.26–7).

So far, 'Helen's' function in *Faustus* is as a pin-up for adolescent university students, a didactic sign of the delicious perils of physical temptation slightly disguised as aesthetic appreciation. But that abruptly changes, once Faustus and Mephistopheles are alone on stage. No longer is the doctor the cool university teacher whose desires are vicariously titillated by his pupils' silent blazon of Helen's topography. Now more Walter Mitty than Clark Kent/Superman, Faustus summons the prosthetic Helen again in order to perform before her. The very fact of her artificialness – her specular fictiveness – is a large part of her allure, for when he looks into Helen's eyes, he hopes to see himself as a great figure. Very much unlike most of the male figures in the *Iliad*, who groan that rash Paris is responsible for great bloodshed, who are openly uncertain about Helen's value in a martial (also homosocial) culture, Faustus is unambiguously thrilled by the virtual Helen[26] that Mephistopheles cheerfully creates. Her presence seems to him to hold out the prospect of a radical metamorphosis of his own identity.

Helen's second appearance in Act 5 is the last moment of magical realism in the tragedy. The laws of ordinary reality are again temporarily suspended to make it possible for Faustus to fantasize an escape from tragedy into another kind of story. As she shimmers into view a second time, the doctor is enraptured. Yet unlike the second scholar, he aims to prove himself worthy of this Helen, for it is not that he wants passively to admire her beauty, but to escape from a world where the walls are coming closer and closer together to crush him. Just as his fantasy of being 'great emperor of the world' (A 1.3.106) is from the first an effervescently bookish aspiration, so too is his apostrophe to Helen a kind of early modern reader response to his own mortality:

> Was this the face that launched a thousand ships
> And burnt the topless towers of Ilium?
> Sweet Helen, make me immortal with a kiss.
>   [*They kiss.*]
> Her lips sucks forth my soul. See where it flies!
> Come, Helen, come, give me my soul again.
>   [*They kiss again.*]
> Here will I dwell, for heaven be in these lips,
> And all is dross that is not Helena.

At this point, like a voyeur, the Old Man silently returns to stage, perhaps standing in for 'weak' Menelaus's marital claim on Helen. Emboldened by being watched, Faustus fantasizes becoming a Trojan prince:

> I will be Paris, and for love of thee
> Instead of Troy shall Wittenberg be sacked,
> And I will combat with weak Menelaus,
> And wear thy colours on my plumèd crest.
> Yea, I will wound Achilles in the heel
> And then return to Helen for a kiss.   A 5.1.91–103

Helen's silence, generically prescribed by the dumb show format, allows Marlowe to concentrate our attention on the doctor's mental processes, as he envisions himself in the pomp of battle.[27] Some time ago, Ian Watt asserted that these lines establish Faustus as a 'heroic lover.'[28] Perhaps. They do reveal some of his fantasy material, but what is revealed would seem to make his character less heroic, not more. For 'Paris' is a deeply problematic role for Faustus to choose. We need only recall how Paris had allowed himself to be bribed by the reward of Helen, while judging whether Hera, Athena, or Aphrodite was most beautiful, to grasp how far afield the role of Paris would have taken Faustus from his early goal of being 'great emperor of the world' (A 1.3.106).

It is important that Marlowe allow Faustus to aspire to, but not become Paris for even a single line. One could argue that his getting into character should have been no problem given that, with

Mephistopheles's help in Act 3, he has easily stolen the identity of a cardinal at the Vatican. But at this late point, the game is up. The play is swinging back toward foundational orthodoxies rejected by Faustus in Act 1. So his apostrophe, more a lament than a request to Mephistopheles, is overdetermined to fail. Its futility draws us to *feel* how Faustus has been neutered by an investment in the rhetoric of what is to us the almost campy hypermasculinity encoded in epic poetry. The collapse of the possibility of heroic playing into the pitiful, abortive gesture that has Faustus competing with 'weak Menelaus' for the affections of a succubus illustrates what is so dangerous about his attempting to borrow identity from a playscript.

Kissing a succubus is surely a perverse reward for any 'Sir Paris,' as Faustus calls his alter ego, to seek for wounding Achilles (A 5.1.23). It makes the idea of playing Paris a demonic violation of being, much as the more vociferous Puritan critics of the theater were then arguing was true of all stage impersonations. That complaint is reinforced, perhaps ironically, by the grotesque image of Helen's lips sucking up Faustus's soul. The slavishness of Faustus's submission may remind us that in the *Iliad*, Paris is criticized by his fellow Trojans for being more of a 'girl watcher' than man-at-arms.[29] In all, Faustus's proposed romance with Helen, with his earlier obsession with having a 'wife' (A 2.1.143), render him beyond the pale of martial glory in any classical sense. While a magically real 'Helen of Troy' penetrates the tedium and terror of Act 5, the figure is unavailable as warp rescuer. Faustus cannot expect to be beamed up.

Flyting Benvolio

The most direct and extensive consideration of soldiering in the play has come earlier, in Act 4. In both 'A' and 'B' Faustus plays the magician usurper in his visit to the court of the Holy Roman Emperor, Charles V, father of England's wartime nemesis Philip II. While at court Faustus is asked to reassure and entertain the emperor by summoning familiars in the shapes of Alexander the Great and his paramour. Their evocation excites Charles to the point of erotic rapture, laying the groundwork for the worshipful apostrophe to the 'Helen' who shows up in Act 5: both of these contacts between a diminished present reality and devilish spirits from a netherworld are simultaneously beautiful but bathetic; both cast aspersions on Faustus's and Charles's ambivalent self-representations here as fighting men; both contacts with the mirages of their respective fantasies make the doctor and emperor seem smaller and desperate rather than larger than life and heroic. Indeed those ambivalent self-representations are linked. As the dumb show vanishes, the emperor's impulsive neediness that it has developed will be encapsulated by his proposed gift to Faustus of 'command' of Germany (B 4.1.172).[30] The timing is auspicious, for the gift is clearly too great for the circumstance, akin to Edward II's impulses to lavish estates on Gaveston when art has swayed that king's fancy. It is almost embarrassing here to see Charles so grateful that he would even casually offer to relinquish control of Germany, a sizable, historically fractious piece of his own empire. The deference implied in such a gesture had been one of Faustus's desires even from his first contact with Mephistopheles in Act 1, though there Faustus had envisioned himself wielding a godlike authority over the Holy Roman Emperor's own life. In time, by the power of 'art,' he had dictated imperiously, even Charles himself 'shall not live but by my leave, / Nor any potentate of Germany' (A 1.3.112–13).

Both 'A' and 'B' juxtapose Charles's tacit acknowledgment of his own vulnerability as emperor (and warlord) with his knights' quite unwarranted sense of invincibility. The emperor's palpable self-doubt is actually stronger in the 'A' version of events. This makes sense if we read *Faustus* as a wartime effort to depict predatory playing: for by the time 'B' was being revised, presumably early in the seventeenth century, Philip II was dead (d. 1598) and the Anglo-Spanish war was subsiding, thus diminishing the incentive for any English playwright or reviser to focus on Charles as an ineffectual weakling beset with anxiety about his legacy. Some ten years earlier, though, Marlowe had had every incentive to bedevil Philip in a patriotic drama by misrepresenting his late father as a weak leader. In a stroke of genius Marlowe undermines Charles in 'A' not by having him suffer physical incursions (a box on the ears, the fate of Pope Adrian in Act 3; or the cuckold's horns, the fate of the Knight in Act 4), but psychological ones that originate within the character of Charles himself. So the weakness confessed by the emperor signals an internally resident blot, and is not simply a sign of his situational misfortune. Direct evidence comes in 'A' as Charles commissions Faustus to bring Alexander to the stage: he confesses to being recently troubled by doubts about his own accomplishments and his heirs' prospects for success as kings. 'As I was sometime solitary set / Within my closet, sundry thoughts arose / About the honour of mine ancestors – / How they had won by prowess such exploits, / Got such riches, subdued so many kingdoms / As we that do succeed or they that shall / Hereafter possess our throne shall, / I fear me, never attain to that degree / Of high renown and great authority' (A 4.1.20–28). In the quiet privacy of his 'closet,' then, Charles has skeptically pondered his achievements, and has found cause to doubt his legacy. The private nature of his anxiety distinguishes his experience from Benvolio's very public withdrawal from stage when he is faced with an uphill battle to restore his own dignity and shore up his reputation. Benvolio had fallen prey to a game that Mark Breitenberg argues was common to early modern men, who would 'stag[e] masculine loss and vulnerability for the purpose of maintaining control of the performance of one's gendered identity.' Benvolio's wager in 'B' would qualify as a game staged in hopes it would pay him large psychic returns on his investment in the joke. As the dramatic 'game' goes awry, however, the rhetoric of masculinity at court is instead utterly subverted.[31]

While 'A' establishes the private circumstances of the emperor's 'fear' about the degree of his own 'renown,' a fear which allows Faustus to transform an ostensible royal entertainment into mockery, the horseplay of 'B' substantially elaborates the merry public attack on the men upon whom he would need to rely to build a greater legacy: the knights who serve the Empire. 'B' tilts the focus away from Charles onto his men. With Philip safely dead by the time *Faustus* is being revised into what we now call 'B', this shift could even be read as a quasi-royalist effort to recuperate the noble status of Charles's kingship (tarnished in 'A') at the expense of common soldiers, a maneuver that would have been consistent with sentiments in England against Roman Catholic knights, not to mention ordinary soldiers of all persuasions. Both 'A' and 'B' further the Marlovian effort to blacken the knights' prowess by having Faustus verbally spar with one particular knight, who is given a pair of cuckold's horns in both versions and the name 'Benvolio' in 'B.' In time, having removed his opponent's horns, the doctor literally recovers his own decapitated head, fights hand to hand, and shames the knights into exile. Introducing the language of shame and exile, 'B' also explicitly draws attention to the tactic of ontological as well as physical assault that is only implicit in 'A'; in 'B' the palace knights of the imperial army are rendered 'incontinent' by Faustus's response to their ambush and decapitation of him (B 4.2.105). The amplifications in 'B' signal that the writers hired by Henslowe to revise *Faustus* after Marlowe's death grasped the paradox of 'A': that the *Faustus* performed before 1593 cultivates nationalist sentiments in order to promote aesthetic resistance to soldiering, even as it celebrates the player as a theatrical predator who can help to keep England's defense strong.

Marlowe imagines knights whose own thought processes and actions against Faustus make plain that they are not up to the job of defending the Empire; they resemble the Catholic monk–soldiers whose indolence and cowardice featured in *The Jew of Malta*. In 'A' they are as self-righteous as they are helpless against Faustus's machinations. Reacting to his very own pair of cuckold's horns, for instance, the Knight can only insult Faustus by impugning his social class status: 'Thou damnèd wretch and execrable dog, / Bred in the concave of some monstrous rock, / How dar'st thou thus abuse a gentleman?' (A 4.1.81–3). As a retort to public humiliation, this is presumptuous but uneventful revenge, words rather than deeds, a formula that Marlowe had to know would make his spectators laugh at the gap between bombast and passivity. Much of the comedy lies in our awareness of the Knight's paralysis in fighting back, a paralysis that comes to overwhelm all of the palace knights in 'B.' Indeed 'B' amplifies the minimal clues to Marlowe's own thinking about the knights' mettle. In 'B' they are debauched, lazy, belligerent, and volatile. They are laughably susceptible to all intimations, however specious, of their inadequacy as knights and men. Lolling about, they embody the formulaic faults of an army suffering from a lack of discipline but no lack of presumption. From the first moment in act 4, their heads aching from too much drink, their conduct reifies military theorists' caveats about drunkenness. In 1590, for example, Sir John Smythe faults the military campaigns in the Low Countries for teaching English soldiers . . . to drink. The vice, he writes, is 'the very mother and nurse of effeminacy, of cowardice, of sensuality, of rebellion, of covetousness, and all other vices that can be imagined.'[32] For Smythe, as for Charles's knights, imagination itself is presented as a potential source of danger to the state. From the beginning, almost inexplicably, the knights are hostile to Faustus; they scorn his reputed magical powers.

Like Sir John Smythe's disgust with drunkenness, the knights are energized to speak out against Faustus by fearful disgust about the loss of control over the somatic body and the effects on military readiness of an imagination gone awry. These fears come across early, alchemized into acidic doubts about the tangible effects of various art forms that are integral to the action in the scene: the use of myth, the dumb show of Alexander and so forth as well as the other prosthetic manipulations of bodies (the cuckold's horns in 'A' and 'B', the false head in 'B'), the intertextual appropriation of epic poetry, and metatheatrical discourse itself. On the one hand, the knights initially express disbelief that black art in particular is capable of doing anything. Yet on the other hand, they soon come to fear what it does to their own control over the world they know. These art forms, even the folk art of cuckolds' horns, cultivate misalliances of social class, genre, and military status that the knights perceive as threats to themselves if not also to Charles and the Holy Roman Empire. These forms of art can be threatening because they invite civilians to blur the lines between genders, nations, and social strata that help an empire demarcate itself from its enemies, foreign and domestic.

The play's exploitation of cultural anxiety about the power of art to cultivate misalliances, to 'admit a plurality of worlds,' as Zamora and Faris say of magical realism, is evident in several ways. Most simply, the word *art* is bandied about indiscriminately. In every case it connotes some form of the capacity to effect advantage and fame if not global dominance and, in doing so, to disturb the status quo. The knight Martino, for example, sarcastically reports 'the wonder of the world for magick art' has arrived from Rome (B 4.1.11), signifying Faustus's fame and reminding his fellows that the doctor is coming from, as it were, the enemy camp; Faustus's rescue of Bruno in Rome is said by Charles to 'add more excellence unto thine art / Than if by powerful necromantic spells / Thou couldst command the world's obedience,' surely a reckless admission of curtailed ambition from the Holy Roman Emperor (B 4.1.52–4); 'by power of art' the doctor is prepared, he replies, to cast 'charms, that shall pierce' hell's gates to make the Furies do as Charles 'commands' (B 4.1.66, 67–8, 70); and Faustus taunts Benvolio for having doubted the power of black magic, vowing revenge 'if my art fail me not' and cutting him with a parodic rejoinder, saying of himself 'The doctor has no skill, / No art, no cunning,' even as Benvolio can feel the horns on his head growing (B 4.1.90–91, 139–40). If the sheer repetition of the word 'art,' with its slippery multiple significations, virtually erases any distinction between the black arts and the arts generally, these repetitions provide elemental evidence that Charles's court assumes that art may be pressed into service as a weapon by which control and consequent fame may be garnered. Even the Chorus plays along. Effecting the transition from the papal chamber in Act 3 to the adventures at court in Act 4, the Chorus speaks of Faustus as a medieval knight, called to a ritual test of his own prowess, in which the term 'art' substitutes for 'martial strength': 'What there he did in trial of his art / I leave untold, your eyes shall see performed' (A Chorus 4, 16–17).

At the heart of the episode in both 'A' and 'B' is the dumb show of Alexander the Great, who appears as a transcendental parrot.[33] Alexander makes an even better choice of idol for Charles than we might expect. His entrance interrupts and calls into question the banal reality at court, but is nonetheless accepted by Charles as raising the conversation rather than threatening his own position. Magically real, the dumb show offers a 'historical allegory' by which Marlowe slyly develops the court's philosophical self-consciousness and his fairly straightforward political criticism of Catholic Charles. Given that Marlowe's Charles teeters on the brink of becoming a laconic sycophant even in 'A', it must have been difficult for contemporary spectators to humor his fantasy of being descended from Alexander's lineage. The misalliance between the classical hero and the star-struck king may well have seemed laughably reductive to playgoers familiar with grander representations of the ancient warrior in other contemporary texts, for Alexander is lionized in late Elizabethan culture. William Harrison glorifies Alexander in *The Description of England* (1577, 1587), for example. Explaining why England is delightfully free of troublesome 'lions, bears, tigers' and other predators, Harrison pauses to praise Alexander's extraordinary heroism as a hunter.

> At vacant times [he] hunted the tiger, the pard [the leopard], the boar, and the bear, but most willingly lions, because of the honorable estimation of that beast, insomuch that at one time he caused an odd or chosen lion (for force and beauty) to be let forth unto him hand to hand, with whom he had much busyness, albeit that in the end he overthrew and killed the beast.

And in *The Arte of English Poesie* (1589) George Puttenham uses Alexander to show that poetry does encourage martial valor. Advancing a claim that poets were more highly valued in previous ages, Puttenham ventures that Alexander held 'the noble poemes of *Homer*' in such esteem that 'every night they were layd under his pillow, and by day were carried in the rich jewell cofer of *Darius* lately before vanquished by him in battaile.'[34] In *Faustus*, then, especially in a culture that regularly celebrated Alexander the Great as a conqueror worthy of emulation, a cameo of Alexander performed by an incubus is perversely designed to shrink Charles by juxtaposition. Nor is Marlowe the first to make the unfavorable comparison between the two emperors. Martin Luther, writing of Charles's lack of support for religious reformers earlier in the sixteenth century, judged him to be unlike an ancient Roman or Greek general in lacking their savvy, ambition, and fortitude. Charles, wrote Luther, 'does not understand our cause, even when someone reads our books to him. Were he a Scipio, an Alexander, or a Pyrrhus, he would break through the papal net and conquer the Germans himself. He begins many things, but completes few. . . . He yields easily in negotiations and this is not because he is a generous spirit. . . . Charles is a melancholy and passionate man, but he is not heroic.'[35]

The dumb show presents Charles in the posture of hero worship. As an art form it also anticipates the development of the masque after Marlowe's death: as Faustus's patron, Charles wants to cross the line from spectator to player by leaving his throne to embrace the illusion of Alexander. In this gesture Charles will seek to cross the frontier of the fantastic; failing to do so will bring him further along in recognizing the power of art to effect the self-consciousness that is prerequisite to the successful pursuit of martial glory in Marlowe's universe. That process is present in 'A' but nicely mirrored and elaborated in 'B,' so the balance of my analysis of the dumb show and the quarrel between Faustus, Benvolio, and his fellow knights will focus on 'B.'

In an extended, marvelously real bit of stagecraft that brings demonic illusions of shades of the dead to stage, Alexander the Great and the Paramour are made to appear first, followed by a pantomime of Alexander's noted defeat of Darius, king of Persia. Helen of Troy these are not. From stage gossip we learn that this incubus Alexander has been summoned to flatter Charles, yet the modern emperor's engagement in the dumb show compounds the specularity of his anxieties of his own weakness. As the knight Martino wryly suggests, Charles is just too keen to be linked via the incubus to 'the race of all his stout progenitors' (B 4.1.13). By having Faustus collaborate in inventing a contrived genealogy to unite ancient Rome and the Holy Roman Empire of contemporary times, Martino hints, Charles hopes to find confirmation of his own credentials as one naturally destined to rule the world.

It is important that Charles is mesmerized by the dumb show. Although the vocabulary of his praise for Alexander's 'warlike semblances' (B 4.1.15) differentiates between the semblance of an incubus costumed as a Roman emperor and the so-called real thing, a differentiation that is even stronger in 'A,' Charles quickly loses his detachment from the show. Forgetting the rules Faustus has laid down, he rushes the stage and '*offers to embrace*' Alexander (B 4.1.102 s.d.). As the doctor stops him, chiding, 'my gracious lord, you do forget yourself. / These are but shadows, not substantial,' Charles is almost breathless: 'O, pardon me. My thoughts are so ravishèd / With sight of this renownèd emperor / That in mine armes I would have compassed him' (B 4.1.103–104). The homosocial vector of Charles's desire for Alexander is unmistakable if also subordinated. It's worth remembering too that in *Edward II*, Alexander's 'companion' is said to be the warrior 'Hephestion' (*Edward II* 1.4.391). And what is cuckoldry if not an 'affair between men,' in Coppélia Kahn's memorable phrase?[36] At the least, Charles is depicted here as being not only foolishly susceptible to the illusions of art, unable to hold in his mind the idea that illusions never prove to be what they seem, but also open to seductive manipulation at the hands of a courtier who produces magnificent objects to be admired, rather more like Edward II early in his tragedy than Charles might want spectators to recognize. Indeed, in the first Chorus there exists a subtle recognition in *Faustus* that soldiers-turned-lovers may be apt to sleep with the enemy instead of fighting him, that the line between sex and conquest, love and war, is in these soldiers' minds a very fine line. As Graham Hammill wryly observes of the Prologue, it seems that in the fields of Trasimene 'the troops perform not fighting but mating.'[37] At Charles's court, then, art is dangerous in part because it opens up the somatic body and the imagination to scrutiny.

More complex evidence of the predatory potential of 'art' lies in the intertwined vignettes of Benvolio's challenge and the subsequent ambush. The first of these is the more provocative, for it taps not only the expected early modern jokes about cuckolds, but also modern chimeras about transvestism, sodomy, and dismemberment. Benvolio's wager is less straightforward than it seems: 'An / thou bring Alexander and his paramour before the Emperour,' he says to Faustus, 'I'll be Actaeon and turn myself to a stag.' The doctor replies, in an aside, 'And I'll play Diana and send you the horns / presently' (B 4.1.98–102).[38] Throwing out a verbal gage, Benvolio flirts with what is to him the outlandish idea of becoming a character in a classical myth (precisely what Faustus hopes to accomplish in Act 5 in his apostrophe to Helen). As the myth goes, Acteon is changed into a stag by Diana for spying on her bath, then torn apart by his hunting dogs, which cannot recognize their master's new identity. (It may be relevant that in the previous scene Rafe has been 'transform[ed]' 'into a dog' by Mephistopheles [A 3.2.38–40].)

The multiple functions of the Acteon myth in *Faustus* are consistent with its role in the early modern period as a meeting place for a wealth of ideas, as Leonard Barkan, Patrick Cheney, Nancy Vickers and others have shown.[39] As Barkan notes is generally the case, Marlowe uses the myth as a semi-covert 'emblem of espionage against a monarch.' Most pertinent to my argument is its function as a 'drama of embarrassment,' a parable of the process of coming into self-consciousness.[40] If the entire scenario at court is set up by Faustus to force soldiers of the Holy Roman Empire into self-consciousness through the medium of drama, then the drama of embarrassment intensifies once the dumb show is dismissed and our attention turns to the court itself. With Alexander et al. gone, Faustus makes good on his earlier threat against his naysayer Benvolio, roasting him with 'spreading horns most strangely fastenèd' (B 4.1.122; '*a pair of horns*' A 4.1.76 s.d.) and calling Charles's attention to the jest. 'See, see, my gracious lord, what strange beast is yon, that / thrusts his head out at window' (B 4.1.119–20). The emperor, invited to play the spectator again, but now with Benvolio substituting for Alexander as the object of his gaze, approves of the doctor's revenge. Saying 'this sport is excellent,' Charles jokes that Benvolio would need no weapon in battle, for his head is 'armed sufficiently' (B 4.1.126, 134). Teasing the braggart about his battle readiness, the emperor is genially amused, not alarmed, by Benvolio's being held up to ridicule. This 'sport' is offered as further entertainment for an emperor who admits that the dumb show of classical battle has 'better pleasest me / Than if I gained another monarchy' (B 4.1.116–17). In this gush we can hear one version of the risks some commentators in early modern London would say that stage entertainments posed to nation or empire – they rob the imperial will of bloodthirst. The probability of this risk is raised further by Benvolio's behavior as the dumb show ends. He is seen perched in the second-floor window, amazed into a stupor, provoking the duke of Saxony who spies him to wonder in jest, 'What, is he asleep, or dead?' (B 4.1.124). Lulled into lethargy by a magic show, Benvolio is seen to be unprepared to defend even himself from shenanigans.

Before falling into a stupor, Benvolio had divulged through his jest with Faustus larger worries about the relative enthusiasm for fiction-making versus war-making within Charles's court. Subsequently, in order to plumb anxieties that the court has now become a space principally for entertainment, and for theatrical pleasure at that, and not for advancing the Empire, Marlowe's revisers in 'B' stretch the Acteon myth across the episode. It recurs as a base text as the knights plot strategy, compare wounds or ruminate on what injury may yet come to them; for example, the ambush is set up in a 'grove' as the soldiers hide 'in an ambush there behind the trees,' as if re-enacting Acteon's surveillance of Diana (B 4.2.16–18). Conversely, it is also a base text in the doctor's machinations against the knights and the emperor; its strategic deployment helps to advance the doctor from peripatetic courtier to sardonic predator. This is plainly seen once the dumb show is dismissed. Faustus reiterates Benvolio's pledge 'in bold Actaeon's shape to turn a stag' (B 4.1.144), then proposes to the emperor another magic trick that suddenly chills the episode by its casual brutality: 'And therefore, my lord, so please your Majesty, / I'll raise a kennel of hounds shall hunt him so / As all his footmanship shall scarce prevail / To keep his carcass from their bloody fangs. / Ho, Belimoth, Argiron, Ashtaroth! (B 4.1.145–9). These lines swerve toward theatricalized sadism, but just as quickly back away. So both Benvolio and Faustus invoke Acteon's story to get advantage over the other. But notice that Faustus's inhabiting the myth is far more aggressive, destructive, and mean-spirited than anything Benvolio musters.

In a knight's hands, as the passage above implies, the Acteon myth can convey the danger of being killed by, as it were, 'friendly fire.' This fear is registered but also neutralized at the scene's end when Martino falters in recognizing his muddy horned comrade. Not knowing him for certain, Martino guesses at his buddy's identity: 'How now, Benvolio?' Then Martino attempts to reassure Benvolio that the knights will hold their fire – 'fear not, man. We have no power to kill' (B 4.3.7, 9) – thus giving an explanation that reminds us of the risks to soldiers in battle who cannot recognize their own kind, for which Acteon's grisly fate could also function as a metaphor in the early modern period. As Martino confesses, although the knights can still distinguish one another on stage, though not with certainty, they have been in effect disarmed – stripped of the 'power to kill' – by Faustus's wrathful art. This outcome was clearly unimaginable to Benvolio when he jested about playing Acteon as a way of tormenting his foe and foreshadows the ending of the knights' engagement with the magician visiting from Rome.

Further, Benvolio's use of the Acteon story to express contempt for Faustian art could be broadened to encompass the knights' contempt for fiction-making in general, or at least for other people's fictions. We have some evidence of that in the knight's debut in 'B'. Awakened from a hangover and egged on by his fellows, who presumably know of his knee-jerk hostility to all things invisible as well as his braggadocio, Benvolio comes to an upstairs window to play the buffoon. He is eager to dismiss the practice of black magic before meeting Faustus. Ironically, he justifies his scorn for Faustian magic by way of a folk-saying about Lucifer that is itself a form of art. 'They say / if a man be drunk overnight the devil cannot hurt him in / the morning. If that be true, I have a charm in my head / shall control him as well as the conjurer, I warrant you' (B 4.1.44–7). A short while later he adds as an aside, 'Blood, he speaks terribly. / But for all that, I do not greatly believe him. He looks as / like a conjurer as the Pope to a Costermonger' (B 4.1.71–3). Benvolio knows only what he can see, dismissing Faustus's Senecanesque rant against him as mere rhetoric: that almost always turns out to be a mistake in Marlowe's universe.

Benvolio's character obviously functions as a comic foil for a more hospitable view of the potential of mimesis. His jest is instantly bounced back to him with a tricky spin, like a tennis ball, raising the stakes, as Faustus offers to 'play Diana and send you the horns presently' (B 4.1.101–2). In some respects this is a puzzling comeuppance. On the one hand, *cuckold's* horns are not part of the Acteon myth, but rather a special gift to Benvolio that shows Faustus' sense of humor.[41] Instead of a stag, Benvolio gets to become a *mere* cuckold, an imitation stag. The blurred etiology of his horns effectively syncretizes a bloody classical story of illicit desire, vision, and knowledge with a medieval and early modern folk tradition that punishes betrayal on these counts far more genially. On the other hand, Faustus's declared intention to 'play Diana' opposite Benvolio's Acteon is startling. It compounds the anxieties of dismemberment and cuckoldry by adding to them the (admittedly unlikely) prospect of his own transgendering from male magician and church doctor to pagan female deity. Aspiring to Christian godhead is one thing, to an Ovidian sex change quite another. The plan to 'play Diana' also threatens to encode Benvolio's sexuality in a way that might expose him to intense shame from his fellow knights. Were Faustus to 'play Diana,' he would be casting himself as the object of Benvolio's passionate gaze, thus trapping Benvolio in his own assignment as Acteon. As Nancy Vickers observes of the Acteon myth generally, it reduces the hunter to the hunted.[42] Extended in this way by Faustus to mark the knight with imputed sodomitical longings, Benvolio's jest instantly boomerangs.

When literary warriors ritually insult each another as Faustus and Benvolio do, Richard Martin calls the exchange 'flyting': a contest of insults between adversaries, an agonistic volley of '"cutting words,"' a 'verbal assault' in lieu of a physical one. As Martin and others point out, flyting is common not only in Germanic epic or the *Iliad*, Martin's particular subject. Flyting is integral to any 'shame or "results-culture,"'[43] such as the one that prevails at the Carolingian court. We get a good example of the practice of flyting as the knights of the Empire prefer to practice it – against a dead foe – just after they jump Faustus and cut off his head, an episode of dismemberment that is perhaps anticipated in 'A' when Faustus is assaulted by the horse-courser and temporarily 'loses' his leg, which is detached from his trunk (A 4.1.174 s.d.). The dismemberment is escalated in 'B' when the knights sever Faustus's false head. They naturally assume that a decapitated foe is dead, yet impulsively they continue to do him harm by flyting his corpse. Their actions indicate that in their world, shame is a fate worse than death, and also that language is at least as powerful a weapon as the sword. They go poetic, vying with one another to deliver the most comically grievous insult. Asks one knight, 'Was this that stern aspect, that awful frown, / Made the grim monarch of infernal spirits / Tremble and quake at his commanding charms?' Another sportingly carries the shaming further: 'Was this that damnèd head whose heart conspired / Benvolio's shame before the Emperor?' (B 4.2.46–50). This blazon of Faustus' face shifts us briefly to the genre of mock epyllion, anticipating Faustus's own apostrophe to Helen of Troy ('Was this the face that launched a thousand ships') discussed above. Having these cads mimic the doctor's later bid to become Paris in Act 5, the reviser of 'B' prepares us to hear that apostrophe, when it gets to us, as silly rather than heroic.

Decapitated in the ambush by the trio of knights who intend to restore their so-called 'honor' by this deed, Faustus performs his greatest trick, the fulcrum of magical realism in the play: he reattaches his own head, resurrecting himself from the dead. At this point in the game he is simply impervious to the mortality of the flesh, to being viscerally 'divided,' as Martino says, evoking a late sixteenth-century technique for eliminating wayward souls (the possessed and the dispossessed) who dared to defy authority of whatever sort (B 4.2.65). The doctor's self-recapitation is unique amongst his tricks because elsewhere 'B' fixates on images of dismemberment. Threats of being 'divided' abound in both 'A' and 'B,' as when the Evil Angel warns Faustus, 'If thou repent, devils shall tear thee in pieces' (A 2.3.80), a threat reiterated by Mephistopheles: 'Revolt, or I'll in piecemeal tear thy flesh' (A 5.1.69). When the scholars find 'Faustus' limbs, / All torn asunder' in 'B''s final scene (B 5.3.6–7), we are invited to imagine him suffering in hell the talionic tortures spelled out earlier in Act 5 by the Bad Angel. These images make the re-membering in 'B' all the more an idiosyncratic retort to the threat of catastrophic corporal dismemberment that pervades both 'A' and 'B.' As a further sign of efforts in 'B' to defy the status quo, the false head is not employed to signify the comic monstrousness of the stage Vice tradition, but to celebrate an oxymoron – a Piconean invincibility and infinity that is, in the terms of Doctor Faustus's bargain, ironically finite.

The plot device of recapitation can produce in audiences an instantaneous warp of causal logic on stage. In effect it transports both Faustus's foes and us beyond representational time and space, beyond the laws of ordinary reality – then back again. Subliminally it invites us to imagine resolving a dispute between factions not with deadly force but with cosmic laughter which, as early modern physiologists understood, rejuvenates the body – reintegrates it, if you will. Our laughing at these knights' efforts to assassinate Faustus cuts through their bombastic claims of authority, which spring from epistemic fantasies and historical realities integral to the Holy Roman Empire, which in Marlowe's lifetime continued to exert control over Europe. While the recapitated head in 'B' may seem like a small gesture toward fracturing that control, it marks and makes possible a swerve in the plot that exhibits one of the most fundamental features of magical realism, the capacity of that momentary rupture of ordinary reality to open a space-time in the narrative for injecting subtle criticism of prevailing historical circumstances, and usually political circumstances at that. The magically real 'parrot' is said to interrupt reality in a way that allows a spectator or reader to grasp that criticism while the narrative maintains the status quo of banal reality at a surface level. It may be objected that Faustus's recapitation does not meet the test of continuous narrative development, for it explicitly disrupts the rest of Act 4: it allows Faustus to avenge Benvolio's slight and indeed to drive the knights into exile *in toto*. But the recapitation is nevertheless an instance of magical realism, I would argue. It transports us across boundaries ontological and otherwise, it disrupts the power–authority differential at court, and it exerts no permanent alteration of the play's ontological landscape, but returns us at the end of Act 4 to Faustus's predicament.

With the emperor gone, *Faustus* 'B' creates a miniature mock-revenge tragedy in the balance of Act 4 that calls attention to the subject of class strife at Charles's court and in the play more generally. Act 4, scene 2 is a comic collage of class consternation masquerading as grand chivalry, where *Faustus's* revisers lay out the architecture of the knights' imperious minds and plumb the depths of their courage, which turns out to be thin bravado, as it does with so many of Marlowe's own soldiers. As *The Jew of Malta* had also done, *Faustus* 'B' uncovers some of the dirty little secrets that debauched knights try to gild in chivalry in the late sixteenth century. For one, they relinquish the pretense that everyone in battle is motivated by high ideals, a fiction they ordinarily rely on to sustain their chivalric program of action, even as they count on the mercenary greed of common soldiers. Among actual soldiers at the time, that ploy was very common, probably essential to sanity. As John Lingham observes in an elegiac pamphlet he published in 1584 to remember English 'captaines and lieuetenants' who have fallen in the Low Countries, they have not gone there seeking 'lucar, wealth, or riches, but only for the good desire they have for the maintenaunce of the trueth, in which cause they have spent and lost their lives.'[44]

Faustus calls attention to the centrality of money to war, showing that knights who with Lingham maintain the chivalric fiction put themselves in paradoxically weak positions. For the common soldiers in 'B' are persuaded to join the reprised assault against the recapitated Faustus only by being paid to risk their lives. Yet those to whom Benvolio and Frederick appeal for aid seem to be members of Charles's army already, suggesting its reliance on mercenaries. Benvolio piques their interest by reporting that he has seen Faustus leaving Charles's castle 'laden with rich rewards,' urging 'Then, soldiers, boldly fight. If Faustus die, / Take you the wealth; leave us the victory' (B 4.2.22–3). Frederick bluntly reinforces the payoff: 'Come, soldiers, follow me unto the grove. / Who kills him shall have gold and endless love' (B 4.2.24–5). It works, of course. When we next see the soldiers they are laying a second ambush, as one tells the other, in order to 'help these noble gentlemen' 'kill the slave' (B 4.2.96, 98).

Does the soldier's use of 'gentlemen' and 'slave' signal that the dichotomy of social class is still intact, because he knows the very words needed to intensify and exploit the knights' class anxieties for the material gain of those commoners who, like Faustus, were born of 'parents base of stock' (A and B Prologue 11)? Or that the dichotomy is intact in spite of Benvolio's worry that his status has been diminished by the cuckold's horns? We know Benvolio is most distressed about what he sees as his public humiliation as a cuckold – as a man who has lost control over his woman and, more specifically, over her body. Pointing to 'my infamy' – cuckold's horns – Benvolio inflates the degree of his humiliation ('so great an injury') against which he prepares to endure a chivalric quest to avenge his honor: 'O, may these eyelids never close again / Till with my sword I have that conjurer slain!' (B 4.2.13, 4, 8–9). One may think of Rafe in *The Knight of the Burning Pestle* and not be far off. It is not that Benvolio feels shame from his fellows – they have urged him to let the great injury pass. As he explains to them, he feels pressure from men who are his social inferiors, and must reply because 'every servile groom jests at my wrongs / And in their rustic gambols proudly say, / "Benvolio's head was graced with horns today"' (B 4.2.5–7). These imagined 'rustic gambols,' a form of folk art, are one further instance of the misalliances created by 'art,' of which Charles's knights live almost inexplicably in fear.

Answering Benvolio's new faux-chivalric challenge, Faustus switches weapons. Instead of cuckold's horns, which inflict symbolic injuries, he commands Mephistopheles to escalate the conflict by using gunpowder against the mercenaries and mischievous physical torture against the trio of knights who persist in carrying out plans to slay him. Faustus relishes the scrimmage, crowing in advance of victory, 'Behold an army comes incontinent' (B 4.2.105). In this exchange spectacle is premium; the stage is noisy. Yet the sortie lacks the pomp, heroic speech, or even the sometimes-ironic gravitas that mark the playscripts that are more fully Marlowe's own. Picking up on cues in 'A,' 'B' seriously reduces the glory of engagement. The soldiers are shortly unnerved and driven from the stage by a muster of devils, equipped with the accoutrements of war. One devil enters '*playing on a drum, after him another bearing an ensign, and divers with weapons*; Mephistopheles *with fireworks*' (B 4.2.105 s.d.). The knights' own conduct during the skirmish does nothing to reverse the reductive nature of the scene's denouement. They return as the devils exit, to complain of the Prosperian revenge inflicted on them. One has been dragged through a lake of mud, a second through a briar; and a third has been hurled down a hill, his bones broken by boulders. Yet plausible proof of the pain of broken limbs is missing. Their worst injury is still the prosthetic horns, which now they all have the pleasure of getting. It is enough to drive them from Charles's court and the stage. As losers they instantly leap to the conclusion that they will be 'laughing-stocks to all the world,' liminal figures of 'brutish shapes' (B 4.3.20, 24), impotent Calibans. 'Sith black disgrace hath thus eclipsed our fame,' says Benvolio, 'We'll rather die with grief than live with shame' (B 4.3.25–6). What is that shame? Neither the somatic physiological transgression so brilliantly elaborated by Gail Paster in *The Body Embarrassed* nor the tropes of cuckoldry in Elizabethan and Jacobean literature that Doug Bruster has traced to anxieties about economic rivalry.[45] Through the drama of artful bodily embarrassment, slinking away from their 'black disgrace,' these Carolingian knights are taking flight from a higher consciousness – from a greater awareness of the limits that art may impose on their 'power to kill.' They dodge coming face to face with the limits on their ability – by making war – to make the world they and Charles wish to inhabit.

In one sense the knights are right – they do become 'laughing-stocks' in the theater if not 'to all the world.' The portraits in both 'A' and 'B' of Charles's knights as dizzy cowards who retreat from adversity makes for great entertainment. But unlike most city comedies of the late sixteenth and early seventeenth centuries, when *Faustus* was extremely popular in theaters, the comic strain here, especially in 'B', is pointed at political targets outside England. That gesture marks these dramas as being designed in part to reify national security risks posed by Roman Catholics and to promote ideological warfare against them rather than, say, against Puritans. The slim portraits of Charles and his army offered up in 'A' and 'B' carry out these functions not by puffing them up as petty tyrants, as Marlowe had done with Ferneze and the Knights of Malta, but by shrinking them. As we know from the playwright's other work, he might have written them into a very different play to produce a more intense reaction to the contemporary Spanish efforts to dominate 'all the world.' Certainly the portrait here is at odds not only with other Marlovian soldiers, but also with the reputation and historical record of Charles and especially the nearly 150,000 men serving in his armies in Europe and Northern Africa at mid-century.[46] They were anything but refugees shrinking back from meeting their enemies in battle.

What others within England and on the Continent thought of Charles V in the sixteenth and seventeenth centuries depended much on their national prejudices. A decade after Marlowe's death, William Segar complained that Charles had granted knighthoods too freely, like James I, 'not only to Gentlemen well borne, but also to Merchants and others, that ambitiously do seek it';[47] his complaint reiterates the struggle between knights and merchants in early modern London that we examined in *The Jew of Malta*. But more representative judgments focused on the very achievements that the stage-Charles had expressed anxiety about. Some suggested that Charles and his army were motivated by blood first, and then gold, and only then honor. The notorious instance of what was often seen even by some Catholics as the troops' ignoble conduct in war had come in 1527, when Charles's quasi-mutinous army, commanded by the constable of Bourbon, sacked Rome. The débâcle was not quickly forgotten, but stuck in Europe's craw for a very long time. Contemporary reactions had fallen along national rather than denominational lines. The Spanish humanist Vives celebrated the victory as a sign of the greatness of his nation and its leader: "'This is the destiny of Charles; to defeat only enemies in great numbers so as to make his victory all the more spectacular.'"[48]

But Luigi Guicciardini, brother of Francesco, the better-known historian of the Italian peninsula, published what he had witnessed in Rome. Unlike the arguably ironic glorifications of battle we get in other Marlowe plays, or the mortal innocuousness of combat in *Faustus*, Guicciardini stresses the blood and other visible and audible signs of carnage in 1527:

> Many nobles lay [in the streets] cut to pieces, covered with mud and their own blood, and many people only half dead lay miserably on the ground. Sometimes in that ghastly scene a child or man would be seen jumping from a window, forced to jump or jumping voluntarily to escape becoming the living prey of these monsters and finally ending their lives horribly in the street.[49]

Unable to get the screams out of his mind, Guicciardini explains he has 'decided therefore to describe these sufferings in detail, even though it was not the custom among past historians to write, except in general terms, about the misfortunes and disasters that occurred in captured cities' (106). Guicciardini's narrative of Rome's sack by Charles's army helps to establish that Marlowe could indeed have written the knights of the Empire into a very different kind of play had he so desired. Instead, Marlowe and his revisers have deliberately abjured that opportunity to make the knights either the focus of the tragedy or its villains, excluding them as cowards unworthy of that genre. Instead they are a society of dupes, vulnerable to the clever pretender who can impersonate the soldier to the point of becoming one himself, an opinion likewise voiced by Barabas in *The Jew of Malta*. Quipping that he once served as an 'engineer' 'in the wars 'twixt France and Germany,' he brags that 'Under pretence of helping Charles the Fifth,' he 'slew friend and enemy with my strategems' (*The Jew of Malta* 2.3.189–92).

'Bowght a robe for to goo invisibell' (*Henslowe's Diary*[50])

At the center of the B-text is a dramatic assault upon a pope, his prelates, and by extension all Roman Catholics. In Act 3, Marlowe dispatches Faustus and Mephistopheles inside the papal chamber, a nerve center of England's spiritual enemy in the Armada period. Throwing food and wine at the pope smacks of slapstick that twentieth-century critics often saw as being out of place in a tragedy. But it is a mistake to take apparently trivial plot events as necessarily signifying nothing beyond anti-popish mischief. However boorish, the Vatican episode seriously engages the secular, martial issues that are more visible in other parts of the play, and takes to a more sophisticated level those claims made elsewhere as to the ways that the stage subliminally, magically transforms what seems to be only the mimesis of aggression into the thing itself.

Faustus's ersatz pilgrimage to Rome to desecrate a holy site would have been taken as a cliché of Reformation polemic in the 1590s. It is not too wayward to read the Vatican episode as a loose imitation of the playwright's own infiltration of the English seminary at Rheims, a place-name mentioned in the episode. At Rheims Marlowe is said to have impersonated a devout Catholic while operating as a double agent.[51] Marlowe complicates the cliché somewhat by demonizing both Catholic and Protestant positions. If Catholicism is popery here, anti-popery is also devilish. Marlowe had available a model of such ideological, metatheatrical obfuscation in *The English Romayne Lyfe*, published by Anthony Munday in 1582. Part *apologia* of a spy, part field study of an expatriate enclave, part propaganda against Catholic monstrosities, *The English Romayne Lyfe*, like Act 3 of *Doctor Faustus*, shuttles its Protestant audience behind the enemy line. Certain details of the two plots are uncannily similar, especially the particulars of attacks on popes by Faustus and a Protestant martyr.

Munday tells an intermittently compelling story. But his assumptions about the theatrics of the insurgency he claims to have been engaged in are unexpectedly impoverished. Recounting a tour he has taken of underground vaults in Rome that house saints' relics, he reports that he abstained from praising any saint or disparaging any English noble loyal to Elizabeth's court. 'And this I may say boldlie, as God is my witnes, that in all the time I was amongst them: I neither offered moitie of misordred [sic] or undecent speech . . . no, nor so much as thought yll.'[52] He smirks at men with 'rash heads' who, safe in London, brag that, were *they* in Rome, 'they would tell the Pope of his lasciuious & vnchristian life, the Cardinals of their Sodomiticall sinnes . . . & the Preestes of their painted Purgatorie, their wafer God, and their counterfeit blood in the Challice' (65). In Rome, Munday avers, such charges against Catholic doctrine and its material props – the 'counterfeit blood' – would provoke 'mercilesse tiranny' (65) from Church Fathers.

The consequence of playing devil's advocate is vividly narrated in Munday's last chapter. It recounts the martyrdom of a Hertfordshire native and Protestant scourge who visited Rome in the summer of 1581. Richard Atkins had attacked the altar of St Peter's as the Eucharist was celebrated, throwing the chalice and its contents on the floor, much as Faustus seizes Adrian's food and wine. For this Atkins was beaten, 'caried to prison,' and sentenced to die for presuming '"to rebuke the Popes wickednesse"' (102). While he awaited the executioner, sundry Catholic Englishmen visited him, urging him to recant. He refused. For his intransigence he initially seems to be admired by Munday as a 'faithfull Soldier and Martir of Christe' (104). The English Catholics who urge Atkins to repent eventually abandon him, when they see how his Protestant faith is fixed. Reporting this, however, Munday also turns against Atkins, saying they abandon him 'to the devill, whom he serves' (104).[53]

Unambiguously, Atkins is said to serve the devil. But he is also depicted as a martyr. The final image in the report is of Atkins smiling at persecutors as they burn him at the stake 'verie cruelly' (104).[54] Then come the platitudes, and an unnerving surprise: Munday concludes Atkins was able to withstand the pain of being burned alive because 'truely I beleeve the devill was in him' (104). So at a point when Atkins's status as a Protestant 'Martir' could have been reaffirmed, à la Foxe, it deliberately is not. Munday instead offers up his countryman as a reprobate infected by trafficking with Lucifer. Proof of his wickedness is in his 'obstinacie.' As with the epilogue to *Faustus*, then, the reversal of Munday's narrative stance warns of the cost of bald resistance of theodicy. *Realpolitik* replaces conscience. A premonition of his expedience lies in the paragraph on his tour of the vaults, where he follows his promise of having spoken plainly by observing, cynically, that a man 'must live as he may, not as he will, favour comes by conformitie, and death by obstinacie' (65).

Like Munday infiltrating Rome, or Marlowe Rheims, or a recusant priest London, Faustus approaches Rome surreptitiously. The episode opens with expository dialogue in which he recollects being aloft on a flying dragon (a sly pun on Philip's ensign?), from where he has seen the vineyards of the 'Rhine,' the treasures of Venice and Padua, and Naples' 'rich Campania, / Whose buildings, fair and gorgeous to the eye' (A 3.1.7, 9–10). In Naples, he has admired 'Maro's [i.e., Virgil's] golden tomb, / The way he cut an English mile in length / Thorough a rock of stone in one night's space' (A 3.1.13–15). Faustus is resurrecting the familiar idea that Virgil, regarded by a few medieval commentators as a magician, had used 'supernatural art' to cut 'a tunnel between the bays of Naples and Baine, through Mt. Posilipo.'[55] Like Faustus's own desire to join 'Afric' to Spain, the image here of 'an English mile' coyly reiterates the nationalistic idea that in the hands of a great poet, art can render physical boundaries, even national borders, perversely plastic.

The exposition of the doctor's journey to Rome concentrates on fortifications. Traveling from Olympus in a chariot drawn by dragons, Faustus has admired Trier's geologically protective circumference of 'airy mountain-tops, / With walls of flint and deepe intrenchèd lakes, /

Not to be won by any conquering prince' (A 3.1.3–5). The fiend, with a tactician's eye, sizes up Rome, too, as more fortress than sanctuary: 'Upon the bridge called Ponte Angelo / Erected is a castle passing strong, / Within whose walls such store of ordnance are, / And double cannons, framed of carvèd brass . . . Besides the gates and high pyramides / Which Julius Caesar brought from Africa' (A 3.1.37–43). Cataloging its defenses, Mephistopheles invites Faustus to see himself as its latest invader. Notice of the castle on Ponte Angelo calls to mind the defenses added to Rome after the 1527 sack. By the mid-1530s, as Frank Tallett notes, the city had become heavily fortified.[56]

Having arrived at the city's edge like a stealthy Caesar, with surprise rather than triumph on his side, within Rome Faustus quickly remakes himself as a surrogate of the Holy Roman Emperor. While Charles's men loll about in Germany, drinking and whatnot, as we have seen, the doctor is busy advancing the Empire's political and military interests in Rome by subterfuge designed to wrest away the election of a pope from the college of cardinals into the hands of the Holy Roman Emperor. Faustus will 'parley with this Pope, / This proud confronter of the Emperor' (B 3.1.117–18). Later, in a 'trial of his art' (A 4.0.16), as the Chorus says, he dons a magic 'girdle' (B 3.2.16 s.d.) to taunt the pope and his legates, while the liberated Bruno 'flies o'er the Alps to fruitful Germany, / There to salute the woeful Emperor' (B 3.2.5–6). These very images recur in the expository material at the head of Faustus's visit to Charles's court, bridging the two episodes and encouraging spectators to see the assault on the pope's privy chamber as part of the centuries-old military hostilities between German kings and the papacy.

Physical spaces and bodies

> All the dividing lines between bodies and objects are erased, even the boundaries between a banquet and war.
> Bakhtin on *Gargantua and Pantagruel*[57]

Faustus's shenanigans in Rome exploit popular criticisms of Catholic rituals as visual spectacles. The peculiarly English strand of the idea that popery is mere playing has been traced by Paul White and others to Henrician reform in the 1530s. The aim of reform was in part to solidify England's ideological war against the papacy, and the strategy was to use theater 'to expose popish priests as actors, their rites as good theater.'[58] Moreover, as historians have documented, these charges were also in circulation among ordinary people. Robert Whiting records that in 1531, Thomas Bennett, an Exeter schoolmaster, was charged with having 'accused the clergy of selling masses for the souls in "feigned purgatory."' Bennett saw the rite of excommunication as a form of 'interludes, played of the priests.'[59] One of the achievements of *Faustus* is its capacity for answering the nationalist call for propaganda, while baiting those reformers whose politics condemned both popery and playing.[60]

Inside the papal chamber, that achievement is at its highest pitch. The injuries inflicted on Adrian and company may derive from a long dramatic tradition of carnival that pre-dates the Reformation, but here the carnival is explicitly labeled a form of theatrical playing, and playing is demonstrated as an ideological weapon fit for action against the Catholic hierarchy. Ironically, the Church's claims of, and devices for, effecting transcendental action are turned against itself: on stage, devices from the liturgy and the Eucharist (rosary beads, the cup) as well as from the mystery plays sponsored by the Church and communities (the iconographic terror of hell, the dirge) are used to parody the transcendental and transubstantial claims such devices customarily substantiated in an earlier dramatic tradition.[61]

For as the apostate doctor is created, his plots in Rome dissolve the boundary between legitimate and illegitimate religious theater. Hence the parodies of prominent Catholic rituals. Even ordination is imitated. While the doctor kneels, the fiend parodically blesses him as an invisible trickster, saying, 'on thy head I lay my hand / And charm thee with this magic wand' (B 3.2.15–16). Moreover, the episode asks spectators to wonder at the legitimacy of transcendental rituals and claims that cannot be verified, but that can be counterfeited on stage. The dirge sung by the friars to protect themselves from an invisible Faustus fails to work; their rosaries may become weapons (B 3.1.84); their iconography of hell is mocked as a fiction. The words *see, perceive, eyes,* and *view* are used eleven times in the sixty-odd lines before a procession of cardinals and bishops enters the stage with Bruno '*led in chaines*' (B 3.1.88 s.d.). Self-consciously the episode is a metadrama, which posits the legitimacy of stage playing by mocking the Roman Church's claim that its rituals alone enjoy an authentic and exclusive status. As Faustus approaches the pope's 'privy chamber' (B 3.1.27) where Adrian is concelebrating his imagined 'triumphant victory' over Charles V and Bruno, he petitions Mephistopheles, 'in this show let me an actor be, / That this proud Pope may Faustus' cunning see' (B 3.1.75–6). While the doctor tropes the Feast of St Peter as a 'show' in which he might take some mischievous part, it is Mephistopheles who voices the doctor's synaptic association of playing and ideological disruption: 'By cunning in thine art, to cross the Pope / Or dash the pride of this solemnity' (B 3.1.80–81). In the devil's hands, theater becomes a parodic technology – a prosthetic voice – through which spectators can vicariously resist oppressive religious authorities. The metadrama aids in what Robert Weimann has noted as a feature of early modern theater: its capacity to 'assimilate' Reformation anxieties opened up by 'newly interactive and precarious relations between language and existence.'[62]

The best single example of the play's parody of the Catholic rhetoric of ontological and epistemological certitude comes in the mock interrogation of Bruno. The episode exploits inquisitorial practices for their entertainment profit, and demonstrates how the stage can function as a counter-inquisitional space that deconstructs the theater of torture practiced by the Inquisition on the Continent. The capricious verdict delivered by 'Faustus' – that Bruno be 'burnt to death' (B 3.2.184) – exposes Adrian's pretended inquiry into Bruno's motives as a charade of policy. This in spite of the fact that as Faustus leads Bruno off to the interrogation, Adrian's minions are instructed to consult Statutes drafted by the Council of Trent in order to discern Bruno's guilt and its statutory consequences; Marlowe exploits for humor the sharp criticism levied by that Council against hypocritical priests who behave with 'depraved morals' while profiting from other people's faults.[63] The verdict mocks prefabricated inquisitorial judgments and the torturous interrogations that often preceded those verdicts on the Continent. Moreover, it may also criticize the threat of torture in obtaining confessions of treason from the missionary priests arrested by the English government, a phenomenon that was becoming more familiar in the late 1580s and 1590s. Elizabeth Hanson notes that English Catholics complained that civil authorities sometimes tortured missionary priests not to elicit 'truth,' but to elicit false confessions that were known to be false, but that would 'justify the government's further repression of Catholicism.'[64] Thus, Hanson concludes, the practice of torture in England was said to be 'merely a parody of the investigation leading to discovery' (55) and not, as on the Continent, an integral part of that discovery process. This is similar to Marlowe's critique of torture in the Vatican episode, albeit the setting is Italian: Faustus, intuiting Adrian's wish that Bruno be tortured for having dared to accept election by Charles V as a rival pope, in effect parodies the process of discovery in which Bruno is supposed to have confessed his treason against the papacy, momentarily making such liberatory playing heroic.

The parody often reaches for the Catholic jugular. Take the practice of excommunication, for instance, which Pius V had infamously levied against the queen in 1570 in the bull *Regnans in excelsis*, and which Sixtus V had renewed in 1588 as Spain launched its armada. Historical evidence suggests that in the late sixteenth century, most Londoners, even the pious ones, would have scoffed at a threat of excommunication, whether delivered by player or priest. Robert Whiting, for one, has shown that excommunication gradually declined as an effective mechanism for policing behavior. While it usually 'evoked fear' in the reign of Henry VIII, he observes, it 'was often treated with derision' as Elizabeth's reign wore on.[65] So in *Faustus*, Adrian's threats against Bruno and Charles V – 'We will depose the Emperor . . . / And curse the people that submit to him. / Both he and thou shalt stand excommunicate' (B 3.1.127–9) – are likely to have been functioning as parody. As a stage tyrant, Adrian rants, but in a campy way that is designed to burn him and not his prisoner in effigy. When Bruno half-demands, half-begs for 'some right of law' (B 3.1.125), for example, Adrian mimics a Tamburlainian answer – 'Is not all power on earth bestowed on us? / And therefore, though we would, we cannot err' (B 3.1.151–2), an answer that furthers the play's project of erasing the boundary between soldiers and priests as well as priests and magicians.[66] Pointing to his 'silver belt' as a token of his apostolic authority, Adrian seems to be sporting a magic girdle no less than Faustus himself, and speaks as if he were Tamburlaine: the silver belt confers 'our sevenfold power from heaven, / To bind or loose, lock fast, condemn, or judge, / Resign, or seal, or whatso pleaseth us' (B 3.1.155–7), echoing the speech Mortimer gives near the end of *Edward II*. Even as the pope mounts 'Saint Peter's chair and state pontifical' by treading on his 'footstool' Bruno, however, his claims to absolute authority are hijacked by Faustus's counterfeiting (B 3.1.91, 89). Although Adrian literally steps on Bruno to ascend his throne, as Tamburlaine does to Bajazeth, Adrian is a mere shell of a conqueror.

Adrian is harshest toward his own kind. Threatening to murder all the priests gathered for the Feast unless they produce Bruno in chains again, Adrian curses them to hell for their presumed betrayal of papal custody: 'By Peter, you shall die / Unless you bring them forth immediately. – / Hale them to prison. Lade their limbes with gyves! – / False prelates, for this hateful treachery / Curst be your souls to hellish misery' (B 3.2.50–54). Adrian's lines stress the *Realpolitik* of getting and keeping St Peter's chair. Even Catholic reformers had lamented the corruption of papal election. Erasmus, the historical Charles V's sometime adviser, had grumbled, for instance, that 'Once bought,' the title of Supreme Holiness 'has to be protected by the sword, by poison, by violence of every kind.'[67] A similar cynicism is voiced in the Prologue of *The Jew of Malta*. But here, Adrian's threats of violence are mocked by the gap between his rhetoric of cosmic terror and the impotence of his regime against theatrical resistance.

As the Feast dissolves into fracas, Adrian's fiery threats turn into self-pitying hyperbole that anticipates the knight Benvolio's whining in Act 4 when Faustus wounds his dignity, too. Crossing himself does no good; Faustus denies the ritual its protective power. Boxed on the ears, Adrian cries out, 'O, I am slain! Help me, my lords. / O, come and help to bear my body hence. / Damned be this soul for ever for this deed!' (B 3.2.88–90). So the episode self-consciously insists that playing the role of anti-Catholic insurgent on stage, much as Anthony Munday had described Richard Atkins's conduct at St Peter's, is a form of aggression that may in some small way lend a hand to the ideological war against Catholic-inspired invasion of England. It's not simply that Faustus plays the part of an 'actor' in the Feast, but that the magical unboundedness of the stage disrupts ancient theological premises about the unique nature of each human being. In a perverse appeal to medieval anxieties that the devil can disguise himself in sheep's clothing, the disruption of certainty of the uniqueness of each soul had been set in motion in Act 1 when Faustus had insisted that Mephistopheles 'go, and return an old Franciscan friar,' coyly explaining that 'that holy shape becomes a devil best' (B 1.3.26–7). Outfitting his master/minion and himself this way, Faustus literalizes his anarchy, degrading the priests' office and the assumptions that go with it.[68] In the papal chamber, wearing scarlet 'fitted well' (B 3.1.161) by the fiend, the doctor not only transgresses the sumptuary laws that protected the divines' sartorial signs of legitimacy and authority, or the holy office itself, but Christian notions of the determinate soul. For as Michael Bristol observes, to impersonate a cardinal is to chip away at the fiction that one's identity is fixed.[69]

Moreover, impersonation is gleefully embraced as identity theft. The costumes that make it possible for the duo to slip undetected into the papal chamber are not created by the fiend *ex nihilo*. As if traipsing through *A Midsummer Night's Dream*, Faustus commands Mephistopheles to tail the cardinals guarding Bruno into the consistory. There the fiend is to 'strike them with sloth and drowsy idleness, / And make them sleep so sound that in their shapes / Thyself and I may parley with this Pope' (B 3.1.115–17). Playing a cardinal leads the doctor to a physical 'parley' with Adrian's crew that not only imitates, but effects an actual battle of sorts on stage. As the episode ends in the A-text, Faustus flings '*fireworks*' among the friars as he beats them (A 3.1.100 s.d.). Likewise in the B-text (B 3.3.106 s.d.), where he presumably is making good on his earlier fantasy of causing their 'shaven crowns to bleed' (B 3.2.27), making them parodic Christ figures and sacking the Vatican with gunpowder and art. As the prelates flee, spectators see that playing can literally become a predatory action. The carnival in the episode may have had a long dramatic history, though not necessarily on the fixed stage, but the effects of the carnival here run precisely counter to the topsy-turvy playing that had been a central feature of medieval carnival. Faustus's theatrics devastate rather than reinforce the Roman Church's authority.

And yet, the play suggests, perhaps the playwright's efforts to collapse that boundary between legitimate ritual and illegitimate magic need not disqualify either the ritual or the playing. Although Act 5 may sober up an audience by depicting an apostate in the throes of divine judgment, the representations of Faustus's damnation again shuttle those spectators back and forth between the verifiable and the fantastic. The Bad Angel of the B-text, sounding very much like a late medieval inquisitor, spells out the miseries awaiting the damned in hell: 'Now, Faustus, let thine eyes with horror stare / Into that vast perpetual torture-house. / There are the Furies tossing damnèd souls / On burning forks; their bodies boil in lead' and so forth (B 5.2.121–4). Arguably, at this moment Faustus experiences an instantaneous, magically real journey through space and time, to see hell '*discovered*' (B 5.2.120 s.d.). Likewise, the audience is invited to skip vicariously from earth to hell and back. Does such mental skipping produce twinges of terror? Or does it coldly resituate an inherited fear of hell within a competing, polyphonic tradition of dissent, in which hell is virtually parodied?

This invitation to skip between worlds – whether heaven, hell, and earth; or Wittenberg, Rome, the zodiac – offers spectators who come to see *Faustus* an opportunity to experience the plasticity of space, time, and human identity. In its medial events in Rome and at the Spanish Charles V's court especially, the play parodies the strategies, the rhetoric, and the very legitimacy of the two groups in sixteenth-century Europe who were most keen to assert claims of epistemic authority, priests and soldiers. *Faustus*-B, I have argued, celebrates the power of the imagination to resist if not defeat both priests and soldiers by conjuring a 'plurality of worlds.'[70]

Notes

1. Tzvetan Todorov, *The Fantastic: A Structural Approach to a Literary Genre*, trans. Richard Howard (Cleveland: Case Western Reserve University Press, 1973), 158.
2. John Michael Archer briefly discusses *Doctor Faustus* as a quasi-autobiographical meditation on espionage, noting that in the play 'Marlowe partly adopted, partly created, a transgressive identity that was of a piece with his reputation as a sojourner on the outer fringes of court society' (74). See his *Sovereignty and Intelligence: Spying and Court Culture in the English Renaissance* (Stanford: Stanford University Press, 1993), 72–6.
3. The formulation is Johannes H. Birringer's in 'Marlowe's Violent Stage: "Mirrors" of Honor in *Tamburlaine*,' *ELH* 51 (1984): 220.

4. On the ways spectators are plunged into theological uncertainty by the play, see Alan Sinfield, *Faultlines: Cultural Materialism and the Politics of Dissident Reading* (Berkeley: University of California Press, 1992), 230–37, who argues persuasively that 'the theological implications of *Faustus* are radically and provocatively indeterminate' (234).

5. Michael Keefer, 'History and the Canon: The Case of *Doctor Faustus*,' *University of Toronto Quarterly* 56 (1987): 507.

6. The textual histories of the plays are notoriously perplexing. The best scholarship on these matters is the Introduction to the Revels Plays edition from which I am quoting *Doctor Faustus A- and B-Texts*, ed. David Bevington and Eric Rasmussen (Manchester: Manchester University Press, 1997), 1–102; Eric Rasmussen, 'Rehabilitating the A-Text of Marlowe's *Doctor Faustus*,' *Studies in Bibliography* 46 (1993): 221–38; Leah S. Marcus, 'Textual Indeterminacy and Ideological Difference: The Case of *Doctor Faustus*,' *Renaissance Drama* 20 (1989): 1–29; Fredson Bowers, ed., *The Complete Works of Christopher Marlowe*, 2 vols, 2d ed. (Cambridge: Cambridge University Press, 1981), 2:123–59; W.W. Greg, *Marlowe's Doctor Faustus 1604–1616: Parallel Texts* (Oxford: Clarendon, 1950); and Constance Kuriyama, 'Dr. Greg and *Doctor Faustus*: The Supposed Originality of the 1616 Text,' *English Language Review* 5 (1975): 171–97.

7. Lois Parkinson Zamora and Wendy B. Faris, ed., 'Introduction,' *Magical Realism: Theory, History, Community* (Durham: Duke University Press, 1995), 5–6.

8. Ibid., 2.

9. See Rawdon Wilson, 'The Metamorphoses of Fictional Space: Magical Realism,' in *Magical Realism*, ed. Zamora and Faris, 209–33; and Rawdon Wilson, *In Palamedes' Shadow: Explorations in Play, Game, and Narrative Theory* (Boston: Northeastern University Press, 1990), 204–5. On 'historical allegory,' see Wilson, *In Palamedes' Shadow*, 202.

10. Zamora and Faris, 'Introduction,' in *Magical Realism*, 3.

11. Alejo Carpentier, 'On the Marvelous Real in America' (1949), trans. Tanya Huntington and Lois Parkinson Zamora, in *Magical Realism*, ed. Zamora and Faris, 81.

12. Philip Henslowe, *Henslowe's Diary*, ed. R.A. Foakes and R.T. Rickert (Cambridge: Cambridge University Press, 1961), 319–21.

13. Wilson, *In Palamedes' Shadow*, 175. As Peter Hyland suggests of the rupture of illusion in revenge tragedies, 'The disguised revenger is, literally, "playing," but the playing becomes reality at the moment of murder' ('Disguise and Renaissance Tragedy,' *University of Toronto Quarterly* 55 (1985–86): 164.

14. Wilson, *In Palamedes' Shadow*, 175.

15. Wilson, 'Metamorphoses,' 210.

16. Barnabe Rich, *A Roome for a Gentleman*, London, 1609, STC 20985, Fv.

17. Edmund Spenser, *The Poetical Works of Edmund Spenser*, ed. J.C. Smith and Ernest de Selincourt, 3 vols (Oxford: Oxford University Press, 1961, 1964), 1:3, 2:485.

18. George Whetstone, *The Honourable Reputation of a Soldier*, London, 1585, STC 25339, Ev, Eiiii–Ev.

19. Philip Sidney, *The Defence of Poesy*, in *Sir Philip Sidney: Selected Prose and Poetry*, ed. Robert Kimbrough, 2d ed. (Madison: University of Wisconsin Press, 1983), 115.

20. Holinshed applies the addiction image to Edward's love for Gaveston in *Chronicles of England, Scotland, and Ireland*, ed. Vernon F. Snow, 6 vols (New York: AMS, 1976), 2:549, 2:547.

21. *A Myrrour for English Souldiers*, London, 1595, STC 10418, A2r–v. 'Overpasse' can mean 'to pass over, travel over, move across or along' and 'to pass through in one's mind' (*OED* [1st ed.] *v.t.* 1 and 5b).

22. D.F.R. de M., 'An Answer to the Untruthes, Published and Printed in Spaine, in Glorie of their Supposed victorie atchieved against our English Navie,' trans. I.L., London, 1589, STC 17132, 19.

23. Michiko Suzuki, *Metamorphoses of Helen: Authority, Difference, and the Epic* (Ithaca: Cornell University Press, 1989), 15.

24. A notable example emerges in the digressive exemplum of the Trojan War in *The Rape of Lucrece*, where Helen's abduction is named a 'rape' (*The Riverside Shakespeare*, gen. ed. G. Blakemore Evans [Boston: Houghton Mifflin, 1974] 1737, l. 1369). In *Faustus*, the third scholar offers an indirect *apologia* of the 'rape': 'No marvel though the angry Greeks pursued / With ten years' war the rape of such a queen, / Whose heavenly beauty passeth all compare' (A 5.1.28–30).

25. See Paul Budra, 'Doctor Faustus: Death of a Bibliophile,' *Connotations* 1 (1991): 1–11 and 286–9.

26. Critics using psychoanalytic theory note Faustus's emotional distance from women but draw different conclusions about it. Kay Stockholder, '"Within the massy entrailes of the earth": Faustus' Relation to Women,' in *'A Poet and a Filthy Play-maker': New Essays on Christopher Marlowe*, ed. Kenneth Friedenreich et al. (New York: AMS, 1988), says Faustus 'thinks himself unworthy of making a sexual claim, and fears paternal reprisal for seeking sexual knowledge' (208); 'he chooses hell and heterosexuality rather than yield to a heaven that contains only a forbidding God' (217). Constance Kuriyama, *Hammer or Anvil: Psychological Patterns in Christopher Marlowe's Plays* (New Brunswick: Rutgers University Press, 1980), reads *Faustus* as in part about Marlowe's struggle to make a 'homosexual adaptation' (120). A number of Marlowe scholars have taken issue with Kuriyama's assumptions and conclusions. See, for example, Claude J. Summers's review in the *Journal of English and Germanic Philology* 81 (1982): 254–8.

27. Having defined the dumb show as 'any piece of silent action where one would normally expect dialogue' (xii), Dieter Mehl mistakenly argues in *The Elizabethan Dumb Show: The History of a Dramatic Convention* (Cambridge, MA: Harvard University Press, 1966) that 'Marlowe does not use dumb shows although his plays are full of impressive stage effects. There seems to be in his plays a particularly close relationship between speech and action which made the introduction of pantomimes unnecessary' (86, n. 1). In this instance, Helen's silence also allows the playwright to convey the selfishness of Faustus's use of Helen.

28. Ian Watt, 'Faust as a Myth of Modern Individualism: Three of Marlowe's Contributions,' in *Faust Through Four Centuries: Retrospect and Analysis*, ed. Peter Boerner and Sidney Johnson (Tübingen: Niemeyer, 1989), 46. I am indebted to both Budra's and Watt's commentaries on Faustus as a reader.

29. Richard P. Martin, *The Language of Heroes: Speech and Performance in the* Iliad (Ithaca: Cornell University Press, 1989), 126.

30. Leonard J. Barkan, 'Diana and Acteon: The Myth as Synthesis,' *ELR* 10 (1980): 328.

31. Mark Breitenberg, *Anxious Masculinity in Early Modern England* (Cambridge: Cambridge University Press, 1996), 6.

32. Thomas Procter, *Of the Knowledge and Conducte of Warres*, London, 1578 (Amsterdam: Theatrum Orbis Terrarum, 1970), iv, v; Whetstone, *The Honorable Reputation of a Souldier*, I4v–K1r; John Smythe, *Certain Discourses Military*, London, 1590, ed. J.R. Hale (Ithaca: Cornell University Press, 1964), 27.

33. Zamora and Faris, 'Introduction,' in *Magical Realism*, 3.

34. George Puttenham, *The Arte of English Poesie*, London, 1589, in *Elizabethan Critical Essays*, ed. G. Gregory Smith, 2 vols (Oxford: Oxford University Press, 1937), 2:17. William Harrison, *The Description of England*, London, 1577, 1587, ed. Georges Edelen (Washington, DC: Folger Shakespeare Library, 1994), 324, 328.

35. *Luthers Werke in Auswahl, Tischreden*, cited in Steven Ozment, *The Age of Reform, 1250–1550: An Intellectual and Religious History of Late Medieval and Reformation Europe* (New Haven: Yale University Press, 1980), 260.

36. Coppélia Kahn, *Man's Estate: Masculine Identity in Shakespeare* (Berkeley: University of California Press, 1981), 19. See also Breitenberg, *Anxious Masculinity*, 15.

37. Graham Hammill, 'Faustus's Fortunes: Commodification, Exchange, and the Form of Literary Subjectivity,' *ELH* 63 (1996): 312. Hammill's point is part of a larger argument about sodomy as a trope (and not a fact) in the play, which he argues 'is a tragedy because of the relation that it establishes between Faustus and the literary,' in which 'the literary is a language that is performative' (309). Hammill's argument and my own both emphasize performativity, yet his interests lie in the psychological and ontological implications of that feature, while mine lie in the consequences for discourses of nationalism and militarism.

    J.B. Steane explains that 'Mars "mated" the Carthaginians, then, in the sense that he entered into them: he was on their side and with his spirit in them they won' (*Christopher Marlowe, The Complete Plays*, ed. J.B. Steane [1969; rpt Harmondsworth: Penguin, 1986], 590, n. 2). Rasmussen calls attention to 'the printer's dedication "To the Gentleman Reader" of *Tamburlaine*,' where 'Richard Jones claims that he has intentionally omitted what seem to have been comic or farcical scenes that were not germane to Marlowe's tragic scenes' ('Rehabilitating the A Text,' 236, n. 37).

38. In 'A,' Benvolio's wager is less a challenge than a denial that borrows the Acteon myth as proof text: If 'You bring Alexander and his paramour before the Emperour,' he says to Faustus, 'I'faith, that's as true as Diana turned me to a stag' (A 4.1.59–60, 62).

39. Barkan, 'Diana and Acteon,' 317–59; Nancy J. Vickers, 'Diana Described: Scattered Woman and Scattered Rhyme,' in *Writing and Sexual Difference*, ed. Elizabeth Abel (Chicago: University of Chicago Press, 1982), 95–109; and Patrick Cheney, *Marlowe's Counterfeit Profession: Ovid, Spenser, Counter-Nationhood* (Toronto: University of Toronto Press, 1998), who widely discusses the functions of the Acteon myth in *Faustus* and *Edward II*.

40. Barkan, 'Diana and Acteon,' 346.
41. See Katharine Eisaman Maus, 'Horns of Dilemma: Jealousy, Gender, and Spectatorship in English Renaissance Drama,' *ELH* 54 (1987): 561–83; and Douglas Bruster, *Drama and the Market in the Age of Shakespeare* (Cambridge: Cambridge University Press, 1992), 47–62.

On a minority tradition in medieval thought that understood horns as a sign of a knight's bravery and victory, and associated with the Horned Moses, see Frederick Elworthy, *Horns of Honour* (London: John Murray, 1900) and Ruth Mellinkoff, *The Horned Moses in Medieval Art and Thought* (Berkeley: University of California Press, 1970), especially 122–3.
42. Vickers, 'Diana Described,' 103.
43. Martin, *The Language of Heroes*, 68–9, citing A.W.H. Adkins on the 'shame or "results-culture."'
44. John Lingham, 'A True Relation of all such Englishe Captaines and Lieuetenants, as have beene slaine in the lowe Countries,' London, 1584, STC 15690.7, A8r.
45. Gail Kern Paster, *The Body Embarrassed: Drama and the Disciplines of Shame in Early Modern England* (Ithaca: Cornell University Press, 1993); and Bruster, *Drama and the Market*, 47–62.
46. Frank Tallett, *War and Society in Early Modern Europe, 1495–1715* (London: Routledge, 1992), 9.
47. William Segar, *Of Honor Military and Civil*, ed. Diane Bornstein (New York: Scholars, 1975), 184.
48. Manuel Fernández Alvarez, *Charles V: Elected emperor and hereditary ruler*, trans. J.A. Lalaguna (London: Thames & Hudson, 1975), 66–7. Vives is cited in Alvarez, quoting Alfonso de Valdés, *Diálogo de Mercurio y Carón*, ed. J.F. Montesinos (Madrid, 1954), 79. Also see Karl Brandi, *The Emperor Charles V: The Growth and Destiny of a Man and of a World-Empire*, trans. C.V. Wedgwood (London: Jonathan Cape, 1954), 253–60.
49. Luigi Guicciardini, *The Sack of Rome*, trans. and ed. James H. McGregor (New York: Italica, 1993), 98. Subsequent quotations of Guicciardini are cited parenthetically. Francesco Guicciardini's account of the invasion and capture of Rome also discusses the ignominy of the soldiers' 'cruel and insolent' treatment of priests especially, but his discussion of the violence is muted by a professional distance from the events that Luigi's account foregoes. Francesco Guicciardini, *The History of Italy*, trans. and ed. Sidney Alexander (New York: Macmillan, 1969), 384.
50. Henslowe, *Henslowe's Diary*, 325.
51. See John Bakeless, *Christopher Marlowe: The Man in His Time* (New York: Morrow, 1937), 82–4; and A.L. Rowse, *Christopher Marlowe: His Life and Work* (New York: Harper and Row, 1964), 28–30, 192–3. Allusions to the seminaries at Douai and, later, Rheims, appear in *The Massacre at Paris*. Cheney, *Marlowe's Counterfeit*, ties Marlowe's espionage activities in the English Roman Catholic seminary in Rheims to the idea of poetry as an avenue of infiltration in *The Jew of Malta* (155).
52. Anthony Munday, *The English Romayne Lyfe*, ed. G.B. Harrison (New York: Barnes and Noble, 1966), 64. Subsequent quotations will be cited parenthetically.
53. Further evidence of the political invocation of the devil comes in the chapter on the vaults that hold saints' relics, where Munday writes that

God has taught Protestants 'not to lust after dreames and fantasies of the devilles invencion' (*The English Romayne Lyfe*, 62).

54. A century after Munday, Aphra Behn will bring her ambiguously hagiographic narrative of Oronooko to a similar narrative conclusion.

55. *Christopher Marlowe's* Doctor Faustus, *Text and Major Criticism*, ed. Irving Ribner (Indianapolis: Odyssey, 1966), 25, n. 14–15.

56. Tallett, *War and Society*, 35.

57. Mikhail Bakhtin, *Rabelais and His World*, trans. Helene Iswolsky (Cambridge, MA: MIT Press, 1968), 335.

58. Paul Whitfield White, 'Theater and Religious Culture,' in *A New History of Early English Drama*, ed. John D. Cox and David Scott Kastan (New York: Columbia University Press, 1997), 136.

59. Robert Whiting, *The Blind Devotion of the People: Popular Religion and the English Reformation* (Cambridge: Cambridge University Press, 1989), 24, 141.

60. White, 'Theater and Religious Culture,' 140.

61. Anthony Esler studies parallel maneuvers designed to ridicule Roman Catholic rituals in 'Robert Greene and the Spanish Armada,' *ELH* 32 (1965): 318, reminding us just how orthodox Marlowe was being in his satire.

62. Kirby Farrell, 'Thinking Through Others: Prosthetic Fantasy and the Cultural Moment,' *The Massachusetts Review* 37 (1996): 224; Robert Weimann, *Authority and Representation in Early Modern Discourse*, ed. David Hillman (Baltimore: Johns Hopkins University Press), 65.

63. *Canons and Decrees of the Council of Trent: Original Text with English Translation*, trans. H.J. Schroeder (1941; rpt St Louis: Herder, 1955), 46.

64. Elizabeth Hanson, 'Torture and Truth in Renaissance England,' *Representations* 34 (1991): 55.

65. Whiting, *Blind Devotion*, 141.

66. The papal efforts to excommunicate Elizabeth after 1570 intensified the English rhetoric of the papacy as just one more military command, albeit a grand and dangerous one. In a typical pamphlet from the period lambasting the Roman Catholic Church, one Henry Bullinger the Elder, writing from Zurich, publishes in London in 1572 his 'Confutation of the Popes Bull,' offering the image of Pius 'rising now out of the throne of his with sword drawn, and pronouncing the extremest sentence against the most vertuous Queene' (*STC* 4044, A3v).

67. Desiderus Erasmus, *The Praise of Folly*, trans. Betty Radice (New York: Penguin, 1971), 178–9.

68. Hyland points out that 'disguise is, after all, essentially anarchic, inverting systems and relationships, creating a distance between appearance and reality, turning the world upside down' ('Disguise and Renaissance Tragedy,' 170).

69. Michael Bristol, *Carnival and Theater: Plebian Culture and the Structure of Authority in Renaissance England* (London: Methuen, 1985), 63–4.

70. Zamora and Faris, 'Introduction,' in *Magical Realism*, 5.

Afterword

It may be more difficult to write on *The Faerie Queene* or *Hamlet* than on *Faustus*, but not much more so. Beneath thick layers of scholarship, supremely daunting texts keep us at bay. Their poetic beauty, their philosophical wiliness, their ambition, their resonance: four centuries later, they continue to fascinate us. They resist being pinned down.

But literary criticism is all about attempting to respond to the elusiveness of such texts by offering a coherent argument that pins them down just enough. In such a game, Marlowe is in my experience trickier to write about (though, again, not necessarily harder) than Spenser or Shakespeare. For his plays seem designed to lure us into heuristic traps. Just as his principal characters fly toward self-destruction like moths to a flame, so are we urged or provoked into surrendering our capacity for thinking about the world in complex ways when we find ourselves taking sides in responding to their predicaments – piously censuring Faustus for his rebellion, perhaps, or admiring his fatal efforts to subvert theology's stranglehold on European consciousness; impiously admiring Barabas for his cunning or laughing at his inability to escape the boiling cauldron that, to the talionically minded, seems like an apposite punishment for his own wicked deeds. More than most early modern literature, the Marlowe plays present zero-sum universes, peopled by absolutists and despots of all kinds who exact their pounds of flesh from the more visibly complex beings in their midst who are trying desperately to inhabit a more symphonic universe.

Enticing an audience to join in the judging of characters' motives, deeds, and desires is a sport that can make spectators feel superior, even as it offers willing moralists blatant opportunities to avert their eyes and thoughts from other kinds of 'problems' with which the plays are engaged. Even a partial list of those problems would include anxieties about the administration of justice, class mobility, aesthetic pleasure, the visceral body, sexual alterity, parental authority, trust, religious identity, the rhetoric of gender, the decline of chivalry, the rise of mercantilism, the threat of civil war, the risks of peace: the plays demonstrate a keen interest in an extraordinary range of human concerns. And yet, as I say, while watching or reading the plays, it does sometimes feel as if they are designed to trap us within the very zero-sum universes their principal characters inhabit, to get us to agree to reduce complexity to the black and white world Edward's captors think they live in, or at least *claim* to

217

think they live in. There is no denying that Marlowe demonstrates a deep fascination with grotesquely bloody ways of responding to the various incarnations of institutional and human weakness he makes into tragic art. In writing this book my challenge has been to resist the magnetic pull of those zero-sum worlds Marlowe creates. Pursuing his seven plays as a series of artistic studies of the effects and implications of martial law across an expanse of geography and history, from ancient Troy and medieval England to sixteenth-century Paris and Malta, I have tried to steer away from their traps, to avoid totalizing claims about the ways they represent martial law and the either/or rhetoric that is often a feature of the principal characters' mentality and language.

In writing about the rhetoric of absolutism and the impulse toward martial law in the plays, I have not intended to make over Christopher Marlowe into some twenty-first-century human rights activist. Not only would it have been anachronistic to assume that he was, for instance, in deep sympathy with the plight of the (relatively few) Elizabethan Jews, it would also not match my experience of watching Marlowe's plays be performed on stage and screen to see in them explicit endorsements of a slate of human rights that were in fact introduced into western culture centuries later. And yet the plays give signs everywhere of Marlowe's attentiveness to what Katharine Eisaman Maus has called the playwright's obsession with 'heretical conscience and theatrical rhetoric.' Studying the plays' immersion in late sixteenth-century heresy disputes and the juridical techniques for discerning an inward 'truth,' Maus concludes that 'just as the incineration of a heretic may produce a terrified recantation of unorthodoxy in one spectator and an increased confidence in the rightness of the heretic's cause in another, so the displays of Marlovian theater are never self-evident, because the responses of individuals are unpredictable, because one person's orthodoxy is another person's heresy.'[1]

I have argued from another angle that Marlowe's dramas exploit the potential energy of heresy and the occasional efforts of Elizabeth's government to suppress it by way of martial law. In the topsy-turvy 1580s and 1590s, as the Anglo-Spanish War became the greatest threat to 'English' security since circa 1066, Marlowe rose up in the London theaters like some Phaeton of the entertainment industry, taking war itself as a central subject of his art. Using the war fever swirling around him in other public scripts to make plays that on one level pander to the public's appetite for bombastic warlords as a sign of the potential fierceness of England's own militias and *ad hoc* armies and navies, Marlowe offered his audiences in return a far more complex experience of that war fever than any other contemporary English playwright, Shakespeare included. Aesthetically, Marlowe raised the stakes for

making plays about war. Asking his spectators to engage in the
contradictions and ambiguities that reside in the rhetoric of war,
Marlowe made it all but impossible to leave a performance of one of his
plays fully convinced that soldiers and the warlords who employ them
do in fact deserve the absolute epistemic control they were bidding for
in the midst of the Armada scares in a London at war. Paradoxically, his
plays suggest, state security may in fact actually be endangered by
soldiers. When they buy into the rhetoric of 'epic masculinity,' a code of
identity requiring them to eliminate virtually all difference from their
local surroundings and from their own characters, soldiers 'protect' the
state in ways that may be fatal – to the civilians who cross them and to
the state they are aiming to protect.

Note

1.   Katharine Eisaman Maus, *Inwardness and Theater in the English
     Renaissance* (Chicago: University of Chicago Press, 1995), 103.

Bibliography

A Larum for London; or, the siege of Antwerpe. London, 1602. Ed. W.W. Greg. Oxford: Oxford University Press, 1913.

Adams, Robert P. *The Better Part of Valor: More, Erasmus, Colet, and Vives, on Humanism, War, and Peace, 1496–1535.* Seattle: University of Washington Press, 1962.

Aelred of Rievaulx. *De spirituali amicitia* [*Spiritual Friendship*]. Trans. Mary Eugenia Laker. Introd. Douglas Roby. Washington, DC: Cistercian Publications, 1974.

Agnew, Jean-Christophe. *Worlds Apart: The Market and the Theater in Anglo-American Thought, 1550–1750.* Cambridge: Cambridge University Press, 1986.

Alvarez, Manuel Fernández. *Charles V: Elected Emperor and Hereditary Ruler.* Trans. J.A. Lalaguna. London: Thames & Hudson, 1975.

Andrews, Kenneth. *Trade, Plunder, and Settlement: Maritime Enterprise and the Genesis of the British Empire, 1480–1630.* Cambridge: Cambridge University Press, 1984.

Aquinas, Thomas. *Summa Theologica. Opera Omnia.* Vol. 8. Rome, 1895.

Archer, John Michael. *Sovereignty and Intelligence: Spying and Court Culture in the English Renaissance.* Stanford: Stanford University Press, 1993.

Ardolino, Frank. '"In Paris? Mass, and Well Remembered!": Kyd's *The Spanish Tragedy* and the English Reaction to the St. Bartholomew's Day Massacre.' *The Sixteenth Century Journal* 21 (1990): 401–409.

Aske, James. 'Elizabetha Triumphans.' 2:545–82. In *The Progresses and Public Processions of Queen Elizabeth.* Ed. John Nichols. 3 vols. London, 1823. New York: Burt Franklin, 1966.

Augustine. *De Ordine. Patrologiae Cursus Completus Series Latina.* Ed. J.P. Migne et al. Vol. 32. Paris, 1845.

Babb, Lawrence. *The Elizabethan Malady: A Study of Melancholia in English Literature from 1580 to 1642.* East Lansing: Michigan State University Press, 1951.

Bakeless, John. *Christopher Marlowe: The Man in His Time.* 1937. New York: Washington Square, 1964.

Bakhtin, Mikhail. *Rabelais and His World.* Trans. Helene Iswolsky. Cambridge, MA: MIT Press, 1968.

Barber, C.L. 'The Death of Zenocrate: "Conceiving and Subduing Both" in Marlowe's *Tamburlaine*.' *Literature and Psychology* 16 (1966): 15–26.

Barish, Jonas. *The Anti-Theatrical Prejudice*. Berkeley and Los Angeles: University of California Press, 1981.

Barkan, Leonard J. 'Diana and Acteon: The Myth as Synthesis.' *English Literary Renaissance* 10 (1980): 317–59.

———. *Nature's Work of Art: The Human Body as Image of the World*. 1975. New Haven: Yale University Press, 1977.

Barnett, Correlli. *Britain and Her Army, 1509–1970: A Military, Political and Social Survey*. New York: William Morrow, 1970.

Barnie, John. *War in Medieval Society: Social Values and the Hundred Years War, 1337–99*. London: Weidenfeld & Nicolson, 1974.

Bartels, Emily C. 'Malta, the Jew, and the Fictions of Difference: Colonialist Discourse in Marlowe's *The Jew of Malta*.' *English Literary Renaissance* 20 (1990): 1–16.

———. *Spectacles of Strangeness: Imperialism, Alienation, and Marlowe*. Philadelphia: University of Pennsylvania Press, 1993.

Battenhouse, Roy. *Marlowe's* Tamburlaine: *A Study in Renaissance Moral Philosophy*. Nashville: Vanderbilt University Press, 1941.

———. 'Protestant Apologetics and the Subplot of *2 Tamburlaine*.' *English Literary Renaissance* 3 (1973): 30–43.

Beaumont, Francis. *The Knight of the Burning Pestle*. Ed. John Doebler. Regents Drama Series. Lincoln: University of Nebraska Press, 1967.

Bec-Crispin, Jean. *The Historie of the Great Emperour Tamerlan*. London, 1597. STC 7263.

Berek, Peter. 'Tamburlaine's Weak Sons: Imitation as Interpretation Before 1593.' *Renaissance Drama* 13 (1982): 55–82.

Bergeron, David M. *Royal Family, Royal Lovers: King James of England and Scotland*. Columbia: University of Missouri Press, 1991.

Bernard. *Commentary on the First Six Books of Virgil's* Aeneid. Trans. Earl G. Schreiber and Thomas E. Maresca. Lincoln: University of Nebraska Press, 1974.

Bevington, David. *Tudor Drama and Politics*. Cambridge: Harvard University Press, 1968.

Birringer, Johannes H. 'Marlowe's Violent Stage: "Mirrors" of Honor in *Tamburlaine*.' *ELH* 51 (1984): 219–39.

Blandy, William. *The Castle, or picture of pollicy shewing forth . . . the duety, quality, profession of a perfect and absolute souldiar, the martiall feates, encounters, and skirmishes lately done by our English nation*. London, 1581. STC 3128. New York: Da Capo, 1972.

Bliese, John R.E. 'Rhetoric and Morale: A Study of Battle Orations from the Central Middle Ages.' *Journal of Medieval History* 15 (1989): 201–26.

Boswell, John. *Christianity, Social Tolerance, and Homosexuality: Gay People in Western Europe from the Beginning of the Christian Era to the Fourteenth Century.* Chicago: University of Chicago Press, 1980.

Bourne, William. *The Arte of Shooting in Great Ordnaunce.* London, 1587. Wing B 3859. New York: Da Capo, 1969.

Bowers, Fredson, ed. *The Complete Works of Christopher Marlowe.* 2 vols, 2d ed. Cambridge: Cambridge University Press, 1981.

Boynton, Lindsay. *The Elizabethan Militia, 1558–1638.* London: Routledge & Kegan Paul, 1967.

———. 'Martial Law and the Petition of Right.' *English Historical Review* 79 (1964): 255–84.

———. 'The Tudor Provost-Marshal.' *English Historical Review* 77 (1962): 437–55.

Braden, Gordon. *Renaissance Tragedy and the Senecan Tradition: Anger's Privilege.* New Haven: Yale University Press, 1985.

Bradner, Leicester. 'Poems on the Defeat of the Spanish Armada.' *Journal of English and Germanic Philology* 43 (1944): 447–8.

Brandi, Karl. *The Emperor Charles V: The Growth and Destiny of a Man and of a World-Empire.* Trans. C.V. Wedgwood. 1939. London: Jonathan Cape, 1954.

Bray, Alan. *Homosexual Desire in Renaissance England.* 1982. Rev. ed. New York: Columbia University Press, 1995.

Bredbeck, Gregory. *Sodomy and Interpretation: Marlowe to Milton.* Ithaca: Cornell University Press, 1991.

Breight, Curtis C. *Surveillance, Militarism and Drama in the Elizabethan Era.* New York: St Martin's, 1996.

Breitenberg, Mark. *Anxious Masculinity in Early Modern England.* Cambridge: Cambridge University Press, 1996.

Brenner, Robert. *Merchants and Revolution: Commercial Change, Political Conflict, and London's Overseas Traders, 1550–1653.* Princeton: Princeton University Press, 1993.

Briggs, Julia. 'Marlowe's *Massacre at Paris*: A Reconsideration,' *Review of English Studies* n.s. 34 (1983): 257–78.

———. *This Stage-Play World.* Oxford: Oxford University Press, 1981.

Bristol, Michael. *Carnival and Theater: Plebian Culture and the Structure of Authority in Renaissance England.* London: Methuen, 1985.

Brooke, Tucker. 'Some Pre-Armada Propagandist Poetry in England (1585–1586).' *Proceedings of the American Philosophical Society* 85 (1941): 71–83.

Bruster, Douglas. *Drama and the Market in the Age of Shakespeare.* Cambridge: Cambridge University Press, 1992.

Budra, Paul. 'Doctor Faustus: Death of a Bibliophile' and 'Doctor

Faustus: The Play-Text or the Play? A Reply to Mark Thornton Burnett.' *Connotations* 1 (1991): 1–11 and 286–9.

Bullinger, Henry. 'A Confutation of the Popes Bull.' London, 1572. STC 4044.

Burke, Peter. *Montaigne*. New York: Hill & Wang, 1982.

Burnett, Mark Thornton. '*Edward II* and Elizabethan Politics.' 91–107. In *Marlowe, History, and Sexuality: New Critical Essays on Christopher Marlowe*. Ed. White.

———. '*Tamburlaine* and the Body.' *Criticism* 33 (1991): 31–47.

———. '*Tamburlaine* and the Renaissance Concept of Honour.' *Studia Neophilologica* 59 (1987): 201–6.

Butler, Judith. *Gender Trouble: Feminism and the Subversion of Identity*. New York: Routledge, 1990.

Calahorra, Diego Ortunez. *The Mirrour of Princely deedes and Knighthood*. Trans. Margaret Tyler. London, 1578. STC 18859.

Canons and Decrees of the Council of Trent: Original Text with English Translation. Trans. H.J. Schroeder. 1941. St Louis: Herder, 1955.

Carpentier, Alejo. 'On the Marvelous Real in America.' 1949. Trans. Tanya Huntington and Lois Parkinson Zamora. 75–88. In *Magical Realism: Theory, History, Community*. Ed. Zamora and Faris.

Cartelli, Thomas. *Marlowe, Shakespeare, and the Economy of Theatrical Experience*. Philadelphia: University of Pennsylvania Press, 1991.

———. 'Shakespeare's *Merchant*, Marlowe's *Jew*: The Problem of Cultural Difference.' *Shakespeare Studies* 20 (1987): 255–60.

Chaucer, Geoffrey. *The Riverside Chaucer*. Ed. Larry D. Benson et al. 3d ed. Boston: Houghton Mifflin, 1987.

Cheney, Patrick. *Marlowe's Counterfeit Profession: Ovid, Spenser, Counter-Nationhood*. Toronto: University of Toronto Press, 1998.

Churchyard, Thomas. *A generall rehearsall of warres*. London, 1579. STC 5235.

Clayton, Giles. *Approved Order of Martiall Discipline*. London, 1591. STC 5376. New York: Da Capo, 1973.

Clayton, Jay. 'Narrative and Theories of Desire.' *Critical Inquiry* 16 (1989): 33–53.

Cole, Douglas. *Suffering and Evil in the Plays of Christopher Marlowe*. 1962. New York: Gordian, 1972.

Cotgrave, Randle. *French–English dictionary*. London, 1650. STC C 6377B.

Cruickshank, C.G. *Elizabeth's Army*. 2d ed. Oxford: Clarendon, 1966.

Cunningham, Karen. 'Renaissance Execution and Marlovian Elocution: The Drama of Death.' *PMLA* 105 (1990): 209–22.

D'Amico, Jack. *The Moor in English Renaissance Drama*. Tampa: University of South Florida Press, 1991.

Danson, Lawrence. 'Christopher Marlowe: The Questioner.' *English Literary Renaissance* 12 (1982): 3–29.

Davis, Natalie Zemon. 'The Rites of Violence: Religious Riot in Sixteenth-Century France.' 203–42. In *The Massacre of St. Bartholomew*. Ed. Soman.

———. *Society and Culture in Early Modern France: Eight Essays.* Stanford: Stanford University Press, 1975.

Dawson, Graham. *Soldier Heroes: British Adventure, Empire and the Imagining of Masculinities*. London: Routledge, 1994.

de M., D.F.R. *An Answer to the Untruthes, Published and Printed in Spaine, in Glorie of their Supposeed Victorie atchieved against our English Navie*. Trans. I.L. London, 1589. STC 17132.

Dennys, Rodney. *The Heraldic Imagination*. London: Barrie & Jenkins, 1975.

Desmond, Marilynn. *Reading Dido: Gender, Textuality, and the Medieval* Aeneid. Minneapolis: University of Minnesota Press, 1994.

Dickens, A.G. 'The Elizabethans and St. Bartholomew.' 52–70. In *The Massacre of St. Bartholomew*. Ed. Soman.

Diefendorf, Barbara. *Beneath the Cross: Catholics and Huguenots in Sixteenth-Century Paris*. New York: Oxford University Press, 1991.

DiGangi, Mario. *The Homoerotics of Early Modern Drama*. Cambridge: Cambridge University Press, 1997.

Digges, Leonard. *Stratioticos*. London, 1579. STC 6848. Amsterdam: Theatrum Orbis Terrarum, 1968.

Digges, Thomas. *A Briefe Report of the Militarie Services done in the Low Countries, by the Erle of Leicester*. London, 1587. STC 7285.

Douglas, Mary. *Purity and Danger: An Analysis of Concepts of Pollution and Taboo*. 1966. New York: Routledge & Kegan Paul, 1970.

Dowriche, Anne. 'The French Historie.' London, 1589. STC 7159.

Drayton, Michael. *Mortimeriados*. 1:305–92. In *Works*. Ed. Hebel et al.

———. *Peirs Gaveston*. 1:157–208. In *Works*. Ed. Hebel et al.

———. *Works*. Ed. J.W. Hebel, K. Tillotson, and B. Newdigate. 5 vols. Oxford: Basil Blackwell, 1961.

Elizabeth I. *Proceedings. A Proclamation against vagarant Souldiers and others*. 13 November 1589. STC 8188.

———. *Proceedings concerning soldiers pressed for the low countries*. 4 October 1588. London, 1588. STC 8175.

———. *Proclamations. A Declaration of the Causes Mooving the Queene of England to give aide to the Defence of the People afflicted and oppressed in the lowe Countries*. London, 1585. STC 9189.

Elton, G.R. 'Government by Edict?' 1:300–307. Reprinted in *Studies in Tudor and Stuart Politics and Government: Papers and Reviews 1946–1972*. 2 vols. Cambridge: Cambridge University Press, 1974.

————. 'The rule of law in sixteenth-century England.' 1:260–84. Reprinted in *Studies in Tudor and Stuart Politics and Government: Papers and Reviews 1946–1972*. 2 vols. Cambridge: Cambridge University Press, 1974.

Elworthy, Frederick. *Horns of Honour*. London: John Murray, 1900.

Erasmus, Desiderus. 'Dulce Bellum Inexpertis.' 107–40. In *Erasmus on his times*. Ed. Margaret Mann Phillips. Cambridge: Cambridge University Press, 1967.

————. *Enchiridion militis christiani* [*The Handbook of the Christian Soldier*]. Trans. Charles Fantazzi. Ed. John W. O'Malley. 66:1–127. *The Collected Works of Erasmus*. Toronto: University of Toronto Press, 1988.

————. *Erasmus on his times: a shortened version of* The Adages. Trans. and ed. Margaret Mann Phillips. Cambridge: Cambridge University Press, 1967.

————. *The Erasmus Reader*. Ed. Erika Rummel. Toronto: University of Toronto Press, 1990.

————. *The Praise of Folly*. Trans. Betty Radice. New York: Penguin, 1971.

Eriksen, Roy T. 'Construction in Marlowe's *The Massacre at Paris*.' 41–54. In *Papers from the First Nordic Conference for English Studies*. Ed. Stig Johansson and Bjørn Tysdahl. Institute for English Studies. Oslo: University of Oslo, 1981.

Esler, Anthony. 'Robert Greene and the Spanish Armada.' *ELH* 32 (1965): 314–32.

Essex, Robert Devereux, 2d earl of (attributed to). *A True Coppie of a Discourse written by a Gentleman, employed in the late Voyage of Spaine and Portingale*. London, 1589. STC 6790.

Estebe, Janine. *Tocsin pour un Massacre: la saison des Saint-Barthélemy*. Paris: Le Centurion, 1968.

'An exhortacion to all English Subjects, to joine for the defence of Queene Elziabeth [*sic*], and their native country.' London, 1588. STC 7582.

Farrell, Kirby. 'Thinking Through Others: Prosthetic Fantasy and the Cultural Moment.' *The Massachusetts Review* 37 (1996): 213–35.

Feld, Maury D. *The Structure of Violence: Armed Forces as Social Systems*. Pref. Charles C. Moskos, Jr. Beverly Hills: Sage, 1977.

Finkelpearl, Philip J. *Court and Country Politics in the Plays of Beaumont and Fletcher*. Princeton: Princeton University Press, 1990.

Flandrin, Jean-Louis. *Families in Former Times: Kinship, Household, and Sexuality*. Trans. Richard Southern. Cambridge: Cambridge University Press, 1979.

Fortescue, J.W. *A History of the British Army*. London, 1910. 2 vols. New York: AMS, 1976.

Foucault, Michel. *Discipline and Punish: The Birth of the Prison.* Trans. Alan Sheridan. New York: Vintage, 1979.

'A Fourme of Common Prayer to be used, by Aucthoritie of The Queenes Majestie, and Necessarie for the Present Tyme and State.' *Church of England Liturgies. Special Forms of Prayer on Various Occasions.* London, 1572. STC 16511.

Friedman, Alan. 'The Shackling of Accidents in Marlowe's *Jew of Malta.' Texas Studies in Language and Literature* 8 (1966): 155–67.

Fulgentius. 'The Exposition of the Content of Virgil according to Moral Philosophy.' 103–53. In *Fulgentius the Mythographer.* Trans. Leslie George Whitbread. Columbus: The Ohio State University Press, 1971.

Garrard, William. *The Arte of Warre.* London, 1591. STC 11625.

Gascoigne, George. 'The Spoyle of Antwerpe.' In *A Larum for London; or The Siege of Antwerpe.* London: Longmans, Green, 1872.

Gates, Geoffrey. *The Defence of Militarie Profession.* London, 1579. STC 11683. New York: Da Capo, 1973.

Gibbon, Charles. *A Watch-Worde for Warre.* London, 1596. STC 11492.

Gill, Roma, ed. *The Complete Works of Christopher Marlowe.* 2 vols. Oxford: Clarendon, 1990.

Girard, Rene. 'The Politics of Desire in *Troilus and Cressida.'* 188–209. In *Shakespeare and the Question of Theory.* Ed. Patricia Parker and Geoffrey Hartman. New York: Methuen, 1985.

Glenn, Garrard. *The Army and the Law.* 1918. Rev. A. Arthur Schiller. New York: Columbia University Press, 1943.

Goldberg, Jonathan. *Sodometries: Renaissance Texts, Modern Sexualities.* Stanford: Stanford University Press, 1992.

Gosson, Stephen. *The School of Abuse.* Ed. John Payne Collier. London, 1841.

Gray, J. Glenn. *The Warriors: Reflections on Men in Battle.* New York: Harcourt, Brace, 1959.

Greenblatt, Stephen. 'Marlowe, Marx, and Anti-Semitism.' *Critical Inquiry* 5 (1978): 291–307.

———. *Renaissance Self Fashioning: From More to Shakespeare.* Chicago: University of Chicago Press, 1980.

Greville, Fulke. *Selected Writings of Fulke Greville.* Ed. Joan Rees. London: Athlone, 1973.

Guicciardini, Francesco. *The History of Italy.* Trans. and ed. Sidney Alexander. New York: Macmillan, 1969.

Guicciardini, Luigi. *The Sack of Rome.* Trans. and ed. James H. McGregor. New York: Italica, 1993.

Guy, John. *Tudor England.* Oxford: Oxford University Press, 1988.

Hacker, Barton C. 'Women and Military Institutions in Early Modern Europe: A Reconnaissance.' *Signs* 6 (1981): 643–71.

Hale, J.R. 'Girolamo Maggi: A Renaissance Scholar and Military Buff.' *Italian Studies* 40 (1985): 31–50.

———. *War and Society in Renaissance Europe, 1450–1620.* New York: St Martin's, 1985.

Hammill, Graham. 'Faustus's Fortunes: Commodification, Exchange, and the Form of Literary Subjectivity.' *ELH* 63 (1996): 309–36.

Hanson, Elizabeth. 'Torture and Truth in Renaissance England.' *Representations* 34 (1991): 53–84.

Harington, John. 'A Preface, or rather a Briefe Apologie of Poetrie.' Preface to *Orlando Furioso.* London, 1591. 194–222. In *Elizabethan Critical Essays.* Ed. Smith.

Harré, Rom, ed. *The Social Construction of Emotions.* Oxford: Basil Blackwell, 1987.

Harrison, William. *The Description of England.* London, 1577, 1587. Ed. Georges Edelen. 1968. Washington DC: The Folger Shakespeare Library, 1994.

Harward, Simon. *The Solace for the Souldier and Saylour.* London, 1592. STC 12923.

Helgerson, Richard. *Forms of Nationhood: The Elizabethan Writing of England.* Chicago: University of Chicago Press, 1992.

Henslowe, Philip. *Henslowe's Diary.* Ed. R.A. Foakes and R.T. Rickert. Cambridge: Cambridge University Press, 1961.

Herford, Charles H. *Studies in the Literary Relations of England and Germany.* Cambridge: Cambridge University Press, 1886.

Holinshed, Raphael. *Chronicles of England, Scotland, and Ireland.* Ed. Vernon F. Snow. 6 vols. New York: AMS, 1976.

Hookham, Hilda. *Tamburlaine, the Conqueror.* London: Hodder & Stoughton, 1962.

Hope, A.D. '*Tamburlaine*: The Argument of Arms.' 45–54. In *Christopher Marlowe.* Ed. Harold Bloom. New York: Chelsea, 1986.

Hoppen, Alison. *The Fortification of Malta by the Order of St. John, 1530–1798.* Edinburgh: Scottish Academic Press, 1979.

Horger, J. 'Derek Jarman's Film Adaptation of Marlowe's *Edward II*.' *Shakespeare Bulletin* 11 (1993): 37–40.

Hotman, François. *A True and Plaine Report of the Furious Outrages of Fraunce, & the horrible and shameful slaughter of Chastillion the Admirall.* Trans. Ernest Varamund. Striveling, Scotland, 1573. STC 13847.

Howard, Jean E. 'An English Lass Amid the Moors: Gender, Race, Sexuality, and National Identity in Heywood's *The Fair Maid of the West*.' 101–17. In *Women, 'Race,' and Writing in the Early Modern*

Period. Ed. Margo Hendricks and Patricia Parker. London: Routledge, 1994.

Howe, James Robinson. *Marlowe, Tamburlaine, and Magic.* Athens, Ohio: Ohio University Press, 1976.

Hughes, Paul L. and James F. Larkin, ed. *Tudor Royal Proclamations.* 3 vols. New Haven: Yale University Press, 1969.

Hulme, Peter. *Colonial Encounters: Europe and the Native Caribbean, 1492–1797.* London: Methuen, 1986.

Hunter, G.K. 'Elizabethans and Foreigners.' 3–30. Reprinted in *Dramatic Identities and Cultural Tradition.* Liverpool: Liverpool University Press, 1978.

———. 'The Theology of Marlowe's *The Jew of Malta.*' *Journal of the Warburg and Courtauld Institutes* 27 (1964): 211–40.

Huston, Nancy. 'The Matrix of War: Mothers and Heroes.' 119–36. In *The Female Body in Western Culture.* Ed. Susan Rubin Suleiman. Cambridge: Harvard University Press, 1986.

Hyland, Peter. 'Disguise and Renaissance Tragedy.' *University of Toronto Quarterly* 55 (1985-1986): 161–71.

Izard, Thomas C. *George Whetstone: Mid-Elizabethan Gentleman of Letters.* New York: Columbia University Press, 1942.

Joplin, Patricia Klindienst. 'The Voice of the Shuttle is Ours.' 35–66. In *Rape and Representation.* Ed. Lynn A. Higgins and Brenda R. Silver. New York: Columbia University Press, 1991.

Jorgensen, Paul A. 'Moral Guidance and Religious Encouragement for the Elizabethan Soldier.' *Huntington Library Quarterly* 13 (1950): 241–59.

Kahn, Coppélia. *Man's Estate: Masculine Identity in Shakespeare.* Berkeley and Los Angeles: University of California Press, 1981.

Keefer, Michael. 'History and the Canon: The Case of *Doctor Faustus.*' *University of Toronto Quarterly* 56 (1987): 498–522.

Keen, Maurice. *Chivalry.* New Haven: Yale University Press, 1984.

Kermode, Lloyd Edward. '"Marlowe's Second City": The Jew as Critic at the Rose in 1592.' *SEL* 35 (1995): 215–29.

Kerrigan, William and Gordon Braden. *The Idea of the Renaissance.* Baltimore: Johns Hopkins University Press, 1989.

Kiefer, Frederick. *Writing on the Renaissance Stage: Written Words, Printed Pages, Metaphoric Books.* Newark, DE: University of Delaware Press, 1996.

Kingdon, Robert M. *Myths about the St. Bartholomew's Day Massacres, 1572–1576.* Cambridge: Harvard University Press, 1988.

Kocher, Paul. 'Contemporary Pamphlet Backgrounds for Marlowe's *The Massacre at Paris.*' *Modern Language Quarterly* 8 (1947): 151–73 and 309–18.

————. 'François Hotman and Marlowe's *The Massacre at Paris.*' *PMLA* 56 (1941): 349–68.

————. 'Marlowe's Art of War.' *Studies in Philology* 39 (1942): 207–25.

Koenigsberger, H.G. 'Introduction.' 1–12. In *The Massacre of St. Bartholomew*. Ed. Soman.

Kuriyama, Constance. 'Dr. Greg and *Doctor Faustus*: The Supposed Originality of the 1616 Text.' *English Language Review* 5 (1975): 171–97.

————. *Hammer or Anvil: Psychological Patterns in Christopher Marlowe's Plays*. New Brunswick: Rutgers University Press, 1980.

Kyd, Thomas. *The Spanish Tragedy*. 1:167–203. In *Drama of the English Renaissance*. Ed. Russell A. Fraser and Norman Rabkin. 2 vols. New York: Macmillan, 1976.

Kyffin, Maurice. *The Blessednes of Brytaine, or A Celebration of the Queenes Holyday*. London, 1588. STC 15097.

Laughton, John Knox, ed. *The Naval Miscellany*. 2 vols. London: Navy Records Society, 1901.

Leicester, Robert Dudley, earl of. *Lawes and ordinances militarie*, Leyden, 1586. STC 7287.7.

Levin, Harry. '*Edward II*: State Overturned.' 9-30. In *Christopher Marlowe*. Ed. Harold Bloom. Modern Critical Views Series. New York: Chelsea, 1986.

Levin, Richard. 'The Contemporary Perception of Marlowe's Tamburlaine.' *Medieval and Renaissance Drama in England* 1 (1984): 51–70.

Lindabury, Richard. *A Study of Patriotism in the Elizabethan Drama*. Princeton Studies in English No. 5. Princeton: Princeton University Press, 1931.

Lingham, John. *A true relation of all suche Englishe Captaines and Lieuetenants, as have beene slaine in the lowe Countries*. London, 1584. STC 15690.7.

Lydgate, John. *Troy Book*. Ed. Henry Bergen. EETS. 3 vols. London: Kegan Paul, 1906–35.

Lyne, R.O.A.M. *Further Voices in Vergil's* Aeneid. Oxford: Clarendon, 1987.

MacCabe, Colin. 'A Post-National European Cinema: A Consideration of Derek Jarman's *The Tempest* and *Edward II*.' 9–18. In *Screening Europe: Image and Identity in Contemporary European Cinema*. Ed. Duncan Petrie. London: British Film Institute, 1992.

MacCaffrey, Wallace T. *Elizabeth I: War and Politics, 1588–1603*. Princeton: Princeton University Press, 1992.

————. *Queen Elizabeth and the Making of Policy, 1572–1588*. Princeton: Princeton University Press, 1981.

MacCary, W. Thomas. *Childlike Achilles: Ontogeny and Phylogeny in the* Iliad. New York: Columbia University Press, 1982.

Machiavelli, Niccolò. *The Art of War.* Trans. Ellis Farneworth. Rev. ed. Indianapolis: Bobbs-Merrill, 1965.

———. *The Discourses.* Ed. Bernard Crick. 1970. London: Penguin, 1981.

———. *The Prince.* Trans. and ed. Peter Bondanella. New York: Oxford University Press, 1984.

Mansfield, Sue. *The Gestalts of War: An Inquiry into its Origin and Meaning as a Social Institution.* New York: Dial, 1982.

Manz, Beatrice Forbes. *The Rise and Rule of Tamerlane.* 1989. Cambridge: Cambridge University Press, 1990.

Marcus, Leah S. 'Textual Indeterminacy and Ideological Difference: The Case of *Doctor Faustus.*' *Renaissance Drama* 20 (1989): 1–29.

Marlowe, Christopher. *Christopher Marlowe's* Doctor Faustus, *Text and Major Criticism.* Ed. Irving Ribner. Indianapolis: Odyssey, 1966.

———. *The Complete Plays of Christopher Marlowe.* Ed. J.B. Steane. 1969. Harmondsworth: Penguin, 1986.

———. *Dido, Queen of Carthage* and *The Massacre at Paris.* Ed. H.J. Oliver. The Revels Plays. Cambridge: Harvard University Press, 1968.

———. *Doctor Faustus: A- and B-Texts (1604, 1616).* Ed. David Bevington and Eric Rasmussen. The Revels Plays. 1992. Manchester: Manchester University Press, 1997.

———. *Edward II.* Ed. Charles R. Forker. The Revels Plays. Manchester: Manchester University Press, 1994.

———. *Edward the Second.* Ed. W. Moelwyn Merchant. New Mermaids Series. London: A.C. Black, 1987.

———. *The Jew of Malta.* Ed. David Bevington. The Revels Plays. Manchester: Manchester University Press, 1997.

———. *The Jew of Malta.* Ed. T.W. Craik. 1966. New Mermaids Series. New York: Norton, 1983.

———. *Marlowe's* Doctor Faustus 1604–1616: *Parallel Texts.* Ed. W.W. Greg. Oxford: Clarendon, 1950.

———. *Tamburlaine.* Ed. J.S. Cunningham. The Revels Plays. 1981. Manchester: Manchester University Press, 1999.

Martin, Richard A. 'Fate, Seneca, and Marlowe's *Dido, Queen of Carthage.*' *Renaissance Drama* 11 (1980): 45–66.

Martin, Richard P. *The Language of Heroes: Speech and Performance in the* Iliad. Ithaca: Cornell University Press, 1989.

Marx, Stephen. 'Shakespeare's Pacifism.' *Renaissance Quarterly* 45 (1992): 49–95.

Massinger, Philip. *The Renegado: A Tragicomedy.* 241–344. In *Three Turk Plays from Early Modern England: Selimus, A Christian Turned*

Turk, The Renegado. Ed. Daniel J. Vitkus. New York: Columbia University Press, 2000.

Matar, N.I. 'English Renaissance Soldiers in the Armies of Islam.' *Explorations in Renaissance Culture* 21 (1995): 81–94.

———. *Turks, Moors & Englishmen in the Age of Discovery*. New York: Columbia University Press, 1999.

Mattingly, Garrett. *The Armada*. Boston: Houghton Mifflin, 1959.

Maus, Katharine Eisaman. 'Horns of Dilemma: Jealousy, Gender, and Spectatorship in English Renaissance Drama.' *ELH* 54 (1987): 561–83.

———. *Inwardness and Theater in the English Renaissance*. Chicago: University of Chicago Press, 1995.

Mauss, Marcel. *The Gift: Forms and Functions of Exchange in Archaic Societies*. Trans. Ian Cunnison. Glencoe, IL: Free, 1954.

McCabe, Richard A. *Incest, Drama and Nature's Law, 1550–1700*. Cambridge: Cambridge University Press, 1993.

McEachern, Claire and Debora Shuger, eds. *Religion and Culture in Renaissance England*. Cambridge: Cambridge University Press, 1997.

Mehl, Dieter. *The Elizabethan Dumb Show: The History of a Dramatic Convention*. Cambridge: Harvard University Press, 1966.

Mellinkoff, Ruth. *The Horned Moses in Medieval Art and Thought*. Berkeley and Los Angeles: University of California Press, 1970.

A Myrrour for English Souldiers. London, 1595. STC 10418.

Montaigne. 'Apology for Raymond Sebond.' 318–457. In *The Complete Essays of Montaigne*. Trans. Donald M. Frame. 1958. Stanford: Stanford University Press, 1985.

Montesquieu. *The Spirit of Laws*. Trans. Thomas Nugent. New York, 1900.

Mueller, Janel M. 'Pain, persecution, and the construction of selfhood in Foxe's *Acts and Monuments*.' 161–87. In *Religion and Culture in Renaissance England*. Ed. McEachern and Shuger.

Munday, Anthony. *The English Romayne Life*. Ed. G.B. Harrison. New York: Barnes & Noble, 1966.

———. *A Watch-woord to England To beware of traytours and tretcherous practices*. London, 1584. STC 18282a.

Murrin, Michael. *History and Warfare in Renaissance Epic*. Chicago: University of Chicago Press, 1994.

Nauert, Charles G., Jr. *The Age of Renaissance and Reformation*. Lanham, MD: University Press of America, 1981.

Nichols, John, ed. *The Progresses and Public Processions of Queen Elizabeth*. 3 vols. 1823. New York: Burt Franklin, 1966.

Nolan, John S. *Sir John Norreys and the Elizabethan Military World*. Exeter: University of Exeter Press, 1997.

Normand, Lawrence. '"What passions call you these?": *Edward II* and James VI.' 172–97. In *Christopher Marlowe and English Renaissance Culture*. Ed. Darryll Grantley and Peter Roberts. Aldershot: Scolar, 1996.

O'Pray, Mike. 'Damning Desire.' An Interview with Derek Jarman. *Sight and Sound* 1:6 (Oct. 1991): 8–11.

Onasander, *The General*. 341–527. In *Aeneas Tacticus, Asclepiodotus, Onasander*. Trans. Members of the Illinois Greek Club. Cambridge: Harvard University Press, 1962.

Ong, Walter J. *Ramus: Method, and the Decay of Dialogue*. Cambridge: Harvard University Press, 1958.

Oxenhandler, Neal. 'The Changing Concept of Literary Emotion: A Selective History.' *New Literary History* 20 (1988): 105–21.

Ozment, Steven. *The Age of Reform, 1250–1550: An Intellectual and Religious History of Late Medieval and Reformation Europe*. New Haven: Yale University Press, 1980.

Pagden, Anthony. *Lords of all the World: Ideologies of Empire in Spain, Britain and France, c. 1500–1800*. New Haven: Yale University Press, 1995.

Parker, Geoffrey. *The Army of Flanders and the Spanish Road, 1567–1659*. 1972. Cambridge: Cambridge University Press, 1995.

———. *The Military Revolution: Military Innovation and the Rise of the West, 1500–1800*. Cambridge: Cambridge University Press, 1988.

———. 'Spain, Her Enemies and the Revolt of the Netherlands, 1559–1648.' *Past & Present* 49 (1970): 72–95.

Parker, Patricia. *Literary Fat Ladies: Rhetoric, Gender, Property*. New York: Methuen, 1987.

Paster, Gail Kern. *The Body Embarrassed: Drama and the Disciplines of Shame in Early Modern England*. Ithaca: Cornell University Press, 1993.

Patterson, Annabel. *Reading Holinshed's* Chronicles. Chicago: University of Chicago Press, 1994.

Patterson, Lee. *Chaucer and the Subject of History*. Madison: University of Wisconsin Press, 1991.

Peele, George. *A Farewell Entituled to the famous and fortunate Generalls of our English forces: Sir John Norris & Syr Frauncis Drake Knights*. London, 1589. STC 19537.

———. *The Works of George Peele*. Gen. ed. Charles Tyler Prouty. 2 vols. New Haven: Yale University Press, 1961.

Perret, Marion D. 'Shakespeare's Jew: Preconception and Performance.' *Shakespeare Studies* 20 (1987): 261–8.

Pigg, Oliver. *Meditations Concerning praiers to Almightie God, for the saftie of ENGLAND, when the Spaniards were come into the narrow Seas. August 1588*. London, 1589. STC 19916.

Procter, Thomas. *Of the Knowledge and Conducte of Warres*. London, 1578. STC 20403. Amsterdam: Theatrum Orbis Terrarum, 1970.

Pryor, John H. *Geography, Technology, and War: Studies in the Maritime History of the Mediterranean, 649–1571*. Cambridge: Cambridge University Press, 1988.

Puttenham, George. *The Arte of English Poesie*. 1–193. In *Elizabethan Critical Essays*. Ed. Smith.

Ralegh, Walter. *A Discourse of Sea-Ports; Principally of the Port and Haven of Dover*. London, 1700. D 1458.

Ramazani, Jahan. *The Poetry of Mourning*. Chicago: University of Chicago Press, 1994.

Rasmussen, Eric. 'Rehabilitating the A-Text of Marlowe's *Doctor Faustus*.' *Studies in Bibliography* 46 (1993): 221–38.

Rebhorn, Wayne A. *The Emperor of Men's Minds: Literature and the Renaissance Discourse of Rhetoric*. Ithaca: Cornell University Press, 1995.

———., trans. and ed. *Renaissance Debates on Rhetoric*. Ithaca: Cornell University Press, 2000.

Rich, Barnabe. *Allarme to England, foreshewing what perilles are procured, where the people live without regarde of Martiall lawe*. London, 1578. STC 20978.

———. *A Path-Way to Military Practise*. London, 1587. STC 20995. Amsterdam: Da Capo, 1969.

———. *A Roome for a Gentleman*. London, 1609. STC 20985.

Roover, Raymond. *Business, Banking, and Economic Thought in Late Medieval and Early Modern Europe*. Ed. Julius Kirshner. Chicago: University of Chicago Press, 1974.

Rose, Mary Beth. *The Expense of Spirit: Love and Sexuality in English Renaissance Drama*. Ithaca: Cornell University Press, 1988.

Rossiaud, Jacques. *Medieval Prostitution*. Trans. Lydia G. Cochrane. London: Blackwell, 1988.

Rowse, A.L. *Christopher Marlowe: His Life and Work*. New York: Harper & Row, 1964.

Salmon, J.H.M. *The French Religious Wars in English Political Thought*. Oxford: Clarendon, 1959.

Sanday, Peggy Reeves. *Divine Hunger: Cannibalism as a Cultural System*. Cambridge: Cambridge University Press, 1986.

Sanders, Eve Rachele. *Gender and Literacy on Stage in Early Modern England*. Cambridge: Cambridge University Press, 1998.

Sanger, Ernest. *Englishmen at War: A Social History in Letters 1450–1900*. Dover, NH: Sutton, 1993.

Scarry, Elaine. *The Body in Pain: The Making and Unmaking of the World*. New York: Oxford University Press, 1985.

Segar, William. *Honor Military and Civil*. London, 1602. Ed. Diane Bornstein. New York: Scholars, 1975.

Serres, Jean. *The Lyfe of the most godly . . . Capteine . . . Jasper Colignie Shatilion*. Trans. Arthur Golding. London, 1576. STC 22248.

Seward, Desmond. *The Monks of War: The Military Religious Orders*. Rev. ed. Harmondsworth: Penguin, 1995.

Shakespeare, William. *The Riverside Shakespeare*. Ed. G. Blakemore Evans et al. Boston: Houghton Mifflin, 1974.

Shapiro, James S. *Shakespeare and the Jews*. New York: Columbia University Press, 1996.

Sharpe, J.A. *Early Modern England: A Social History 1550–1760*. 2d ed. New York: Arnold, 1997.

Shepard, Alan. 'William Patten's *Expedition of Somerset into Scotland* (1547) as English Imperial Discourse.' *Scottish Literary Journal* 22 (1995): 22–34.

Shepherd, Simon. *Amazons and Warrior Women: Varieties of Feminism in Seventeenth-Century Drama*. New York: St Martin's, 1981.

———. *Marlowe and the Politics of Elizabethan Theatre*. Brighton: Harvester, 1986.

Sidney, Mary. *The Tragedy of Antonie*. 13–42. In *Renaissance Drama by Women: Texts and Documents*. Ed. S.P. Cerasano and Marion Wynne-Davies. New York: Routledge, 1996.

Sidney, Philip. *The Defence of Poesy*. 99–158. In *Sir Philip Sidney: Selected Prose and Poetry*. Ed. Robert Kimbrough. 2d ed. Madison: University of Wisconsin Press, 1983.

Sinfield, Alan. *Faultlines: Cultural Materialism and the Politics of Dissident Reading*. Berkeley and Los Angeles: University of California Press, 1992.

Singerman, Jerome. *Under Clouds of Poesy: Poetry and Truth in French and English Reworkings of the* Aeneid, *1160–1513*. New York: Garland, 1986.

Slyngisbie [or Slingsby], William. *Relation of the Voyage to Cadiz, 1596*. Ed. Julian S. Corbett. 1:23–92. In *The Naval Miscellany*. Ed. Laughton.

Smith, Bruce. *Homosexual Desire in Shakespeare's England: A Cultural Poetics*. Chicago: University of Chicago Press, 1991.

Smith, G. Gregory, ed. *Elizabethan Critical Essays*. 2 vols. 1904. Oxford: Oxford University Press, 1937.

Smythe, John. *Certain Discourses Military*. London, 1590. Ed. J.R. Hale. Folger Library Series of Documents in Tudor and Stuart Civilization. Ithaca: Cornell University Press, 1964.

Snow, Edward A. 'Marlowe's *Doctor Faustus* and the Ends of Desire.' 70–110. In *Two Renaissance Mythmakers: Christopher Marlowe and*

Ben Jonson. Ed. Alvin Kernan. Selected Papers from the English Institute, 1975–76. Baltimore: Johns Hopkins University Press, 1977.

Soman, Alfred, ed. *The Massacre of St. Bartholomew: Reappraisals and Documents*. The Hague: Martinus Nijhoff, 1974.

Somerset, Anne. *Elizabeth I*. New York: St Martin's, 1991.

Somogyi, Nick de. *Shakespeare's Theatre of War*. Aldershot: Ashgate, 1998.

Spenser, Edmund. *The Poetical Works of Edmund Spenser*. Ed. J.C. Smith and Ernest de Selincourt. 3 vols. 1909. Oxford: Oxford University Press, 1961–64.

Stevenson, Laura. *Praise and Paradox: Merchants and Craftsmen in Elizabethan Popular Literature*. Cambridge: Cambridge University Press, 1984.

Stockholder, Kay. '"Within the massy entrailes of the earth": Faustus's Relation to Women.' 203–19. In *'A Poet and a Filthy Play-maker': New Essays on Christopher Marlowe*. Ed. Kenneth Friedenreich et al. New York: AMS, 1988.

Stubbs, John. *The Discoverie of a Gaping Gulf*. Ed. Lloyd Berry. Charlottesville: University Press of Virginia, 1968.

Styward, Thomas. *The Pathwaie to Martiall Discipline*. London, 1581. STC 23413.

Summers, Claude J. Rev. of Constance Kuriyama's *Hammer or Anvil*. *Journal of English and Germanic Philology* 81 (1982): 254–8.

Sutcliffe, Matthew. *The Practice, Proceedings, and Lawes of Armes*. London, 1593. STC 23468.

Suzuki, Michiko. *Metamorphoses of Helen: Authority, Difference, and the Epic*. Ithaca: Cornell University Press, 1989.

Tallett, Frank. *War and Society in Early Modern Europe, 1495–1715*. London: Routledge, 1992.

Tartaglia, Niccolo. *Three Bookes of Colloquies Concerning the Arte of Shooting*. Trans. Cyprian Lucar. London, 1588. STC 23689.

Theweleit, Klaus. *Male Fantasies*. Trans. Erica Carter et al. 2 vols. Minneapolis: University of Minnesota Press, 1987, 1989.

Thurn, David H. 'Economic and Ideological Exchange in Marlowe's *Jew of Malta*.' *Theatre Journal* 46 (1994): 157–70.

Todorov, Tzvetan. *The Fantastic: A Structural Approach to a Literary Genre*. Trans. Richard Howard. Cleveland: Case Western Reserve University Press, 1973.

Tuck, Anthony. *Richard II and the English Nobility*. London: Edward Arnold, 1973.

Turner, Victor. 'Colour Classification in Ndembu Ritual.' 47–84. In *Anthropological Approaches to the Study of Religion*. Ed. Michael Banton. New York: Praeger, 1966.

Turner, W. Craig. 'Love and the Queen of Carthage: A Look at Marlowe's *Dido*.' *Essays in Literature* 11 (1984): 3–9.

Turville-Petre, Thorlac. *England the Nation: Language, Literature, and National Identity, 1290–1340*. Oxford: Clarendon, 1996.

Tymme, Thomas. *A Preparation against the Prognosticated dangers of this yeere, 1588*. London, 1588. STC 24420.

Vermeule, Emily. *Aspects of Death in Early Greek Art and Poetry*. Berkeley and Los Angeles: University of California Press, 1979.

Vickers, Nancy J. 'Diana Described: Scattered Woman and Scattered Rhyme.' 95–109. Reprinted in *Writing and Sexual Difference*. Ed. Elizabeth Abel. Chicago: University of Chicago Press, 1982.

Virgil. *Aeneid*. Trans. Allen Mandelbaum. Berkeley and Los Angeles: University of California Press, 1971.

Vita Edwardi Secundi. Trans. and ed. N. Denholm-Young. London: Thomas Nelson, 1957.

Vitkus, Daniel J., ed. *Three Turk Plays from Early Modern England: Selimus, A Christian Turned Turk, The Renegado*. New York: Columbia University Press, 2000.

Waith, Eugene. 'Tamburlaine.' 69–91. In *Marlowe: A Collection of Critical Essays*. Ed. Clifford Leech. Twentieth-Century Views. Englewood Cliffs, NJ: Prentice-Hall, 1964.

Watt, Ian. 'Faust as a Myth of Modern Individualism: Three of Marlowe's Contributions.' 41–52. In *Faust Through Four Centuries: Retrospect and Analysis*. Ed. Peter Boerner and Sidney Johnson. Tübingen: Niemeyer, 1989.

Weil, Judith. *Christopher Marlowe: Merlin's Prophet*. Cambridge: Cambridge University Press, 1977.

Weimann, Robert. *Authority and Representation in Early Modern Discourse*. Ed. David Hillman. Baltimore: Johns Hopkins University Press, 1996.

Wernham, Robert B. *After the Armada: Elizabethan England and the Struggle for Western Europe, 1588–1595*. 1984. Oxford: Clarendon, 1986.

———. *The Making of Elizabethan Foreign Policy, 1558–1603*. Berkeley and Los Angeles: University of California Press, 1980.

Wettinger, Godfrey. *The Jews of Malta in the Late Middle Ages*. Malta: Midsea, 1985.

Whetstone, George. *The English Myrror*. London, 1586. New York: Da Capo, 1973.

———. *The Honorable Reputation of a Souldier*. London, 1585. STC 25339.

White, Paul Whitfield, ed. *Marlowe, History, and Sexuality: New Critical Essays on Christopher Marlowe*. New York: AMS Press, 1998.

————. 'Theater and Religious Culture.' 133–51. In *A New History of Early English Drama*. Ed. John D. Cox and David Scott Kastan. New York: Columbia University Press, 1997.

Whiting, Robert. *The Blind Devotion of the People: Popular Religion and the English Reformation*. Cambridge: Cambridge University Press, 1989.

Wiggins, Martin. *Journeymen in Murder: The Assassin in English Renaissance Drama*. Oxford: Clarendon, 1991.

Wilkinson, C.P. Seabrook. 'The Transmutation of Rhetoric in *Edward II*.' *Shakespeare Bulletin* 14 (1996): 5–7.

Williams, Gordon. *Technique and Ideas in the* Aeneid. New Haven: Yale University Press, 1983.

Williams, Roger. *The Actions of the Lowe Countries*. Amsterdam: Theatrum Orbis Terrarum, 1970.

————. *The Actions of the Lowe Countries*. Ed. D.W. Davies. Folger Library Series in Documents of Tudor and Stuart Civilization. Ithaca: Cornell University Press, 1964.

Willis, Deborah. 'Marlowe Our Contemporary: *Edward II* on Stage and Screen.' *Criticism* 40 (1998): 599–622.

Wilson, Rawdon. 'The Metamorphoses of Fictional Space: Magical Realism.' 209–33. In *Magical Realism*. Ed. Zamora and Faris.

————. *In Palamedes' Shadow: Explorations in Play, Game, and Narrative Theory*. Boston: Northeastern University Press, 1990.

Wilson, Richard. 'Visible Bullets: Tamburlaine the Great and Ivan the Terrible.' *ELH* 62 (1995): 47–68.

Wilson, Thomas. *Arte of Rhetorique*. Ed. Thomas J. Derrick. The Renaissance Imagination Series. 2 vols. Gen. Ed. Stephen Orgel. New York: Garland, 1982.

Wind, Edgar. *Pagan Mysteries in the Renaissance*. Rev. ed. New York: Norton, 1968.

Zamora, Lois Parkinson and Wendy B. Faris, ed. and introd. *Magical Realism: Theory, History, Community*. Durham: Duke University Press, 1995.

Index

238